Evangelism in Europe

Hannes Wiher (ed.)

Bibliographic information published by the Deutsche Nationalbibliothek
The Deutsche Nationalbibliothek lists this publication in the Deutsche Nationalbibliografie; detailed bibliographic data are available in the Internet at http://dnb.dnb.de.

ISBN: 978-3-95776-081-4

© 2018, VTR Publications, Gogolstr. 33, 90475 Nürnberg, Germany
www.vtr-online.com

Réseau de missiologie évangélique pour l'Europe francophone (REMEEF), rue du Village-Suisse 14, 1205 Geneva, Switzerland
www.missiologie.net

French Version:
Hannes Wiher, ed., L'évangélisation en Europe francophone
© 2016, Éditions Excelsis, 385 chemin du Clos, 26450 Charols, France
www.xl6.com

This book includes a wide diversity of evangelical authors and hence various views in the evangelical community. No individual contribution necessarily represents the preferred position of REMEEF leaders.

Scripture quotations in text, unless otherwise indicated, are taken from the Holy Bible, *New Revised Standard Version*, © 1989.

Photo credits: © Nuggets Poulet
https://commons.wikimedia.org/wiki/File:Europe_en_couleur.png

Layout: VTR Publications
Cover design: VTR Publications

Summary

Preface v
Preface to the French Version *(Bernard Huck)* vii
Introduction 1

Part One:
Understanding Europe 13

Chapter 1: Evangelism in Europe: Historical Background
Neal Blough 15

Chapter 2: European Context Today and Evangelism
Julien Coffinet 26

Chapter 3: Paradox of Europe and Christianity Barriers and Bridges
Evert van de Poll 47

Chapter 4: How "Christian" Is Europe Today?
Towards a Post-Secular Situation?
Evert van de Poll 67

Chapter 5: Particular Difficulties Facing our French Fellow Citizens
in Understanding and Receiving the Gospel
David Brown 88

Chapter 6: Interdisciplinary In-Depth Analysis
Hannes Wiher 104

Chapter 7: The Mosaic of Cultures: A Challenge for European and
International Churches
Johannes Müller 137

Part Two:
Communicating the Gospel in Europe 159

Chapter 8: What Is Evangelism? Biblical Hints for the
European Context
Léo Lehmann 161

Chapter 9: Cross-Cultural In-Depth Evangelism
Hannes Wiher 182

Chapter 10: Outreach amongst African-led Churches
  in Switzerland: A Case Study
  Johannes Müller 215
Chapter 11: Demonology: A Forgotten Dimension
  Hannes Wiher 234
Chapter 12: What Kind of Church for Postmodern Europeans?
  David Brown 261

Conclusion 272
Appendix 280
List of Authors 305
Bibliography 307
Index of Names 331
Index of Subjects 336
Table of Contents 343

Preface

Many English books have been translated into French. This time we are doing it the other way around. The Network for evangelical missiologists in French speaking Europe (*Réseau de missiologie évangélique pour l'Europe francophone*, REMEEF), is translating its book "Evangelism in French speaking Europe" (*L'évangélisation en Europe francophone*) from French to English. It desires to share its findings and ideas with Christians and missiologists from all over Europe, something France did repeatedly in the past, especially during the Enlightenment epoch.

The title of this English version is *Evangelism in Europe*. Why is the subject no longer limited to "francophone Europe" like in the French version? There was a debate among the members of the network about the two options. The main experience of the authors has been gained in French speaking Europe. On the other hand, Europe passed through a history with a particular characteristic which distinguishes it from other continents, i.e. the European Enlightenment, which has left its mark on the continent down to the present day, although of course not in all countries to the same degree. Evert van de Poll formulates this fact in the introduction to chapter 3 in the following way:

> Our subject is evangelism in Europe as a whole – that is, including the countries outside the European Union. When we look at such a vast field, our approach can only be a general one. This is a deliberate choice, for I am persuaded that when we try and see the overall picture of Christianity and religion in Europe, we will gain a better understanding of what is happening in each particular country on this continent. Together they constitute a specific context for the communication of the Gospel.

This English version is thus not a word for word translation of the French book, but rather an adaptation to Europe as a whole and to the Anglophone socio-cultural and missiological context.

Profiting from an overview of Europe, we are at the same time aware of the particularities that each country presents. The commonalities and the differences will both shape the evangelistic approach adopted in each European country. Looking at the whole of Europe, we will also become more conscious of Europe's specific challenges and opportunities. Jiří Unger, the President of the Czech Evangelical Alliance and former President of the European Evangelical Alliance, summarises some of them in the preface to Deborah Meroff's book *Europe: Restoring Hope*:

- Europe was and still is the world's most important exporter of secularism and atheism, and of ideologies that are in opposition to Christianity;
- We are no longer living in Jerusalem where people follow our rules and prescriptions, but in a new Babylon;
- We can learn to be a minority without suffering from an inferiority complex;
- We can contribute to God's plan for the future of Europe.

Unger deplores the fact that many European Christians have what he calls a "grasshopper mentality" (Num 13:33). Faced with the European "giants," they are paralysed by fear, shame and resignation. Calebs are needed, Christians who see the many possibilities to share the Gospel and enter the open doors. Speaking about Europe as a new Babylon, Unger observes that we need many Daniels in Europe, Christians who are faithful to God in everyday life, render quality service in their professional involvement, and witness to Him in their daily relationships.

I want to thank the authors, who agreed to translate and adapt their chapters, for their additional effort, and the other authors for their consent and trust in those doing the translation and adaptation. Thanks go also to the proof-readers Elizabeth Johnston and Barbara and Derek Cheeseman for their competent and enjoyable collaboration. Finally, I thank Thomas Mayer from VTR Publications for his diligent and efficient handling of the project.

The Network of evangelical missiologists in French speaking Europe (REMEEF) hopes that this book will be an encouraging read and provide the tools and innovative ideas for those eager to be Daniels and Calebs for our fellow Europeans.

Hannes Wiher

Preface to the French Version

Some years ago my wife and I were invited by long-time friends to make a trip to Bulgaria. What a surprise to discover an oriental but European country marked by years of Soviet domination, but whose European roots had not disappeared! As everywhere else in Europe, the magnificent Roman ruins were still standing; the Christian monasteries (here orthodox), real cultural and spiritual fortresses, had resisted all the assaults, the town centre district with its splendid architecture recalled the prosperity of old, the magnificent churches had survived, and some mosques recalled the conflicts that had shaken the country severely over the centuries. Regarding the population, the contrast was striking between the older generations with sad and closed faces, and the carefree youth turned towards the West, somewhat disoriented, but full of questions and hope. There was a similar strong contrast between the Orthodox Church making a huge effort to recover the hegemony of old, and the young evangelical churches, enthusiastic but fragile, without forgetting this venerable Presbyterian Church, still present after more than one and a half centuries, and still very alive. Last surprise: to discover a Francophile country which has links with the Francophonie, whose youth has only one aspiration: to master English.

In fact, Europe. The old Europe, culturally and socially perceptible, despite all the disruptions throughout the centuries. A Europe that has deep roots, which is a reality but also an enigma. How can populations, who kept killing each other throughout history and were constantly in conflict, still perceive a common identity? The contemporary politico-economic Europe is an eloquent reflection of this. Nevertheless, it functions more or less.

To think Europe represents a challenge. A challenge that may seem foolish to take up, but which corresponds to a reality. Some great personalities accepted this challenge, just after the awful conflict of 1939-1945. It was really necessary to do something! As regards missiology, it took more than a half century to confront the task. However, it must be said that the spiritual damage caused by two centuries of Enlightenment influence, militant atheism, and the return of spirituality through the arrival of sects, Esotericism and oriental religions, is daunting. The new challenges due to massive immigration and Islam added to the complexity.

It is time to meet our responsibilities. The churches and missions have certainly not waited for the 21st century to tackle it. Since the end of World

War II, the efforts at evangelism were considerable, with a certain success. But they did not stop the unfurling wave mentioned above. The gravity of the situation and its extreme complexity call for a deep awareness of the situation in Europe, an analysis of contemporary practices, a theological reflection on the spiritual condition of Europeans, the witness of old and new churches, and the nature of the Gospel that has to be announced.

This is a considerable enterprise. Many have been engaged in it recently. The Network of evangelical missiologists in French speaking Europe (*Réseau de missiologie évangélique pour l'Europe francophone*, REMEEF) wants to make its modest contribution. This book presents the papers given on the subject during several conferences of members of the Network and of several specialists. I want to thank the authors for their contribution, particularly Evert van de Poll, who has also participated in preparing the outline of this book.

Modest contribution, I said, but a determined contribution. Now we have to summon up the courage to examine ourselves and face the situation – and this not only by multiplying activities, but by stepping back in order to reflect, to consult, and propose a new step. This book wants to contribute to this new dynamic. I wish you an inspiring reading!

Bernard Huck

Introduction

Hannes Wiher

After twenty centuries of Christian history evangelism in Europe cannot be envisaged along the same lines as during the first evangelisation of Europe. If we do not have innovative approaches to contemporary Europeans, the enterprise may well fail. A complete rethink of our approach to evangelism seems inevitable. On the basis of the new developments in the science of mission, the Network of evangelical missiologists for French speaking Europe (REMEEF[1]) has reflected on the ways by which the message of the Gospel can be communicated in the different European contexts, particularly in Western Europe, in a way that is faithful to Scripture and relevant for contemporary Europeans.

The aim of this book is not to present the full picture of evangelism in Europe. Through some presentations at the meetings of our network REMEEF and at the evangelical seminaries in Paris, France,[2] and in Heverlee, Belgium,[3] we will put forward some suggestions for context analysis and evangelistic approaches. We have to emphasise that Europe is not a virgin "mission field." Many Europeans would say: "We have already tried it and have seen that it does not work." The Frenchman Jean Delumeau formulates the problem well:

> Christendom as a constituted body has constantly disclaimed itself despite the faith, piety and charity of a great number of particular individuals.[4]

If we do not want to be considered naïve, we must think about a new approach to evangelism in a scientific way with the help of all the tools that theology and missiology (including the social sciences) offer us today, and this on the sound basis of a missional spirituality.

In this introduction, we will first reflect on the definitions of evangelism, evangelisation and mission (the definition of Europe follows in chapter 2). Then we have to think about a good way to integrate the social sci-

---

[1] Réseau de missiologie évangélique pour l'Europe francophone (REMEEF).
[2] Faculté libre de théologie évangélique de Vaux-sur-Seine (FLTE), France.
[3] Evangelische Theologische Faculteit (ETF), Heverlee (Leuven), Belgium.
[4] Jean Delumeau, *Le christianisme va-t-il mourir?* (Paris: Hachette, 1977), p. 41.

entific data into a missiological analysis, and thirdly we will present a concise review of research on the topic. Detailed statistics and a literature review figure in the Appendix.

Definition of Evangelism, Evangelisation and Mission

When defining evangelism or mission, we find ourselves embarrassed by the multiplicity of definitions. Different people understand the three terms differently, and the definitions are not as clear as it might seem, judging by the frequent use of the terms. Most people use evangelism and mission more or less as synonyms, covering the whole spectrum from narrow to broad understandings. Others distinguish evangelism and mission, for example by assigning evangelism geographically to local monocultural endeavours and mission to foreign cross-cultural activities, or attributing the term evangelism to activities targeted at people who are *no longer* or nominal Christians, and mission to those who are *not yet* Christians. This view has been generally held by Lutheran and Reformed Churches as well as by the Vatican II documents. Among those who distinguish between the two terms, for some evangelism is the broader term covering the whole ministry of the Church, while for others it is the narrower term covering only the heart of mission, in terms of verbal proclamation of the Gospel. The older term evangelism is dominant in mainline Protestant churches. The Roman Catholic Church and Evangelicals have partly dropped the ambiguous terms mission and evangelism and prefer the newer term evangelisation, as is apparent in the Catholic concept of "new evangelisation" and the exact name of the Lausanne Movement: the Lausanne Committee for World Evangelisation (LCWE).[5]

One way to get an orientation in this chaos is an historical approach to the development of the definitions in the major documents of the Lausanne Movement and their evaluation by theologians and missiologists.[6] The reason why the Lausanne Movement has avoided the term mission in its name seems to be the widening of the concept in ecumenical and Roman Catholic circles during the years prior to the foundation of the Lausanne Movement. The term "evangelisation" seemed to lend to less misunderstandings.[7]

---

[5] For a detailed discussion, see David J. Bosch, "Evangelism: Currents and Cross-Currents in Theology Today," *International Bulletin of Missionary Research* 11, 3 (1987), p. 98-103; idem, *Transforming Mission: Paradigm Shifts in Theology of Mission* (Maryknoll: Orbis, 1991), p. 409-411.

[6] Lausanne Covenant (1974), Manila Manifesto (1989), Cape Town Commitment (2010), and some thirty Lausanne Occasional Papers (LOP), at www.lausanne.org.

[7] Bosch, *Transforming Mission*, p. 411; Ralph Winter, "The Highest Priority: Cross-

Paragraph 4 of the Lausanne Covenant (1974) entitled "The Nature of Evangelism" gives the following definition (I quote the paragraph here completely):

> To evangelize is to spread the good news that Jesus Christ died for our sins and was raised from the dead according to the Scriptures, and that as the reigning Lord he now offers the forgiveness of sins and the liberating gifts of the Spirit to all who repent and believe. Our Christian presence in the world is indispensable to evangelism, and so is that kind of dialogue whose purpose is to listen sensitively in order to understand. But evangelism itself is the proclamation of the historical, biblical Christ as Saviour and Lord, with a view to persuading people to come to him personally and so be reconciled to God. In issuing the gospel invitation we have no liberty to conceal the cost of discipleship. Jesus still calls all who would follow him to deny themselves, take up their cross, and identify themselves with his new community. The results of evangelism include obedience to Christ, incorporation into his Church and responsible service in the world.[8]

According to the Lausanne Covenant's definition, evangelism comprises presence, dialogue, proclamation and persuasion. The element lacking compared to a more holistic definition of mission is social action. This aspect is included in the concept of mission by Latin American authors in an alternative Lausanne Covenant.[9] The official Lausanne Covenant mentions social action in paragraph 5 under the heading "Christian Social Responsibility:"

> We express penitence both for our neglect and for having sometimes regarded evangelism and social concern as mutually exclusive. Although reconciliation with other people is not reconciliation with God, nor is social action evangelism, nor is political liberation salvation, nevertheless we affirm that evangelism and socio-political involvement are both part of our Christian duty.

Paragraph 5 seeks a balance between a dichotomist view (evangelism and social responsibility, a "Northern" view), and a holistic view of "both [being] part of our Christian duty" (a "Southern" view). This fact mirrors John Stott's median position. He was mainly responsible for the formula-

---

Cultural Evangelism," in *Let the Earth Hear His Voice*, ed. J.D. Douglas (Minneapolis: Worldwide Publications, 1975), p. 213-225.

[8] Bible references given: 1 Cor 15:3,4; Acts 2:32-39; John 20:21; 1 Cor 1:23; 2 Cor 4:5; 5:11,20; Luke 14:25-33; Mark 8:34; Acts 2:40,47; Mark 10:43-45.

[9] "Theological Implications of Radical Discipleship," in Douglas, *Let the Earth Hear His Voice*, p. 1294-1296; see also Valdir R. Steuernagel, "Social Concern and Evangelization: The Journey of the Lausanne Movement," *Occasional Bulletin from the Missionary Research Library* 15, 2 (1975).

tion of the first two Lausanne declarations and the paper of the Grand Rapids Consultation on the Relationship between Evangelism and Social Responsibility (1982). The latter maintains the same position – for it has the same main author. About the relationship between the two, it affirms under the fourth heading that social responsibility can be a consequence of evangelism, a bridge to evangelism and a partner of evangelism. "They are like two wings of a bird." However, evangelism has priority (primacy) over social responsibility.[10] The concept of priority maintains the dichotomist view.

In his *Transforming Mission* (1991), David Bosch distinguishes between evangelism and mission, evangelism being the narrower concept. He defines evangelism,

> as that dimension and activity of the church's mission which, by word and deed and in the light of particular conditions and a particular context, offers every person and community, everywhere, a valid opportunity to be directly challenged to a radical reorientation of their lives, a reorientation which involves such things as … embracing Christ as Savior and Lord; becoming a living member of his community, … [and] placing all things under the rule of Christ.[11]

For Bosch, evangelism is thus "the core, heart, or center of mission; it consists in the proclamation of salvation in Christ to nonbelievers."[12] However, in the 18th affirmation on evangelism, Bosch specifies: "Evangelism is not only verbal proclamation." His position differs thus from most others who opt for a narrow concept of evangelism and see in evangelism the strictly verbal proclamation of the Gospel. On the other hand, according to Bosch, "mission denotes the total task God has set the church for the salvation of the world … Mission is the church sent into the world, to love, to serve, to preach, to teach, to heal, to liberate." In doing this, "it crosses all kinds of frontiers and barriers: geographical, social, political, ethnic, cultural, religious, [and] ideological."[13]

In 2007, Tormod Engelsviken, a member of the Lausanne Theology Working Group, formulates the Lausanne consensus in a similar way to Bosch:

> Although there is no consistent way of speaking of mission, evangelization and evangelism with the Lausanne movement, we may say that while mission and

---

[10] "Lausanne Occasional Paper No. 21: Evangelism and Social Responsibility," at www.lausanne.org/content/lop/lop-21.

[11] Bosch, *Transforming Mission*, p. 420. See also his 18 affirmations on evangelism p. 411-421.

[12] Bosch, "Evangelism," p. 100.

[13] Bosch, *Transforming Mission*, p. 412; idem, "Evangelism," p. 100.

evangelization are the broader, more comprehensive terms including both proclamation and social concern, evangelism is a more narrow [sic] concept being defined primarily in terms of proclamation.[14]

The embarrassment of defining evangelism and mission continues. Another step on the road to a broader definition is proposed by the Micah Network. Pushed by the mounting pressure of "radical Evangelicals" from the Global South, the Micah Network introduced in 2001 the concept of "integral (or holistic) mission:"

> Integral mission or holistic transformation is the proclamation and demonstration of the gospel. It is not simply that evangelism and social involvement are to be done alongside each other. Rather, in integral mission our proclamation has social consequences as we call people to love and repentance in all areas of life. And our social involvement has evangelistic consequences as we bear witness to the transforming grace of Jesus Christ.[15]

The Micah Network adopts a holistic approach to the definition of evangelism/mission. In 2010, it was followed by the Theological Commission of the Lausanne Movement composed of a majority of Southern theologians under the leadership of Christopher Wright. The Cape Town Commitment affirms, under the heading "Bearing witness to the truth of Christ in a pluralistic, globalised world:"

> As disciples of Christ we are called to be people of truth. (1) We must *live* the truth. To live the truth is to be the face of Jesus, through whom the glory of the gospel is revealed to blinded minds. People will see truth in the faces of those who live their lives for Jesus, in faithfulness and love. (2) We must *proclaim* the truth. Spoken proclamation of the truth of the gospel remains paramount in our mission. This cannot be separated from living out the truth. Works and words must go together.[16]

When defining witness, the Lausanne Movement avoids the terms evangelism and mission, both now open to misunderstandings. The Cape Town Commitment starts with "living the truth," seconded by "proclaiming the truth," whereas the Micah Network, nine years earlier, still started with proclamation. The holistic approach to mission appears to be ac-

---

[14] Tormod Engelsviken, "Mission, Evangelism and Evangelization – from the Perspective of the Lausanne Movement," *International Review of Mission* vol. 96, Nos. 382/383 (July-October 2007), p. 204-209.

[15] "Micah Network Integral Mission Declaration (2001)," at www.micahnetwork.org/integral-mission.

[16] "Cape Town Commitment (2010)," IIA1a, at www.lausanne.org/ctcommitment.

knowledged by the Lausanne Movement. However, not all Western Evangelicals follow this line; many still prefer a dichotomist definition maintaining the priority of evangelism.[17]

Relationship between Theology and Social Sciences

As a missiological approach is an interdisciplinary endeavour, we also have to think about how the social sciences can be integrated with theology in a good way.[18] In practical theology and missiology the relationship between theology and social sciences is usually thought of in terms of three models:[19]

1) The social sciences are *preliminary* to theological reflection in order to help those involved in mission and pastoral work to better understand the world around them, and particularly their target population.

2) The social sciences have a role as an *adviser* who gives them help in order to find the best practices.

3) The social sciences are in constant *dialogue* with theological reflection, recognising that all viewpoints are relative.

As we intend to include an analysis of the socio-cultural context in our missiological approach, we must first study the legitimacy of the above models of integration.

The Incarnation of the Word is the basis of the Christian understanding of the person of Jesus of Nazareth. On the one hand, he is the son of a Pal-

---

[17] See also the discussions in chapters 8 and 9.

[18] In this section we build on Julien Coffinet's discussion of the relationship between theology and sociology in the French version of this book. Cf. Julien Coffinet, "Le rapport entre théologie et sociologie," in Wiher, *L'évangélisation en Europe francophone*, p. 38-40.

[19] See for example Edward Rommen & Gary Corwin, eds., *Missiology and the Social Sciences: Contributions, Cautions and Conclusions* (Evangelical Missiological Society Series No. 4; Pasadena: William Carey Library, 1996); Paul G. Hiebert, "Reflections on Epistemological Foundations," in *Anthropological Reflections on Missiological Issues* (Grand Rapids: Baker, 1994), p. 19-52; Pierre Bühler et al., *Humain à l'image de Dieu: La théologie et les sciences humaines face au problème de l'anthropologie* (Lieu théologiques 15; Genève: Labor et Fides, 1989); Jean Joncheray, "Théologie et sciences humaines," in *Précis de théologie pratique*, eds. Gilles Routhier & Marcel Viau (Bruxelles/Montréal: Lumen Vitae/Novalis, 2004); N. Mette & H. Steinkamp, *Sozialwissenschaften und Praktische Theologie* (Düsseldorf: Patmos, 1983).

estinian carpenter, an Aramaic, Hebrew and Greek speaker who lived under the reign of the Roman Emperor Augustus, and at the same time he is the Son of the eternal God. The Incarnation of God in Jesus Christ is the manifestation of his love to us humans (Jn 3:16), the model of his communication and thus the matrix of contextualisation.[20] In his book *Center Church*, Timothy Keller proposes the following definition of contextualisation:

> [Contextualization is] giving people *the Bible's answers*, which they may not at all want to hear, *to questions about life* that people in their particular time and place are asking, *in language and forms* they can comprehend, and *through appeals and arguments* with force they can feel, even if they reject them.[21]

On this basis we think that to give oneself the means to engage with our fellow Europeans, in order to understand them in their real life setting, can be seen in very spiritual terms. In this perspective the social sciences represent an intellectual act of humility before God and an act of respect before our contemporaries. It helps us to encounter our fellow humans beyond our egocentric projections and through a thoughtful effort before we even start to communicate. The social sciences make more transparent our cultural presuppositions which form the framework in which we have understood and integrated the Gospel.

This being said, the collection of data and their interpretation by the social sciences have necessarily certain limits which require vigilant attention:

1) Jesus Christ knows each one of his sheep by its name (Jn 10). On the other hand, the social sciences can give us at the maximum phenomenological and partial approaches to the reality of persons and cultures. The collective subconscious, the aspects of common culture or the apparent preoccupations of a survey are never sufficient to really know people, because they cannot be reduced to the collective determinants that we can model intellectually. "Such knowledge is so high that I cannot attain it" (Ps 139:6).

2) "The light shines in the darkness" (Jn 1:5). In the interpretation of surveys one insists very often on the distance between "perception"

---

[20] See Dean S. Gilliland, "The Incarnation as Matrix for Appropriate Theologies," in *Appropriate Christianity*, ed. Charles H. Kraft (Pasadena: William Carey Library, 2005), p. 493-520.

[21] Timothy Keller, *Center Church: Doing Balanced, Gospel-Centered Ministry in Your City* (Grand Rapids: Zondervan, 2012), p. 89 (italics in the original).

and "reality" as well as the subjectivity of the self-definition of persons. All these reservations of the surveyors and of the sociologists who interpret the data can be worked on within a phenomenological framework of self-perception. In a biblical perspective it seems to us that we reach the limits of the capacity to know the real core of persons. It is paramount not to give an excessive importance to expectations expressed by persons who do not know the Gospel, because God is infinitely beyond all we can think or imagine (Eph 3:20). On the other hand, the preaching of the Gospel targets a renewed life which radically turns human aspirations upside down.

3) The collection of data on real life has no end. The social sciences have at their disposition a great number of fields and methods of investigation. It is of paramount importance that the missiologist has a mastery of the epistemological[22] aspects of missiology in the transition from social scientific data to theological reflection. It is the missiologist's task to guide the procedure of the social sciences towards the objective which he has fixed theologically beforehand. This does not hinder him from being challenged by the social scientific data. Nevertheless, he has to make intentional use of the social sciences subordinated to his theological project, and not undertake a "preliminary" procedure in the sense that the theological reflection only takes second place.

4) Finally, the missiologist has to keep in mind that the social sciences function according to a methodological atheism. Therefore, a critical distance has to be maintained regarding the social scientific interpretations. Jean-Marie Donegani writes: « As a metalanguage sociology wants to introduce an insurmountable distance between knowledge and faith while theology positions itself as a critical authority within the worldview of the believer and starts from revelation that constitutes the point of departure of its procedure."[23] From this point of view it will be the missiologist's task to go beyond a preliminary social scientific procedure and to contest the interpretative contention

---

[22] Epistemology (from Greek *epistêmê* "knowledge" and *logos* "discourse") is the study of knowledge and asks the question how it is possible to know.

[23] Jean-Marie Donegani, "Les récits de vie" (the narratives of life), in Routhier & Viau, *Précis de théologie pratique*, p. 113-114, quoted by Jean-Georges Gantenbein, *Mission en Europe: Une étude socio-missiologique pour le 21ᵉ siècle* (Ph.D. thesis, Faculté de théologie protestante Strasbourg, Université Marc Bloch, 2010; Studia Œcumenica Friburgensia 72; Münster: Aschendorff, 2016), p. 26.

of the social sciences to exhaust the interpretation of a social fact through the analysis of other social data. He will have to find the appropriate moment to reintegrate the spiritual interpretation, and ultimately the sovereignty of God over history and human behaviour, in this closed system.

In response to the initial question how a good integration of theology and the social sciences can be envisaged, we can draw the following conclusion: The social sciences are at the same time offering a *preliminary* investigation to the theological reflection, and they are a concomitant *adviser* and *dialogue partner* of the theologian. However, the missional theologian and practitioner will keep his critical distance from the social scientific data in order to integrate them in his findings by making a critical evaluation of them. In this way, the particular data from different sciences found on the basis of a secular worldview can be integrated in the overall biblical worldview.

Review of Research

Our interdisciplinary missiological approach also includes an assessment of the research on evangelism in Europe in the areas of theology, philosophy, sociology, cultural anthropology and missiology. We do this in the form of a statistical and a literary review. The interested reader will find the detailed statistics and literature in the appendix.

At this point we want to give just a glance at some intriguing statistical data:[24]

- Nine of the twelve atheistic/agnostic countries, which are statistically at the top, are located in Europe.
- Among the 738 million Europeans less than 2 % actively follow Jesus Christ. And in at least 20 European countries there are less than 1 % evangelical Christians.
- Islam is the fastest growing religion in Europe.
- The countries with the highest suicide rates are located in Europe: Belarus, Lithuania and Russia.
- The number of marriages has dropped in the European Union from 6.3 per 1000 inhabitants in 1990 to 4.9 per 1000 inhabitants in 2008;

---

[24] Selected from Deborah Meroff, *Europe: Restoring Hope* (Nürnberg/Linz: VTR/OM, 2011), p. 11.

one third of all children in these 27 countries were born outside of marriages.
- In 2002 the Netherlands was the first country to legalise euthanasia, even though it has been practised there since 1973. Dutch medical doctors end the life of 900 to 1000 patients per year without request or consent. In Belgium, euthanasia has also been legalised, and Switzerland allows medically assisted suicide. Based on this fact, Switzerland has become the target of "suicide tourists."

Our literature review includes particularly elements inherent in a missiological approach: a history of evangelism in Europe, an analysis of the socio-cultural context, a theology of the Gospel and of evangelism, and a reflection on the communication of the Gospel and church planting in the European context.[25]

Concerning the history of evangelism in Europe, Neal Blough and Sébastien Fath agree that there can be no sensible approach to evangelism without a thorough knowledge of the history of Christianity in Europe: the quality of the first evangelism among the animistic Germanic peoples, the Renaissance and the Enlightenment, Protestant and Catholic Reforms with the religious wars, Pietism and the revivals with the first evangelism and discipleship schemes of the evangelical movement, and finally the de-Christianisation during the 20th century and the arrival of postmodernity.

In the same line of thought, an evangelism which wants to be relevant to our European contemporaries cannot ignore socio-cultural analysis. In recent decades there has been a real boom in studies on European values and milieus, and a whole realm of new concepts in the sociology of religion. The main reflection centred on the de-Christianisation of Europe, and consequently the question what the convictions of the so-called secular people outside of the church were. Going beyond the concepts of secularisation and de-secularisation, Grace Davie has introduced the catch-phrases of "the paradox of Europe," "vicarious religion," "religion by default," and "believing without belonging." In the same vein, Danièle Hervieu-Léger introduced the notions of "lost religion" and "the religious everywhere." For her, religious awareness is not only defined in terms of the religions, but is a transversal dimension of the human phenomenon. She also proposed a typology of contemporary Christian believers with the stable "practitioner," the mobile "pilgrim" and the "convert" who changes religion and finds a new identity. In her contribution to the collective book *La*

---

[25] See the appendix 2 for detailed references.

globalisation du religieux (2001), she observes the contemporary trends in religion and makes three interesting statements: The more belief individualises, the more it homogenises; the more belief homogenises, the more the believers circulate; the more the beliefs circulate, the less they determine and respond to practical belonging, and the more they favour a communitarian voluntarism liable to evolve towards sectarian forms.

On the other hand, studies on a theology of evangelism were rather rare. Here we have to mention Karl Barth's Catholic colleague in Basel, Hans Urs von Balthasar, who has adopted in his Trilogy the missiological approach indicated at the beginning of this review: a history and analysis of European philosophical thought, a fundamental theology, and in the last part of his triptych a reflection on theologising in the European context, a "theo-logic." The Catholic concept of "new evangelisation" gives the impression that it represents a rather nostalgic attempt to return to the first evangelism of Europe. However, James Russell deconstructs Europe's Christianisation during the medieval epoch so that a rather disillusioned picture remains. Newer attempts on the Catholic side (Marie-Hélène Robert) and in evangelical circles (Stefan Paas, Christophe Paya, Friedemann Walldorf, Klaus Müller, Markus Müller) are more encouraging. Very encouraging and interesting are some recent projects of theological reflection for Western culture proposed by systematic theologians and missiologists. We mention only the Gospel and Our Culture Network (GOCN) initiated by Lesslie Newbigin, and the books of N.T. Wright and Kevin Vanhoozer. The pragmatic side of American-influenced missiology has also produced many reflections on the communication of the Gospel and church planting in the European context. We mention the proposals of Raphael Anzenberger and Yannick Imbert in apologetics, of David Brown in discipleship, the concept of dialogue in the ecumenical movement, and manifold practical advice by Timothy Keller, the Redcliffe Nova Research team, Johannes Reimer and Gabriel Monet on the idea of a missional church based on the reflections around the concept of "emerging church." The reader will find more details in the appendix.

Concluding Considerations

What are the lessons on evangelism in Europe that we can learn from our literary review? We find that there are many different approaches: historical (Blough, Fath), economic and political (Van de Poll), sociological (European Values Study, Sinus-Milieus, Davie, Hervieu-Léger, Champion, Gantenbein), apologetic (Beyerhaus, Anzenberger, Imbert), communicative (Brown, Reimer, the concepts of presence and dialogue of the ecumenical movement), practical (Keller, Monet) and some theological reflections (the concept of "new evangelisation" of the Catholic Church, Robert, Paas, Paya, Walldorf, Müller, Newbigin, Wright, Vanhoozer). However, there is no reflection that comprises all four steps of a missiological procedure mentioned above: a history of evangelism in Europe, an analysis of the socio-cultural context, a theology of evangelism, and a reflection on the communication of the Gospel and church planting in the European context. A praiseworthy exception is the contribution of Marie-Hélène Robert who goes the farthest in this direction.

In conclusion we want to introduce briefly Markus Müller's and Deborah Meroff's reflections on the contemporary challenges for Europe and the Christian response they require. According to Müller,[26] the life of a contemporary European is marked more and more by its rapidity and complexity. One attractive response would be a simple and decelerated life style in the church. The centrifugal forces in our societies are increasing. The church offers the option to focus on the Centre who is Jesus Christ. Europe will know scenarios of deprivation in the future. The Europeans must thus learn how to be happy in trials and in situations of deprivation. Furthermore, according to Müller, there exists a menace of a culture shock. The church should propose solutions for multicultural life in general and for co-existence with Islam in particular. In Europe cultural pluralism will have to be recognised by everyone. Personal, cultural and economic differences are a fact. The migrants, on their side, must accept to learn how to live in Europe. Müller suggests that the state should oblige them to learn the local language in order to promote integration and ask that they respect the constitution and the judicial code of the welcoming country. Finally, Müller perceives a spiritual battle over Europe.

Deborah Meroff[27] proposes in her book *Europe: Restoring Hope* (2011) that Christians and Christian communities that are eager to reach fellow Europeans assist marginal groups, love Muslims, start capacity building among children and youth, make outreach to secular and nominal European neighbours and organise partnerships among churches.

We hope that this book can give some basic information on evangelism in Europe and present some innovative paths, and that more complete reflections will follow.

---

[26] Markus Müller was the former international director of Chrischona in Basle.

[27] Deborah Meroff is an American journalist who has done research on evangelism in Europe on behalf of Operation Mobilisation (OM).

Part One

Understanding Europe

Chapter 1
Evangelism in Europe: Historical Background

Neal Blough[1]

The first Gospel in the NT starts with a genealogy. This simple fact allows one to understand that one cannot announce the Gospel without placing it in a long term perspective. One cannot understand Jesus without Abraham or David. Likewise, evangelism in contemporary Western Europe cannot be understood without Irenaeus, Constantine, Charlemagne, Calvin, Loyola, Louis XIV and the Enlightenment.

This chapter tackles the "larger" historical context of evangelism in Europe by going back to the 2nd century. It would be naïve to pretend that one can evangelise Europe as if one started from zero, as if our evangelism were not part of a very complex historical process, and as if we and our contemporaries were not marked by this history. The mentality of a people is not necessarily conscious. It is forged along the centuries, transmitted from generation to generation.

In this chapter, we raise some important general issues in order to ask some questions and make some observations in relation to our reflection and our contemporary practice of evangelism in Europe. The history of Christianity in Western Europe will serve as a framework for our more general reflection.

Pre-Constantine Epoch

In South Western Europe, the Church has been present since the 2nd century AD (and perhaps even before). In the second half of the same century, Christianity was already well planted in the Greek speaking communities of Vienna and Lyon where Irenaeus had become a figure of prime importance for the Church of his epoch. It is interesting to realise the man-

---

[1] This text is a translated and adapted version of the article: Neal Blough, "Évangéliser en France: Regards en arrière," in *La mission de l'Église au 21ᵉ siècle: Les nouveaux défis*, ed. Hannes Wiher (Charols: Excelsis, 2010), p. 35-47.

ner by which Christianity expanded throughout the Roman Empire during the first centuries. The historians estimate that by 312 the Christians represented between 5 % and 25 % of the population of the Empire.[2] This number reflects a very remarkable growth during a difficult period when there was no social advantage in professing the Christian faith.

When trying to understand and explain this growth, historians remark that there was no explicit strategy for evangelism, very few if not any public sermons to the masses, no institution to propagate the faith, no prayer for the conversion of the non-Jews nor exhortation to engage in evangelism.[3] On the contrary, in the Christian communities of this pre-Constantine period, it was difficult to become a member. A non-Jew was not able to take part in Christian worship services; those who manifested their interest in the faith had to go through a period of catechism that lasted two or three years.

Yet, how did it happen that the Church grew in numbers? The most frequently suggested reason is the quality of the personal and collective life of the Christians. Worship services and catechisms of this period were intended to set up a new mentality, to form a people that lived according to the Spirit of Christ, to bring to life a communal reality where there was neither Jew nor Greek, neither man nor woman, neither slave nor free man.

> The heart of the newness, the pre-Christendom Christians sensed, was the person and teaching of Jesus Christ. He and his words were good news to people. Jesus' words were, according to the mid-third century *Didascalia Apostolorum*, "incisive words." Origen testified that they had a "charm" that drew people to follow him. In Justin's experience Jesus' words possess a terrible power in themselves, [...] Pagans, the Christians testified, were drawn to Jesus and his Sermon on the Mount teachings.[4]

If this teaching attracted many people, it questioned also certain fundamental values of the Empire, resulting in rejection and persecution on the part of several Roman emperors. For some, the voluntary death of the martyrs reinforced the attractiveness of Christianity, for others, it confirmed the folly of the members of this strange sect.

---

[2] Alan Kreider, *Worship and Evangelism in Pre-Christendom* (Joint Liturgical Studies, 32; Cambridge: Grove Books Limited, 1995), p. 11.
[3] Idem, p. 6-7.
[4] Idem, p. 11.

Constantine and the Medieval Epoch

The severe persecution at the beginning of the 4th century stopped suddenly with Constantine's "conversion." From that moment on Christianity experienced an important "growth." Under Constantine Christians began to be tolerated, under Theodosius paganism was proscribed, under Clovis and Charlemagne Europe saw numerous populations calling themselves Christians following the application of missionary methods that were more than dubious. Besides the use of political and military means to spread Christianity, one should also mention the patient evangelism and teaching accomplished by the monastic communities.

Nevertheless, the understanding of what a Christian is began to change. Catechism and baptism altered in character. In 370, Bazile of Caesarea could insist on the fact "that one has to be first a disciple before receiving baptism," while in the 5th century, Augustine says: "first baptise them, and then one can teach them a transformation of life and customs."[5]

We enter the period of Christendom, that is, a civilisation where everything, at least in theory, is derived from the Christian base and foundation: ethics, economy, politics, philosophy, science. In theory, everybody is or should be Christian, and the methods of converting non-Christians (Jews or Muslims) are sometimes less than ideal.

This period lasted for a long time, and left a profound mark on European civilisation. One was born Christian just as today one is born an Englishman, a Frenchman, German, Swiss, Hungarian, Polish, Romanian, or Russian. The reflection on this phenomenon by Jean Delumeau is illuminating:

> Christian theology has certainly been in power and the authorities in place have forged the term *res publica christiana* to indicate the territories as a whole – where one should have recited – the *Credo*, but:
> 1. This Christendom has been more an authoritarian construction and a system with a strict control of the populations than a *conscious* adhesion of the masses to a *revealed* faith ...
> 2. As a constituted body, Christendom has constantly disclaimed itself, despite the faith, piety and charity of numerous particular persons.[6]

---

[5] Idem, p. 41.
[6] Jean Delumeau, *Le christianisme va-t-il mourir?* (Paris: Hachette, 1977), p. 40-41.

Epoch of Reformation (16th and 17th Century)

As a Protestant, one normally regards the medieval period as a decadent period of decline, both in the papacy and in theology. Fortunately, we say, the Reformation has arrived.

The Reformation asks, in fact, important theological questions. But it also raises the question of evangelism, or more precisely of the "Christianisation" of Europe. If the Roman Catholic Church is mistaken, as the Reformers claim, we have to "teach" or "Christianise" the towns, the landscapes and the entire countries again.

Where there was only one church, only one official Christianity, Europe now found herself confronted with several gospels that seemed to exclude each other mutually. For Luther, the pope is the anti-Christ; for the pope, Luther merits excommunication. This marks the beginning of a race for the "true evangelism" of Europe. New "true" churches (Lutheran, Reformed, Anabaptist) are created, along with a new catechism, because it is discovered that the people do not know very much about the Christian faith. Faced with the Protestant reforms, Rome also undertakes hers, especially by means of the Council of Trent. Both find their political support, both find their means (peaceful or otherwise). Certain territories become Protestant (entirely). Others remain Roman Catholic; others again, like France and Germany, become a subject of dispute, for a period at least.

And because everybody believes that they possess the truth, tolerance or dialogue are not considered. It is apparent that the methods of evangelism in medieval Christendom are seldom questioned during the epoch of Reformation. Since Clovis or Charlemagne had not hesitated to Christianise their territories by force, the Europe of the 16th and 17th century saw no reason to reject similar endeavours of evangelism. The political powers continued to legislate in matters of the Christian faith, in other words to "Christianise" entire populations, at Geneva, Paris, Rome or Munster. And in the disputed territories, like France and Germany, one resorted without scruples to war when legislation did not succeed, all in the name of Christianisation.

One arrives at things that are hard for our 21st century minds to believe. A whole series of wars were necessary until Protestantism was recognised in France, while later Cromwell and his dissident armies executed a king in England whose reign claimed to be of divine right. Towards the middle of the 17th century, after the end of the Thirty Years War, Europe became tired of confessional wars and of forced "Christianisation," which did not prevent Louis XIV from revoking the edict of Nantes. One is far away from the Gospel and one can in fact question the means used to evangelise

Modernity

The chief challenge that the Enlightenment poses to Christianity is an intellectual one. It is claimed that the Gospel is no longer credible because of the developments of modern science and philosophy. Modern man, product of Voltaire, Rousseau, Marx, Nietzsche and Freud, cannot believe.

Be that as it may, in the context of modernity[7] it has become difficult to evangelise. The ideal of the French Revolution challenges Christianity and the old order. For many, Europe cannot be a modern continent without rejecting its Christian past. Additionally, urbanisation, industrialisation and secularisation are advancing and destroying everything in their path that resembles a "religious" mentality, at least as medieval Europe has conceived it. However, in the 19th century, Protestantism has become more open to the emerging modernity than the Roman Catholic Church. Pluralism and secularism have made vital room for religious minorities.

In our contemporary context, the sphere that is reserved for the Christian faith has become smaller. Today we can believe what we want under the condition that it remains confined to the private sphere; faith is only one opinion among others and is increasingly excluded from the public sphere i.e. politics, school, the economy, and the space where we live, work, and seek to witness daily. We have arrived at a situation where all the churches realise that something has changed, that the situation is new, and are asking themselves what "evangelism in Europe" could mean in the context of modernity and secularisation. In trying to answer this question, in our opinion it is necessary to reconsider at the same time the past history that we have described above and to take into account the spiritual context in which we live.

---

[7] Here we do not enter into the debate concerning the differences between "modernity" and "post-modernity." We believe that even if post-modernity introduces important differences that characterise the contemporary Western world, it is nevertheless in continuity with "modernity," being its end state which demonstrates the contradictions of certain fundamental presuppositions of the Enlightenment. When we use the term "modernity" in this chapter, we are referring to European history since the 18th century including our own epoch.

Five Observations

1. Gospel between Pluralism and Relativism

In certain respects, we have returned to the beginning of the historical process. Christianity finds itself to be a minority in a world where relativism and pluralism reign. It is by the way important to observe how many think that relativism and pluralism are totally new phenomena. However, already in the Roman Empire every religion or philosophy was only admitted as long as the dominant ideology (the emperor's divinity) was not questioned. Today we live in the paradoxical situation that on the one hand the most diverse ideas can coexist without problems, and on the other hand certain ideas like the sacredness of the free market are seemingly untouchable. There is another element that recalls the first centuries of our era: there is a dominant culture and civilisation. It is not the *pax romana*, but globalisation.

At the same time, we cannot go back because the history, which we have presented above, is indeed over, and it seems that it has inoculated many of our contemporaries against the Christian faith. Therefore, when we talk about evangelism in Europe, we have to take into account the fact that the Europeans have buried this history somewhere in their memory, even if most know very little. For many Europeans, the Church and the Gospel are a "solution" that has already been tried, but which is disqualified in advance.

2. Imported Religion

From a chronological point of view, many churches or evangelical movements arrived very late in this history, and this fact becomes even more complex with the American influence and presence in evangelical circles since the Second World War. Some forget too quickly that until the 16th century the history of evangelism in Western Europe was entirely linked to the history of the Roman Catholic Church. It was only later that the Reformed and Lutheran Church entered this history in Western and Northern Europe. We do not always draw the conclusions of this observation. For many Europeans, and especially for the media, to be a Christian is synonymous with being Catholic or Orthodox. Even if the theology of the majority church or the "historic" church is not ours, we cannot simply behave as if this church did not exist, or as if nothing good were within it.

Protestantism has often been considered as a foreign element in Catholic or Orthodox countries. Since the 16th century the Protestants have been suspected of being under English, German or Swiss influence. Today the American influence (positive or negative) in the evangelical movement reinforces the impression of a foreign presence for many Orthodox, Catholic or Protestant believers. True evangelism of Europe implies a solid deep-rootedness in its history and culture. Many evangelism efforts of Evangelicals are conceived as if it were necessary to turn the past into a *tabula rasa* or as if one could start from zero.

Today the other churches are also realising the necessity of evangelism and thinking about the same questions as we are. Is this the moment for us to stay apart? We could profit from the deep-rootedness of the majority churches in the history and culture of their respective countries.

3. Logic of Division

Roman Catholicism introduced a division in Christianity in the 11th century, and Protestantism did the same in Western Christianity in the 16th. Since then we have become used to this situation, forgetting that Luther's goal was not to fracture the Church but to heal it. In this way, a logic of continuous division and fragmentation has been set up.

In the history of Protestantism, differences have been settled too often by schism. Luther and Zwingli as well as their successors did not get along with each other and their dissensions were foundational to the creation of two churches: a Lutheran and a Reformed Church. The Anabaptists diverged from Zwingli, and out of this disagreement the Anabaptist communities were born. Henry VIII created the Anglican Church; the Puritans dissented, leading to the birth of the Presbyterians, Baptists, Congregationalists and Quakers.

Later during the 17th century, the Lutheran Church lost its fervour; Spener tried to renew it. In this way Pietism came into existence, a movement that attempted to remain in the official church but ended up creating new churches and new movements like Wesley's Methodism. One can trace similar splits throughout history down to the present day, but these examples may suffice.

We Evangelicals have been in the habit of dividing when theological differences arise among us, and generally this does not seem to bother us. Everyone creates his own Church, his movement, his evangelistic strategy, forgetting too often that we are members of Christ's body, and thus members of each other, and that maybe we can learn things from one another. In this logic of division, our theology or the invention of new evangelistic strategies are sometimes nothing more than the justification of the division. Since we must distinguish ourselves from the others, we underline the importance of the points of division rather than create a more comprehensive theology.

At the same time, we have difficulties in seeing beyond individual faith or the local church. By contrast, there reigned a kind of "congregationalism" or "episcopal synodalism" in the early church within which the local communities were linked together. We have a too limited sense of Church, a deficient ecclesiology that is not without any connection with our way of doing evangelism, which is very often exclusively linked to a particular concept of "revival."

We are really dependent on revival movements, which also often represent breaches. Without denying all the positive aspects that have originated from this tradition, it sometimes reinforces our incapacity to be rooted in history.[8]

One can hardly be against revival, but to insist on the phenomenon at the expense of a church or structures, which enable continuance in the long term, can falsify our vision of evangelism. The insistence on an evangelism based exclusively on the concept of revival can morph into a constant search for something new. Every time the church falls asleep, this tendency can lead to the creation of a new revival movement or church, which will develop the same problems after one or two generations just like the church we have left. As a result this new movement will sense the necessity to give itself structures, to answer questions that it had entirely refused to take into account because of the urgency to generate a "revival" or to "evangelise."

4. Facing Modernity

Very often "modernity" is considered to be the enemy of evangelical theology. According to this view, it is modernity that engenders liberal theology or the contemporary relativism. One wants to defend the universal truth of the Gospel. This hinders us from seeing at which point our own circles can be dependent on this same modernity, even if it is otherwise.

We forget that the social and political functioning of "pre-modern" Christian Europe is largely responsible for the rejection of Christianity. When we make appeal to history, it is sometimes a way of evoking a certain nostalgia for the epoch when Christendom prevailed and a secret de-

---

[8] We do not experience the great revivals of the Wesleyan type but certain contemporary tendencies that seem to use the concept of revival in order to bring about ever "new" or "spectacular" experiences. See our article: "Réveil ou *ecclesia semper reformanda*?" *Théologie Évangélique* 7, 1 (2008), p. 31-39.

sire to return to a situation when the Church was dominant (desire that is nourished by certain currents of American or global evangelicalism). Let us not forget that it is exactly that dominant Christendom which has been rejected by Europe and that the Gospel has always been a scandal for some and a folly to others.[9] In order to evangelise today it is necessary to have courage and stick to one's convictions and to know that they will not always be shared, especially if our message is not afraid to challenge the idols of our epoch.

Seen under a different angle, Jacques Ellul has taught us to what extent modernity is shaped by technology and the search for efficacy.[10] This simple observation implies that our efforts to develop global strategies and methods for evangelism are not without problems. The concepts of "strategy" and "efficacy" are not far from the ideology of modernity and can falsify our understanding of the Gospel. From a theological point of view, it seems better to talk about "contextualisation" than about "strategy."

5. Strategy towards Contextualisation

A strategy runs the risk of a short-term vision and of sacrificing faithfulness to the Gospel in the name of the expected results. It is precisely in the name of modern efficacy (called also "globalisation") that one is levelling the cultures and forgetting history, which provokes by the way dangerous identity reactions. In her analysis of the contemporary context, Danièle Hervieu-Léger talks about religion in terms of a memory reduced to crumbles.[11] Technology and efficacy do not need memory or history. But human beings need roots and sense. To contextualise means to understand the situation in which one lives and works, and to take root, looking at the context in the light of the Gospel. This perspective allows to discern the idols (*idôlos*) of the context, that is, the values, mentalities and behaviours that contradict what God teaches us in Jesus Christ.

The early church offers us a model of contextualisation. This church grew despite being a minority in a hostile environment. And yet, we have noted an apparent absence of evangelistic strategy. By contrast, we see

---

[9] See 1 Cor 1:23. Despite of its discourse on liberty, the same desire to "dominate" nature, economy or other peoples (through colonialism) is an integral part of the ideology of modernity.

[10] See his fundamental work: *The Technological Society* (transl. John Wilkinson; New York: Vintage, 1964). Original French edition: *La technique: Enjeu du siècle* (Paris: Economica, 1954).

[11] See Danièle Hervieu-Léger, *La religion comme mémoire* (Paris: Cerf, 1993).

thriving churches, which does not exclude that they had their problems; we see churches, the members of which knew why they existed; we see churches that knew how to cross the frontiers of the epoch: in their midst there was no longer Jew or Greek, slave or free, male and female (see Gal 3:28). We see communities whose sermons answered the deep needs of their contemporaries, which proposed adequate answers to practical problems of society, while questioning the idols of the epoch.

Additionally, they offered, at least in part, an answer to our logic of division and to our individualism. During the first centuries, the local church became the bridgehead of evangelism, together with the other communities. The individual and collective life of the Christians was sufficiently visible to address questions to the people of the epoch. The great challenge of evangelism in a context of modernity is to refuse to let the faith remain a private matter and so be excluded from the public sphere. But as we have already mentioned, we have to remain conscious of the fact that the Church bears a great part of the responsibility for the withdrawal of religion into the private sphere. Faced with the dominant church of Christendom and the wars of religion, one can indeed understand why Europeans have wished that the faith become a private matter.

The Christian faith concerns the public sphere insofar as the Gospel depends on an eschatology and announces the Lordship of Christ. It derives from a vision of history founded on the crucified and risen Christ who reigns and will reign. This message always takes form in the world. But this form takes Christ as a model who has refused domination while being Lord. In this world where exclusion and racism are such great issues, a world where a certain economic ideology determines more and more both our social and individual choices in life, we do not have to announce a particular political strategy instead of the Gospel, but we can never forget the practical implications of the Gospel. We cannot separate the individual destiny from the new earth and heaven where justice will reign.

Suggestions and Questions

1) We need to root our evangelism better in history and culture. How can we do this, and how far are we ready to go in order to do it, especially concerning our relationship with the other Christians? Do we see ourselves as the only true Christians who are not forced to take into account the presence of other churches? Or are we part of a larger family, where we have certainly to conduct difficult conversations, but always a family of which we are members with others, which would not be without implications for our evangelism.

2) We need to have a better ecclesiology: that means on the one hand leaving the logic of division, and on the other hand understanding that the existence of thriving communities turned towards the outside world is an integral part of evangelism. The Church is the public place of the Gospel, the space where the values of the Gospel are actualised, a community of peace, forgiveness, healing and reconciliation. How can we get out of the logic of division? How can we better integrate the life of the local church into evangelism?

3) We need to contextualise the Gospel in European modernity; for this we need to understand how much the Evangelicals are influenced by modernity. We need to discover the Gospel as "speaking in public" without trying to dominate society. How can we have the necessary hindsight to perceive our syncretism, and how can we distinguish between critical and acceptable elements of the modern culture? How can we identify our idols?

Further Reading

Blough, Neal, "Mission in Europe," in *Evangelical, Ecumenical and Anabaptist Missiologies in Conversation*, ed. J.R. Krabill, W. Sawatsky, C. Van Engen (Maryknoll: Orbis, 2006), p. 216-222.

Blough, Neal, "Réveil ou *ecclesia semper reformanda?*" *Théologie Évangélique* 7, 1, 2008, p. 31-39.

Hervieu-Léger, Danièle, *La religion comme mémoire* (Paris: Le Cerf, 1993).

Kreider, Alan, *Worship and Evangelism in Pre-Christendom* (Joint Liturgical Studies, 32; Cambridge: Grove Books Limited, 1995).

Russell, James C., *The Germanization of Early Medieval Christianity: A Sociohistorical Approach to Religious Transformation* (New York: Oxford University Press, 1994).

Chapter 2
European Context Today and Evangelism

Julien Coffinet[1]

This chapter considers the question of the European context by using the tools of historical and sociological analysis, especially its contemporary situation with regard to evangelism. Our approach is shaped by the missiologist's question: "Where is Europe with God and the message of the Gospel?" In order to be able to answer this question, we will proceed by progressively integrating social scientific data and asking three sub-questions: What is the state of Europe today? What do Europeans believe? And what about the Christian Churches and the European Christians? The first question to be tackled is: "What is the state of Europe today?"

Geographical Definition

Geographically, Europe is a small continent or part of the supercontinent Eurasia or Afro-Eurasia. As we will see later, the unity of Europe is above all an idea. The Eastern geographical limits are unclear in Russia and Georgia as well as Turkey, as these states have a great part of their territory in Asia.

With a total surface estimated at 10.4 million km^2 of which 40 % are in Russia, the continent of Europe is four times smaller than Africa or North America, and five times smaller than Asia.[2]

In Europe we can discern four zones of coherent cultural and religious influence in the form of a cross:
- North West: mainly Protestant including important Roman Catholic minorities in some countries
- South West: mainly Roman Catholic

---

[1] This text is based on a paper presented on January 7, 2013, in a Master's seminar at the *Faculté libre de théologie évangélique de Vaux-sur-Seine* (France).
[2] Evert Van de Poll, *Europe and the Gospel: Past Influences, Current Developments, Mission Challenges* (Maastricht/Aachen: Shaker/de Gruyter, 2012), p. 22f. The statistics are available online: http://statistiques-mondiales.com/europe.htm (accessed on November 1, 2012).

- East: ethnically populated by Slaves who are mainly Roman Catholic in the Western part, and Orthodox in the Eastern part
- South East: depending on the region mainly Roman Catholic, Orthodox or Muslim.[3]

Demographic Data

All the data below represent rounded estimates. We have updated them with recent figures, the tendencies being confirmed by Evert van de Poll's studies on which we have largely based this presentation.

Total Population

In 2015 the United Nations estimated the European population at 738.5 million inhabitants (including the Russian Federation with its 143.5 million inhabitants, but without Georgia with its 4 million inhabitants, and Turkey with its 78.5 million inhabitants.[4]

Population Growth

With a growth rate of 0.08 % for the period of 2010-2015, Europe is the continent of the world that has the slowest growth (world mean of 1.18 %; in comparison North America with 0.78 %). In the projections for the period of 2015-2020 and later, the demographists estimate that the European population will decrease.

Fertility Rate

In 2015 Europe's fertility rate was the lowest in the world with 1.6 births per woman (world mean 2.51; North America 1.86).

Number of Migrants

In the period of 2010-2015 the number of migrants arriving in Europe was estimated at 4 million (compared to 6.2 million in North America). These numbers will probably be much higher during the following period. In different demographic models the closure of frontiers as a result of the

---

[3] Van de Poll, *Europe and the Gospel*, p. 41-46.
[4] The UN statistics are available online: http://esa.un.org/unpd/wpp (accessed on December 29, 2015).

pressure of the population on governments is a factor taken into account in proportion to the increase of the number of migrants.

Ageing Process

In 2015 the median age for the world population was 29.6 years, as compared to 41.7 years for Europe, and 38.3 years for North America. The European population is thus the oldest in the world. The projections for the following period confirm this ageing process. The world demographic data are summed up in the following table:[5]

Country	Total Population (in thousands)	Birth Rate	Mortality Rate	Life Expectancy	Child Mortality Rate	Number of Births per Woman	Growth Rate	Population of 65 years and more (in thousands)
Africa	1 166 239	34.6	10.0	59.1	59.9	4.54	24.2	40 726
Latin America & Caribbean	630 089	17.3	5.9	75.3	16.4	2.12	10.5	48 109
North America	361 128	12.9	8.2	79.5	5.6	1.94	8.0	53 443
Asia	4 384 844	17.1	7.2	71.9	28.8	2.16	9.6	328 266
Europe	743 123	10.7	11.7	76.5	5.5	1.60	0.4	128 770
Oceania	39 359	16.7	6.8	78.0	19.5	2.37	13.6	4 672
World	7 324 779	19.0	8.0	70.5	34.7	2.47	11.0	603 986

---

[5] Source: World Population Prospects, United Nations, 2015: http://esa.un.org/unpd/wpp (accessed on December 29, 2015).

Economic Data

Europe, a World Economic Power

In this section we are basing our findings on Van de Poll's data:[6]
- The capital flow in Europe is 2378 billion Euros (as compared to 1416 for the USA and 2235 for all Asia).
- The investment in Europe is 230 billion Euros (as compared to 100 for the USA and 80 for China).

Van de Poll notes that 55 % of the world humanitarian aid comes from the European Union alone. Beyond what this number indicates about the abundance of life in Europe, the international influence of Europe is important and also has consequences for its attractiveness for migrants.

Persistant Important Inequalities

According to the French *Observatoire des inégalités*, the poverty rate in Europe varies from 5.8 % to 16.9 % depending on its definition. At 60 % of the median revenue, the rate oscillates from 10.1 % in Norway to 23.1 % in Greece.[7]

According to an OXFAM Media Briefing Report published in 2015, the most disturbing numbers concern the dramatic recent downgrade of persons at the limit of poverty. This concerns 123 million Europeans today.

Urbanisation

In Europe urbanisation has been a marked phenomenon since the industrial revolution. Today 80 % of Europeans are urbanised. Even though the largest cities of the world are located elsewhere, this continent remains the most densely populated, with extremes like the agglomerations in the Rhine delta and the empty regions of Scandinavia. Today the growth of megacities is an increasing phenomenon, involving a reorganisation of the territory, together with an impact on habitat, transport, and the daily mobility of Europeans.

---

[6] Van de Poll, *Europe and the Gospel*, p. 31-32.
[7] Observatoire des inégalités, "La pauvreté en Europe:" http://www.inegalites.fr/spip.php?article388 (accessed on December 29, 2015).

Heritage of the Great European Ideas

Greco-Roman Roots

Among European roots Jean-Georges Gantenbein discerns first the Greco-Roman civilisation with its conceptual focus, the Greek literary and dramatic capacity, the Greek vision for the modern state (democracy), the Roman administrative precision, Roman law and the idea of a civilisation with the vocation to enlighten the barbarians. Notable is also the Roman tolerance welcoming foreign beliefs under the condition of absolute allegiance to the emperor. This golden age of Europe under Roman rule enlightened by the Greek philosophical schools is present in the collective imaginary of Europe. It returns cyclically in the arts and culture contributing to the implanting of some great ideas of Antiquity in the individual and collective subconscious of the Europeans.[8]

Pagan Cults

New Age is a quest for symbols and mysteries that has been inspired by pre-Christian spirituality in order to structure identity in the midst of a destructive and technological modernity. Among the explications of the fall of Christianity in Europe, some authors are interested in the way the European territories have been evangelised. Wessels considers that the influence of Celtic cults on the first Christian leaders and on the structuration of Christian spirituality is important. On the basis of the study of conversion narratives, he insists on the considerable influence of the Germanic ancestor cult and mythology on Christianity.[9] During the postmodern quest for identity, the resurgence of these cults and their deep-rootedness is apparent. However, the sociologist of religion Grace Davie notes that the adhesion of Europeans to pre-Christian spirituality seems to be linked to an intended particularisation but that this desire for particularisation remains at this moment marginal among Europeans.[10]

---

[8] Van de Poll, *Europe and the Gospel*, p. 204.

[9] Anton Wessels, *Europe: Was It Ever Really Christian? The Interaction between Gospel and Culture* (London: SCM, 1994), p. 47-54, 94-95, 154-160, summarised in Jean-Georges Gantenbein, *Mission en Europe: Une étude socio-missiologique pour le 21e siècle* (Münster: Aschendorff, 2016), p. 166.

[10] Van de Poll, *Europe and the Gospel*, p. 294.

Enlightenment

The Enlightenment has considerably influenced Europe by entering it into the epoch of modernity through the emancipation of human reason and the exaltation of individual liberty. By rejecting the concept of a divine law and by promoting the notion of the sovereignty of the people, the Enlightenment had a decisive influence not only on the French Revolution but in a much larger sense on the contemporary idea of parliamentary democracy. Human rights are a powerful heritage of this European idea (there is a European concentration of institutions and NGOs inspired by and established on this vision). They constitute a universal value in the European conscience. The most powerful heritage that has structured the European mentality until today comprises: the exaltation of individual liberty, and consequently societal pluralism and the privatisation of belief, the exaltation of critical reason and consequently the distrust of religious experience, and the persuasive nature of the universal value of European ideas.[11]

Postmodernity

The deconstruction of pre-modern values by the Enlightenment is arriving at its end by deconstructing itself. This is implied in the sociological concepts of ultra-modernity or postmodernity which evoke on the one hand the end of modern pretentions (reason, science and the idea of universality), and on the other hand the resurgence of irrationality and the place of emotions and of subjective experience as the basis of judgment. Relativism, which is a central concept for understanding the European mentality, is derived from pluralism and individualism (heritage of the Enlightenment), but at the same time overcoming it through the emphasis on subjectivism (post-Enlightenment heritage).[12]

Christian Heritage

Van de Poll draws attention to the impregnation of European culture by Christian elements: the omnipresence of the cross in the names of locations, families, hospitals, and national flags; Christian references in literature and music; Church buildings marking the territory, the crosses at the

---

[11] Idem, p. 209-211. See also François Bousquet, "The Enlightenment: The Foundation of Modern Europe," *International Review of Mission* vol. 95, n° 378-379 (July-October 2006), p. 236-246.

[12] Van de Poll, *Europe and the Gospel*, p. 267-268.

entry of villages, and the impregnation of the languages by expressions and proverbs derived from the Bible.[13] Even on the negative side, the great European ideas are (in collaboration or opposition) closely linked with Christianity from the Enlightenment to the philosophies of suspicion.

European history is inseparable from the history of the Church because Europe is the continent which has been the most durably evangelised and thus the most profoundly marked in its culture by Christianity. We have to take into consideration the fact that this (real or imagined) heritage had both a positive impact on society through the Gospel, in terms of ethics and the creation of charitable organisations, but also a negative impact: the history of the crusades, colonialism, the wars of religion, the ambiguity maintained in relation to slavery, the antisemitism of the Holocaust, etc. In one of his last chapters, the one on the idea of post-Christianity, Van de Poll evokes the conceptual idea of a post-evangelical Europe as a continent where the inhabitants have some awareness of the biblical message, sometimes even experiencing goodwill towards it, but are not personally touched. Beyond the fact that the balance of the benefits and failures of Christianity might be positive in the historic conscience of the Europeans, we have to realise that this continent has already been evangelised and that the Europeans may say: "We have already tried and it has not worked." Neal Blough emphasises: It is the failure of a "pre-modern" situation, where Christianity was socially and politically dysfunctional, that has caused the rejection of Christianity by modernity.[14]

Religions and Beliefs of Europeans

European and National Statistics

On the website Eurel.info, which records sociological and judicial data on religion in Europe, two surveys are presented. The first, the European Values Survey (EVS), dates from 2008, and concerns the religious affiliation and practice of Europeans. The second, Gallup International, dates from 2014, and targets religious feelings. We present the results of the two surveys (the two include Russia and Turkey) in this following section.[15]

---

[13] Van de Poll, *Europe and the Gospel*, p. 37, see also p. 223-249.
[14] Neal Blough, "Evangelism in Europe: Historical Background," chapter 1 of this book.
[15] See also the statistics in Appendix 1.

European Values Survey (EVS) 2008

The percentages represent the proportion of valid responses.
Do you belong to a religious confession?[16]
    yes 76.4 %, no 23.6 %.

To which religious confession are you affiliated? (% of valid responses):
- Roman Catholic   36.7 %
- Protestant   14.5 %
- Free Church/non-Conformist/Evangelical   0.6 %
- Jewish   0.2 %
- Muslim   15.0 %
- Hindu   0.1 %
- Buddhist   0.1 %
- Orthodox   30.6 %
- Other   2.3 %
- Total   100.0 %

How often do you take part in religious services?[17]
- More than once per week   4.8 %
- Once per week   13.5 %
- Once per month   11.0 %
- Only for certain holidays   25.9 %
- Once per year   7.0 %
- Less frequently   9.9 %
- Never, practically never   27.9 %
- Total   100.0 %

Do you think personally that it is important to celebrate a religious service at one of the following events?

	No	Yes
Birth	26.9 %	73.1 %
Marriage	26.8 %	73.2 %
Death	18.1 %	81.9 %

Almost 28 % of Europeans declare that they never (or practically never) participate at a religious service. However, the attachment to religious

---

[16] http://www.eurel.info/spip.php?rubrique574 (accessed on December 29, 2015).

[17] http://www.eurel.info/spip.php?rubrique576 (accessed on December 29, 2015).

celebrations remains strong for certain events of life. More than 80 % of respondents estimate that it is important to have a religious funeral.

Gallup International 2014

Would you say that you are ...[18]

	A Religious Person	Not a Religious Person	A Convinced Atheist	Does not Know / Does not Respond
Poland	86 %	10 %	2 %	2 %
Turkey	79 %	13 %	2 %	6 %
Romania	77 %	16 %	1 %	6 %
Italy	74 %	18 %	6 %	3 %
Greece	71 %	15 %	6 %	8 %
Russia	70 %	18 %	5 %	8 %
Portugal	60 %	28 %	9 %	2 %
Bulgaria	52 %	36 %	3 %	8 %
Ireland	45 %	41 %	10 %	5 %
Belgium	44 %	30 %	18 %	7 %
Denmark	42 %	40 %	12 %	7 %
France	40 %	35 %	18 %	7 %
Latvia	40 %	41 %	9 %	10 %
Austria	39 %	44 %	10 %	6 %
Switzerland	38 %	46 %	12 %	4 %
Spain	37 %	35 %	20 %	8 %
Germany	34 %	42 %	17 %	7 %
United Kingdom	30 %	53 %	13 %	4 %
Netherlands	26 %	51 %	15 %	8 %
Czech Republic	23 %	45 %	30 %	2 %
Sweden	19 %	59 %	17 %	6 %

---

[18] http://www.eurel.info/spip.php?rubrique574 (accessed on December 29, 2015).

Four Particular Situations in Europe

Gantenbein's study on evangelism in Europe concentrates on four particular regional situations: France, United Kingdom, Romania, and the new East German federal states. These four situations overlap with the partition in form of a cross which we have presented in the section on the delimitation of the European space. This partition is mentioned by Van de Poll, with the exception of the new East German federal states, which represent a mainly Lutheran, not a Catholic or Orthodox context, even though they are in Eastern Europe and were part of the Warsaw Pact. Gantenbein specifies in his study that he does not consider these four countries as typical of their region nor as unique. Rather they represent for him areas of questioning and of instruction in view of his method of contextualisation.[19]

France

Despite the quasi unique separation between Church and State in the French laicity system, France fits naturally among countries modelled by Southern and Western European Roman Catholicism. Based on the French historian Émile Poulat, Gantenbein describes a triangular conflict between the Roman Catholic Church, the liberal bourgeoisie and socialism, which exists since the 16th century, with a modification during the 20th century after the rallying of Roman Catholics to the Republic. In the second half of the 20th century, French Roman Catholicism became extremely politicised. The Second Vatican Council has not stopped the decline of French Roman Catholicism which continues until today despite the vitality of charismatic movements (recognised in 1975 by Pope Paul VI).[20]

Despite a rapidly falling practice, in 2007 51 % of French people still declare themselves to be Roman Catholic. However, there exists a notable discrepancy between this declaration and the adhesion to dogmas by French people who say they belong to the Church. Based on Frédéric Lenoir, Gantenbein's conclusion is that the Roman Catholics adhere both to the values of modernity and to the symbols of the Church.[21] In parallel, we note with Yves Lambert a rapprochement between the practising Roman

---

[19] Gantenbein, *Mission en Europe*, p. 112.

[20] Émile Poulat, *Église contre bourgeoisie: Introduction au devenir du catholicisme actuel* (Tournai: Castermann, 1977), p. 109-133, 173-205, discussed in Gantenbein, *Mission en Europe*, p. 50.

[21] Frédéric Lenoir, "Vers un catholicisme minoritaire?" *Le monde des religions* n° 21 (jan.-fév. 2007), p. 5, quoted in Gantenbein, *Mission en Europe*, p. 59.

Catholics and the persons "without religion" in the field of ethics (examples: divorce, homosexuality, etc.). This rapprochement is due to the diminishing permissiveness of the persons "without religion" and the increasing tolerance of the practitioners.

In 2004 French Muslims numbered 5 to 6 million, the second largest religious group, of which 36 % declare themselves practitioners and 42 % declare themselves to be "believers."

Protestants are a minority represented especially in certain regions (Alsace, Paris region, South). Within Protestantism a "cultural," "ageing" and "museum" current is declining substantially, while Evangelicals and Pentecostals are growing, accelerated by the ethnical Protestant wing of migrant believers.

There are other minorities: the Jews, oriental Christians, Hindus and Buddhists, including the minority sects more or less close to traditional Christian teaching. On the basis of Cholvy and Hilaire, Gantenbein reports a presence of approximately 140 000 Free Masons without commenting on the fact.[22]

Beyond an analysis of religious confessions, an analysis of convictions gives results that cross established confessions and must interest the missiologist. If belief in a personal God, his general importance or the dimension of sin are still declining in the studies, belief in "a spiritual being" or "a vital force," the assurance of a life after death in general and the beliefs which are particularly connected to it (hell, paradise, reincarnation) are growing. The responses of the 18-29 years old deserve to be mentioned especially: they believe more than the same group ten years ago that "the Church can give answers to spiritual needs." They are more convinced than the rest of the population of the importance of ceremonies (baptism, marriage, funerals). They believe more and more in life after death (especially the notion of hell). This tendency is registered even among those "without religion" and even among the "convinced atheists," while it decreases or maintains itself among the young Roman Catholics. Gantenbein concludes:

> Being a Catholic or an atheist does not mean the same thing as before: the first open themselves to a more diffuse belief and move away from doctrine; the second open themselves to a more general belief ... We are thus faced with "believing without belonging."[23]

---

[22] Gérard Cholvy & Yves-Marie Hilaire, *Le fait religieux aujourd'hui en France: Les trente dernières années (1974-2004)* (Paris: Cerf, 2004), p. 118-141, discussed in Gantenbein, *Mission en Europe*, p. 65.

[23] Gantenbein, *Mission en Europe*, p. 67.

Chapter 2 – European Context Today and Evangelism 37

United Kingdom

Gantenbein bases his study on the (outdated) findings of Grace Davie who has done research on the situation in the United Kingdom. She initiated the catchphrase "believing without belonging." In this country, the historical religion is Anglicanism which represented 1.8 million active members in 1992 as compared to 25.5 million "latent" Anglicans. The practising Roman Catholics are thus more numerous than the practising Anglicans. They have counted 2 million practitioners already in 1992. Between 1981 and 1990 70 % of the British declared that they "believe in God." The civil society is still under the Anglican influence even though the British do not adhere any more to its doctrinal and religious base.

All the statistics that Grace Davie had access to were outdated. But they allowed her to construct different models, in addition to the one mentioned above those of "vicarious religion" and "consumer religion."

> The first stipulates that a majority of religiously non-practising persons approves of the active religious minority of a society. The second describes the definitive abandoning of the compulsory adhesion to a religion in favour of pluralism, of relativism and a religion of "choice."[24]

Romania

During the 20th century, Romania has passed from a mono-confessional and mono-ethnic state to a mainly Orthodox but multi-ethnic and multi-confessional state where the confessional affiliation of its citizens corresponds closely to the ethnic composition of the country.

During the communist persecution up to 1989 the churches submitted to the regime without compromising themselves. After the fall of the communist regime, the reputation of the recognised cults has permitted them to reinforce the links with the new state. The churches have known a complete renaissance. The Orthodox Church prospers and enjoys great confidence in the population today.

This situation is similar to the majority of countries in Eastern Europe in terms of the re-emergence of post-communist religiosity. But if on the one hand Romania is the least secularised and the most religious country of Europe, one notes on the other hand an increasing privatisation of religious life and an erosion of the adhesion to Christian doctrines and a de-

---

[24] Gantenbein, *Mission en Europe*, p. 80, summarising Grace Davie, "Is Europe an Exceptional Case?" *Hedgehog Review* spring-summer 2006, p. 23-34, reprint *International Review of Mission* vol. 95, n° 378-379 (July-October 2006), p. 247-258.

creasing influence of the Church on ethical positions of Romanians (for example in the Orthodox Church 57.4 % are favourable to induced abortion, and 35 % to euthanasia).

New German Federal States

In this region, which is very marked by Lutheranism, the percentage of Christians decreased after 1989, contrary to what happened in numerous other Eastern European countries and despite an active involvement of the Church in the process of the reopening of East Germany. 75 % of the inhabitants of these new federal states are today no longer part of any church. Religious indifference is by far the primary feature. Contrary to Western European countries, the New Religious Movements (NRM) and the esoteric movement (which we will discuss below) have had a very small impact on the population of these new federal states.

None of the proposed interpretations seem to explain satisfactorily the unique religious situation of this country: the communist system has apparently succeeded in interrupting the cultural continuity of an ancient Christian tradition by persecution and replacing it with a non-religious culture.

Islam in Europe

Islam has a long history in Europe. According to Gantenbein, we have to take into account the heavy weight of the medieval crusades and the Spanish *reconquista* on European conscience, and not forget "the expansionist warrior policy of the Muslim world from the 7th to 17th centuries surpassing in brutality the two quasi exclusive examples of the opposite camp."[25]

If one defines Europe geographically as the area between Ireland and the Carpathians (all the member states and the candidates of the European Union plus Norway and Switzerland, but without Turkey and its 70 million Muslims, totalling 34 countries), there are approximately 23.8 million Muslims, which corresponds to 4.6 % of the total population. One third of

---

[25] Gantenbein, *Mission en Europe*, p. 177, summarising Philip Jenkins, *God's Continent: Christianity, Islam and Europe's Religious Crisis* (Oxford/New York: Oxford University Press, 2007), p. 10, 103-111: "The stories that we regard as the tragedies of interfaith intolerance, the Crusades and the Spanish Reconquista, are the two great – and rather isolated – examples in which Christian forces won major military victories" (Jenkins, *God's Continent*, p. 105).

the 24 million Muslims in Europe have been established here for a long time. The European country with the highest number of Muslims is France.

Gantenbein and Van de Poll emphasise the importance of relativizing these numbers because of the asymmetry between the auto-definition of Europeans of Muslim culture regarding their affiliation to Islam and Europeans of Christian culture regarding their affiliation to Christianity. If a cultural definition of affiliation is used, Jenkins shows that the Christians would be twenty times more numerous than the Muslims.[26]

Van de Poll devotes a chapter to the question of Islam and evokes different forecasts of demographic growth of Islam in Europe. The demographic projections depend on the birth rate and the immigration rate of Muslims in Europe.[27] Van de Poll then reflects on the relationship of Europeans with Islam. Questions about identity and ideology are raised, and fear and ignorance exist, particularly regarding the ability of Muslims to adapt to European laws and customs.[28]

Islam and Anti-Occidentalism

According to Van de Poll, the radicalisation of young Muslims is very weak in Europe, even if the media put a strong accent on it during terrorist attacks. Radicalisation is a phenomenon which cannot be explained without taking into account economic, social and psychological causes (the quest for identity). Regarding the desire of European Muslims to create a space under the rule of sharia law, Van de Poll draws on several sociologists and missiologists to affirm that it is an idea of a small minority in the Muslim community. According to him, we have to consider the particularity of a European Islam evolving in a Western secular and pluralist society.[29]

Finally, according to Van de Poll, it seems that the missionary activity of Islam produces especially fruit among Muslims of the second and third generation, and that the majority of conversions of Europeans of non-Muslim culture to Islam is simply the result of mixed marriages.[30]

---

[26] Jenkins, *God's Continent*, p. 17-19, 155-157, cited in Gantenbein, *Mission en Europe*, p. 179.

[27] Van de Poll, *Europe and the Gospel*, p. 193-205.

[28] See also the statistics on Islam in Europe in Appendix 1.

[29] For further information on European Muslims' concerns and worldview, see: www.pewglobal.org/2006/07/06/muslims-in-europe-economic-worries-top-concerns-about-religious-and-cultural-identity (accessed on December 29, 2015).

[30] Van de Poll, *Europe and the Gospel*, p. 205.

Mystical-Esoteric Nebula and the Recomposition of Religion

As indicated in the religious statistics at the beginning of this chapter, the auto-definition of Europeans regarding their religion is oriented very little towards religions other than Christianity or Islam. The other "great religions" remain marginal in Europe (Judaism 0.2 %, Hinduism and Buddhism 0.2 %). On the other hand, the number of persons "without religion" is increasing constantly. However, as Gantenbein indicates for France, a study of the "convictions" rather than the "confessional affiliation" gives paradoxical results because the persons "without religion," and even the "convinced atheists" can develop convictions that the sociologist considers as religious beliefs. At the same time, the heterodoxy of European Christians is very marked in his study, particularly in French Roman Catholicism and Romanian Orthodoxy.

The French sociologist of religion Françoise Champion has developed the notion of "mystical-esoteric nebula" (*nébuleuse mystique-ésotérique*) in order to evoke in an intentionally fuzzy way the elements of clairvoyance, astrology, parallel medicine, reincarnation, near death experience or esotericism. Françoise Champion emphasises that this nebula emerges in reaction to Western culture: 1) the decline of the Church has favoured this form of belief in wonders, magic and mystery; 2) the battle against obscurantism has first profited science, but the latter's incapacity to respond satisfactorily to postmodern fears after having promised a lot leaves space for parallel interpretations disregarding scientific explanations; 3) contemporary individualism is the third facilitator of the expansion of this nebula because non-critical subjectivity has become a criterion of experience and of validation. Françoise Champion's studies on France lead her to say that she has almost never met somebody who does not affirm to "believe in something."[31]

According to Gantenbein, in order to understand the de-Christianisation of Europe, it is important to raise the issue of the impregnation of Christianity by the spirituality of the indigenous culture in Europe. Despite the statistical importance of the persons "without religion" the French sociologist of religion Danièle Hervieux-Léger interprets the de-Christianisation of Europe not as a progression of atheism, but as a recomposition of religiosity with a "religious patchwork" (*bricolage de croyances*). This aspect of

---

[31] Françoise Champion, "L'univers mystique-ésotérique et croyances parallèles," *Futuribles* n° 260 (Jan. 2001), p. 49-59, quoted in Gantenbein, *Mission en Europe*, p. 155.

religiosity in Europe concerns of course both the persons "without religion" and the "religious" persons.[32]

European Christianity

Typology of European Christians

The differences between practice and adhesion to Christian doctrines among the Europeans who consider themselves as Christians have led sociologists to establish different typologies in order to account for the difference in religious realities behind affiliation to a Christian confession, even beyond ecclesial practice. Van de Poll reports on several models with different criteria giving more or less equivalent results.[33]

Some:
1) observe certain Christian traditions such as Christmas and commemorative ceremonies
2) insist on getting married in Church, baptising their children and being buried with a Christian funeral
3) respect Christian values and norms regarding marriage, sexuality, family, education, protection of human life and tolerance
4) believe that God exists, that Jesus is his Son, that paradise and hell exist
5) read their Bible and pray in private.

We have to take into consideration Grace Davie's observations on the United Kingdom for the whole of Europe, particularly the concept of "believing without belonging" with its corollary "belonging without believing" that is well developed in Eastern Europe. We also have to note the high level of "minimal church membership," which means that many members of Christian churches are not very committed, a typical European phenomenon.

Religion by Default and Vicarious Religion

These two models have been introduced by Grace Davie in order to take into account the "European exception" where abandoning the Christian faith does not mean adopting a new religious affiliation. The other

---

[32] Gantenbein, *Mission en Europe*, p. 154-157; Danièle Hervieu-Léger, *La religion pour mémoire* (Paris: Cerf, 1993).
[33] Van de Poll, *Europe and the Gospel*, p. 285-286.

option is that after abandoning the Christian faith Europeans turn towards pre-Christian spirituality, New Age or oriental religions. This is a particular individual choice. But the classical option (particularly for funerals) remains to go and see a member of the Christian clergy.[34]

Vicarious Religion corresponds to what we have reported for the United Kingdom: a largely non-involved majority approves of the practice of the minority and even its readiness to believe. In practical theology and in pastoral ministry these sociological findings are taken into account in different ways. Felix Moser for example introduces the notion of "non-practising believers" when he analyses his ministry in Basse Normandie (France) and French speaking Switzerland. Moser refuses the stereotypes of "non-believers" and "regulars," re-evaluates the concept of "popular religion" within Protestantism and reconsiders positively the requests for church rites.[35]

Christian Potential for Mission in Europe

World mission is in transition. In an article published in 2010 in a book on the mission of the Church in the 21st century, Van de Poll has analysed the missionary forces present in Europe.[36] He observes first that the classical missionary-sending nations (USA, UK, New Zealand, Protestant Europe), send fewer and fewer missionaries, but that there seems to be at the same time more short-term missions (Van de Poll himself asks for a verification of this affirmation). This has consequences for the non-European nations that used to receive many missionaries.

The article reflects also on the change in the motivations and the ways of thinking of the missionary as a function of the generation they belong to. The article asks more questions than it gives answers. But using the findings of sociology in order to understand the future potential of missionary work is an interesting approach for missiology. Beyond employing sociology to understand the context of evangelism, it can turn out to be useful to reflect on the ways to generate the calling and training for these ministries.

---

[34] Grace Davie, "Is Europe an Exceptional Case?" *International Review of Mission* vol. 95, n° 378-379, July-October 2006, p. 247-258.

[35] Felix Moser, *Les croyants non pratiquants* (Genève: Labor et Fides, 1994).

[36] Evert van de Poll, "Mission, malaise ou transition?" in *La mission de l'Église au 21e siècle: Les nouveaux défis*, ed. Hannes Wiher (Charols: Excelsis, 2010), p. 71-82.

In the same volume on mission in the 21st century, Djamba-Albert Watto reflects on the potential of the migrant churches for mission in Europe.[37] If the first concern of these migrant churches is the migrants themselves, in future these churches could develop strategies to evangelise the Europeans. In this dynamic he cites the initiative GATE (Gift from Africa to Europe), which brings together African leaders with the vision to evangelise Europe. Finally, the article mentions the attractiveness of African and Caribbean worship services for certain Europeans. However, the question of the identity of Europeans in relation to these worship services seems complicated in view of any future important mission in Europe by migrants.

Sleepiness and Awakening

To conclude this section, we need to put into perspective the state of Christianity in the course of history and the contemporary de-Christianisation of Europe. In his study on the mission in Europe, Gantenbein cites the critical comments of Jean Delumeau and Le Goff on the past history of the European Church. In 1977, Jean Delumeau reported in his book, *Le Christianisme va-t-il mourir?*: "Towards 1500, Christendom was almost a mission receiving area." Agreeing with Le Goff, Delumeau observes that during certain periods of the Middle Ages Europe was extremely de-Christianised, while the Church was manifesting a great heterodoxy and heteropraxis.[38] According to Gantenbein, the golden age of Christendom in Europe seems to have been between 1750 and the end of the 19th century. Gantenbein reports on historical studies that tend to relativise the Christianisation of the peoples of Europe, which was sometimes obtained by sacrificing evangelical truth. The same remark is made by Neal Blough concerning the reigns of Theodosius, Clovis and Charlemagne.[39]

On the other hand, the awakenings are also historical realities which witness to the possibilities of "religious renewal" in a society not interested in religion. It is in this perspective that Philip Jenkins emphasises the signs of renewal in the Roman Catholic Church, particularly in the charismatic

---

[37] Djamba-Albert Watto, "L'engagement des Églises issues de l'immigration pour la mission," in Wiher, *La mission de l'Église au 21e siècle*, p. 83-92.

[38] Gantenbein, *Mission en Europe*, p. 167f.

[39] See Neal Blough, "Evangelism in Europe: Historical Background," chapter 1 of this book; James C. Russell, *The Germanization of Early Medieval Christianity: A Sociohistorical Approach to Religious Transformation* (New York: Oxford University Press, 1994).

movements of the 1960s onwards and the revitalisation of monastic movements like *Paray-le-Monial* and Taizé in France, as well as the renewal signs in the Anglican Church with the movement of *Holy Trinity, Brompton* (HTB) and the figure of David Pytches in the ministry *Soul Survivor* since 1993.[40]

Conclusion

At the end of this chapter we want to make a final assessment and summary, and answer succinctly the three questions introduced at the beginning of this chapter: What is the state of Europe today? What do the Europeans believe? What about the Christian Churches and the European Christians?

What Is the State of Europe Today?

Europe is a very populated but ageing continent. Its population growth will probably soon be negative despite a strong attraction of migrants. Its economy is prosperous, but the inequalities persist dangerously. The majority of its population lives in urban areas inducing the phenomenon of metropolisation that imposes significant social restructuring.

The unity of the continent is fundamentally cultural and ideological while having complicated geographical borders. In order to understand this unity in diversity, we have discerned four cultural zones which overlap largely with the majority historical Christian confessions. Among the great European ideas we have emphasised the powerful impact of postmodernity accompanied by secularisation and spiritual and ethical relativism. Linked to its Christian history during many centuries, Europe remains profoundly marked in its culture and identity by biblical symbols and those inherited from Church tradition, without being really clear and easy with this dimension of its identity.

This quest for identity seems present in many countries of this continent. The demographic and sociological data allow the prediction that this quest will become more and more significant. In fact, Europe is a continent that figures high in the development indices and has dominated the world by its culture, its diplomacy, its technology and economy. However, at a time when the other continents are progressing and Europe is seeking her identity philosophically and ideologically, the complex of superiority of

---

[40] Philip Jenkins, "Godless Europe?" *International Bulletin of Missionary Research* 31, 3 (2007), p. 115-120.

past centuries, still visible in issues like human rights, seems to lead to a profound crisis of purpose and insecurity about the future of its civilisation.[41]

What Do the Europeans Believe?

The second question targets the religions and beliefs of Europeans. A great majority of Europeans continues to consider themselves as "believers." According to the auto-definition of Europeans, the affiliation to the different large historical Christian confessions remains the main feature in Europe. In many countries the majority church remains a structuring point of reference for the population despite substantial erosion, and continues the practice of and the adhesion to the teaching of these churches. This disaffection towards the majority churches does not produce other affiliations, with the result that the other "great religions" remain a minority. Islam confirms more and more its place as second religion in Europe. But it is an Islam closely linked to immigration, and it seems that few convert. On the other hand, this Islam is itself influenced by the European secular, humanist and relativist "ambiance." Finally, European spirituality, which is shared by believers and atheists, consists of this mystical-esoteric nebula or individual religious construct à la carte.

The results of sociological studies seem to confirm that the Europeans do not know very well what the religions profess nor what they are ready to believe. They seem to have generally a very cultural vision of religion, and this is by the way very often what the clergy (in the broader sense) effectively suggest. Regarding their spiritual quest the Europeans cobble together a lot. They seem to aspire profoundly to a reconnection of their ideologies with their emotions and experiences without finding full satisfaction anywhere.

What about the Christian Churches and the European Christians?

The third question concerned the characteristics of European Christians. European Christianity is multiform and comprises a great variety of affiliation of those auto-defining themselves as Christians. The Europeans who agree to the teachings of the Church are less and less numerous among its

---

[41] See Jean-François Thiry, "Devant l'indifférence religieuse en Europe: croire sans appartenir à une Église, et appartenir à une Église sans croire. Une proposition culturelle et spirituelle," in *Donner une âme à l'Europe: Mission et responsabilité des Églises* (Rencontre européenne de culture chrétienne, Vienna, Mai 3-5, 2006; Vienna: Pro Oriente, 2007).

members, and more and more of its members are involved very marginally. At the same time there are more and more Christians who do not belong to any church. Certainly, the perseverance of the Europeans to request rites in the Church manifests a religious and spiritual longing. However, it is apparent that the Church is profoundly worldly if it is evaluated by the faith of its members. Beyond this, it is often marginalised in its mission, only called upon for occasional ceremonies than for the daily needs of its members. The task of evangelism in Europe will thus encounter a Christianity which is neither challenging nor inspiring, at the same time known and recognised for its easily accessible religious offer and its loss of contact with the daily life of its contemporaries. Historical analysis helps to show the lack of novelty of these observations and offers examples that allow one to envisage that evangelism could also renew these historically planted churches.

Further Reading

Bousquet, François, "The Enlightenment: The Foundation of Modern Europe," *International Review of Mission* vol. 95, n° 378-379 (July-October 2006), p. 236-246.

Davie, Grace, "Is Europe an Exceptional Case?" *International Review of Mission* vol. 95, n° 378-379 (July-October 2006), p. 247-258.

Gantenbein, Jean-Georges, *Mission en Europe: Une étude missiologique pour le 21e siècle* (Ph.D. thesis, Faculté de théologie protestante, Strasbourg, 2010; Studia œcumenica Friburgensia 72; Münster: Aschendorff, 2016).

Jenkins, Philip, *God's Continent: Christianity, Islam and Europe's Religious Crisis* (Oxford/New York: Oxford University Press, 2007).

Jenkins, Philip, "Godless Europe?" *International Bulletin of Missionary Research* 31, 3 (2007), p. 115-120.

Van de Poll, Evert, *Europe and the Gospel: Past Influences, Current Developments, Mission Challenges* (Maastricht/Aachen: Shaker/de Gruyter, 2012), at http://www.degruyter.com/view/product/209760.

Wessels, Anton, *Europe: Was It Ever Really Christian? The Interaction between Gospel and Culture* (London: SCM, 1994).

Chapter 3
Paradox of Europe and Christianity Barriers and Bridges

Evert Van de Poll[1]

According to Swiss theologian Christine Lienemann, mission is "the theory and the practice of the Church meeting strangers," that is, people who are strangers to the Church and the Christian faith.[2] This simple and modest definition is very appropriate for the mission of the Church in Europe because it makes us aware that a large part of the population in our countries has indeed become alienated from the Christian worldview and religious practice. So much so that one could turn this definition around and say that communities of practising Christians have become minorities, and even strangers, in the modern world. We can simply observe this situation all around us, but the perplexing element of the matter is that this happens in Europe, the most Christianised of all continents where the message of Jesus Christ has been proclaimed for many centuries and in many forms. This makes Europe such a specific context for evangelism.

Our subject is evangelism in Europe as a whole – that is, including the countries outside the European Union. When we look at such a vast field, our approach can only be a general one. This is a deliberate choice, for I am persuaded that when we try and see the overall picture of Christianity and religion in Europe, we will gain a better understanding of what is happening in each particular country on this continent. Together they constitute a specific context for the communication of the Gospel.

This is a vast and fascinating field of study. Those who reflect on evangelism in Europe have different angles from which they try to understand

---

[1] This chapter is a slightly modified version of my article "Evangelism and the Paradox of Europe," *European Journal of Theology* vol. 25, 2 (October 2016), p. 151-161. It develops the paradoxical barriers and bridges for the communication of the Gospel.

[2] Quoted by Benedict Schubert, "Témoigner: Responsabilité personnelle, communautaire, ecclésiale," Paper presented at the *Association Francophone Œcuménique de Missiologie* (AFOM), Paris, on June 21, 2014.

the characteristics of this context. In this chapter we shall shortly discuss the three most frequently used ones. We will then propose another approach, one that does not replace the three preceding ones but rather places them in a particular perspective and should be useful to understand our European context.

Why Europe?

Before we go into the subject, we have to answer the preliminary question: why look at Europe as a whole? What justification is there for taking this frame of reference? I will give three reasons.

First, on a sociocultural level, the peoples and the countries of Europe are very similar. I agree with social scientists like Pamela Sticht that these peoples constitute a cultural zone or a family of cultures that have common roots, a common history and to a certain extent common values.[3]

Second, sociologists of religion have characterised Europe as "the exceptional continent." In Europe, the rise of modernity (the dominance of rational science and technology) has been accompanied by secularisation of the public sphere and the decline of religious practice, but this is not a universal phenomenon. In other parts of the world, the development of a society along the lines of Western technology and rational science does not seem to hamper religious practice as can be seen in the United States, Canada, Korea, China and Latin America. So the European combination of modernity and secularisation is the exception to the rule.[4]

Third, there is the missionary experience. One cannot just adopt approaches and methods simply because they have proven to be successful in other countries with similar Western cultures. Many who try to do this discover that for some reason or another, things work differently here.

The Angle of Secularisation

The first angle from which we can look at Europe as a context for evangelism is secularisation. The terms secular and secularisation can have several meanings. Here I will use them in the sociological sense: the decline of the social and political influence of the Church and Christian institutions, and the public sphere becoming secular, i.e. neutral, a-religious.

---

[3] Pamela Sticht, *Culture européenne ou Europe des cultures? Les enjeux actuels de la politique culturelle en Europe* (Paris: Harmattan, 2000).

[4] Grace Davie, *Europe, the Exceptional Case: Parameters of Faith in the Modern World* (London: Darton, Longman & Todd, 2007), p. 137, 145.

Since the twentieth century, "secular" refers to people who have no religious affiliation and hold no "religious" beliefs. So secularisation is the decline of Church membership. All of this has given rise to a secular worldview, which often becomes an ideology called secularism. According to this view, a universal, neutral rationality is normative in politics, science, economics and society.

Only a minority of secular people are convinced atheists. Most of them are agnostics who just don't know, or who suppose that there is something like a divine being or force, but generally speaking they are not interested in relating to that "something." But practically speaking, they live "as if there is no God." They manage their life without religious practice related to a transcendent Being.

Major Barrier: Non-Religious Worldview

When in terms of culture and religion, secularisation is seen as the main characteristic of European societies, then the major barrier for evangelism is unbelief in the existence of God. Or, to put it more generally, a worldview and a lifestyle that do not take into account any divine or transcendent reality.

The secularisation of Europe partly explains why some evangelism models that have worked well in Latin America or in Africa do not yield much fruit in Europe. In those parts of the world, the Gospel is communicated among people with some kind of religion: Roman Catholic, Animistic or others. They already believe in God or at least in a divine reality. No need for them to change this religious worldview in order to accept the Gospel and become a Christian. What changes for them is their image of God, their doctrinal convictions, religious practices and spiritual experience. Perhaps they only change denominational attachment.

For secularised Europeans, the situation is completely different. Before they can even consider the invitation of the Gospel, they need to should become religious, have their secular worldview transformed into a religious one. The question is not, which God, which religion? But, why God, why religion in the first place? Does God exist? What does the word "God" mean, and to whom or what does it refer? Are you talking about a force, a person, an idea, a projection of a human father figure? Can we experience this God? And if so, why is this important? What is the relevance of religion anyway? When I'm not poor, depressed, lonely, ill or jobless, what would I need a religion for? What does this "God" add to my life?

Moreover, many secularist intellectuals maintain that religion is a past stage in the development of humanity. Viewed from such a perspective, secularisation is a stage that comes after Christianity. What is the next step? There is no next step, at least not a religious one, because secular humanism considers itself to have advanced beyond all religions. As Marcel Gauchet puts it: "Christianity is (or was) the religion of the end of all religion."[5]

This view is based on the evolutionary development of cultures, already put forward by Herbert Spencer, Lewis Morgan, Edward Tylor and others towards the end of the nineteenth century. While this is an old theory that is now disputed by scholars, it is still widely held and propagated, for instance by the French philosopher and former cabinet minister of education, Luc Ferry. He argues that the God of the Bible is a human creation. "In the past, people needed this imagined divine being, but we have to do without, and we can do without."[6] For a secularised European, to become Christian really amounts to a conversion in the truest sense of the word; a complete turnaround in direction, which goes against the thrust of history, against the whole cultural and intellectual development of our world! Embracing a religion, even Christianity, is seen as a step backward.

Secular-3 and the Challenge of Exclusive Humanism

Sociology, theology and missiology have been discussing secularisation for several decades now. Charles Taylor has taken this reflection a step further because in his *A Secular Age* (2007) he analyses at length and in great detail how secularisation has come about in history.[7] Although Taylor is a Canadian, his analysis is particularly relevant for the European situation, because secularisation is a European "invention," a phenomenon that has arisen on our continent. In fact, Taylor pretty much writes and argues like a European, for Europeans.

Taylor makes an important distinction. What people have been discussing so far, he says, is the worldview and lifestyle of non-religious or unchurched people, as well as the idea of a secular science or secular politics, in the sense of a-religious, neutral, unbiased, "objective." He calls this

---

[5] Marcel Gauchet first presented this argument in *Le désenchantement du monde* (Paris: Gallimard, 1985), and repeated it in several subsequent publications, lastly in *Le religieux et le politique: Douze réponses de Marcel Gauchet* (Religion & Politique; Paris: Desclée de Brouwer, 2010).

[6] Luc Ferry, *La révolution de l'amour* (Paris: Plon, 2010), p. 7.

[7] Charles Taylor, *A Secular Age* (New York: Harvard University Press, 2007), p. 2-3.

secular-2. Then he introduces another sense of the term, secular-3. This stands for a society in which religious belief or belief in God is understood to be one option among others. Moreover, many secular people find the option to believe quite contestable, and they strongly contest it. The major problem of our "secular age," says Taylor, is that our religious beliefs are considered to be unbelievable. Under such conditions it is difficult to believe in God.

Believers are continually challenged by the alternative of not believing. Taylor speaks of an "exclusive humanism, a radically new option in the marketplace of beliefs, a vision of life in which anything beyond the immanent is eclipsed."[8] In other words, our neighbours and colleagues are coping with the difficulties of life without looking to God for help. They find our convictions simply unbelievable. Taylor describes several "conversion experiences" of people who have abandoned religious beliefs and turned to atheism. Many of them say that this felt like "becoming an adult, coming of age, getting rid of childish Sunday school images." Such stories make Christians look like naïve people who "still" believe in some sort of fairy tale.

Response: Apologetics

The usual response of Christians to secularisation is to make a case for believing in God, showing the plausibility of the Christian faith. This is the apologetic attempt to remove the barrier of a worldview without God by showing the "plausibility of the Christian worldview," as David Brown puts it.[9] A recent example of this approach in the Netherlands is a book by Stefan Paas and Rik Peels entitled *Proving God*.[10] Apologetic arguments may not convince others, but they certainly have an important function to reassure believers that what they believe is not irrational or childish.

Bridges

However, apologetics is not enough. We should find points of contact and common ground on which we can build bridges of understanding. As

---

[8] Summary of James K.A. Smith, *How (not) to be Secular: Reading Charles Taylor* (Grand Rapids: Eerdmans, 2014), p. 22-23.

[9] See David Brown, "Particular Difficulties of Europeans to Understand and Accept the Gospel," chapter 5 of this book.

[10] Stefan Paas and Rik Peels, *God bewijzen: argumenten voor en tegen geloven* (Amsterdam: Balans, 2013).

Elaine Storkey puts it: building bridges "enables us to cross over into a non-Christian cultural context and begin to understand it from within, [to gain] some knowledge of who we are speaking to, and what matters to them." And they provide ways for non-Christians to "cross the great cultural chasm between the worldview of Christianity and the worldviews of our contemporary world, so that the Gospel can be heard for what it is."[11]

The question is how we can build bridges in what Taylor called a secular-3 situation. What starting points do we find there? Taylor himself shows us the way. He makes every effort to place himself in the position of an exclusive secular humanist. How does it feel to live without God, to have a closed worldview, to live with the idea that death is the total extinction of life? In anthropology, this would be an *emic* approach.

Taylor examines what he calls the "unquiet frontiers" of secular people. "Our age is very far from settling into a comfortable unbelief. The secular age is deeply cross-pressured."[12] This means that people experience a kind of emptiness that makes everything look useless. They are frequently haunted by the happy memories of religious belief. In particular, many moderns are uncomfortable with death, "the giving up of everything."[13] Secular belief is a shutting out: "The door is barred against further discovery." But "in the secular waste land ... young people will begin again to explore beyond the boundaries."[14] And so there is an explosion of all kinds of spirituality, of quasi-religious experiences.

Here we have many starting points to build bridges of understanding. An interesting example of such a bridge is the television documentary *Heureux naufrage* (happy shipwreck), produced by a team of French-speaking Canadians and Europeans. Several philosophers, journalists, educators and writers talk about how they manage in a world after faith in God. As one author puts it, "I do not believe in God but I miss Him." Others talk about their way to faith, as a post-secular experience.

---

[11] Elaine Storkey, "Bridges to the Gospel," UCCF The Christian Unions, 2015, at www.bethinking.org/apologetics/bridges-to-the-gospel (accessed on August 1, 2015).

[12] Taylor, *A Secular Age*, p. 727.

[13] Idem, p. 725.

[14] Idem, p. 769, 770.

The Angle of Post-Modernity

The second angle from which we can look at Europe as a context for evangelism is post-modernity. Numerous descriptions and definitions of postmodernism are given and there is considerable debate on which one is right. Let me just give some key elements. Postmodern means that you are critical towards the pretention of rational science, that it knows the truth about reality itself. This truth is hidden from us; we can only see parts of it. Postmodernists mistrust any religion or political ideology that presents something like the final truth for everybody. According to postmodernists, such "metanarratives" are used as a mask for a power play.[15]

Besides this philosophical stream, there is a more widespread postmodernism on a popular level. People with a postmodern mind-set or outlook are "sceptic about technology, objectivity, absolutes, and total explanations." At the same time, they highly value "image and appearance, personal interpretation, pleasure, and the exploration of every spiritual and material perspective."[16]

Major Barrier: Unbelief in Absolute Truth

Some consider postmodernism as the main characteristic of our societies. Of course, this is not to say that everybody in Europe has a postmodern outlook. But when you see postmodernism as the major cultural characteristic of European societies, the main obstacle for evangelism is the refusal to believe in absolute truth. This includes the message that Jesus "is the truth." As a human being, Jesus is highly esteemed, but the postmodern outlook finds it difficult to admit that he could be the Christ, the unique Saviour of mankind.

Response: Dialogue and Respect for Others

Lesslie Newbigin comes to mind. In his writings he has dealt with the pluralist society, in which religious truth is separated from the truth claims of rational science. In a pluralist world, religion is a matter of values and personal experience, and no one can pretend that their religion is superior to that of another. This is the major challenge for evangelism in Europe, says Newbigin.[17] He counters this by arguing that scientific truth is as

---

[15] E. David Cook, *Blind Alley Beliefs* (2nd ed.; Leicester, IVP, 1996).
[16] James W. Sire, *The Universe Next Door: A Basic Worldview Catalogue* (3rd ed.; Downers Grove/Leicester: IVP, 1997).
[17] Lesslie Newbigin, *The Gospel in a Pluralist Society* (London: SPCK, 1989).

much based on presuppositions as religious truth is based on faith. So we should not accept the pluralist idea that scientific reason stands above all religious affirmations, as their ultimate arbiter. On the other hand, we cannot convince others by our rational arguments either. We can and must speak the truth only in the humble confidence that the Spirit convinces the heart of the hearer.[18]

In his writings, Newbigin did not use the term postmodern, but what he described is indeed a major element of post-modernity. Many churches, mission organisations and theologians see post-modernity as the key characteristic of Europe today. For instance, in 2008 the German *Arbeitsgemeinschaft für evangelikale Missiologie* organised a colloquium on mission in Europe, at which the main angle of approach was postmodernism.[19] Similarly, the international mission conference in Edinburgh 2010, which marked the centenary of the historic world mission conference of Edinburgh 1910, placed post-modernity in the centre of its theological deliberations. At this point, I also want to mention Marie-Hélène Robert. In her recent book on the theology of evangelism she analyses the documents of the Roman Catholic Church on "new evangelism," as well as the European context in which this takes place. In line with these texts, she too defines this context in terms of post-modernity.[20]

The main thrust of all these conferences and publications is a call for a new kind of evangelism, in the form of dialogue, based on respect for the opinions and lifestyles of others. The issue of absolute truth cannot be avoided, but we should make it known in ways that allow others the freedom to respond. Another important element of our witness are acts of charity, as concrete signs of God's love. Marie-Hélène Robert combines that with the notion of respect, which she defines as granting others the liberty to respond as they desire. She writes:

> Postmodern cultures adapt easily to charity and liberty, but they do not consider the truth as Christianity presents it, neither the objective truth (its divine origin and universality), nor the subjective truth (its human reception and

---

[18] See Lesslie Newbigin, *Proper Confidence: Faith, Doubt and Certainty in Christian Discipleship* (London: SPCK, 1995).

[19] See the publication based on this colloquium: Klaus W. Müller (ed.), *Mission im postmodernen Europa: Referate der Jahrestagung 2008 des Arbeitskreises für evangelikale Missiologie* (Mission Reports 16; Gießen: Edition AfeM, 2008).

[20] Marie-Hélène Robert, *Pour que le monde croie: approches théologiques de l'évangélisation* (Lyon: Profac, 2014).

translation). Evangelism is the proclamation of a real liberty: man is free to respond in love to the offer of love ...[21]

On the basis of charity (practical love) and granting others this liberty, we can speak the truth of salvation, says Robert.

Bridges

What points of contact do we find in the postmodern world to build bridges of communication? Elaine Storkey identifies the following starting points for making the Gospel understood:
- A new involvement in spirituality
- Fascination with the narrative
- Cultural openness to worldview questions (film, novel, music)
- Shared issues of justice, meaning, compassion and suffering[22]

Postmodernism is not a reaction to any religious experience and practice. It is not against religion, nor does it present itself as an alternative religion. People with a postmodern outlook are not closed off to religious belief and spiritual experience, quite the contrary. One can be postmodern and practise a religion – as long as one remains tolerant of other forms of "truth." Tolerance is the key postmodern value, including tolerance of Christian religious experience. This openness provides many points of contact.

The Angle of Post-Christendom

The third angle from which theologians, and missiologists in particular, look at the European context is that of post-Christendom. This term needs some clarification. Christendom is not the same as Christianity (the religion, the faith) but denotes the Christianised society in which the state Church is closely connected with the political powers. Another term for this is Constantinianism, because it was the Roman emperor Constantine who, in the fourth century, introduced the alliance between the political powers and the established Christian Church. In *Evangelism after Christendom*, Bryan Stone gives the following description:

> In the Constantinian state of affairs, which is also called Christendom, church and state are fused together for the sake of governance in such a way that

---

[21] Robert, *Pour que le monde croie*, p. 297, 300.
[22] Storkey, "Bridges."

Christianity becomes a project of the state, or an appendage to the state, subject to its violent ends.[23]

This situation has come to an end with the separation of church and state, although there are many vestiges of the old system in every European country. We are now in a post-Christendom, post-Constantinian situation as Christianity is no longer the dominant religion. Practising Christians have become a minority and the churches are pushed to the margins. The problem is that the many forms of church life from the old situation are retained. Stuart Murray is a typical example of those who look at Europe from the post-Christendom angle. He describes this situation as follows:

> Post-Christendom is the culture that emerges as the Christian faith loses coherence within a society that has been definitively shaped by the Christian story, and as the institutions that have been developed to express Christian convictions decline in influence.[24]

In short, post-Christendom means that Christians are moved from the centre to the margins. From being a majority they have become a minority. They have lost privileges and have become a community among others in a plural society. The shift from Christianity to another religion is not new in history. It has happened in several regions of the world, such as North Africa, but in Europe this shift was different. Stuart Murray explains:

> Here the Christian story has not been replaced by another [religious] story but [by] the scepticism about all explanatory and culture-shaping stories. In this sense, post-Christendom in Western Europe is different from earlier versions: we really have not been here before.[25]

Major Barrier: the Image of Church

When we look at Europe through this angle, then post-Christendom is in terms of culture and religion considered to be the main characteristic of our societies. Viewed from this angle, the major problem or barrier is the Church, or rather the image people have of Church. Through the historic forms of established Churches and Christian institutions, people have been

---

[23] Bryan Stone, *Evangelism after Christendom: The Theology and Practice of Christian Witness* (Grand Rapids: Brazos, 2007), p. 118.
[24] Stuart Murray, *Post-Christendom: Church and Mission in a Strange New World* (Milton Keynes: Paternoster, 2004), p. 19.
[25] Murray, *Post-Christendom*, p. 19-20.

given a wrong picture of the Christian faith. It really is quite different from the Christendom kind of religion.

Response: Other Kinds of Churches, New Forms of Evangelism

The response, then, is to do something about the Church. The emphasis should change from maintenance, keeping what you have, to mission; from being an institutional church to being a movement of followers of Christ. Stuart Murray is an example of this approach because he analyses the current situation and proposes new ways of communicating the Gospel as well as new forms of church life. His work has inspired a whole network of so-called "new expressions." Murray agrees with those who find that post-Christendom is not an easy environment for discipleship, mission or Church. He notices that Post-Christendom can easily be perceived as a threat and associated with failure and decline, but he himself takes a different perspective:

> [This response] celebrates the end of Christendom and the distorting influence of power, wealth and status on the Christian story. It grieves the violence, corruption, folly and arrogance of Christendom. It rejoices that all who choose to become followers of Jesus today do so freely without pressure or inducements. It revels in a context where the Christian story is becoming unknown and can be rediscovered by Christians and others. It welcomes the freedom to look afresh at many issues seen for so long only through the lens of Christendom. It anticipates new and liberating discoveries as Christians explore what it means to be a church on the margins that operates as a movement rather than an institution. And it trusts that history will turn out how God intends with or without Christians attempting to control it.[26]

Post-Christendom also implies that Christians have to evangelise in a new way, not through control as in the old days, but through the witness of our lifestyle, through personal testimony and through the communal witness of churches that are signs of the new society that only God can build. In the words of Bryan Stone, another author who has reflected on evangelism in the post-Christendom situation,

> The most evangelistic thing the Church can do today is to be the Church, to be formed by the Holy Spirit through core practices such as worship, forgiveness, hospitality and economic sharing into a distinctive people in the world, a new social option, the body of Christ. This is ... the witness to God's reign in the world. [Mission] is neither the individual, private, or interior salvation of individuals nor the Christianisation of entire cultures, but the creation of a people

---

[26] Murray, *Post-Christendom*, p. 21.

... The Church does not really need an evangelistic strategy, the Church *is* the evangelistic strategy.[27]

The Paradox of Europe and Christianity

As far as we can see, there is not one angle that suffices to get an overall picture of religion and society in Europe; the three angles discussed so far are complementary. So I propose to place them, and other possible angles, in a wider framework, which I call the "paradox of Europe and Christianity." One could also say: the love-hate relationship between these two.

Clearly, Europe is the most Christianised continent; no other part of the world has been exposed to the message of the Bible for such a prolonged period of time and in such a consistent way as this continent. Nowhere else is there such a rich Christian heritage. Its cultures are still rooted in Christian values and symbols, and Christian institutions were at the basis of the current social benefit systems. Without the spread of the Gospel, the impact of the Bible, and the influence of institutional churches, Europe as we know it today might never have come about. A sweeping statement indeed! But a justified one, given the crucial role of Christianity in the political and cultural development of Europe as a whole, and of each European country in particular. Several historians and political scientists bring this out.[28]

At the same time, Europe is now marked by the abandonment of Christianity more than any other part of the world. Nowhere is the desertion of the Christian faith and the retreat from institutional churches as widespread as in Europe, and nowhere else has this been going on for such a prolonged period of time. It is here that a secularised worldview, atheism, secular lifestyles, and secular political ideologies have emerged – so much so that Europe is now called "post-Christian," although it is much more precise to say "post-Christianised."

This is the paradox of Europe; its societies are marked as much by the Christian faith as by its abandonment and rejection, by an enormous varie-

---

[27] Stone, *Evangelism after Christendom*, p. 15 (our italics).

[28] Several historians and political scientists take this view, e.g. Philip Jenkins, *God's Continent: Christianity, Islam, and Europe's Religious Crisis* (Oxford: Oxford University Press, 2007); Norman Davies, *Europe: A History* (Oxford: Oxford University Press, 1996); Urs Altermatt, Mariano Delgado, Guide Vergauwen (eds.), *Europa: Ein christliches Projekt? Beiträge zum Verhältnis von Religion und europäischer Identität* (Stuttgart: Kohlhammer, 2008).

ty of expressions of Christian faith and a rich heritage of historical European Christianity, and by a variety of alternative, secular worldviews and ideologies, a secularised public sphere and the spread of secular lifestyles. Failing to take in account both sides of the coin leads to misrepresentations: either we draw a picture that is too optimistic with respect to the influence of the Church or we depict an image that is too much the opposite.

From whatever angle we look at Europe as a context for the mission of the Church, we should take into account this paradox, namely that our societies are at the same time marked by Christianity and by the abandonment of Christianity. This approach does not replace the angles mentioned above. It should rather refine our perception, as we realise that there is always the other side of the coin. The contradicting aspects of the same reality fall into place.

When studying the context in which we as a Church are called to bear witness to our faith, I find this paradox of Europe and the Gospel a helpful tool to come to grips with the different characteristics and apparent contradictions of our societies, in relation to Christianity and the Gospel. Therefore, let us take a second look at the other angles.

Much Christianity in Secularisation

First, there is so much Christianity in secularisation. This is not only a barrier for the Gospel. Secularisation has not just replaced the religious practice of Christianity, but it is at the same time very "Christian" because it is permeated by originally Christian ideas and values. Secularisation, to be precise, is the secularisation of Christianity. Some Christian elements are retained, such as the idea of the intrinsic value of humans, ideas of individual responsibility, freedom, and social and cultural values. Secularisation is "post-Christian" but only in a partial manner. People take the humanist values of Christianity out of their original religious "envelope."

This means that secular humanism is not only a barrier but also provides common ground to build bridges of understanding. Take for instance the issue of which values are to be considered foundational to create cohesion in our multicultural societies. This is a matter of ongoing debate, and the interesting thing is that the values in question are to a large extent secularised biblical and Christian values.[29] What will become of them in the

---

[29] Here I follow the lead of several historians, such as the contributors to Francis Jacques (ed.), *Les racines culturelles et spirituelles de l'Europe: Trois questions sur la place de la source chrétienne* (Paris: Parole et Silence, 2008).

long run if they are cut off from their original religious foundation? Here is where Christians come in and take part in the debate.

Look for instance what happened to Jean-Claude Guillebaud, a leading left-wing intellectual in France. He set out to define the basic values that are needed to restructure our multicultural societies. Listening to a host of secular philosophers and social scientists he came up with a list of six values, which he described in a lengthy book, *La refondation du monde*.[30] Towards the end he came to the surprising conclusion that five of the six foundational values had biblical, Christian roots. This was the beginning of an intellectual pilgrimage that led him a few years ago to publicly embrace the Christian faith.

Another example is the French philosopher Luc Ferry. In his recent book *The Revolution of Love*, Ferry develops what he calls a "secular spirituality" based on the biblical concept of love. He thinks highly of Jesus, qualifying him as "the supreme example of an altruistic lifestyle." He takes the teachings of the Church seriously when it comes to the practical application of the commandment to love your neighbour, and summarises it in the principles of solidarity, the primacy of the common interest, and the value of selfless service.[31] What he says about love would largely fit in a manual on practical Christian discipleship. However, contrary to Guillebaud, he did not turn to the Christian faith. So here we have the paradox again.

Human rights are yet another example. They are key values in European societies, but it is not without coincidence that they have emerged in the history of European Christianity, not elsewhere. How many secular people (and Christians for that matter) realise that Baptist and other non-conformist leaders were the first to define the universal right of religious freedom and freedom of conscience? This was the starting point of a process that led to the declaration of universal human rights. Some atheist philosophers admit this. Michel Onfray says: "Their language is rational, but their quintessence is Judeo-Christian ethics."[32] John Gray calls them "a hangover of Christianity."[33] This again provides an interesting point of contact for introducing the biblical message.

---

[30] Jean-Claude Guillebaud, *La refondation du monde* (Paris: Seuil, 1999).

[31] Luc Ferry, *La révolution de l'amour* (Paris: Plon, 2010), p. 7.

[32] Quoted by Frédéric Lenoir, *Le Christ philosophe* (Paris: Plon, 2007), p. 262.

[33] John Gray, *Straw Dogs: Thoughts on Humans and Other Animals* (London: Farrar, Straus and Giroux, 2007).

Postmodern Critique and Christian Experience

Secondly, our paradox shows another side of the postmodern outlook. The Christian community, particularly in evangelical circles, often takes a suspicious, negative stance towards this mode of thought, because of its critical attitude towards the message that Jesus is *the* truth and *the* way to fullness of life. Yet at the same time, Christians can join postmodernism in its critique of totalitarian regimes such as Nazism. Reacting against social structures and ideologies that claim to represent absolute truth, postmodern thinkers argue that such claims for absolute loyalty really were (and are) instruments of power. Following the line taken by Jacques Derrida, Jean-François Lyotard and others, they set out to deconstruct these systems in order to bring to light the political and economic interests behind them. By excluding all rivals, these "great stories about reality" lead to oppression of individual freedom. This critique of the terrors of atheistic, totalitarian regimes such as Nazism and Soviet Communism reminds us of the biblical critique of any Tower of Babel kind of system based on human pride.

Postmodernism is not only suspicious of religious claims to knowing "the only way" to salvation and happiness, but in a similar vein, it also criticises the dogmatic attitude of secular rationalism. It deconstructs the idea, based on the Enlightenment, that modern science leads humanity on a triumphant march towards a brave new world. In fact, what are the grounds of this "belief" in progress? What kind of knowledge do scientists have of reality? Are there no other things to know than phenomena that meet the rational eye? And are there no other ways of obtaining knowledge than rational enquiry? Human beings are fundamentally a mystery even to themselves, so instead of relying on the limited power of reason, this mystery can often be better explored by means of music, aesthetics, intuition, religion and other rich worlds of experience.

We can take up these "postmodern" questions and bring to light the pretentions of secular scientific rationalism as it tries to impose its worldview. This creates an opening for Christians to come up with plausible answers to the questions people are asking today. A religious answer is not by definition less valid than a secular one. On what grounds can secular rationalists "absolutely" exclude the existence of God, the validity of religious experiences, and the biblical story of the origin of humankind?

Moreover, postmodernism is not in opposition to religious experience and practice. The postmodern outlook is not an alternative to religion as such, but a reaction to the dominance of truth systems. People with a postmodern outlook are not closed off to religious belief and spiritual experience, quite the contrary. One can be postmodern and practise a religion

– as long as one remains tolerant of other forms of "truth." From the Christian standpoint, the great problem of postmodernism is its pluralism, which leads to relativism.

Heritage of European Christianity

Thirdly, let us look at the legacy of European Christianity. Surely, established churches have a very dubious historical record because of their implication in power politics, wars, oppression and so on. Moreover, they suffer from a negative image among a considerable part of the population. At the same time, they enable us to build bridges for making known the Gospel today. For a start, the message of the Bible has permeated every sector of our society. An Indian author, Vishal Mangalwadi, puts it this way: "This is the book that shaped European culture, indeed the soul of the whole Western civilisation."[34] We should keep in mind that this came to pass not only through Christian counter-movements and apostolic preachers, but to a much larger extent through established churches and their social institutions.

Moreover, European Christendom has left us with an enormously rich heritage: art, music, paintings, cathedrals, monasteries, universities, social customs, festivals, names, symbols. This heritage abounds in all European countries; it is there for everybody to see and hear, read about, touch and visit. The question is: who will be a guide? Many people visit cathedrals without understanding their symbolism. They enjoy sacred music and admire famous paintings of biblical figures without understanding the real meaning. They use the benefits of hospitals and schools that were once Christian institutions but they have no idea why and how they came about. They give their children names of Christian saints while ignoring their history.

Finally, there is a growing interest in the roots of our culture. As Christians, we represent the major religious root of Europe and this provides us with countless occasions to build bridges for the message. We only need to explain general culture, quite simply. Because we are familiar with the Bible, we have the key to unlock the meaning of this rich cultural heritage to our contemporaries. As Christians, we are ideally equipped to explain European culture to our contemporaries who are ignorant of its background.

Christian heritage centres have been developed in several locations, and they organise lectures and heritage tours. This is not a difficult endeavour, and every church can try to see what Christian heritage there is in their city

---

[34] Vishal Mangalwadi, *The Book that Made your World. How the Bible Created the Soul of Western Civilization* (New York: Thomas Nelson, 2011).

and in the region and make efforts to study it. Before long, they can offer city walks, guided tours and heritage talks. Throughout Europe, people are generally fond of discovering culture, ranging from local music to local cuisine and local customs, and also natural sites with history, architecture and so on. In most cases, there is a link with the history of the Church. Find out about it and transmit it to others. One just has to explain the meaning of this painting, that building, a popular custom, or tell the story of a famous person in the past, and there is a natural occasion to explain the Bible.

Ambivalent Attitudes towards Christianity

Are we not drawing a much too optimistic picture of the socio-religious context of Europe with respect to the communication of the Gospel? This would indeed be the case if we were to forget the paradox. The long history of Christianity in Europe and all the efforts of evangelisation that have been going for ages have led to a paradoxical situation in which there are ambivalent attitudes towards Christianity. We need to be aware of this when we attempt to gain an understanding for the Gospel.

Attachment and Indifference

On the on hand, there is a widespread cultural attachment to the heritage of Christianity. The Bible and its moral values and its picture of God, the Gospel stories of Jesus and the cross, the names of the apostles, and countless traditions of the Church have become part and parcel of European cultures. While many people feel attached to this heritage, they are often indifferent to the message of Christianity.

One can observe this ambivalence for example among the electorate of patriotic, political parties that are on the rise all over Europe (also labelled as "extreme right" or "populist"). High on their agenda is the defence of the "European" identity, that is, the culture of the indigenous autochthone people in the context of a multicultural society and ongoing immigration of non-Europeans. It is commonplace for these movements to appeal to the Christian or Judeo-Christian roots of our societies, but, as political scientist Pascal Perrineau points out, "they attract more non-religious voters and nominal, non-practising Catholics than among practicing Catholics."[35] In

---

[35] Pascal Perrineau, "Le FN est désormais présent dans toutes les catégories," interview in *La Croix*, December 11, 2015, p. 5. This phenomenon is further developed

France, Catholicism is the main form of Christianity, in terms of numbers and of historical influence.

This ambivalence is characteristic for society as a whole, at least in Western Europe. Benedict Schubert, Reformed inner city pastor and lecturer at the *Theologisches Alumneum* in Basel, summarises it as follows:

> In our country, there is an extraordinary inhibition to speak of faith in public. This leads, in fact, to a particular ambivalence. To begin with, this reluctance does not mean that people want to do away the visible signs of Christian presence that are everywhere around us: the crosses on the mountain tops, chapels beside the trail and churches in the village centre. On the contrary, people seem to be attached to them. In the debates on migration, there is much emphasis on the fact that we are a "Christian country." However, and this is the other side of this ambivalence, this does imply an openness to publicly discuss the meaning and the scope of such a statement. Asking someone what faith and religion mean to him, usually causes discomfort.[36]

Readers all over Europe will recognise this combination of cultural attachment to the heritage of Christianity and indifference to the message of this religion for today. Since churches have been around for ages, how can their message still surprise? How can it be heard as good news? People certainly need to hear it as something "new" in order to be willing to change their minds, but precisely because of our "Christian" history it is not easy to present the Gospel as good news.

Ignorance

The two phenomena of attachment and indifference are intertwined and point to another ambivalence. Nowhere else in the world have Christian beliefs and practices been taught and transmitted from generation to generation as in Europe, so much so that it is considered to be a Christian continent. About 75% of the population is affiliated to a Church (at least nominally). This is the average figure for the whole of Europe, with peaks in some countries like Italy, Ukraine or Poland to mention a few. In secularised countries like France, the Netherlands or Czech Republic, the percentages can be as low as 50%, but that is still considerable. Yet at the same time, we notice widespread ignorance with respect to what it means to be a Christian.

---

in his book on right wing populist movements, *La France au Front: Essay sur l'avenir du FN* (Paris: Fayard, 2014).

[36] Schubert, "Témoigner."

Chapter 3 – Paradox of Europe and Christianity: Barriers and Bridges

When people hear about Jesus and the Christian faith, their first and automatic reaction is: "We know all that." The problem is that they think they do, while in fact false presuppositions, preconceived ideas and traditional misrepresentations abound. They are much harder to correct than ignorance.

Most people are superficially familiar with the person of Jesus. From what they know, they will generally have a positive impression of his ethical conduct, and as such Jesus enjoys a certain popularity. But being a disciple of Jesus is quickly associated with not so attractive images of the institutional Church. Some associate Jesus with outdated songs, long sermons, prescribed rituals and a whole list of forbidden pleasures, others with a child in the arms of Mary and a dying man on a crucifix. This also pertains to the influence of historical Christianity, with its paradoxical mix of Bible truth and human traditions.

We can take our paradox even further. Precisely in Europe with its rich history of Christian practice, where Christian symbols still abound, more and more people no longer understand what religious language really means. Everyday language owes much to the Bible and Christian tradition, but today, the language in which Christians express their faith often meets with incomprehension. Generally speaking, people are indifferent to what is abracadabra to them. Benedict Schubert hits the nail on its head when he says that in Europe of all places (!) we are faced with the tremendous challenge to make new translation efforts:

> Find phrases, metaphors, illustrations, lines of argument that allow us to express our faith, to talk about our experiences with God in a way that is meaningful for our secularised contemporaries. This begins with listening to them, their songs, their books, their films. In what context and with what connotations did you recently come across the word "sin" for example?[37]

For those who are involved in evangelism, this other side of the coin is all too familiar. However, if we only look at that, we can draw a very pessimistic picture of the religious state of Europeans, to the detriment of the other side of the reality, i.e. the far-reaching influence that this same message has exerted and still exerts on the cultures and social institutions of our continent. These two sides of reality should not be treated as mutually exclusive.

---

[37] Schubert, "Témoigner."

Conclusion

We bring our reflection on the paradox of Europe and Christianity to an end by emphasising once again that everywhere in Europe we see signs of the impact of the Bible and the Gospel, even in the ways in which it has been rejected and abandoned. Many churches, organisations and individual believers today find ways to add new chapters to this ongoing story!

Further Reading

Davie, Grace, *Europe, the Exceptional Case: Parameters of Faith in the Modern World* (London: Darton, Longman & Todd, 2007).

Jenkins, Philip, *God's Continent: Christianity, Islam, and Europe's Religious Crisis* (Oxford: Oxford University Press, 2007).

Mangalwadi, Vishal, *The Book that Made your World. How the Bible Created the Soul of Western Civilization* (New York: Thomas Nelson, 2011).

Murray, Stuart, *Post-Christendom: Church and Mission in a Strange New World* (Milton Keynes: Paternoster, 2004).

Stone, Bryan, *Evangelism after Christendom: The Theology and Practice of Christian Witness* (Grand Rapids: Brazos, 2007).

Taylor, Charles, *A Secular Age* (New York: Harvard University Press, 2007).

Van de Poll, Evert, *Europe and the Gospel: Past Influences, Current Developments, Mission Challenges* (London: de Gruyter/Versita, 2013).

Chapter 4
How "Christian" Is Europe Today?
Towards a Post-Secular Situation?

Evert Van de Poll[1]

The person on the other end of the line spoke very poor French. From what she said, I gathered that she was trying to find *la Chapelle*. On a shivery winter day in 2004, she had decided to contact a pastor. By some inexplicable means she had obtained a tract of the Baptist congregation of which I was the pastor. Our meeting hall was the basement of an apartment building, located at a corner somewhere in the complicated system of alleys, squares, shop windows and restaurants that make up the commercial centre, *Saint Georges*, in the middle of the historic centre of Toulouse. We called it *la Chapelle*. Apparently, the person had not been able to find it (no wonder!), but fortunately the tract listed a phone number, so she called it and that's how she got me on the line. I guided her by phone through the labyrinth to the front door of our chapel.

She came in and we got talking. I learned that she was a Japanese immigrant, staying with a friend in an apartment not far from the chapel. She was hoping to find a steady job. For the time being, learning French was the main challenge. Then she told me the reason for contacting me: "I want to become a Christian; could you tell me what I should do?" I must admit that I was rather taken aback, and immediately felt suspicious. In France, this is not the question people will ask you right away. Was this just a way of getting a residence permit, by becoming a member of a church? Was the next question perhaps of a financial nature, or a demand for lodging? Working in downtown Toulouse had made me careful. However, when she told me her story, I heard nothing to raise my suspicions.

Her name was Akiko. As she didn't speak English and as her Japanese was all Greek to me, we had no language alternative but French. She had searched for spiritual truth in her home country, but found no peace in

---

[1] This chapter is a modified and enlarged version of chapter 17 of my book *Europe and the Gospel: Past Influences, Current Developments and Mission Challenges* (London: de Gruyter/Versita, 2013), entitled "How Christian is Europe Today?"

traditional religion. She had travelled and lived in several other countries. She believed that there was a God who cared for us, but she didn't know how to contact him, how to have peace of heart with this God. Which religion can help me, she wondered. After her arrival in Europe she noticed that there were churches everywhere she went. Gradually, she arrived at the conclusion that in Europe, one needs to be a Christian to approach God. As simple as that!

But then, how does a young Japanese woman become a Christian? Good question. She tried to find out in several Catholic churches in the centre of Toulouse, but to no avail. Finally, she decided to try the Protestant way of becoming a Christian. This was the beginning of a whole year of preparation for baptism. My wife and I took all that time to explain the Christian faith, making sure that her motivation was sincere. Akiko faithfully attended all church services, and began to participate in prayers.

Easter Day 2005 arrived, the day of her baptism. When she rose up from the water in the baptistery, she smiled and heaved a deep sigh: "Finally, she whispered, now I really am a Christian!" Akiko has continued to follow the Lord, even after she left France. We have occasionally received news from her, confirming that she was keeping to her faith commitment.

This is certainly a remarkable story! But notice what triggered Akiko's search for faith in the first place: church buildings, cathedrals, chapels. Christian edifices communicated to this Japanese immigrant the message that in our part of the world one should approach God through the Christian faith. In her eyes, Europe of all places, and even France, was Christian.

In the preceding chapter, we have described in what way Europe has become post-Christianised, but this is only one side of the paradox of our continent. The other side is that Christianity still occupies a very important place in society. We should therefore ask the question: how "Christian" is Europe today? A closer look reveals that the presence of the Christian religion is more widespread and our societies are more Christianised than we are often made to think.

Christians in a Secularised and Multi-Religious Society

Until the 1960s, European societies were largely mono-ethnic, with a European culture and Christianity as the dominant religion. Since then, large scale immigration has changed the traditional white face of Europe into a multi-coloured one. Our societies have become multi-ethnic, multi-cultural and multi-religious.

Meanwhile, the number of practising Christians has been in constant decline during recent decades. Conversions of Christian or secularised Europeans to other religions are exceptional. Consequently, it would be a simplification to describe European societies either as multi-religious or as secularised. To be precise, we should say that we live in largely secularised societies with various religious minorities: Christians, Muslims, Buddhists, religious Jews, etc.

Special Position of Christianity

Europe is becoming increasingly pluralist, yet only partly so, because the traditional culture of the country remains the dominant one. Sociologists call it the *Leitkultur* to indicate that in a multicultural society there is always one culture that takes the lead. This is invariably a European one. This implies that the religion that was (and still is) part of the *Leitkultur* also maintains a special position. In one country, it is the Lutheran Church, in another one the Anglican Church, or the Reformed or the Roman Catholic or the Orthodox Church, but in all cases it is Christianity that remains the frame of reference. For this reason, Europe is still considered to be Christian, as we saw in the preceding chapter.

Consequently, the position of Christianity remains a special one. The scope of its action extends beyond its constituency of practising members. The situation is paradoxical. A large majority of Europeans lead a secular life. Yet many of them maintain a certain level of association with Christianity.

Churches are losing the ability to define the beliefs and influence the behaviour of the vast majority of Europeans. Nevertheless, they continue to have a significant role in the lives of both individuals and communities, most obviously at times of celebration or loss. They are no longer able, however, to exert any form of control. This is a European story, brought about for European reasons, quite different, for example, from the continuing religious vitality of the United States, or indeed the rest of the world.

Even so, despite the pluralist ethos according to which all religions are of equal value, Christianity remains the most attractive one when secularised Europeans are seeking for spiritual meaning.

A Solid Minority

We have stated that our societies are marked by the abandonment of Christianity. But the loss in numbers is not as complete as it looks. It depends on whom you count as "Christians." Numbers of practising Christians are relatively small. When one takes church attendance on an average

Sunday as a criterion, the percentage in most European countries is less than ten. Exceptions are staunchly Catholic countries like Italy, Poland and Ireland. Some Orthodox regions in Eastern Europe also show higher percentages. But then, not every committed Christian goes to church every Sunday.

Philip Jenkins speaks of a "solid minority of committed believing Christians." Some sixty million to seventy million West European Christians assert that religion plays a very important role in their lives, and many of those attend church regularly.[2] If Jenkins is right, we should put the figure for the whole of Europe at 100 to 120 million, i.e. fifteen to eighteen percent of the population.

The Limitations of Quantitative Approaches

Counting Christians is a complicated matter. Distinguishing "real" from "nominal" Christians is even more complicated. Quantitative approaches have serious limitations. Quite often, they only take into account one or two parameters of adherence to Christianity, namely church attendance and/or church registration. You can count the number of people in the pews, you can count the number of names on the church register, but how do you count those who believe in their heart that Jesus died for their sins? Clearly, other criteria are equally valid in determining whether someone is a Christian. For example:
- Belief in basic Christian doctrines
- Individual religious practice (prayer, reading the Bible)
- Lifestyle related to Christian ethical and socio-cultural values
- Requesting Christian ceremonies such as rites of passage (birth, confirmation or religious adulthood, wedding, and funeral)

All these criteria are not necessarily linked to church attendance. Church members who hardly ever attend church (the classic sociological definition of a nominal Christian) can:
- Observe Christian traditions such as Christmas and other holidays, religious ceremonies related to national commemorations, etc.
- Insist on a church wedding ceremony, want their children to be baptised (or "christened" as Anglicans say), and their loved ones given a Christian burial

---

[2] Philip Jenkins, *God's Continent: Christianity, Islam, and Europe's Religious Crisis* (Oxford: Oxford University Press, 2007), p. 56.

- Hold to Christian norms and values with respect to marriage, sexuality, family and education, protection of human life, bioethics, and tolerance
- Believe that God exists, that Jesus is the Son of God, that there is a heaven and a hell
- Read the Bible and/or pray in private

These variants show that a more refined approach is needed to get an idea of the scope of Christianity beyond the visible community of believers assembling for worship on any given Sunday.

Marginal Church Membership

To begin with, there is the typical European phenomenon of marginal church membership. It comes in two forms: nominal Christianity and minimal Church practice.

Nominal Church Members

Nominal means that a person is registered as Protestant, Orthodox or Roman Catholic but does not practise this religion. Some nominal Christians come to a point where they demand deregistration, but their percentage is very small indeed. Meanwhile, the nominal ranks are continually swelling. There are two ways of "becoming" nominal (although it is usually not a decision but rather a quiet process):
- Being baptised as infants because their parents wished to express their adherence to a certain community, follow the tradition of the grandparents, do not personally connect to any form of church life.
- No longer participating in church when once they did.

Notice, however, that nominal Christians do not sever all links with the institutional church. Although their daily life is largely secularised, and although they may have a secular worldview, they wish to maintain at least an administrative link with organised religion. Reasons may vary:
- It is useful to maintain membership to ensure a Christian burial.
- The church does good work for the poor and I want to support that.
- In times of need, I might need the church.
- Maybe God would be offended if I deregister.
- I want to end up in paradise, not somewhere else.

Minimal Church Practice

In many countries, there is a notion of minimal church practice. That means that one has to meet minimum requirements in order to benefit from the services of the Church in times of need, and to be sure that at the end of your earthly existence your family will have a Church funeral. This notion is particularly widespread among Roman Catholic and Eastern Orthodox populations. In the past, the Roman Catholic Church has defined minimum requirements of church attendance: go to confession and mass at least once a year. The typical period of the year varies from country to country: Christmas, or Easter, or Palm Sunday. If not, people run the risk of no longer benefiting from the grace of God as it is mediated by the Church. Orthodox churches have similar guidelines.

Many church members opt for the minimum requirements to ensure a good conscience. A few years ago, I talked with Ronaldo Diprose, then academic dean of the Italian Evangelical Bible Institute in Rome, about the place of Roman Catholicism in Italian society. I also asked him about the level of religious practice. Over ninety percent of the Italians are baptised Catholics. He explained that this is even part of the national identity.

> However, the overwhelming majority hardly ever attend a mass, but that doesn't mean that the Church is not important for them. Almost all Italians consider themselves to be good Catholics. They honestly believe that if you're baptised in the Church, if you have done First Communion, if you're married in church, and if you go to confessional and to mass once a year at Easter, then you're a good Catholic.[3]

Minimal church practice is based on the idea that although you are not interested in church life, you still want to keep on good terms with the Church in order to be acceptable to God. Today, this notion is often subconscious. For many people, it has become automatic to do the minimum thing and be comfortable. It almost goes without saying.

A Typical European Phenomenon

Marginal church membership is widespread in Europe. In some countries, it entails more than half of the population! One might even go as far as to say that this phenomenon is typical of the religious situation in the "Old Continent." Nowhere else in the world is there such a large percentage of nominal Christians.

---

[3] This conversation took place during my stay at the Italian Evangelical Bible Institute in Rome, March 22, 2010.

During the nineteenth and early twentieth centuries this phenomenon affected large sections of the working class in the industrialised parts of Europe. After the Second World War, it has become more generalised, especially since the 1960s. It can be observed in all historic churches, Roman Catholic, Orthodox and Protestant. In passing, we notice that a similar process of estrangement from traditional religion can be observed among the Jewish and Muslim communities in Europe.

Two examples serve to illustrate the scope of what we are talking about. In France, some sixty-five percent of the population defines itself as Roman Catholic (or Christian, which in this country commonly amounts to the same). An even higher percentage has been baptised in this church. Roughly half of the marriages include a church ceremony. But only seven to nine percent attend mass at least once a month. For the younger generation, the figures are considerably lower.[4]

In the past, the Spanish population was overwhelmingly and staunchly Roman Catholic, but this is rapidly changing. While 82.4 percent of the population still identify as Roman Catholic, only 47.7 percent of them, that is thirty-nine percent of the population, "practise" Catholicism, according to the same criteria as used in the case of France.

It should be noted that the number of nominal Christians is considerable in countries whose history has been dominated by Roman Catholicism and Orthodoxy (Italy and Greece are the most telling examples). This is less common in countries historically dominated by Protestantism. Historic Protestant churches have lost a considerable proportion of their nominal members.

Interestingly, Evangelicalism is far less affected by nominal membership. The major reason seems to be that it is a conversion movement rather than an historic tradition. However, there are signs that the phenomenon is also beginning to make inroads in these circles.

Different Criteria, Different Variants

Notice that definitions of nominal Christianity vary. It is a confusing term that can mean different things. Historic churches practising infant baptism consider all baptised members as Christians. Some give them a provisional status, considering them as Christian in view of a confirmation at a later stage in life. The fact that they hardly ever show up in church is not a reason to exclude them.

---

[4] See e.g. Frédéric Lenoir, *Le Christ philosophe* (Paris: Plon, 2009), as well as the survey published by *Le Monde des religions* (July 2005).

Evangelical churches, however, link Christian identity to a faith decision. People are consciously incorporated into the church through baptism or public confession or both. Viewed from this angle, nominal church members still need to receive salvation, and therefore are not "real" Christians. Here, for example, is the definition proposed by the influential Lausanne Committee of World Evangelisation.

> A nominal Christian is a person who has not responded in repentance and faith to Jesus Christ as his personal Saviour and Lord. He is a Christian in name only. He may be very religious. He may be a practising or non-practising church member. He may give intellectual assent to basic Christian doctrines and claim to be a Christian. He may be faithful in attending liturgical rites and worship services, and be an active member involved in Church affairs. But in spite of all this, he is still destined for eternal judgment (cf. Matt 7:21-23, James 2:19) because he has not committed his life to Jesus Christ (Rom 10:9-10).[5]

Obviously, different criteria of determining Christian identity result in different statistics. Evangelical authors put the percentage of Christians at less than one percent in countries with a Roman Catholic or Orthodox tradition, and at an average of four to five percent in countries with a Protestant tradition. On the contrary, government statistics are usually based on church attendance, so they present quite another picture, as do historic churches who present figures from their registers. They mention percentages ranging from fifty to sixty in countries that are most secularised, to more than ninety percent in countries where church membership is still assumed.

Evangelical churches, generally speaking, closely relate Christian identity to active church membership. This explains why nominal membership is not so widespread among them, although it exists.

According to the criteria generally adopted in socio-religious studies, a nominal Christian is someone registered as a church member while not practising his religion in terms of attending church services, except occasionally.

Believing and/or Behaving without Belonging

When we look at forms of "Christianity" outside the circle of practising believers, we notice more than only nominal Christians. In order to bring this out, it is useful to use more variables than church attendance or official membership.

---

[5] Lausanne Committee of World Evangelization, *Christian Witness to Nominal Christians among Roman Catholics* (Lausanne Occasional Paper No. 10; Charlotte, NC: LCWE, 2002), p. 4.

Believing without Belonging

To begin with, we should distinguish "belonging" and "believing." These technical terms were introduced by Grace Davie in 1994, and adopted by most sociologists of religion in Western Europe, as they analysed the outcomes of the European Values Study (EVS).
- Belonging stands for church attendance.
- Believing stands for holding Christian beliefs in God, life after death, heaven, hell, sin, etc.

The European Values Studies (EVS) are a series of surveys conducted by a number of universities in several European countries at regular intervals (1981, 1990, 1999). The latest survey dates from 2008. What makes the EVS interesting is that they use more criteria to assess the religious situation of modern Europe: denominational allegiance, reported church attendance, attitudes towards the church, indicators of religious belief and subjective religious dispositions. From the data a widespread phenomenon emerges, known as "believing without belonging," the name given to it by Grace Davie.[6] There are two types of variables to measure religious practice, she says: on the one hand those concerned with feelings, experience and the more numinous religious beliefs, on the other hand those which measure religious orthodoxy, ritual participation and institutional attachment.

> It is only the latter (i.e. the more orthodox indicators of religious attachment) which display an undeniable degree of secularisation throughout Western Europe. In contrast, the former (the less institutional indicators) demonstrate considerable persistent religious adherence. With this in mind, I am hesitant about the unqualified use of the term secularisation even in the European context. Indeed, it seems to me considerably more accurate to suggest that West Europeans remain, by and large, unchurched populations rather than simply secular. For a marked falling-off in religious attendance (especially in the Protestant North) has not resulted, yet, in a parallel abdication of religious belief – in a broad definition of the term. In short, many Europeans have ceased to connect with their religious institutions in any active sense, but they have not abandoned, so far, either their deep-seated religious aspirations or (in many cases) a latent sense of belonging.[7]

---

[6] Grace Davie, *Religion in Britain since 1945: Believing without Belonging* (Oxford: Blackwell, 1994).

[7] Grace Davie, *Europe, the Exceptional Case: Parameters of Faith in the Modern World* (London: Darton, Longman & Todd, 2007), p. 7f.

On the basis of the most recent EVS data, Grace Davie even comes to an opposite conclusion. "Religious belief is *inversely* rather than *directly* related to belonging." In other words, as the institutional disciplines decline, belief not only persists, but becomes increasingly personal, detached and heterogeneous, and particularly among young people.

Believing without belonging has quickly become a catch phrase that rings a bell with most people who study the religious situation in their country. It describes the phenomenon that Christian beliefs are widespread beyond church institutions. It is found among nominal church members, and even among those who are no longer registered as such. Many Europeans seem to be secularised at face value, but retain a "latent sense of belonging" because they share a number of beliefs inherited from the Christian past.

Behaving without Belonging – Cultural Christians

However, this distinction does not suffice to discern the spread of "Christianity" outside the visible church community. We should enlarge the two variables (belonging-believing) to a triangle: belonging-believing-behaving. This helps us to see more clearly yet another category of persons. We owe this insight to Allan Billings. Together with some colleagues, this British Anglican priest analysed the religious situation in his region. According to the 2001 census in the UK, over seventy-six percent of people identified themselves with "a faith tradition" (answering this question was not compulsory!). These faith traditions comprise not only Christianity but also other religions, as well as vague notions of "spirituality." Unsatisfied with the secularisation theories, they used the idea of believing without belonging as a tool to better understand these people in their cities, towns and villages. But this didn't give much more clarity. Most people who were not churchgoers appeared to be quite eclectic in what they believed. "They thought of Christianity more in terms of praxis, a way of living, than a set of beliefs." Billings describes them further:

> They live Christian lives; they are Christians because their lives reflect the life and values of Jesus Christ. Like him they acknowledge that we live in a creation; that God cares for us, that we should care for one another, and so on. It is the religion of the golden rule: do unto others as you would have them do to you. Sometimes they feel the need to attend a Church on such occasions as a Christmas Carol Service or Midnight Mass. They want family weddings and funerals to be held at a Church. They watch and feel uplifted by *Songs of Praise* on Sunday-night television. Sometimes they might want to hear inspir-

ing music at a cathedral Matins or Evensong. They see the Church, in other words, as a spiritual resource. But they do not want to belong.[8]

We could call this "behaving without belonging." Granted, this is a diluted form of practising Christianity. It only touches the social behaviour side of it, omitting the belief side and the worship side almost entirely. Allan Billings calls such people "cultural Christians." He distinguishes them from "Church Christians" (who go to church and adhere to its basic beliefs). This term should not be confused with the *Kulturchristentum* in nineteenth-century Germany, although there are similarities. As I talk with people in my French surroundings and look at their attitude to Christianity, I recognize this description. In this country, I meet many cultural Roman Catholics, as Billings meets many cultural Anglicans in Britain. I suspect that the reader could meet them in any European country.

This cultural Christianity is the effect of more than a thousand years of Christianity that has left behind a legacy of stories, words, images, and rites, through which Christian beliefs are transmitted. Think of the popular idea of Saint Peter at the gate of heaven, of the deceased floating on a cloud to heaven, of a horned devil that tempts people to commit a deadly or "capital" sin. It has above all left us with values and a morality, notices Allan Billings:

> The way we treat one another – especially the sick, the aged, the poor, the stranger in our midst – owes a great deal to the Biblical notion that all people are created in God's image and deserving of care. We are a people who have been shaped and continue to live by Christian values.[9]

He goes on to say that many people want to abide by social values that have a Biblical origin, and which they do not hesitate to call Christian values.

> They feel that they are doing what can be expected of any Christian. And God, if he exists, will certainly approve. He will accept them. It is lived Christianity. It is hardly a matter of "believing without belonging," since most people are not much interested in beliefs; the attachment is more emotional and practical than intellectual.[10]

---

[8] Alan Billings, *Secular Lives Sacred Hearts: The Role of the Church in a Time of no Religion* (London: SPCK, 2004), p. 11.
[9] Idem, p. 15f.
[10] Idem, p. 18.

Belonging without Believing and/or Behaving

Pastors who "know their flock" will add to this that the inverse phenomenon also exists. They are usually saddened to observe that people belong to the church without believing and/or without behaving as Christians should. But that is an alternative way of defining the phenomenon of nominal Christianity described in the preceding paragraph.

Vicarious and Default Religion

We cannot limit the scope of Christianity to the number of practising Christians only, nor even to the percentages of marginal Church members and un-churched people holding to Christian beliefs.

There is yet another way in which Europe is more Christian than one would have thought when looking at the ongoing secularisation of society. While the vast majority of the people do indeed live a secular life, they do not disregard Christianity altogether. In the pluralist society of today, all religions are tolerated and treated as equal before the law. According to the postmodern worldview no religion can claim absolute authority in matters of social ethics. Even so, Christianity is not reduced to just one of the many religious options. Even in the multicultural society where secular humanism dominates the public sphere, many un-churched people maintain an indirect, often unconscious link with Christianity. Two phenomena confirm this.

Vicarious Religion

The first phenomenon is called "vicarious religion." The term was introduced by Grace Davie and Danièle Hervieu-Léger, a British and a French sociologist of religion. They noticed that the church embodies the collective religious memory of the whole nation, including people who do not practise the Christian religion. In this respect, the church has a function for the society at large. People appreciate that there are churches; they find them useful. Moreover, they see them in relation with the history of their nation. The Church is part of the national cultural heritage, so the Church should go on, even when they do not participate themselves. Grace Davie has this to say:

> For particular historical reasons (notably the historic connections between Church and State), significant numbers of Europeans are content to let both churches and churchgoers enact a memory on their behalf (the essential meaning of vicarious), more than half aware that they might need to draw on the capital at crucial times in their individual or collective lives. The almost uni-

versal take up of religious ceremonies at the time of a death is the most obvious expression of this tendency; so, too, the prominence of the historic Churches in particular at times of national crisis or, more positively, of national celebrations.[11]

This is a typical European phenomenon, sociologists notice. Everybody in Europe seems to be able to easily understand it, but in other parts of the world people find it difficult to grasp, as if it is something outside their experience.

Default Religion?

Related to this is a second idea in which Christianity is the default religion of Europeans. If you are not religious yourself, but want something religious, this is the religion you turn to, as long as you do not have a particular preference for another one. Secularised people who wish a religious funeral for their deceased loved ones are unlikely to approach a rabbi or an imam. Either they ask a professional undertaker to organize an eclectic mix of texts and traditions with a more or less spiritual connotation, or they request the services of a clergyman.

What is the default setting to which Europeans return when they are thinking about spiritual matters, about God, prayer, after-life, sin, the origin of man? Two options seem to be prevalent. Either an esoteric New Age kind of spirituality made up of elements of Asiatic religious traditions and/or of elements from pre-Christian pagan religions in Europe. For this option, one needs to have a more than average acquaintance with such traditions. One needs to be a deliberate seeker of spiritual meaning in order to follow this track. In computer terms, this is not a default setting, but a customisation, based on personal configurations.

The other option is taking up Christian traditions that linger in the collective subconscious of European people. For this option, one doesn't have to make much effort. It is there, disseminated in our culture, to be found in any church around the corner. If you're looking for spiritual meaning and you don't customise, this is what you get: a Christian image of God, a Christian image of man, a Christian idea of prayer, and so on.

What about other religions? As far as we can observe, and generally speaking, neither Islam nor Hinduism are attractive options for Europeans in search of spirituality, inner peace or whatever term we could use for a renewed religious interest. Certainly, Muslims are actively engaging in

---

[11] Grace Davie, *Europe, the Exceptional Case*, p. 19.

missionary activities, but apparently, these are aimed mainly at the second and third generation of Muslim migrants who are drifting away from the religion of their parents. Islam is still very much a communitarian religion. "Old stock" Europeans who convert to Islam almost always do this in the context of a mixed marriage. More research is needed to learn about conversions for other reasons. From the available publications on the spread of Islam in Europe, we get the impression that the number of converts from a European cultural background to Islam is limited.

Many Europeans have a benevolent attitude towards Judaism. Christians in particular are interested in its traditions, but in the eyes of both insiders and outsiders, this remains a religion of and for Jewish people. This feeling is enhanced by the fact that Judaism is not at all a missionary religion. Rabbis do not encourage non-Jews to become Jews. Very few take this step. In fact, this happens mainly in the context of mixed marriage.

Buddhism and other Asiatic spiritualities seem to be attractive to European society in search of a non-religious spirituality, in harmony with nature. This is often interconnected with interest in esoteric sources. Usually denoted as New Age or as New Religious Movements, these movements remain typically European. Instead of fully converting to the original Asiatic religion, its adherents usually take over its ethical elements, without its religious practices.

Many non-religious people in Europe have the idea that the appropriate religious practice in Europe, for those who wish "to have one," is Christianity. While they have no problem with churches continuing to function, considering that "they have always done so," they are often apprehensive about the presence of mosques. They tolerate them, as they think modern citizens should, but nevertheless, they often feel that Islam is foreign to "our country," "our way of life." In the eyes of a considerable percentage of the population, a mosque is considered to be a kind of edifice that is not "home" to Europe, representative of a way of life they would rather not like their children to adopt.

A Typical Example

A few years ago, Catherine, a middle-aged business woman lady, joined our congregation. Having studied psychology, she took a keen interest in matters of well-being and "spirituality." This is how her pilgrimage led her to our small Protestant Church in a largely secularised small town:

Born in a Roman Catholic family, I abandoned religion as a teenager. Later in life I began searching for more spirituality in my life, but I didn't want to learn Tibetan words and become Buddhist like my son. I tried, but that made me feel far away from home, so I went to a church because that is much closer to my culture. At first I went to a Roman Catholic parish church, but felt not really welcomed. A few months later, I discovered a small Protestant church building just down the road, where Bible study discussions were held every Wednesday. I asked whether I, as a Catholic, could attend, and the group welcomed me without asking questions. Gradually I have drawn closer to experiencing a relationship with God. This was like returning to my lost spiritual roots.

What made this woman decide to come back to a church? It was her awareness that Buddhism was "far from home," while a church is "much closer to my culture." In the eyes of many, Christianity is the most appropriate religion of Europe.

Europe Still Considered a "Christian" Part of the World

Despite massive secularisation and the development of a multi-religious society, Europe is still considered to be Christian.

In a Cultural Sense

Christianity has left Europe with a rich cultural heritage of values, ideas and images, artistic expressions, traditions, festivals, wedding and funeral rituals, local social customs, symbols, etc. This heritage can be found everywhere. It gives a Christian ring to our national and regional cultures. We also noted the existence, all over Europe, of a plethora of Christian schools, hospitals, social institutions, welfare programs, rehabilitation centres, television and radio networks, publishers, newspapers, humanitarian and development agencies, and so on. They constitute a "presence" of Christianity that goes far beyond the Christian community or even the marginal Church members. The same can be said of confessional political parties, trade unions and influence organisations (so-called "lobbies"). Not to mention individual politicians in other parties who take Biblical values and Christian beliefs as their frame of reference.

All of this makes Europe still look Christian, particularly to outside observers. When tourists come to get an idea of Europe, they come and visit the outstanding works of art that are part of our Christian heritage. Among Europeans as well there is a widespread popular feeling that "we are a Christian country" – that is, in a cultural sense.

One thinks of the recent row over the Swiss referendum resulting in a vote against the construction of minarets (2013). One thinks of the popular outcry in Italy when action groups wanted to have crucifixes removed from public schools (2012). One also thinks of the political parties who attract voters with the message that the Muslim presence is becoming a threat to our cultural heritage, saying that after all, "'we' are a Christian country."

Other faith communities do not fit easily into our societies which regard the privatisation of religion as normal practice. Muslims in particular find it normal to practice religious customs both privately and publicly. This has led to heated controversies about wearing head veils in public schools, medical treatment by doctors from the opposite sex, subsidising the construction of non-Christian religious buildings, etc.

But public signs of Christian faith do not arouse the same level of protest. Instead, they are taken for granted as part of the landscape. One will find that secularised people actively oppose the destruction of a chapel because they consider it a beautiful element of the cultural heritage of the village. All these examples illustrate that Christianity is seen as a normal part of the cultural landscape of Europe.

In a Civilisational Sense

The French political scientist Jean-François Susbielle has recently published a study on the decline of "the European Empire." His scenario of future doom is debatable. What makes his argument interesting for our subject is his repeated claim that "in this twenty-first century, the European Union remains the cradle of the Christian West, a community of countries who share common values ... Christianity is indeed one of the foundations of Europe."[12] Statements to the effect that Europe is part of Western Christian civilisation can be found in many other essays on global issues and geopolitical developments.

Moving to Post-Secular Situations?

There is a widespread assumption that secularisation is definitive, a no-return phase in cultural or human development. Entering the secularised phase means the end of all religion. Only people with a residual religious worldview might link up with the church again, but people with no notion

---

[12] Jean-François Susbielle, *Le déclin de l'empire européen: qui domine l'Europe ?* (Paris: First, 2009), p. 187, 192.

of divine reality whatsoever, are unlikely to change. Such is the assumption. Secularist philosophers give ample food to this idea. They argue that religion is a temporary phase in the development of humanity. Once this phase is past, there is no turning back. Massive decline in church membership in the post-war decades seems to substantiate this scenario. But is it realistic? Several indicators seem to point to the contrary.

The past century has been marked by secularisation, but this does not mean that the present century will simply follow the same path. We cannot draw a straight line from yesterday to tomorrow. This is what the old secularisation theory did, according to which Europe will inexorably become less religious. But there are several signs that the future might well be different, less secularised.

Return of Religion in the Public Sphere

Notice the "return of religion" in the public sphere, in the arts, in popular music, in philosophical debates. There is a growing interest in spiritual matters among a wide range of people raised in a secular environment. So much is happening in the area of religion and society. Look at the new religiosity that has spread among Europeans who have not been brought up in a religious context. Often labelled as New Age or New Religious Movements, this can take the form of Eastern meditation, esoteric speculation, an interest in heretical movements of the past (Catharism for example), neo-paganism (Celtic cults revisited), or an ethical form of Buddhism combined with a bit of "spirituality:" seeking transcendental truth in the inner self.

There is also a new interest in Christianity. The number of adult baptisms in Roman Catholic churches, the popularity of Gospel music, the number of people taking part in spiritual retreats in a monastery, the ongoing success of Taizé, the charismatic movements in historic churches, the young people with no Christian background whatsoever, who are attracted to Evangelical musical events, and so on. Although the people concerned are often nominal church members, we also find among them people who have come out of a completely secularised environment.

Several social scientists see signs that the decline of Christianity is about to come to a standstill. The American investigative journalists John Micklethwait and Adrian Wooldridge were so intrigued by the ongoing news of religious communities and by people in their highly secularised environment who appeared to have linked up with the Christian faith again, that they decided to concentrate their research on this subject; not only in the US but also in Europe. The result is a most challenging book called *God is Back*.[13] Quoting research in the area of religion, collecting data about religious practice, reading publications and talking to opinion leaders in society, they arrived at the conclusion that "a global revival of faith is changing the world." Not only Christianity but also Islam, Hinduism and other religions are progressing in highly modernised societies, including Europe.

Leaving journalistic hyperbole aside, the facts they collected are telling us that a new kind of religious adherence is winning ground all over Europe. While fewer people are inclined to remain faithful to the tradition of former generations, hence the decline of historic churches, a growing number of people are receptive to the Christian faith through a process of personal enquiry, leading to a spiritual experience and to some kind of conversion. This corresponds with the observations of sociologists like Danièle Hervieu-Léger that the typical twenty-first-century believer is a "pilgrim" and a "convert."[14] For this reason, Evangelical, Pentecostal and Charismatic faith expressions are finding increasing response, as Micklethwait and Wooldridge point out.[15] According to the *World Christian Encyclopaedia*, these churches and movements accounted for 8.2 percent of Europe's population in 2000, nearly double to that in 1970.[16] Pentecostalism is France's fastest-growing religious movement. Meanwhile, migrant churches are thriving in all the larger cities in Western Europe, thus changing the perceptions of Christianity among the general population.

On the one hand, Europe is becoming markedly more secular. Traditional Christian values are being set aside; legislation follows majority opinions that run counter to what the Church has always taught. On the other hand, there is an upsurge in religious practice, even in the urban areas. This comes as a surprise to the largely secularised world of social sciences. Moreover, the place of religious communities and their customs in society is a regular issue in political discussions.

Secular and Religious Trends

What is the overriding trend in Europe? Is it secular or religious? "Predicting the future about religion in Europe is tricky, as more than one thing

---

[13] John Micklethwait and Adrian Wooldridge, *God is Back: How the Global Revival of Faith is Changing the World* (New York: Penguin Press, 2009).

[14] The title of one of the main publications of Danièle Hervieu-Léger *Le pèlerin et le converti: la religion en mouvement* (Paris: Flammarion, 1999).

[15] Micklethwait and Wooldridge, *God is Back*, p. 356ff.

[16] Quoted by Micklethwait and Woolbridge, *God is Back*, p. 136.

is happening at once," says Grace Davie, whose analyses we have found useful to get a picture of the place of Christianity in today's society. A few years ago, a journalist with *The Guardian* put this question to her: "Is Europe's future Christian?" Her answer was:

> The historic Churches of Europe are losing the ability to discipline both the beliefs and behaviour of the vast majority of Europeans. The process is unlikely to be reversed and will lead, other things being equal, to an increase in secularisation in most parts of the continent. Other things, however, are not equal, given that the rest of the world is arriving in Europe – pretty fast. New communities have arrived, which understand their religious lives very differently from their European hosts. Among them are forms of Christianity which challenge the historic Churches of Europe – in terms of fervour as well as belief; they are markedly more conservative. Among them also are other-faith communities, some of which do not fit easily into our societies which regard the privatisation of religion as "normal." Hence the series of heated controversies about the wearing of the veil in public school, for instance.[17]

In our time, religion is becoming increasingly important in society. Traditional religious practices are not disappearing as secularist intellectuals have thought they would, but remain important for a considerable part of the population. This creates problems: should ritual slaughter by Jews and Muslims be allowed; should the state help migrant communities to build better places of worship; what kind of religious education should be taught in public schools? Politicians are often ill-equipped to take decisions. Here we notice the effects of secularisation, one of which is the systematic loss of religious knowledge. It follows that necessarily sensitive debates are very often engaged by people who, literally, do not know what they are talking about – with respect to their own faith, never mind anyone else's. "It is little wonder that things get out of hand," notes Grace Davie, who emphasises that "little will be gained, conversely, by denying the realities of the past, by contempt for the seriously religious, and by the (sometimes deliberate) cultivation of ignorance about faiths of any kind." She adds that Europeans should be better informed about their religious heritage, and build on its positive dimensions – those of generosity and welcome. Europeans, moreover, should ensure that there is a place in their societies for those who take faith seriously, whatever that faith might be. "The largest proportion of these people will still be Christian, but in ways rather different from their forebears."[18]

---

[17] Grace Davie, "Is Europe's Future Christian?" interview in *The Guardian*, June 1, 2009.
[18] Idem.

Is Europe becoming post-secular? While the process of secularisation is still going on, we are witnessing new forms of church life (all kinds of missionary and "emerging" churches, religious communities) and a host of revitalised existing churches. Micklethwait and Wooldridge conclude their research by saying:

> Give people the freedom to control their lives and, for better or worse, they frequently choose to give religion more power. Give religious people modern technology and they frequently use it to communicate God's Word to an ever-growing band of the faithful. ...
>
> Religion is proving perfectly compatible with modernity in all its forms, high and low. It is moving back toward the centre of intellectual life. But it is also a vital part of popular culture, with Christian barbershops and tattoo artists, skateboarders and stand-up comedians. Christian rock-music is ubiquitous.[19]

In his book on the future of religion in Europe, Philip Jenkins has devoted a whole chapter to these phenomena, aptly called "Faith among the ruins."[20] These may be portentous days in which the Gospel will gain a larger hearing still.

Hope

At the end of our investigation we want to quote once more Lesslie Newbigin. We don't need promises of coming revival or statistics of church growth, he says, to have confidence for the future. Instead, we must accept the facts. We are a minority, but that should not worry us, because our hope is not based on figures but on the faithfulness of God.

> In a pluralist society, there is always a temptation to judge the importance of any statement of the truth by the number of people who believe it. Truth, for practical purposes, is what most people believe. Christians can fall into this trap. It may well be that for some decades, while Churches grow rapidly in other parts of the world, Christians in Europe may continue to be a small and even shrinking minority. If this should be so, it must be as an example of that pruning which is promised to the Church in order that it may bear more fruit (John 15). When that happens, it is painful. But Jesus assures us, "My Father is the gardener." It is a summons to self-searching, to repentance, and to fresh commitment. It is not an occasion for anxiety. God is faithful, and he will complete what he has begun.[21]

---

[19] Micklethwait and Wooldridge, *God is Back*, p. 355.
[20] Philip Jenkins, *God's Continent*, chapter 3.
[21] Lesslie Newbigin, *The Gospel in a Pluralist Society* (London: SPCK, 1989), p. 244.

The last phrase reminds us of the words of the Psalmist as they are echoed in the traditional greeting pronounced at the beginning of Protestant church services: "Our help is in the name of the Lord, who is faithful in eternity, who never abandons the work that his hand began."

If we can say that he began a work through the apostles who set foot on the shores of Macedonia at the beginning of the Christian era, and that he has continued the work during many ages in what has come to be called Europe, then we may have confidence that he will not abandon it, but bring it to completion, according to his good purposes.

Further Reading

Billings, Alan, *Secular Lives, Sacred Hearts: The Role of the Church in a Time of no Religion* (London: SPCK, 2004).

Davie, Grace, *Europe, the Exceptional Case: Parameters of Faith in the Modern World* (London: Darton, Longman & Todd, 2007).

Mangalwadi, Vishal, *The Book that Made your World: How the Bible Created the Soul of Western Civilization* (New York: Thomas Nelson, 2011).

Lausanne Movement, *Christian Witness to Nominal Christians among Roman Catholics* (Lausanne Occasional Paper No. 10; Report on the Consultation on World Evangelization held at Pattaya, Thailand, June 16 to 27, 1980; Charlotte, NC: LCWE, 2002).

Micklethwait, John and Wooldridge, Adrian, *God is Back: How the Global Revival of Faith is Changing the World* (New York: Penguin Press, 2009).

Newbigin, Lesslie, *Proper Confidence: Faith, Doubt and Certainty in Chrstian Discipleship* (London: SPCK, 1995).

Pope John-Paul II, *Ecclesia in Europa*, Post-Synodic Apostolic Exhortation (Rome: Vatican Press, 2003).

Robert, Marie-Hélène, *"Pour que le monde croie:" Approches théologiques de l'évangélisation* (Lyon: Profac, 2014).

Stone, Bryan, *Evangelism after Christendom: The Theology and Practice of Christian Witness* (Grand Rapids/New York: Brazos/Harvard University Press, 2007).

Van de Poll, Evert, *Europe and the Gospel: Past Influences, Current Developments, Mission Challenges* (London: de Gruyter/Versita, 2013).

Chapter 5
Particular Difficulties Facing our French Fellow Citizens in Understanding and Receiving the Gospel

David Brown[1]

The first point to clarify is this: who are these fellow citizens who find it so difficult to understand the Gospel? When I was asked to present this paper, the suggested title mentioned "our European fellow citizens." Now it may turn out that this paper is valid in a wider European context, but my main experience is in France. I am convinced that the cultural diversity of Europe (albeit with undeniable common features) leads us to the conclusion that the difficulty in understanding and accepting the Gospel is greatly influenced by the history and the cultural evolution of each constituent nation.

So who are these French fellow citizens mentioned in the title of this paper? In my way of thinking, they are all those members of the French nation who have been strongly influenced by the mental picture of reality transmitted via French culture. Sometimes these people are called Franco-French or ethnic French. But these two terms are an oversimplification because they presuppose that there is a French lineage, whereas people born in France but with foreign parents have undergone this cultural conditioning. It would be preferable to use another expression to designate the people in my title such as "our fellow citizens with a French culture".

Now let's take our thinking a step further. It is valid to ask the question whether these "fellow citizens with a French culture" can really understand the message of the Gospel in the way churches habitually communicate it, using words such as "sin," "retribution," "expiation" or "justification." How can we help them understand these biblical truths in a language which is accessible and contextualised, without losing the substance during the process? This is how one pastor put it:

---

[1] This paper was presented at the REMEEF meeting on February 23, 2015. The oral style has been retained.

How can we communicate the central message of the Gospel in a way which a French citizen can sufficiently understand in order to accept it or reject it as an informed decision? I have sometimes heard people say that the French have rejected the Gospel. But I wonder whether the present generation has the slightest awareness of what the Gospel is, in particular the notion of God's wrath against sin necessitating substitutionary atonement. I'm not suggesting we do away with these concepts: I am asking the question as to how we communicate them in our context.

Different approaches have been suggested in relation to this observation, in particular the need to re-examine the vocabulary we use, the need to fight against ignorance and the need to take cultural issues more seriously. We shall examine these responses and then suggest four avenues which could lead to a better communication of the Gospel while remaining faithful to Biblical fundamentals.

Particular Difficulties

Vocabulary

It is legitimate to ask whether the Gospel is not understood first and foremost because of the vocabulary used by Christians. Would it not be preferable to communicate with words which are not drawn from theological discourse? After all, the success of the "for dummies" series has shown the need for intelligent popularisation of ideas and concepts. Why should it be any different when it comes to the Christian faith? In fact, in all areas of life there is a marked tendency to resort to specialised and targeted vocabulary which keeps the uninitiated at a distance. However, Christians do want to communicate their faith in a way which makes sense to unbelievers, and so much creativity is needed to find synonyms and expressions which allow the message to be received. Several people have given thought to this question and made some useful suggestions.

For example in the GBU-IFES,[2] students are invited to take part in a quiz "Rather than say ... say instead". For example:

- Rather than say "sin", say "turn your back on God."
- Rather than say "repentance," say "realise that you are wrong in rejecting God and decide to come back to him and obey him."
- Rather than say "conversion," say "give a new direction to your life".

---

[2] *Groupes Bibliques Universitaires*, the French University Christian Unions affiliated to the International Fellowship of Evangelical Students (IFES).

In this vein, Édouard Nelson and Gordon Margery affirm:

> We must work on our language, our images, our communication so as to make the Gospel as accessible as possible but without losing its content. This a difficult balance to maintain ... We must strive to communicate without ever using deception or distorting the word of God, aiming to set forth the truth plainly (2 Cor 4:2). Using contemporary language, avoiding Christian jargon; that is true faithfulness, because our effort to be understandable is faithfulness to the Gospel.[3]

Here are two examples the authors give in this article. "Turn to Christ, trust him with your life and comply with his teaching" could help to communicate the concepts of repentance and faith. And a car doing an about-turn is part of a family of images which can help to make the notion of conversion more tangible.

It seems important to bear in mind this thinking on the language we use. The apostle Paul who wanted to be "all things to all men in order to save some" (1 Cor 9:22) has given us a fine example in the book of Acts, with vocabulary adapted to different situations: at the synagogue (Acts 13), with the farmers in Lystra (Acts 14), and with the intellectuals in Athens (Acts 17).

However, this approach alone does not seem adequate to counteract the particular difficulties facing our French fellow citizens in their understanding and acceptance of the Gospel.

Ignorance

It is indisputable that there is today a growing ignorance about all things religious. This is sometimes called a lack of religious culture because knowledge of culture no longer includes a knowledge of religions, even Christianity which has forged our European identity for centuries.

Twenty years ago a survey showed that only 15% of the French population could name the authors of the four gospels. What would the figure be today? Bearing this in mind, the secular school system has started teaching objective facts about religions, (*"le fait religieux"*). What was the motivation behind this decision? Firstly, and quite simply, the need to understand our own culture – the paintings in art galleries, the literary texts studied for the end of secondary school exam (*le baccalauréat*), classical musical works, and of course French history from the Reformation through the Wars of Religion, the age of Enlightenment, the Dreyfus affair and the

---

[3] Édouard Nelson and Gordon Margery, « Conversion », *Le Journal du Réseau FEF* no. 140 (2014).

Chapter 5 – Particular Difficulties Facing our French Fellow Citizens

1905 law establishing a separation between churches and the State. But there was also a more pragmatic motivation: promoting the idea of "living together" within schools and more widely in the community. Over the last thirty years a variety of issues have cropped up with a religious basis: wearing the Muslim veil in schools, mixed education and the food supplied for school meals. Then there was the debate about cults in France, leading to the setting up in 1998 of an agency called the "The Inter-ministerial Mission to Combat Cults" (MILS) which later became "The Inter-ministerial Mission of Vigilance to Combat Sectarian Excess" (MIVILUDES).[4] More recently, France has had to face the threat of jihadist terrorism. And to come full circle, some people are claiming that a lack of culture also includes the notion of the secular state because secularism is seen by many young people as the fight against all religions.

The teaching of religious facts, an objective and rational approach to religions, aims therefore to help pupils rediscover their human heritage in order to understand the world, to appreciate culture in the widest sense, and to live together within the nation as it is in today's world. But several questions remain unanswered:

- Is it possible to understand a religion from the outside, especially if you are not religious yourself? I think it probable that a believer, whatever his or her religion, shares a certain notion of transcendence and a certain approach to life with other believers which facilitates dialogue. Can an atheist enter this field? Can he experience enough resonance with someone who practises a religion to enable him to have a benevolent attitude towards the teaching of "religious facts"?
- Bearing in mind the extent of ignorance about religion, are teachers themselves able to teach the subject accurately and objectively? Do they even want to?
- Are even so-called specialists capable of communicating objective facts? I was surprised to read some comments written by Odon Vallet, a historian of religions and a specialist in religious anthropology in an article published in *Le monde des religions*: "We use the term *born again* for evangelical Protestants who consider that their adult baptism is a "new birth" ... thus undermining the single Christian baptism recognized by the Orthodox, by Catholics and by Protestants."[5]

---

[4] *Mission interministérielle de lutte contre les sectes* (MILS); *Mission interministérielle de vigilance et de lutte contre les dérives sectaires* (MIVILUDES).

[5] Odon Vallet, "Your questions answered by Odon Vallet: who are the born again?" *Le monde des religions* no. 33 (January-February 2009).

Basically, it is not at all clear that all the efforts made to redress the lack of religious culture are adequate to help the general population grasp the issues raised by different religions. It has been said that France has a high level of integration of the concept of tolerance but that French culture finds it more difficult to accept pluralism (especially religious pluralism). In other words, the willingness to accept another person is higher than the ability to accept their ideas, to admit that they may have different convictions which must be understood in order to coexist peacefully. Here is a concrete example: most atheists have rejected the Roman Catholic Church, but deep down they have retained the Catholic dogma that "outside of the Church there is no salvation". Consequently, when they have moved away from Catholicism, they think they have rejected Christianity altogether. It doesn't occur to most of them that there may be another form of Christianity which they might consider.

So we see the weight of the surrounding culture. This context is very much the cause of the lack of religious culture in France, and this leads us to consider culture as the main explanation of the difficulty our fellow citizens have in understanding and accepting the Gospel.

The Worldview Conveyed by French Culture

Why is it so hard to understand an idea? Basically, it is because the whole life of an individual is incorporated in a particular culture and each culture is totally encompassing. We have no choice but to live within a particular culture.

> In its widest sense, culture may now be said to be the whole complex of distinctive spiritual, material, intellectual and emotional features that characterize a society or social group. It includes not only the arts and letters, but also modes of life, the fundamental rights of the human being, value systems, traditions and beliefs.[6]

That is how UNESCO defined culture in the Mexico City Declaration on Cultural Policies which was adopted in 1982, and reaffirmed in the Universal Declaration of Cultural Diversity (Paris, 2001).

Culture provides landmarks to give us identity: a certain way of looking at reality as it is conveyed via the family, the school, institutions and the media.

> Culture is everything which, transmitted by education, is passed on from one generation to the next leaving an imprint which expresses the identity of the

---

[6] UNESCO, "Universal Declaration of Cultural Diversity" (Paris: UNESCO, 2001).

human being and allows him to identify with the group to which he belongs by birth or by choice.[7]

Culture provides codes of behaviour which make our life easier in all sorts of circumstances. Should I shake hands with this person or kiss her on the cheek? Or make a polite bow? What kind of food should I offer a guest who comes to my house? What is an appropriate time and place to make an appointment for a business meeting?

But behind codes of behaviour, there is a worldview which is to a greater or lesser extent held in common with the other members of the group: prohibitions and duties, shared values. I would like to illustrate this with two examples which are relevant to the issue which we are examining.

First, the French notion of *laïcité* (the relationship between religions and the state) is not just a legal concept. It is much more in the area of the mental image which citizens have of what is allowed or not allowed, and this often has no connection to what the courts have ruled.

Second, via the culture a French citizen already has a mental image of what a "normal" religion is. In fact, it is Roman Catholicism seen through the lenses of French geography, history and sociology. Every village has its church and steeple, every city has its magnificent cathedral, every local government area (*département*) covers roughly the same area as a diocese (and the hierarchy of both the church and the state are very similar). Then, the history of France, as taught in schools, communicates that religion leads to wars and that the Roman Catholic Church was always on the side of the king and the nobility. And on the sociological level, the average French citizen is totally ignorant of the existence of "professing churches" to which members adhere by choice. The more learned among them have heard of the work of Max Weber (1864-1920) on the sociology of religion, examining the different ways in which Christian groups are organised socially and their relationship to the economy, in particular those groups he called sects. But by this term "sect" Weber meant "confessing churches," or evangelical churches in the French context. However, in the course of the 20th century, the meaning of the word "sect" changed, and today the work of Weber is even more incomprehensible to the average French citizen. In my book, *Servir à nos Français*,[8] I quote an article by Nathalie Luca, "Sects, churches and new religious movements," published on the

---

[7] Charles-Daniel Maire, *Parole de Dieu et cultures des hommes* (Valence: LLB, 2006).

[8] David Brown, *"Servir à nos Français"* (Marne-la-Vallée: Farel, 2009), chapter 17.

site of the National Education Ministry. There we can read a fine definition of the difference between a "church" and a "sect":

> In a church there is no need to adhere voluntarily: you belong practically from birth without making any request to do so. There is no individual selection. The unbeliever, the righteous and the pious rub shoulders. The church has a universalist flavour. On the other hand, the "sect" by its very essence has renounced universality. It is composed of individuals who have made the deliberate choice to convert and belong.[9]

But the author of these lines then goes on to give an extraordinary opinion: "This typology ... does not correspond to reality ... it must be regarded as an "ideal-typical" accentuation drawn from observation of Christianity in periods of crisis." This tends to lead us to conclude that she has never heard of professing churches. In fact, she even goes as far as to say that "this typology is still valid today in order to analyse fundamentalist Christian groups such as the Jehovah's Witnesses."[10]

We have seen that culture is all encompassing. There is therefore a high risk that mental maps take on a normative character, in that there is a confusion between culture and universality as people give their perception of things an absolute value. Several sociologists have noted this phenomenon.

For Peter Berger,[11] "reality" is a social construct and it is impossible to escape the ideology conveyed by one's social context. Several mechanisms contribute to this process. Mental representations come from forces of habit which, once they have been transmitted, become less pliable. One's social context is an all-encompassing reality which is transmitted to the following generations via the institutionalisation of their interactions, and in their eyes this context is comparable to the reality of natural phenomena. Thus, a structure of plausibility is built up: a body of knowledge is developed which explains why the structure is plausible with forms of legitimations which give it meaning. The structure of plausibility guarantees that social reality will not be questioned. Symbolic universes are the products of social history but they are perceived as being totally inevitable.

On this side of the Atlantic, Pierre Bourdieu adopted the Latin word *habitus*:

---

[9] http://eduscol.education.fr (accessed on February 4, 2016).

[10] Idem.

[11] Peter L. Berger & Thomas L. Luckmann, *The Social Construction of Reality: A Treatise in the Sociology of Knowledge* (Harmondsworth: Penguin, 1967).

> The habitus is the product of a process of inculcation and appropriation which is necessary so that these products of collective history, which are objective structures ... manage to reproduce, in the shape of permanent dispositions, in all the organisms (that you can call individuals if you like) which are permanently subjected to the same material conditions of existence.[12]

In other words, norms are fixed by culture, not by the individual. But the individual is not aware of this. He has the impression that he is acting freely. So we can see that culture in the widest sense is at the root of the difficulty which our fellow citizens experience in understanding and accepting the Gospel. The missiologist Lesslie Newbigin suggests that this barrier to the knowledge of the Gospel corresponds to the biblical expression "authorities and powers."[13] There is a fight to be fought in the invisible world since Satan is trying to worm his way in to every culture. "For our struggle is not against flesh and blood, but against the rulers, against the authorities, against the powers of this dark world and against the spiritual forces of evil in the heavenly realms" (Eph 6:12). The Good News is that victory belongs to the Lord through the death and resurrection of Jesus Christ: "And having disarmed the powers and authorities, he made a public spectacle of them, triumphing over them by the cross" (Col 2:15).

The Plausibility of the Message of the Gospel

As we have just seen, the fundamental problem concerning the communication of the Gospel is the plausibility of the message. The Gospel just doesn't seem possible for a person who is living in the plausibility structure of French culture. It just does not seem likely or credible. Paul Ricœur used the expression "what is available to be believed" (*le croyable disponible*) to indicate this reality.[14]

Furthermore, for some theologians of a liberal persuasion, the biblical message is just not plausible in itself. Rudolf Bultmann wrote the following thoughts on the subject:

> We cannot use electric lights and radios and, in the event of illness, avail ourselves of modern medical and clinical means and at the same time believe in the spirit and wonder world of the New Testament. Whoever thinks he can for himself, must recognize that by defining this as a Christian attitude of faith, he

---

[12] Pierre Bourdieu, *Esquisse d'une théorie de la pratique* (Paris: Seuil 2000), p. 282.
[13] Lesslie Newbigin, *The Gospel in a Pluralist Society* (Grand Rapids: Eerdmans, 1989), p. 201, 209.
[14] Paul Ricœur, quoted by Henri Blocher, *Bible et histoire* (Lausanne: Presses Bibliques Universitaires, 1980), p. 32.

is making the Christian message incomprehensible and impossible for our time.[15]

This argument confirms the basic idea of postmodern thought: if we find it impossible to discover a meaning to life through our use of reason, everything comes back to one's own personal choice of lifestyle, validated by one's feelings. "It's my choice," people say. In fact today nobody reproves a believer for choosing to exercise faith – it's his choice! In fact, our fellow citizens are quite willing to accept any personal lifestyle choice, since all options are all equally valid. However, what is unacceptable is to try to "impose" your choice on someone else.

In this context every attempt to communicate the Gospel is all too easily criticised and called "proselytizing" (of which we must naturally be aware). In the course of a television program on iTélé, two speakers experienced great difficulty in trying to reconcile freedom of expression and suspicion towards religion. Geneviève Fioraso, Secretary of State for Higher Education, said: "We must stop students from proselytizing in our universities." But Jean-Loup Salzmann, president of the Paris 13 University, affirmed that "freedom of speech must be total in the universities."[16]

In this case two mental representations, two ideas conveyed via the ambient culture, clashed head on. And Christians trying to communicate the Gospel are the collateral victims.

How Can Christians Deal with These Mental Representations?

In his well-known book *The Gospel in a Pluralist Society* (1989), Lesslie Newbigin states:

> What really needs to be said is that where the Church is faithful to the Lord, there the powers of the kingdom are present and people begin to ask the question to which the Gospel is the answer. And that is why, I suppose, the letters of St. Paul contain so many exhortations to faithfulness but no exhortations to be active in mission[17].

A survey commissioned by the Evangelism Commission of the National Council of Evangelicals of France (CNEF[18]) bears out this affirmation

---

[15] Rudolf Bultmann, *Neues Testament und Mythologie* (München: Kaiser, 1941), p. 4.
[16] "*Le grand décryptage*," *iTélé*, February 12, 2015.
[17] Newbigin, *The Gospel in a Pluralist Society*, p. 119.
[18] *Conseil national des évangéliques de France.*

of Lesslie Newbigin. A clear consensus is emerging that the Gospel must be spread through relationships rather than methods. When pastors were asked the question: "What are the best means of evangelism today?" the vast majority opted for relationships (73.9 % "agree somewhat" and 13.7 % "agree fully" making a total of 87.6 %, much higher than any other option).

The logical corollary can be seen in the answers to another question of this survey: "What types of training would be the most useful in the contemporary context?" 75.3 % of respondents chose: "How to build healthy relationships with non-Christians and speak of the Gospel;" 70.2 % favoured training about the role of prayer; 68.8 % on personal witness, 61.4 % on understanding the Gospel, and 59.3 % desired training on "how to reconfigure the church to make it a place of discovery of the Gospel through its regular activities."

As we have seen, Lesslie Newbigin is convinced that "where the Church is faithful to the Lord, there the powers of the kingdom are present and people begin to ask the question to which the Gospel is the answer." But what does this faithfulness look like in our French context? What are the essential biblical components and how should we live them out in the reality of today's world? I would like to suggest three ways which may help our fellow citizens understand and accept the Gospel: the life of each Christian, the life of the church, and the notion of freedom.

The Life of Each Christian

The disciple is called to live his Christian life in a transversal way, in other words, in every area of life. My personal analysis of the New Testament has led me to suggest that there are four basic aspects of discipleship.[19]

The Disciple Worships God

Worship is an attitude of the heart which does not accept the sacred / secular divide because the Christian cultivates a continual consciousness of the presence of God (while respecting the laws of the separation of Church and State). Our fellow citizens will end up by seeing that our worship of God is not just a liturgical act reserved for sacred occasions in church buildings, but the reflection of the relationship with God, which we have all throughout the day, whether we are eating, drinking or in fact in what-

---

[19] David Brown, *Disciple 24/24* (Marne-la-Vallée: Farel, 2015).

ever we're doing (1 Cor 10:31). Rather than complain continually, we thank God in all things.

The Disciple Trusts God

People around us have so many fears and worries! But worrying has never provided a single solution to a problem. Jesus said: "Who of you by worrying can add a single hour to his life?" (Matt 6:27). Whether it concerns mere details or big life decisions, people will see our trust in God, our heavenly Father. Faced with our worries about food and clothing, Jesus invites us not to worry because "your heavenly Father knows that you need them" (Matt 6:32). This is the only way in which our fellow citizens living in the here and now will see the reality of our faith. Many of them are seeking a stress-free life, a good life, but the only thing which they think can help them are the "techniques" of self-development that they find on the Internet or in self-help books. But what false hopes are raised! It is not through benevolent thoughts about themselves that they will find their inner unsuspected qualities which will help them to experience lasting change. God alone is our shelter faced with the uncertainties and vagaries of life.

The Disciple Obeys God and Fights the Good Fight

Yes, our fellow citizens are seeking a stress-free life, they want to be "zen" as they say. But to be really "zen," the only option is to go down the Buddhist path or to focus on yourself as popular psychology advocates. On the other hand, the only way to live in a relationship with God, to love others, and to know God's forgiveness is by faith in Jesus, in the real world. But this world has no longer been normal since the fall recounted at the beginning of the Bible. Consequently our environment ("the world"), our inner life ("our flesh"), and the challenge to God's rule ("the devil") are pitted against our wish to live a satisfying life. The Christian proves his serious desire to live according to his convictions by the daily fight he leads against evil (but not against people). His fight against evil is similar to the way in which Alcoholics Anonymous leads the struggle against alcoholism. The biggest problem is to stay abstinent in the here and now. The 24 hours which make up today are the only period of one's life when someone can act on one's problem. Yesterday has gone. Tomorrow is yet to come. But today (the member of AA can say), "today I will not drink a glass." In the same way, the Christian joyfully fights the good fight day by day.

The Disciple Loves His Neighbour as Himself

This is the greatest commandment on the horizontal level, love for our fellow humans. To love is to be interested in others, to do them good. "Therefore, as we have opportunity, let us do good to all people, especially to those who belong to the family of believers" (Gal 6:10). We should be always looking out for opportunities to do good, to grasp the opportunities to witness ("redeeming the time" as older translations of the Bible put it):

> Be wise in the way you act toward those who are not believers, making good use of every opportunity you have. Your speech should always be pleasant and interesting, and you should know how to give the right answer to everyone (Col 4:5-6, Good News Bible).

When each Christian lives out his faith without complex in his environment, there will necessarily be an impact on the nation. Our fellow citizens need to see examples of faith lived out all day and every day. If they think our "religion" is limited to a Sunday service and a conservative stance on ethical issues, there is little chance that they will want to know more. But the same does not apply when they rub shoulders with Christians who are happy to live in the world God created, despite the afflictions of this life. And I might just add that it serves no purpose to make Christians feel guilty if they do not witness or "make new disciples:" that is no way to help him or her to show his joy at belonging to the Lord. In the same way, training someone to witness is not enough if the love of God is not spread out of his heart. Does a young woman need to attend a course of training to tell her friends that she has just got engaged? Does a young man need training to talk about his favourite football team? It is only when he has a genuine love for his neighbour that a Christian will begin to look out for the times when he can speak a word of testimony or explain a Bible verse. This is the true adventure of living the Christian life in relationship with the sovereign God.

The Life of the Local Church

Over the last few years, the biblical vision of the Church as a "community" has been highlighted again. Of course, it had never been really forgotten, since the time of the apostles and the Church Fathers (for whom the witness of the Christian community contrasted sharply with surrounding pagan society). Partly through the impetus of what was known as "emerging churches," practically every church and denomination today would echo Paul's words: "You yourselves are our letter, written on our hearts, known and read by everyone" (2 Cor 3:2). Every local church, as a manifestation of the Body of Christ, makes Christ visible in its locality. The church is God's tract.

Jesus clearly taught it to his disciples: "By this all men will know that you are my disciples, if you love one another" (John 13:35). This is the test offered to unbelievers, and it is in fact remarkable that churches are indeed composed of men and women from every walk of life and of different temperaments, and that they bring together children, young people, families and older people. Intergenerational and multicultural communities fascinate and challenge our fellow citizens. "Accept one another, then, just as Christ accepted you, in order to bring praise to God" (Rom 15:7).

Lesslie Newbigin links this role of the church to the sociological concept of "plausibility structures." As we have already seen when thinking about culture, the plausibility structure determines what ideas seem credible to its members. Newbigin states that the Christian community is an alternative plausibility structure in which Christians will learn to live out their faith in a way which is consistent with it. The Christian community will affect the people who see that Christians are really trying to live in the truth and live in their culture, taking their place in human history as God has revealed it, attempting to live out all the implications of the mighty declaration: "Jesus Christ is Lord."

Consequently Christians should never "domesticate" the Christian message by adapting it to the surrounding ideas of plausibility. It is impossible to explain one's new way of thinking in terms of one's former way of seeing the world. The Christian can but invite the non-Christian to stand next to him and hope he begins to see the same reality that the Christian does.

Freedom

Freedom (French *la liberté*) seems to be the absolute priority for our fellow-citizens with a French culture. A few examples will suffice to show this.

Freedom is the very first value mentioned in the watchword of the French Republic: *liberté, égalité, fraternité* "freedom, equality, brotherhood." It is also at the heart of the national anthem, la Marseillaise: one of the verses contains a very well-known expression *"liberté chérie"* (freedom we cherish).

> Drive on sacred patriotism
> Support our avenging arms
> Liberty, cherished liberty
> Join the struggle with your defenders.

Generations of school children have learnt by heart the poem written by Paul Eluard in 1942: here is a short extract.

On my school books
On my desk and trees
On the sand and snow
I write your name

On all pages read
On all white pages
Stone sand paper or ashes
I write your name

And by the strength of one word
I start over my life
I was born to know you
To name you

Liberty.

When the French Christian student movement (GBU) did a series of surveys on university campuses, a recurrent question was: "Do I have to choose between God and my freedom?" This was one of the seven questions selected for the book "Questions about God."[20] It is interesting to note that similar books published by other European student movements do not include this objection to faith. This question is simply not asked in the same way in France's neighbouring countries.

In a totally different context, a program broadcast on the France-Inter radio station on February 21, 2015, discussed the subject of young people from France going to the Middle East as jihadists. The issue was how to "deradicalise" these young people, and the journalist presented various approaches which have been used in different European countries. At the end of the broadcast, there was a consensus that the important thing was not to bring them back on the right track but to help them find their freedom!

Now the Bible presents the Christian life as a way of freedom: "If the Son sets you free, you will be free indeed" (John 8:36). The Christian must learn to live out and articulate this freedom since it is a subject which has not been sufficiently thought out in French churches despite the ardent desire of our people for freedom. And it should be noted that evangelical Christians have good arguments and assets when it comes to freedom!

---

[20] GBU, *Questions autour de Dieu* (Marne-la-Vallée: Farel/GBU, 2009).

- In the history of ideas, the revolution initiated by Christianity led to the Universal Declaration of Human Rights since it became clear that all human beings are of equal dignity in that they were created in the image of God.
- Christianity also gave birth to the idea of the equal worth of every citizen, which is at the heart of modern democracy.
- Baptism after a personal confession of faith (as compared to infant baptism) is a sign of the individual's free choice.
- The way churches are run locally under the provisions of the law on religious associations (*associations cultuelles*). We need to point out to our fellow citizens that this democratic ideal of the professing church is very close to Republican values.
- Concerning our spiritual life, freedom is a good way to explain concepts such as "guilt" and "justification:" the Gospel is a way of true freedom by removing the burden of malaise and existential distress.

We as Christians must make the most of this thirst for freedom by being free ourselves, and by pointing out the dangers of other paths towards this goal: "You, my brothers, were called to be free. But do not use your freedom to indulge the sinful nature; rather, serve one another in love" (Galatians (5.13)

Conclusion

So what I am suggesting concerning the difficulties of our fellow citizens to understand and accept the Gospel is that the problem is neither just a question of vocabulary (even though this has its importance) nor a question of ignorance (even if this problem must be taken seriously). The real issue is the very acceptance of biblical Christianity in the present day cultural climate.

The life of the individual Christian, the community life of the church and the thirst for freedom are certainly three paths towards the Christian faith for our fellow citizens. But that raises a whole series of further questions. Is this merely a pragmatic approach? Or is it based on a model of evangelism which we can find in the New Testament? And how exactly can we, must we, live it out in the present day French context?

Personally, I maintain that these approaches are much more in line with what we find in the New Testament than much of what is done in the name of evangelism (but of course I do not question the sincerity of this action). I have looked closely at all the New Testament texts which bear on evangelism and discipleship, and the three-pronged approach recommended in this chapter seems to reflect the experience of the early church and to be of timeless value.

So if that is the case, why do we continue to use ineffective methods of evangelism (although I admit that some of them can be useful in giving a greater visibility to the Gospel and to a local church)? Why not commit all our energy to going down these paths in order to reach our fellow citizens? How is it that churches do not do more to encourage Christians to live out their faith confidently within their family and among friends and colleagues? That is why the Father sent the Son, and that is why the Son sends us.

As you sent me into the world, I have sent them into the world (John 17:18).

As the Father has sent me, I am sending you (John 20:21).

Chapter 6
Interdisciplinary In-Depth Analysis

Hannes Wiher[1]

The literature review of research on evangelism in Europe[2] has shown an essential fact: to be able to communicate the Gospel to contemporary Europeans in an innovative and relevant way, an in-depth analysis is essential. This analysis should be both collective and individualised. To attain this goal, this chapter presents some reflections on the deep structures of persons, cultures and religions. The widely accepted technical term for deep structures is "worldview." It is true that values represent deep cultural elements. But despite the fact that certain approaches of the reviewed research start from an analysis of values, the choice of these values does not always seem to be of great help in communicating the Gospel.

This is why, as a first step, we make some preliminary reflections on an in-depth analysis using the concept of worldview. In a second step, we then propose a choice of four worldview models that are appropriate for biblical, sociological and anthropological analysis. We then apply these models, in a third step, to an interdisciplinary in-depth analysis of the European context.

Preliminary Reflections on an In-Depth Analysis

Before presenting the worldview models, it is necessary to make a brief observation on the "deep structures" of persons, cultures and religions, the role of models in the sciences, on the worldview as a "model," and on the relationship between Bible and culture.

---

[1] This chapter is the second part of a paper presented at the meeting of the *Réseau de missiologie évangélique pour l'Europe francophone* (REMEEF) on November 20, 2013.

[2] Interested readers can access a general overview of literature in the Introduction and the details in Appendix 2, as well as some statistical data in Appendix 1.

Biblical and Anthropological Approaches to the Deep Structures

To better understand the deep structures of personality, culture and religion, we will first discuss the key terms of the Bible and the concepts proposed by the social sciences.

The biblical expressions describing the deep structures of man are principally "inner man," "the heart" and "the conscience."[3] In the OT, "inner man" (*qereb*, Ps 103:1; Isa 16:11) is situated deep in the body. It is often associated with the "soul" (*nefech*), the invisible part of man, with the belly, the bowels (*me'im*) and the womb (*bethen, rehem*), with the fat close to the diaphragm that was to be burned but not eaten during sacrifice rites (Lev 1-7), with the liver (*kabed*) and the kidneys (*kelayot*), themselves often associated with the heart (*leb*, Ps 7:9; 26:2). In the NT, "inner man" (*eso anthropos*) is the part of man that functions according to the Spirit and can be influenced by him (Rom 7:22; Eph 3:16).

The second notion describing the deep structures of man, "the heart" (*leb, kardia*), is considered to be the centre and source of personality. Proverbs 4:23 exhorts us: "Keep your heart with all vigilance, for from it flow the springs of life." The heart reflects the cognitive (Prov 2:10; Rm 1:21), affective (Ps 13:2; Mt 22:37-39), volitional (Prov 16:1; 2 Cor 9:7) and spiritual (Ezek 6:9; 2 Cor 3:3) aspects of the personality.

The third notion that influences the behaviour of man, "the conscience" (*suneidesis*), was introduced to the biblical vocabulary primarily by the apostle Paul. It is the structure in man that "knows with" God, particularly his laws (Rom 2:14f). Yet God is an authority beyond the human conscience (2 Cor 4:2; 1 John 3:20).

The behavioural sciences have developed the notion of "black box" to avoid having to speak of the deep structures of man, inaccessible to empirical research. Empirical psychology and sociology limit themselves to studying the influences on the black box and its outcomes (the behaviour). However, Sigmund Freud's hermeneutic psychology, for instance, develops the notions of ego, id, ego ideal and super ego, which determine the behaviour of man, the latter two corresponding loosely to the notion of conscience.

In their sociology of knowledge, Peter Berger and Thomas Luckmann develop the notion of social construction of a unified structure of meaning,

---

[3] Cf. Hans-Walter Wolff, "V. *Leb(ab)* – Reasonable man," and "VII. The Inner Parts of the Body," in *Anthropology of the Old Testament* (transl. Margaret Kohl; London: SCM, 1974), p. 40-58, 63-66; Herman Ridderbos, *Paul: An Outline of His Theology* (transl. John R. de Witt; Grand Rapids: Eerdmans, 1975), p. 115-130.

which serves the orientation of man in the midst of a chaotic universe that is empty of meaning and orientation.[4] According to Peter Berger, religions are like "sacred canopies" that offer a protective cover under which one can envisage one's life in security. At the same time, Berger and Luckman propose "plausibility structures" that serve as securing landmarks for man.[5]

Philosophy has developed the concept of "worldview" as an underlying factor of man's behaviour. During the late 19th century, this technical term was widely accepted in scientific vocabulary. Together with the psychological concept of "identity," it has largely replaced the old term "conscience" in scientific discourse. The concept of worldview has found a particularly warm welcome in the evangelical movement. Consequently, in this chapter, we will use this term when talking about the deep layers of man.

When trying to define worldview, it is important to note that every definition is itself influenced by the definer's worldview.[6] Therefore, one finds many different definitions depending on the personality and the academic background of the author.

According to the American philosopher David Naugle, "worldview is a [semiotic] system of narrative signs that establishes a powerful framework within which people think (reason), interpret (hermeneutics), and know (epistemology)."[7] This definition refers to the cultural influence on ways of knowing, thinking (logic), and evaluating. It includes the cognitive and evaluative dimensions of worldview.

The Dutch philosopher Herman Dooyeweerd extends the concept of worldview to include the affective and religious dimensions.[8] He was professor of law at the Free University of Amsterdam between 1926 and 1965, a disciple of Abraham Kuyper, and considered to be the most creative phi-

---

[4] Peter L. Berger & Thomas L. Luckmann, *The Social Construction of Reality: A Treatise in the Sociology of Knowledge* (Harmondsworth: Penguin, 1966).

[5] Peter L. Berger, *The Sacred Canopy: Elements of a Sociological Theory of Religion* (New York: Doubleday, 1967).

[6] David K. Naugle, *Worldview: The History of a Concept* (Grand Rapids: Eerdmans, 2002), p. 253.

[7] Naugle, *Worldview*, p. xix, see a similar formulation p. 253, explained p. 291-330.

[8] Herman Dooyeweerd, *A New Critique of Theoretical Thought*, vol. 1 (transl. David H. Freeman, William S. Young, et H. de Jongste; Jordan Station, Ont.: Paideia Press, 1984), p. v.; see also Jacob Klapwijk, "On Worldviews and Philosophy," in *Stained Glass: Worldviews and Social Science*, ed. Paul A. Marshall, Sander Griffioen, Richard J. Mouw, Christian Studies Today (Lanham, MD: University Press of America, 1989), p. 51.

losopher among the Calvinists of the 20th century. For Dooyeweerd, philosophy and the concept of worldview have both a concern for totality and for the "fundamental religious motive."[9] The difference between them is that worldview is pre-theoretical and popular, whereas philosophy represents a theoretical system of thought developed by professional thinkers.[10] For Dooyeweerd, every philosophy is itself constructed on a worldview.

According to the American anthropologist Clifford Geertz, worldviews are a people's "picture of the way things, in sheer actuality, are, their concept of nature, of self, of society."[11] They are in fact looking through tinted spectacles. For people are not aware that what they see is not necessarily the reality, but their conceptualised picture of it. In this vein, worldview includes for the anthropologist Charles Kraft the presuppositions, the basic values, and the conceptualisations of a culture.[12] In a functionalist perspective, Lothar Käser understands worldview as a strategy: a set of interpretations of the world, of society and of self that serve to answer everyday questions and solve everyday problems.[13] Paul Hiebert then defines worldview as "the foundational cognitive, affective and evaluative assumptions and frameworks a group of people makes about the nature of reality which they use to order their lives."[14] According to Hiebert's definition, worldview does not only have a cognitive dimension emphasised by theologians and philosophers.[15] The affective and evaluative aspects of worldview (the values) reach deeper layers of personality, culture and religion than the cognitive aspects.[16]

---

[9] Because of the transcendental and integral structure of our experience, Dooyeweerd is convinced that the point of departure of every philosophy is the "fundamental religious motive," which has its origin either in the action of the Holy Spirit or in the spirit of apostasy.

[10] Dooyeweerd, *A New Critique of Theoretical Thought*, vol. 1, p. 128.

[11] Clifford Geertz, *The Interpretation of Cultures* (New York: Basic Books, 1973), p. 303.

[12] Charles Kraft, *Christianity in Culture: A Study in Dynamic Biblical Theologizing in Cross-Cultural Perspective* (rev. ed.; Maryknoll: Orbis, 2005 [1st ed. 1979]), p. 53-56.

[13] Lothar Käser, "Culture as a Strategy," in *Foreign Cultures* (Nürnberg: VTR, 2014; German ed. 1997), p. 36-37.

[14] Paul G. Hiebert, *Transforming Worldviews: An Anthropological Understanding of How People Change* (Grand Rapids: Baker, 2008), p. 15, 25.

[15] See for example Naugle, *Worldview*, p. 68-185; Brian J. Walsh & J. Richard Middleton, *The Transforming Vision: Shaping a Christian Worldview* (Downers Grove: IVP, 1984).

[16] Already Talcott Parsons and his associates have attributed the central role to the evaluative dimension because persons evaluate through their values, the cognitive

According to Hiebert and Kraft, we can discern the following functions of worldviews: 1) they are our "plausibility structures" that provide answers to our ultimate questions, 2) they give us emotional security, 3) they validate our deepest cultural norms, 4) they integrate the different elements of our culture, 5) they monitor cultural change, 6) they provide psychological reassurance that the world is truly as we see it, and a sense of peace and of being at home in the world in which we live.[17]

From an anthropological perspective, religion is an expression of culture. Both religion and culture are functions of worldview. Lothar Käser sees the relationship between language, culture and religion in the following way:

> Religion [is] the second cultural area in which people identify one another as similar or different [additionally to language, and] is just as complicated and all-embracing as language. It forms a similar high-level classification system within the individual culture and is one of the most significant auxiliary strategies people employ to shape and master their existence.[18]

As one of the central strategies for mastering life, religion – like culture – is closely linked to worldview. Worldview is thus situated at the centre of personality, culture and religion. It is largely unconscious.[19] In metaphorical language, worldview "formats" behaviour, personality, culture and religion, just like the BIOS determines how the hard disk of a computer functions. It resembles the deeper part of an iceberg, which represents personality, culture and religion in its upper parts. These are the "tinted spectacles" through which people look at reality.[20]

Operational Approach to the Deep Structures

Just like the concepts of culture, religion and identity, worldview is a fuzzy concept with many different definitions. For this reason, many theologians, philosophers and anthropologists have abandoned these concepts.

---

themes in order to know what is true and false, and the affective themes in order to know what is beautiful, and these values lead to action. Talcott Parsons & Edward Shils, ed., *Toward a General Theory of Action* (Cambridge, MA: Harvard University Press, 1952).

[17] Hiebert, *Transforming Worldviews*, p. 28-29; Kraft, *Christianity in Culture*, p. 54-56.

[18] Käser, *Foreign Cultures*, p. 159.

[19] Hiebert, *Transforming Worldviews*, p. 47.

[20] Hiebert, *Transforming Worldviews*, p. 46; Klapwijk, *Stained Glass*.

In this chapter, we will adopt the opposite approach. We propose to put the notion of worldview into practice by using practical models drawn from theology, philosophy and the social sciences. If this approach succeeds, we will have acquired a tool for in-depth understanding of personalities, cultures and religions. The choice has fallen on models where Scripture and the social sciences draw near each other. Being aware of the issues at stake, we want to be careful when integrating the selected concepts drawn from the social sciences into the worldview and epistemology of the Bible.[21]

Role of Models in the Sciences

What is the role of models in the sciences, particularly in social sciences? Since reality is very complex and entails human understanding and paradoxes that mutually exclude each other, the models represent a coherent simplification of reality, Weberian ideal types.[22] In metaphorical language, models represent "maps" or "blueprints." Talking about a landscape, one can conceive political maps showing the frontiers, or geographical maps indicating mountains, rivers, lakes, towns and villages. Thinking of a building, one can imagine plans with the walls, the carpentry, the sanitary or electric installations, and front or side view. According to the objective, one selects relevant elements in relation to the target. The aim of models in in-depth evangelism is to better understand certain aspects of persons, cultures and religions in order to find guidelines for an evangelistic approach.

---

[21] For a more detailed discussion, see Edward Rommen & Gary Corwin, eds., *Missiology and the Social Sciences: Contributions, Cautions and Conclusions* (Evangelical Missiological Society Series No. 4; Pasadena: William Carey Library, 1996); Paul G. Hiebert, *Missiological Implications of Epistemological Shifts: Affirming Truth in a Modern/Postmodern World* (Harrisburg, PA: International Trinity Press, 1999).

[22] The ideal type is a concept introduced by Max Weber into the sociology of religion, from where it was then accepted in the social sciences in general. In short, an ideal type is an abstract category that helps to understand or conceptualise certain phenomena, without pretending that the characteristics of the type are always and perfectly present in the observed phenomena. An ideal type aims to construct a model of a social phenomenon, in other words a "map." It represents a simplification of reality and reflects a perspective linked to the objective of this model, in our case the communication of the Gospel.

Worldview as a "Model"

Worldview as a selective choice of coherent and plausible elements of a very complex reality fills the criteria of a model in the world of sciences. As a selective choice, it depends on the socialisation of persons, cultural and religious elements. It is therefore relative, itself a function of a worldview. However, the American anthropologist Michael Kearney discerns in worldviews not only particular aspects, but also five universal dimensions: self and other, the relationship between self and other, the classification of the other, causality, space and time.[23]

The concept of worldview has been widely accepted by the evangelical community. The reason for this is certainly that it offers the possibility to explain the whole of reality, and demonstrates the rational coherence of biblical revelation.[24] David Naugle considers that

> Conceiving of Christianity as a worldview has been one of the most significant developments in the recent history of the church. ... [The concept of worldview] offers the church a fresh perspective on the holistic nature, cosmic dimensions, and universal applications of the faith. Plus, the explanatory power, intellectual coherence, and pragmatic effectiveness of the Christian worldview not only make it exceedingly relevant for believers personally, but also establish a solid foundation for vigorous cultural and academic engagement.[25]

In the Reformed tradition, the elaboration of a Christian worldview has become an important enterprise. Reformed theological institutions and the International Association for the Promotion of Christian Higher Education (IAPCHE)[26] have produced an impressive number of publications on the subject.[27] They continue the heritage and tradition of works such as Augus-

---

[23] Michael Kearney, *Worldview* (Novato, CA: Chandler and Sharp, 1984), p. 208. See also Naugle, *Worldview*, p. 239-244; Hiebert, *Transforming Worldviews*, 19f. Michael Kearney has drawn these universal elements from Robert Redfield, *The Primitive World and Its Transformations* (Harmondsworth, UK: Penguin, 1968).

[24] Carl F. H. Henry, "Fortunes of the Christian World View," *Trinity Journal* 19 (1998), p. 163.

[25] Naugle, *Worldview*, p. 4-5.

[26] www.iapche.org.

[27] See for example Bennie J. van der Walt, *The Liberating Message: A Christian Worldview for Africa* (Potchefstroom: Potchefstroom University, 1994); idem, *Transformed by the Renewing of Your Mind: Shaping a Biblical Worldview and a Christian Perspective on Scholarship* (Potchefstroom: Potchefstroom University, 2001); idem, *The Eye Is the Lamp of the Body: Worldviews and Their Impact*

tine's *City of God*, Thomas Aquinas' *Summa theologica*, and John Calvin's *Institutes of the Christian Religion*, which all aim to provide an all-embracing life system and the vision of Scripture as a coherent whole.

Relationship between Bible and culture

When adopting an interdisciplinary approach, we need to ask the epistemological question of whether a concept developed by the sciences can be integrated into the theory (theology) and practice of the Christian faith. And if the answer is yes, then how can it be done?

The apostle Paul provides an example of this procedure. He took several notions present in the society where he lived (their cultural forms) by transforming their content: for example, the titles of the Roman emperor (Lord and Saviour: *kyrios kai soter*) and of his coming (*parousia*), which he applied to the coming of Jesus Christ. One can also think of concepts drawn from the mystery religions: *metamorphosis* "transformation" which he applies to the regeneration, *mysterion*, the mystery of the initiation into the religion which he applies to Jesus. Paul's strategy was "to take every thought captive to make it obedient to Christ" (2 Cor 10:4). After him, Augustine developed the analogy of the "Egyptian gold," recovered by the Israelites based on Exodus 11-12. He exemplified how a cultural concept can be integrated into Christian life.[28] On the contrary, by rejecting philosophy, Karl Barth also refused the concept of worldview.[29] We thus have three of the four types that Dean Flemming discerns in the apostle Paul's attitude towards integrating cultural elements: to confirm (Augustine), to oppose (Barth), to transform (the apostle Paul), and to relativize (when the apostle Paul relativizes the Jewish calendar and Jewish dietary rules).[30]

(Potchefstroom: Institute for Contemporary Christianity in Africa, 2008); Roy Clouser, "A Blueprint for a Non-Reductionist Theory of Reality," *Contact* 19, 2 (December 2007); Danny McCain, "Battle for the Mind," *Contact* 21, 4 (June 2010); David Naugle, "The Educational Power of Great Tradition Christianity," *Contact* 22, 1 (September 2010); see also the different issues of the two journals of IAPCHE: *Christian Higher Education*, and *Christian Scholars Review*, and the bibliography under the rubric "Research" at www.iapche.org.

[28] Augustine, *De Doctrina Christiana*, Corpus Christianorum 1 (Paris: Brepols, 1982), § 2, 60.

[29] Karl Barth, *Church Dogmatics*, III/3 (transl. T.H.L. Parker; Edinburgh: T. & T. Clark, 1976), § 49, 2.

[30] Dean Flemming, *Contextualization in the New Testament: Patterns for Theology and Mission* (Leicester: Intervarsity Press, 2005), p. 118-151.

The philosopher David Naugle answers the question about the integration of Scripture and science favourably.[31] But how can we envisage a *good* integration of the concept of worldview, which is a product of modernity, into the Christian faith? To do this well, we must recognise not only the subjectivity and relativity of (scientific) thought systems which have their root in the plurality of cultures and worldviews, but we must also recognise the objectivity of God's revelation. For the evaluation of worldviews, Naugle proposes three criteria which more or less correspond to the epistemological criteria of coherence, correspondence and pragmatic efficiency.[32] The rational test views the coherence of a worldview. The empirical test demands that the worldview be global and heavily explanatory. The existential and pragmatic test evaluates whether a worldview is practical and satisfactory in relation to personal needs. Naugle is convinced that with these three criteria a worldview that is founded on Scripture can demonstrate its philosophic integrity, have a superior credibility to other worldviews, and provide the conceptual space for understanding the all-encompassing scope of the fundamental doctrines.[33] The spiritual benefit of the Christian faith conceived as a worldview will result from its intellectual coherence, its empirical and trans-empirical comprehensiveness, its interpretative power, its practical viability, and its power for personal and cultural transformation. Its biblical wholeness puts away with the vicious dualisms and reductionisms such as the dualism between time and eternity, body and soul, faith and reason, the sacred and profane, earth and sky.[34] A Christian faith conceived as an all-encompassing worldview "imparts to believers a cognitive confidence, an apologetic strategy, a cultural relevance, and a sound, spiritual basis for life in the coherent picture of God's larger story."[35]

Four Operational Models for Worldview

On the basis of these considerations, we propose four worldview models: the stratigraphic model of creation (containing the classification of the other and the concept of space), the five basic soteriological concepts (including the relationship between self and other, and the aspects of causali-

---

[31] Naugle, *Worldview*, p. 258. In this section, we follow Naugle, p. 253-345.
[32] Idem, p. 327f.
[33] Idem, p. 339f.
[34] Idem, p. 342f.
[35] Idem, p. 341.

ty), the conscience orientation (which represents self and other and their relationship, aspects of the classification of the other and of the concept of space) and the time concept (which includes also aspects of causality). The stratigraphic model of creation, the five basic soteriological concepts and the concept of time represent principally the cognitive aspects of worldview. The affective and evaluative aspects of worldview are represented in the conscience orientation. The latter thus represents the deepest layers of worldview.

Stratigraphic Model of Creation

A simple way to approach the concept of worldview is the stratigraphic model of creation. How does a worldview organise (stratify) the different elements of creation as matter, plants, animals, humans, spiritual beings and gods? We can classify the different worldviews of our planet in four groups representing four Weberian ideal types: the holistic, Hebrew, dichotomist, and secular worldview.

First, in the holistic worldview, the universe is an integrated whole. Examples of holistic cultural and religious systems are Animism, Esotericism, Hinduism, Taoism, Chinese and Tibetan Buddhism, Shintoism and the popular religions. Second, the Hebrew worldview has developed starting from a holistic (animist) worldview. The books of Genesis and Leviticus insist on the fact that God is the creator of the universe separated from creation, that he is "holy" (cf. Gen 1-2; Lev 19:2). As a reform movement of Judaism and Christianity, Islam has stratified the elements of creation in the same way as the Hebrew worldview. However, in other aspects of worldview, for example the five basic soteriological concepts, there are great differences between the Islamic and the Hebrew worldview. Third, the dichotomist worldview separates the material and visible world from the immaterial and invisible world. One example is Plato's philosophy. In medieval Roman Catholic Europe, influenced by Neo-Platonism, the "middle sphere" of existence has been excluded from the worldview.[36] It is this sphere which regroups the spiritual beings that are considered to be responsible for misfortunes and diseases in the animist worldview. It is this

---

[36] The concept of the "excluded middle" was introduced by Paul G. Hiebert, "The Flaw of the Excluded Middle," *Missiology: An International Review* 10, 1 (1982), p. 35-47; reprint in *Anthropological Reflections on Missiological Issues* (Grand Rapids: Baker, 1994), p. 189-201; see also Paul G. Hiebert, Daniel R. Shaw, Tite Tiénou, "Split-Level Christianity," in *Understanding Folk Religion: A Christian Response to Popular Beliefs and Practices* (Grand Rapids: Baker, 1999), p. 89-91.

sphere that dominates everyday life in animist and esoteric worldviews. Fourth, the Enlightenment philosophy has gone one step further: it has excluded the whole aspect of the invisible world. It considers only what is observable and measurable. The European Enlightenment philosophy with its secular worldview has drawn its main ideas from Aristotelian philosophy. For Europe, "largely, secularization has resulted from potent social and economic pressures, from greater individualism, and the dominance of new values about family, gender, and sexuality."[37] In Asia, the representatives of a secular worldview are the original philosophies of Confucius and Buddha. The latter corresponds to Sri Lankan and Indochinese Buddhism, the form of Theravada Buddhism, which is actually a materialist philosophy.[38] Later these two philosophies adapted themselves to the Chinese holistic worldview. The latter has been transformed into Mahayana Buddhism. The graphic on the next page visualises schematically the way in which the different worldviews stratify creation and where the religious and philosophical systems fit in.[39]

It becomes evident that a person who converts from Hinduism or from a secular society to the Christian faith cannot change their worldview straightaway. They have to make substantial and continuous efforts in order for the presuppositions and conceptualisations acquired during early childhood to be transformed.[40] Evidently, several of these ideal types of worldviews can be combined in one person. As an evangelical Christian, I have a Hebrew worldview. But through my socialisation and through my training at school and university, I have included some dichotomist and secular elements in my worldview. These different worldviews are opera-

---

[37] Grace Davie, *Europe, the Exceptional Case: Parameters of Faith in the Modern World* (London: Darton, Longman & Todd, 2002).

[38] The French philosopher Luc Ferry says that "philosophy is always secularisation of a religion." Luc Ferry & Lucien Jerphagnon, *La tentation du christianisme* (Paris: Grasset, 2009), p. 100. In this vein, Greek philosophy of the Platonian or Aristotelian type are secularisations of Greek Animism, and Enlightenment philosophy is a secularisation of Christianity, just as Sri Lankan (Theravada) Buddhism is a secularisation of Hinduism, and Taoism and Confucianism secularisations of the Chinese religions (with an important component of Animism). Later on, Taoism, Confucianism and the Chinese (Mahayana) Buddhism integrated (again) into the Chinese holistic worldview.

[39] Adapted from Paul G. Hiebert, *Anthropological Insights for Missionaries* (Grand Rapids: Baker, 1985), p. 158.

[40] For a more detailed discussion, see Hannes Wiher, "Worldview and Identity across Conversion," *Evangelical Review of Theology* 38, 4 (2014), p. 307-323.

tional in different situations of my daily life: when I am ill, I have the natural inclination to take medicine, a thought influenced by the secular worldview. But through my Hebrew worldview I am also motivated to pray. My dichotomist worldview allows me to continue working while I am ill, even though I know that I should relax.

Holistic Worldview	Hebrew Worldview	Dichotomist Worldview	Secular Worldview
	God		
Supreme Being		Spirit	Invisible Aspect
Spirits Ancestors	Angels Spirits	Excluded Middle	("Supernatural") Excluded
Humans Animals Plants Matter	Humans Animals Plants Matter	**Humans** Animals Plants Matter	**Humans** Animals Plants Matter
Animism Hinduism Taoism Chinese and Tibetan Buddhism Shintoism Popular Religions	Judaism Christianity	Plato	Confucianism Sri Lankan Buddhism Aristotle Enlightenment

On the other hand, a Muslim, Hindu or Buddhist migrating to Europe will be influenced by the prevailing secular worldview. Additionally, European Islam, Hinduism and Buddhism will not be the same as their corresponding socio-religious systems in the countries of origin of the migrant workers. Secondly, basic soteriological concepts will be adapted to corresponding European notions. However, because of their secular worldview, a minority of contemporary Europeans are likely to be attracted to exotic aspects of the new religions.

Five Basic Soteriological Concepts

The second selected model consists of the five basic soteriological concepts (God, man, evil, sin, and salvation). Traditionally, evangelism started by announcing the Good News of Jesus Christ, the heart of Scripture. But the coming of the kingdom of God through Jesus Christ (Mark 1:15) and the forgiveness of sins (Rom 3:24-26) are not good news where there is no sin to be forgiven, as for example in a secular worldview and in Islam. For contemporary Europeans, the only aspect of the concept of sin that remains is one's "little weaknesses". The Quran says that man is created good but weak (Surah 2:36; 4:28). It is thus normal for him to sin.

Consequently, it makes no sense to announce the liberation of sin where sin is not a problem. The notion of sin is closely linked to the concept of evil. In a secular Europe, the only notion of evil that subsists is the one of misfortune and illness. How did evil enter the world for the monotheistic religions? Is evil linked to the good or evil destiny sent by the supreme God? (Surah 35:15). Or else, as the Bible says, was evil introduced into the world through the initiative of the Adversary, Satan (Gen 3:1), in an entirely good creation, created by an entirely good God (Gen 1:31)? Moreover, the concept of sin is closely linked to the concept of man. Is man created in the image of God (Gen 1:26), or does this idea represent a blasphemy? (Surah 112). Is it normal that man sins or is it sin that separates him from fellowship with God (Gen 3)?

The concept of man leads to the concept of God. Is it futile to reflect on metaphysics in its strict sense, about the existence of a soul and of God? These are not only the thoughts of the European Enlightenment and those of contemporary European atheists or agnostics, but equally of the Buddha of Indian origin.[41] Islam has retained the stratigraphic order of the Hebrew worldview: God is separated from creation, he is "holy." However, the moral quality of Allah's holiness is quite different from the biblical God's holiness. Generally speaking, the holiness of the biblical God has a moral quality that is difficult to find in other religions where the divinities represent the whole spectrum of human character, for example, in Greek mythology or in the Hindu pantheon. The conception that God is holy and separated from the universe as we find it in the Hebrew worldview is opposed to oriental notions of divinity that are monist and pantheist, where the supreme divinity is part of the universe and in everything (pantheism

---

[41] See the Sanskrit concept of *anatman* or Pali *anatta* (no-soul) and the absence of the reflection on God in Theravada Buddhism.

and pan-en-theism). The majority of oriental religions have a holistic worldview.

In conclusion, we maintain that the offer of salvation only makes sense where evil and sin are recognised. These latter are founded on the concepts of man and God. Scripture teaches these concepts from the three first chapters onwards but in the opposite order: the concepts of God and man (Gen 1-2), the concepts of evil and sin (Gen 3) and the concept of salvation (from Gen 3:15 on through the whole Bible).

Based on these reflections, missiologists have developed the concept of "chronological evangelism," which consists of teaching Scripture chronologically starting with Genesis 1. Its pioneer book is *Building on Firm Foundations* by Trevor McIlwain with sixty Bible story lessons.[42] On the basis of Luke 24:44-46 where Jesus explains the messianic prophecies of the OT to the two disciples of Emmaus, shorter versions with fourteen lessons of Bible stories have been produced for different contexts.[43] For oral or "digit-oral"[44] cultures, this teaching has to be transmitted in a narrative form. The chronological Bible teaching in oral form has been further developed in a great variety of presentations by the International Orality Network (ION).[45]

What is the relationship between the model of the five basic soteriological concepts and worldview and its transformation? In fact, these five basic soteriological concepts build a worldview, whether it is biblical or not. One has to work on them before or after conversion in order to transform a cultural worldview into a biblical worldview. If these chronological, transforming Bible studies are not integrated into a discipleship process, the worldviews of believers will not change. John Calvin's example in Geneva is very meaningful: during only eighteen years, the Reformer preached more than two thousand sermons across the whole Scripture. In this way, he transformed the worldview of the Genevans, probably in spite of them.

---

[42] Trevor McIlwain, *Building on Firm Foundations* (9 vol.; Sanford: NTM, 1991).
[43] John R. Cross (pseudonym), *The Stranger on the Road to Emmaus*; an adaptation for a secular context: idem, *By This Name* (with the Gospel of John as a template); an adaptation for a Muslim context: Yehia Sa'a, *All that the Prophets Have Spoken* (with minor modifications of *The Stranger*). These texts are produced by Goodseed and available on www.goodseed.com in English, French, German, Arab, Chinese, Korean, Russian, and other languages.
[44] For the concept of "digit-orality" see the section "Literate Culture / Orality" below.
[45] www.orality.net.

This fact also casts light on the question whether the OT is replaceable as "preparation of the Gospel" (*praeparatio evangelica*) by other cultural and religious systems in the different regions of the world[46]. Evidently, other religious systems will construct other worldviews than that of Scripture and cannot replace the OT with its particular worldview, built on the basis of the stratigraphic model of creation, the five particular soteriological concepts and the time concept.

Conscience Orientation

Whereas the two former models represent the cognitive aspects of worldview, conscience orientation integrates the affective and evaluative aspects in our approach to worldview and therefore reaches the deepest layers of personality, culture and religion. Contrary to the other three worldview models, conscience orientation does not construct a specifically biblical worldview but is presented in the Bible in a balanced way.

The model of conscience orientation is a theological-psycho-anthropological model that is particularly useful for cultural analysis in missiological perspective. The path from sin to salvation passing through forgiveness is placed at the heart of biblical concern, at the same time describing the most profound human desire, and is reflected in the basic functioning of the conscience from anxiety, shame or guilt through forgiveness to harmony and peace. In the social sciences, the model is used particularly in psychology and cultural anthropology. These sciences deal specifically with the feelings of shame and guilt, which we use to define our model of conscience orientation. Defined this way, this model deals with notions that are important to the Bible, psychology and cultural anthropology. It is an extremely rare case that a concept is so central to the Bible and the social sciences. The conscience is easily understood based on its development during childhood.[47]

---

[46] The term was introduced by Eusebius of Caesarea in his work *Praeparatio evangelica*. The concept probably comes from Origen of Caesarea and forms the basis of the anthropological model of contextualisation adopted by Matteo Ricci, John Mbiti, and subsequently liberal Catholic and Protestant missiologists. For a detailed description of the anthropological model and other contextualisation models, see A. Scott Moreau, *Contextualization in World Missions: Mapping and Assessing Evangelical Models* (Grand Rapids: Kregel, 2012).

[47] For a more detailed discussion of this model, see Hannes Wiher, *Shame and Guilt: A Key to Cross-Cultural Ministry* (Bonn: VKW, 2003), available at www.worldevangelicals.org/resources/rfiles/res3_234_link_1292694440.pdf.

Development of the Conscience

At birth, the conscience is present in the form of a genetic disposition. According to the socio-cultural context during early childhood, it can develop in different ways. The American anthropologist Melford Spiro has made observations in an Israeli kibbutz.[48] He remarked that the children raised by few attachment figures (*significant others*), for example their father and mother in the framework of a nuclear family, integrate[49] not only the norms presented, but also the educators themselves in their conscience. These children function with a fixed set of norms and develop a personality centred on rules (norms). They organise their life according to a program; the desire to be punctual and to fix for themselves well defined objectives. Work is more important for them than relationships. As their conscience functions in an autonomous way, they tend to become individualists. And when they violate a norm, they feel guilty. This is why Spiro calls this rules-centred conscience a guilt-oriented conscience.

If the children are raised by many attachment figures reference persons, for example in a nursery or an extended family, they integrate the norms but cannot integrate the educators in their conscience. They thus remain dependent on the presence of their significant others in order for their conscience to be operational. If the mother is present, the norms of the mother are functional; and if the grandmother is present, the norms of the grandmother are operational. These person-oriented children have a tendency to develop a relational personality with a group identity. They prefer personal interactions to work, and when they work, they prefer to do it in a team. Their focus is rather on status and prestige than on the accomplishment of their objectives. And when no significant other is present, no norm is functional. This fact represents the basis for the phenomenon of corruption. Such a person says: "As long as nobody sees it, I can do anything." But when the violation of the norm becomes publicly known, a feeling of shame arises. This is why Spiro calls this relational conscience a shame-oriented conscience.

With the number of reference persons as a factor in the development of the conscience, Spiro gives us an interesting model for the development and transformation of worldview. But of course, this does not show the entire reality of the development of the conscience. A Chinese child that is

---

[48] Melford E. Spiro, *Children of the Kibbutz* (Cambridge: Harvard University Press, 1958), chapter 15, particularly p. 408f.

[49] The exact psychoanalytic term is "introject". Spiro makes his analysis based on the psychoanalytic theory.

raised in a nuclear family in a rural zone of China will still have a relational conscience, even though it is raised by few significant others. The reason is that there are other factors that influence the development of the conscience, particularly the methods of education. If the educators present the norms by giving explanations and arguments (rules), the child's conscience will be rules-centred. If the educators emphasise the relational aspects of the norms, the child's conscience will become relational. They say for example: "If you do this, papa will spank you;" or "What will the neighbours say?" If very few norms are presented to the child, the conscience can either become relational or does not develop properly. This happened for example in the 1968 Movement that rejected the traditional norms of Western society. Their children have either relational or underdeveloped consciences, which have inadequate functioning, neither relational nor rules-centred. A child or adolescent with an underdeveloped conscience can kill a peer without remorse, a phenomenon that one encounters increasingly today in suburbs of megacities around the globe. Another nuancing factor is that both conscience orientations are present in one and the same person in a very specific mixture that gives a particular profile to the personality. In the next section, we reflect on the influence of conscience on personality.

Conscience and Personality

By adapting the model of basic values introduced by Sherwood Lingenfelter and Marvin Mayers,[50] one can develop a typology of personalities on the basis of conscience orientation. By combining basic values and conscience orientation, this model becomes more nuanced. As indicated above, the two types represent Weberian ideal types. Every person is a specific mixture of the two conscience orientations. Thus, a person will have a very specific profile of the six value-pairs in this typology. It is useful to know one's own profile of preferred values and that of others, in order to better understand oneself and others, how and why people behave as they do, specifically one's partner, friend, colleague, and neighbour, that is the people to whom we want to bring the Gospel.

The rules-centred conscience has an autonomous functioning. It has a tendency to produce individualists who fix for themselves rules and objectives like a program, a tight agenda, or a to-do list. As individualists, they engage easily in new initiatives. The relational conscience needs the pres-

---

[50] Sherwood G. Lingenfelter & Marvin K. Mayers, *Ministering Cross-Culturally: An Incarnational Model for Personal Relationships* (Grand Rapids: Baker, 1986).

ence of the significant others to function well. It tends to produce persons with a group identity who are person-oriented and focused on status and prestige. They take few initiatives out of fear of losing face in the case of failure or when leaving the security of the group.

Rules-Centred Personality	Relational Personality
Individualism	Collectivism
Time Orientation	Event Orientation
Task Orientation	Person Orientation
Achievement Focus	Status Focus
Analytic Thinking	Holistic Thinking
Courage to Lose Face	Fear of Losing Face

Knowing our own and the other person's profile will improve our relationships with others, and our communicatory approach to contemporary Europeans of all sorts of origins and backgrounds.

Soteriological Model of Conscience

As shame and guilt can be expressions of sin, the model of conscience orientation is a soteriological model that means a model regarding salvation. It thus has close links with the model of the five basic soteriological concepts. The relational conscience tends towards peace expressed by harmony, while the rules-centred conscience tends towards law. The latter seeks to repair the faults in order to restore innocence by reparation of individual guilt, reparation by the God who forgives (the doctrine of justification). The relational conscience seeks to restore harmony and honour with the significant others by reconciliation. As these persons are prisoners of shame after violating the norms of a significant other present, they need a third person as mediator for reconciliation. The emphasis of rules-centred persons is on law and rights, while relational persons seek harmony, prestige, power, prosperity and well-being. For rules-centred persons and societies, human rights are important, whereas for relational persons and cultures the collective honour is the priority. This fact was operational during the events around the Muhammad cartoons,[51] and is continuously responsible for so-called "honour killings."

A deep personality structure like conscience orientation will not change automatically around conversion. The only way to transform the different

---

[51] Copenhagen (Denmark) and Charlie Hebdo (Paris).

values is by influencing them intentionally. The deep layers of personality that were acquired during early childhood will allow less transformation than the layers acquired during adulthood. Relational elements can be added by a relational (self-) education or lifestyle, for example an intimate relationship with the biblical God. Rules-centred elements can be introduced in people's lives by the introduction of rules, for example the Ten Commands, or a tight agenda.

The table below presents the positive and negative values in a schematic way. On the left, the biblical notions are presented, in the centre the judicial axis (from guilt to law and right), and on the right the relational axis (from shame to harmony and honour).

Biblical Notions		Judicial Axis		Relational Axis
Salvation Justice Blessing	↔	Innocence Right Law	↔	Harmony Honour / Prestige Power Prosperity Wellbeing
↑		↑		↑
Forgiveness Repentance	↔	Reparation Justification	↔	Reconciliation (Mediator)
↑		↑		↑
Sin Anxiety	↔	Guilt Anxiety	↔	Shame Anxiety

Understanding our own perception and conception of the three concepts of sin, forgiveness and salvation and that of our communication partners, will be likely to improve our missiological approach to the people around us.

Conscience and Scripture

After analysing personalities, cultures and religions, we want to analyse the biblical message to be communicated and the context in which it has been communicated by God, the prophets, Jesus and the apostles. Starting from the animist relational context of the ancient Near East, God builds a specific worldview during the course of the OT by means of the stratigraphic model of creation, the five basic soteriological concepts and the development of the time concept.

This becomes evident in the creation account when God emphasises the fact that he is the Creator and all elements of the visible and invisible universe are parts of creation (Gen 1-2; Col 1:16). This means that the Creator-God is outside of his creation, holy and separated from it (Lev 19:2; 20:26). God intends to change the conception that the Supreme Being is part of the universe as is the case in the animist worldview. Thus, God induces a transformation from an animist holistic worldview into a Hebrew worldview where God is apart from creation.

Another way God builds his society starting from the animist background is demonstrated in the first books of Scripture, particularly in Leviticus.[52] From the point of view of conscience orientation, the Hebrew language with its very large and fuzzy semantic domains reveals a relational conscience orientation. However, beyond an intimate relationship, God desires that his people obey his commands. Thus, we find the following often repeated formula in both Testaments: "Love God and obey his commands."[53] It is our hypothesis that this formula, among other elements, shows God's will to lead his Hebrew people towards a balanced conscience.[54] This is the foundation for the introduction of all the complicated rules in Exodus and Leviticus.

Based on the fact that Greek culture is an animist culture, its worldview is likely to be holistic and relational.[55] However, the materialist and dichotomist Greek philosophies promoting fragmented worldviews, together with the Greek language, witness to an analytic thinking which creates a certain balance of the conscience orientation. Thus, the authors of the NT, the majority of whom are Jews, communicate the message of the OT principally in continuity with the Hebrew worldview, as far as the worldview is concerned, yet adopt some aspects of the Greek language and worldview. Consequently, we can expect the NT authors to have a somewhat balanced personality and communication of the Gospel, a fact that can be largely confirmed.

For Roman culture, which was also animist, one can also expect a holistic and relational worldview. However, the well-structured Latin language and the importance of the Roman law witness to a well-developed judicial axis.

---

[52] Mary Douglas, *Leviticus as Literature* (New York: Oxford University Press, 1999).
[53] Deut 6:5f; 7:9; 11:1,13; 30:16; Josh 22:5; 23:6,8; 1 Kgs 9:4; Neh 1:5; Ezek 36:26f; Dan 9:4; John 14:15,21,23f; 15:10; 1 John 3:23f.
[54] Wiher, *Shame and Guilt*, p. 159, 178, 180, 215, 277, especially 280f.
[55] Idem, p. 295-311.

From the point of view of the science of religion and cultural anthropology, it should be noted that Christianity is the only religion with a sacred book written in three languages: Hebrew, Aramaic, and Greek. In this way, Bible translation is unavoidable and cultural pluralism is programmed in advance. The Trinitarian God who desires to dwell in us through the Holy Spirit does not depend on fixed cultural forms, but expresses himself through very diverse personalities and cultures.

Knowing the conscience orientation of the Hebrew, Greek and Roman cultures and the biblical authors will help us to understand and interpret Bible passages in line with the conscience orientation of the original text and its author, and will also be likely to improve our Bible competency.

Conscience and Theology

Theology was largely developed during the Patristic and medieval periods, in a Europe that was marked by Roman culture and law, and a Christianity founded on the Latin translation of the Bible and Roman Catholic tradition. In this way, theology shows the fingerprint of analytical thinking and thus a systematic theological approach. Western theology has developed a rules-centred doctrine like no other theology.

Rules-Centred Theology	**Relational Theology**
Analytic Thinking (dictionaries)	Holistic Thinking
"Scientific" Epistemology (subject-object distance)	"Relational" Epistemology (subject-object intimacy)
Dogmatic Theology	Relational Theology (allegiance encounter)
Systematic Theology	Narrative Theology (chronological storying)
Apologetics (truth encounter)	Spiritual Warfare (power encounter)

Since the middle of the 20th century, a counter-current has become evident in the West, well reinforced by theologians from the Global South. It has developed narrative and relational theologies and emphasises reconciliation rather than justification put forward by the Reformers. The approach becomes more holistic and relational. Because the background of a great number of Christians in the Global South is animist, the subject of spiritual warfare receives more attention.

Time Concept

In this section, we present the fourth model, the time concept. It takes up one of the values of the typology of personalities based on the conscience orientation, and deepens the analysis because of its particular importance in peoples' lives and in contemporary theological discourse. Rules-centred people are particularly managed by time, their agenda and programs. They prefer to be punctual. On the contrary, relational persons will pay little attention to time and punctuality, and orient themselves rather towards people, relationships, and the events experienced with them.[56] The famous passage drawn from Ecclesiastes 3:1-8 presents an event orientation, typical for the relational dimension of Hebrew culture.

However, there is an additional aspect of the time concept: past or future orientation.[57] Many peoples on our planet, just like the Hebrews, focus on their ancestral traditions. They are looking backwards like the rowers of a ship and thus have the future in their back (Hebrew *'aharît*: Ps 143:5; Isa 46:10; Jer 29:11).[58] The genealogies in the OT witness to this past time orientation. However, it is not an incapacity to conceive the future as Mbiti proposed,[59] but a difference in the dominant time orientation, either past or future.[60] In their personality typology, Lingenfelter and Mayers call the past orientation logically "absence of crisis orientation" because it is not preoccupied with future problems, and the future orientation or "crisis orientation."[61] For persons with a future time orientation it is easy to plan

---

[56] See Lingenfelter & Mayers, "Tensions about Time," in *Ministering Cross-Culturally*, p. 37-50.

[57] See Wiher, *Shame and Guilt*, p. 286f.

[58] Wolff, "X. The Old Testament Concept of Time," in *Anthropology of the Old Testament*, p. 83-92; see also Andrew E. Hill, "*'aharît*," *NIDOTTE*, vol. 1, p. 361f.

[59] John S. Mbiti, "The Concept of Time as a Key to the Understanding and Interpretation of African Religions and Philosophy," in *African Religions and Philosophy* (London: Heinemann, 1969), p. 15-28; idem, *New Testament Eschatology in an African Background* (London: SPCK, 1969), p. 24ff.

[60] Mbiti has been criticised by Leonard Nyirongo, "The African and Biblical View of Time, History and Progress," in *The Gods of Africa or The God of the Bible?* (Potchefstroom: Potchefstroom University, 1997); Van der Walt, *The Liberating Message*, p. 203f; idem, "Time Moving 'Past' Man Versus Man Moving 'Through' Time," in *Afrocentric or Eurocentric?* (Potchefstroom: Potchefstroom University, 1997), p. 64-66. See also Edward T. Hall & Mildred R. Hall, *Understanding Cultural Differences* (Yarmouth, MA: Intercultural Press, 1990), p. 17; Wiher, *Shame and Guilt*, p. 286f.

[61] Lingenfelter & Mayers, "Tensions associated with Handling Crises," in *Ministering Cross-Culturally*, p. 65-76.

into the future, to adopt for example a strategy of "planning by objectives." On the other hand, for persons with a past time orientation it is very difficult to plan ahead and to foresee potential problems that might occur in the future, like for example a stock depletion.

How did the transition from past orientation towards future orientation come about in the OT? According to Gerhard von Rad, it is by following the constant prophetic preaching about the day of YHWH that the Israelites have started to look towards the future and that the time concept has become linear.[62] This future orientation, particularly the eschatological orientation towards "the last days," becomes an important parameter of the time concept in the NT. The NT authors situate themselves in the "eschatological interim" between the two comings of Christ and are oriented towards an eschatological future.[63]

Interdisciplinary In-Depth Analysis

After presenting the four worldview models, we will now apply them to the European context in an interdisciplinary and in-depth analysis. We will first present the interdisciplinary aspect, and then secondly the cultural in-depth dimension of the analysis.

Interdisciplinary Analysis

An interdisciplinary analysis integrates the different approaches discussed in the literary review presented briefly in the Introduction, and in more detail in Appendix 2. It includes a historical analysis which takes into account the Greek, Roman and Christian heritage, the predominance of the Roman Catholic Church over the centuries, the influence of the Protestant Reformation, the impact of religious wars in the collective memory of Europeans, and especially the Enlightenment influence. For worldview this means that in the collective memory of Europeans there will be a mixture of stratigraphic models of creation: holistic, dichotomist, secular and Hebrew worldviews. Depending on the cultural and religious influences on a person, one will also meet a mix of basic soteriological concepts. The time concept will be impregnated by a strong future orientation, thus planning

---

[62] Gerhard von Rad, "Israel's Ideas about Time and History, and the Prophetic Eschatology," in *Old Testament Theology, vol. 2: The Theology of Israel's Prophetic Traditions* (transl. D.M.G. Stalker; London: Oliver & Boyd, 1965), p. 99-127.

[63] Oscar Cullmann, *Christ and Time: The Primitive Christian Conception of Time and History* (London: SCM, 1951).

by objectives in several sectors of life. As far as conscience orientation is concerned, its analysis will have to be strongly individualised.

The philosophical analysis will consider the influence of Christianity on philosophy. It will be interested in the change of the philosophical concepts during the progressive abandonment of the Christian basis in the different historical periods. As Luc Ferry indicates, philosophy in the line of Enlightenment thought is a secularisation of Christianity.

The economic-political analysis will retain the influence of industrialisation which focuses on efficiency and the material well-being in the contemporary world. This materialism expresses itself in a secular worldview and the emphasis on efficiency within the framework of a rules-centred conscience orientation. The analysis of the recent past also includes the history and influence of the European Union.[64]

The sociological analysis is interested in the changes that have taken place in Europe during the last fifty years, a transitional process from an epoch called modernity to a new paradigm called postmodernity or late modernity.[65] The psychological analysis will take into account the multiple models of socialisation that exist in Europe producing very diverse personalities. After the mass arrival of migrant workers, the anthropological analysis will be more necessary than ever. Immigrants from very diverse cultural and religious backgrounds are bringing all imaginable worldviews with them to Europe in regard to the four operational models: the stratigraphic model of creation, the five basic soteriological concepts, conscience orientation, and the time concept. Each model will bring its own particular contribution. In this way, one arrives at a perspective of Europe in terms of all important aspects – theology, psychology, sociology, anthropology, economics and politics. The transformations in the different disciplines create an enormous complexity in European societies. Consequently, the analyses, and later the approaches to evangelism, will have to be individualised.

Cultural In-Depth Analysis

From another perspective, and in order to deepen our analysis towards the deep "core of the iceberg," we apply the four proposed worldview models to the understanding of the European context. We start with the

---

[64] See Evert van de Poll, *Europe and the Gospel: Past Influences, Current Developments, Mission Challenges* (London: de Gruyter/Versita, 2013).

[65] For a more detailed discussion, see the section "Modernity / Postmodernity" below.

deepest model, the conscience orientation, which reaches the affective and evaluative level of worldview by means of an examination of values.

Conscience Orientation

In the second half of the 20th century, and even more so since the arrival of migrants who have gone through all sorts of socialisations in different corners of the world, European societies have experienced a cultural explosion. The evangelist (and all Christian engaging with their fellow Europeans) will be faced with all kinds of conscience orientations. One will find every possible mixture of value profiles indicated in the section on personality typology. With its emphasis on efficiency, the importance of punctuality and professional requirements, Europe produces predominantly conscience orientations in the sense of achievement focus and task orientation, or transforms persons and socio-religious systems in this direction. By contrast, migrants bring all sorts of relational consciences.

Modernity / Postmodernity

The changes that have come about in Europe during the epochs of the Renaissance, the Protestant Reformation, the Enlightenment and industrialisation, are called "modern times" or epoch of "modernity." Modernity is characterised by the rise of "empirical science and technology, of industrialization and capitalism, of urbanization and social mobility, of legal bureaucracy, democracy and the nation states."[66]

> Modernity promotes individualism, privatization, and the dominance of a scientific worldview that makes obsolete religious claims to provide healings or miracles. The modern welfare state provides the social services and education once supplied by religious-based charities or movements, so that citizens know they can comfortably rely on government-provided assistance in time of crisis. Once ordinary believers can assert with confidence that "the state is my shepherd," organized religion declines sharply. This does not mark the end of religion as such, since a notion of higher powers appears to be hard-wired into our consciousness, but now the religious instinct is manifested in a more personal, autonomous, non-dogmatic and non-judgmental spirituality.[67]

---

[66] Loek Halman et al., eds., *Religion in Secularizing Society: The Europeans' Religion at the End of the 20th Century* (Leiden: Brill, 2003), p. 1.

[67] Philip Jenkins, *God's Continent: Christianity, Islam, and Europe's Religious Crisis* (Oxford: Oxford University Press, 2007), p. 43.

Modernity favours thus a secular worldview. Following the philosophy of Neo-Platonism, the basis of Christendom during the scholastic period, the Roman Catholic Church maintained basically a dichotomist worldview. During the epoch of modernity, Europeans became more and more inclined to efficiency, to emphasise work, achievement and punctuality. The inclination to analytic thinking has favoured philosophy and the sciences. By generalising (in the logic of an ideal type), modernity has produced a type of person with a rules-centred conscience orientation.

During the second half of the 20th century, a trend has appeared which the different sciences call postmodernity, advanced modernity or late modernity.[68] The debate on the interpretation of this new trend is ongoing. According to philosophers and sociologists, it is a radicalisation, an acceleration and a crisis of modernity. On the contrary, psychologists and anthropologists observe a deep change in behaviour between older and younger generations, a post-modernity as counter current of modernity.[69]

Luc Ferry observes three reactions to this crisis of modernity which could be perceived as three currents of postmodernity: the return to pre-modern tradition (in a theological perspective this can be called the "orthodox" reaction in which one could classify a part of the evangelical movement), an attempt at deconstruction (for example Jacques Derrida and

---

[68] Or also hyper-modernity, ultra-modernity, trans-modernity, meta-modernity. See especially French authors: Jean-François Lyotard, *The Postmodern Condition: A Report on Knowledge* (transl. from the French by Geoff Bennington and Brian Massumi; Minneapolis, MN: University of Minnesota Press, 1993 [French version 1979]): "post-modernity"; Gilles Lipovetsky, *Les temps hypermodernes* (Paris: LGF, 2008); Frédéric Lenoir, *Les métamorphoses de Dieu: La nouvelle spiritualité occidentale* (Paris: Plon, 2003), p. 211: "ultra-modernity" (this is also the term preferred by Jean-Paul Willaime and Danièle Hervieu-Léger); Élie Théofilakis, ed., *Modernes, et après?* (Paris: Autrement, 1985), p. 10: "trans-modernity"; Marc Augé, *Non-Lieux: Introduction à une anthropologie de la surmodernité* (Paris: Seuil, 1992); Denis Müller, *L'éthique protestante dans la crise de la modernité* (Paris/Genève: Cerf/Lavor et Fides, 1999), p. 129: "meta-modernity"; François Dubet, *Le déclin de l'institution* (Paris: Seuil, 2002), p. 52: "late modernity".

[69] See for example J. Andrew Kirk, *The Future of Reason, Science and Faith: Following Modernity and Post-Modernity* (Aldershot: Ashgate, 2007); J. Andrew Kirk & Kevin Vanhoozer, ed., *To Stake a Claim: Mission and the Western Crisis of Knowledge* (Acts of a Conference in Paris of the Epistemology Group of the Missiology of Western Culture Project; Maryknoll: Orbis, 1999); Yves Bonny, *Sociologie du temps present: Modernité avancée ou postmodernité?* (Paris: Armand Colin, 2004). The promotors of the Emerging Church Movement perceive postmodernity rather as a counter current.

Thomas Althizer) or at reconstruction (in a theological and ecclesiological perspective one could situate here Process Theology and the Emerging and Missional Church Movement).[70] In a similar vein, Heinzpeter Hempelmann sees three basic positions ("premodern," "modern" and "postmodern") and interprets them as co-existing "basic mentalities" rather than historical epochs. With this view, he positions himself in line with the concept of worldview and also with the Sinus Milieus developed by the Heidelberg research institute, the three "basic mentalities" representing the horizontal coordinate of the Sinus diagrams.[71]

Concerning the position of Evangelicals reacting to this crisis, the French sociologists of religion Jean-Pierre Bastian, Françoise Champion and Kathy Rousselet make the following interesting observation:

> The Evangelicals ... present the apparent paradox of constituting a powerful reactive pole to a certain cultural modernity and to the homogenising globalisation while being at the same time perfectly in phase with the new modes of communication that permit its worldwide development, and which are precisely one of the most important factors of standardisation.[72]

Thus, the current of postmodernity presents itself in very diverse ways. In this vein, let us note first that the concepts of modernity and postmodernity are complex and fuzzy. Then we have to consider that, during a cultural change, elements of continuity and discontinuity can exist side by side. Depending on whether one emphasises continuities or discontinuities, a divergence of points of view is not surprising.[73] The continuation of achievement focus and time orientation, and the emphasis on individual-

---

[70] Luc Ferry, *Homo aestheticus: L'invention du goût à l'âge démocratique* (Paris: Grasset, 1990), p. 311-319, discussed in Gabriel Monet, *L'Église émergente* (Berlin: LIT, 2014), p. 174-179. Ferry engages here in a reflection on art and philosophy, but we think with Monet that one can make an extrapolation of this analysis on the whole society.

[71] Heinzpeter Hempelmann, *Prämodern, Modern, Postmodern: Warum „ticken" Menschen so unterschiedlich? Basismentalitäten und ihre Bedeutung für Mission, Gemeindearbeit und Kirchenleitung* (Neukirchen-Vluyn: Neukirchener Verl., 2013).

[72] Jean-Pierre Bastian, Françoise Champion & Kathy Rousselet (eds.), *La globalisation du religieux* (Paris: Harmattan, 2001), p. 16.

[73] This interpretation of postmodernity as cultural mutation corresponds to the fifth option proposed by Yves Bonny. According to him, postmodernity can be seen as 1) an aesthetic sensitivity, 2) a state of mind, 3) a set of philosophical and epistemological orientations, 4) a set of moral and political positions, 5) a cultural mutation. Bonny, *Sociologie du temps présent*, p. 65-89.

ism and analytic thinking indicate a rules-centred conscience orientation. At the same time, anthropologists and sociologists observe a transition of a rules-centred conscience orientation in the generations born between the two World Wars and after World War II, towards an increasingly relational conscience in the contemporary younger generations.[74] On the one hand, one is inclined to speak of a continuity of the characteristics of a rules-centred modernity, on the other hand rather of a new epoch with a relational functioning of the conscience.

However, even during modernity the general profile of persons was already a mixture of the two orientations. In the Mediterranean region, and in Eastern Europe under the influence of the Orthodox Church, this mixture was more relational than the one in the United Kingdom, Germany and Scandinavia under the influence of the Protestant churches. Since the cultural explosion of European societies and the arrival of migrants, the diversity of the mixture has increased, and with it the relational tendency, because immigrants have mostly a relational functioning. Compared with the English-speaking world which has produced most of the literature on postmodernity, the difference between conscience orientations during modernity and postmodernity is thus less noticeable in the Mediterranean region, in France and in Eastern and South Eastern Europe.

The characteristics of a relational personality are person and event orientation, status focus and group identity, whereas the emphasis on efficiency, punctuality and tasks are less important. This relational orientation inclines a person to prefer oral functioning rather than reading newspapers and books, a subject that we want to study in the next section.

---

[74] This is the sociological theory of generations that distinguishes a consequence of different generations, first in American society, then equally elsewhere. For a secular analysis, see for example W. Strauss & N. Howe, *Generations: The History of America's Future, 1584 to 2069* (New York: Quill, 1992). For an analysis of the generation X in an evangelical, missiological perspective, see for example Kath Donovan & Ruth Myors, "A Generational Perspective into the Future," in *Too Valuable to Lose: Exploring the Causes and Cures of Missionary Attrition*, ed. William D. Taylor (Pasadena: William Carey Library, 1997), p. 41-73, esp. the synoptic table p. 48; Gary L. McIntosh, *Make Room for the Boom... or Bust: Six Church Models for Reaching Three Generations* (Grand Rapids: Revell, 1997), p. 14-15, 18-21 (synoptic tables); Jürg Pfister, "The Characteristics of Generation X," in *Motivating the Generation X: The Potential of Generation X as a Challenge for Christians and for Missions* (Nürnberg: VTR, 2004), p. 22-43 (synoptic tables p. 114-117); Wiher, *Shame and Guilt*, p. 363-365.

Literate Culture / Orality

The preceding reflections allow us to say that relational persons, cultures and religions tend to prefer oral functioning. They like to listen to stories and tell stories, either their own stories[75] or Bible stories.[76] In relation to communication, they may like to tell the stories several times by varying some details and expressions, one might say playing with language and communication. For the Hebrew language, the latter phenomenon is called "Hebrew parallelism." Generally speaking, it is a synonymous parallelism. However, the phenomenon is not specific to Hebrew. It can also be found in other languages of relational cultures.[77]

One can conclude that persons with oral preference have the following basic values: collectivism, event and person orientation, group identity, indirect communication, status and prestige focus, holistic thinking and fear of losing face. Their priority objectives in life are harmony, honour, prosperity and well-being. They have to be situated in the relational conscience orientation. We can discern allusions to current familiar notions: the "prosperity gospel" and the "fun generation" (as generation X is often called).

In our contemporary globalised world, one can also observe a phenomenon that one could call "digit-orality:"[78] Literate persons can function like oral persons sending written messages by SMS, WhatsApp or in a chat on the internet. This shows that social media are attractive for relational persons through the promotion of oral functioning. At the same time, it becomes evident that we are a mixture of two conscience orientations, orality belonging rather to a relational personality and literate competences rather to a rules-centred functioning.[79] Being a highly literate person, I still prefer

---

[75] See www.mystory.com; www.mystory.me; www.god.tv/videos.

[76] See the method of Chronological Bible Storying at www.orality.net.

[77] Cai Zong-Qi, "Synthetic Parallelism as a Cultural Expression: A Cross-Cultural and Cross-Disciplinary Study," *Tamking Review* 20, 2 (1989), p. 151-167; James Fox, "Roman Jakobson and the Comparative Study of Parallelism," in *Roman Jakobson. Echoes of His Scholarship* (PdR Press Publications on Roman Jakobson; Lisse: Peter de Ridder Press, 1977).

[78] Samuel E. Chiang, "Three Worlds Converged: Living in an Oral, Literate, and Digital Culture," in *Worship and Mission for the Global Church: An Ethnodoxology Handbook*, ed. James R. Krabill et al. (Pasadena: William Carey Library, 2012), p. 179-183. Cf. idem, "Editor's Note," *Orality Journal* vol. 1, n° 1 (2012), p. 8, accessible on www.orality.net.

[79] See the section "Conscience Orientation" above, and Walter J. Ong, *Orality and Literacy* (London/New York: Routledge, 1982).

listening to an audio-Bible and to the news on the radio and television rather than reading Scripture and newspapers.[80]

Relational postmodern persons generally have a holistic worldview rather than a secular worldview, which was typical for modernity. It is this phenomenon that will be studied in the next section on Esotericism.

Esotericism / Animism

The term Esotericism (from Greek *esôteros* "inside") refers to spiritual currents that emphasise, contrary to the evident and superficial external aspects of reality and religiosity, the hidden and invisible side of reality and spirituality. The fundamental idea is that of correspondence between all objects. Everything belongs to the same all-encompassing universe, material or non-material, and all objects have relationships between them. Esotericism thus includes a holistic cosmology and anthropology.[81] It has links with theosophy and anthroposophy, Rose-Cross, Free Masonry, Occultism, Neo-Druidism and New Age. The latter emerged in the 1970s and is the "New Age of Aquarius" which replaces the "Age of the Fish." It is a period of harmony and peace characterised by meditation and mysticism, an influence of oriental religions, and of rituals drawn from European and other traditional religions. Through the notion of unity between the universe and man, its thinking is holistic. The idea of correspondence of every object in the universe witnesses to a relational conscience orientation. The concept comes close to the notion of "spirit double" in Animism.[82] Both Esotericism and Animism are relational systems with a holistic worldview. The attractiveness of oriental and traditional religions on young Europeans thus has its source in a relational conscience orientation with a holistic worldview. The evolution towards it corresponds to the current of postmodernity as discussed above.

---

[80] For a more detailed discussion, see my article: Hannes Wiher, "Worldview and Oral Preference Learners and Leaders," in *Beyond Literate Western Practices: Continuing Conversations in Orality and Theological Education*, ed. Samuel E. Chiang and Grant Lovejoy (Hong Kong: Capstone Enterprises, 2014), p. 109-125, available at www.orality.net.

[81] See for example Svetoslava Toncheva, *Out of the New Spirituality of the Twentieth Century: The Dawn of Anthroposophy, the White Brotherhood and the Unified Teaching* (Berlin: Frank & Timme, 2015).

[82] Lothar Käser, "Concepts of Man in Different Societies," "Concepts of the World in Different Societies," and "Man and his Spirit-Double," in *Animism: A Cognitive Approach* (Nürnberg: VTR, 2014), p. 40-55, 56-65, 158-185.

Spirituality / Religions

After the classical religions (especially Roman Catholicism and Protestantism) were dismantled by the religious wars, the Enlightenment, and the two world wars, especially World War II, the return to a holistic worldview opens the door to an interest in the spiritual world. Spirituality can be practised in a free mixture drawn from Asian, European or traditional religions, or without any linkage to any religion. Sociologists of religion speak of "religious patchwork" (*bricolage religieux*) or of a "religious supermarket." Additionally, as Danièle Hervieu-Léger and Françoise Champion show clearly, one can find religious elements in many secular events in European societies: the adoration of music or sports idols, the rituals before football matches which are regularly held on Sunday mornings, atheist celebration meetings held on Sunday mornings or atheist "baptism," and the religious symbolism of certain advertisements and costumes. On the basis of the transformation from a rules-centred to a relational conscience orientation linked to a change from a secular to a holistic worldview, "spiritual" practices such as pilgrimages, meditation and contemplation are becoming very attractive again.

Parallel to these developments, and through the arrival of migrant workers, Islam, Hinduism and Buddhism are making their entry into Europe. They represent alternatives to Christianity by the fact that they offer themselves as relational religious systems to corresponding majority conscience orientations. There is also the so-called "popular" religious component that is the animistic aspect, which turns Islam and the oriental religions into relational systems. Additionally, and opposed to Christianity, Islam offers a simple system of doctrines and practices to the believer, a basis of orientation in a confusing world. On the other hand, Tibetan and Zen Buddhism offer open holistic and relational systems without any doctrinal confinement. The practices of meditation and certain rituals that are rich in symbols can render this exotic approach popular for a minority in Europe.

Result of the Interdisciplinary In-Depth Analysis

What is the conclusion on the usefulness of the four selected worldview models after this analytic tour through the European cultures? The change from a rules-centred to a relational conscience orientation linked to a transition from a secular or a dichotomist to a holistic worldview is the result of many factors that are summarised in the concepts of "crisis of modernity" and "postmodernity." The latter opens the door to movements such as

Esotericism and a regain of interest in spirituality, based on a holistic worldview. Grace Davie speaks about the "fragility of European secularism,"[83] and Andrew Greeley remarks that "religion is always declining and always reviving."[84] This development proceeds against the background of modernity through institutions that continue to require efficiency, punctuality and achievement focus, the respect for rules in general. Rules-centred persons will not be attracted at all by the new holistic spirituality and prefer to remain at a distance from any religion. This is still the case for the majority of Europeans, as sociological research has shown. For Muslims, Philip Jenkins observes that "converts do not represent a vast proportion of European Muslims." He concludes:

> The recent experience of Christian Europe might suggest not that the continent is potentially a graveyard for religion but rather that it is a laboratory for new forms of faith, new structures of organization and interaction that can accommodate to a dominant secular environment.[85]

The observed mixture is typical for a period of cultural change during which one finds characteristics of the two epochs, modernity and postmodernity. The influx of migrants increases the complexity of the mixture in European societies. The Christian believer and the evangelist reaching out to contemporary Europeans face a perplexing diversity of worldviews that oblige them to individualise the approach to evangelism using a refined cultural in-depth analysis of the person or subculture targeted.

Further Reading

Davie, Grace, *Europe, the Exceptional Case: Parameters of Faith in the Modern World* (London: Darton, Longman & Todd, 2002).
Davie, Grace, *Religion in Modern Europe: A Memory Mutates* (New York: Oxford University Press, 2005).
Käser, Lothar, *Foreign Cultures: A Cognitive Approach* (Nürnberg: VTR, 2014).
Lingenfelter, Sherwood G. & Mayers, Marvin K., *Ministering Cross-Culturally: An Incarnational Model for Personal Relationships* (Grand Rapids: Baker, 1986).

---

[83] Davie, *Europe, the Exceptional Case*.
[84] Andrew M. Greeley, *Religion in Europe at the End of the Second Millennium* (New Brunswick, NJ: Transaction Publishers, 2003).
[85] Jenkins mentions 100 000 ethnic Germans, 100 000 ethnic French, and 20 000 to 50 000 Italians (*God's Continent*, p. 226). The quote is from p. 19.

Naugle, David K., *Worldview: The History of a Concept* (Grand Rapids: Eerdmans, 2002).
Van de Poll, Evert, *Europe and the Gospel: Past Influences, Current Developments, Mission Challenges* (Maastricht/Aachen: Shaker, 2012).
Wiher, Hannes, *Shame and Guilt: A Key to Cross-Cultural Ministry* (Bonn: VKW, 2003).

Chapter 7
The Mosaic of Cultures: A Challenge for European and International Churches

Johannes Müller[1]

In recent years, a true mosaic of cultures has emerged in most European countries. How can churches react to this reality in their environment? In the first part, this article describes three basic models on how to deal with cultural diversity in churches. These can help churches to consider their options in facing cross-cultural challenges. In the second part, practical indications are given of how the mosaic of cultures can be dealt with inside a church and how contacts with churches of other cultures can be established.

Cultural Diversity in Churches

God's ultimate objective for mankind is a multitude of people from diverse backgrounds all over the world living in unity in his presence.[2] For centuries, this perspective has been perceived as an abstract truth and its realisation was expected in a distant afterlife. Over the last few years, however, God has introduced a surprise: he is already letting us experience a tangible foretaste of this global diversity in many places in this world. The inflow of refugees and migrants from more and more distant countries has brought this diversity all the way to European cities and villages. A true mosaic of cultures has formed in our immediate environment.

This reality does not stop at the doors of Christian congregations. Interestingly, churches sometimes experience more difficulties in dealing with

---

[1] This text is an expanded and updated version of the following articles in German and French: Johannes Müller, "Mosaik der Kulturen: Eine Herausforderung für einheimische und internationale Gemeinden in Europa," *Evangelische Missiologie* 32, 4 (2016), p. 177-189; idem, "La mosaïque des cultures: un défi pour les Églises européennes et les Églises issues de l'immigration," in *L'évangélisation en Europe francophone*, ed. Hannes Wiher (Charols: Excelsis, 2016), p. 157-173.

[2] Gal 3:28; Col 3:11; Rev 5:9-10; 7:9-10; 21:23-27.

diversity than other groups such as football clubs. Through their knowledge of the Bible, the unifying power of Christ's love and the power of the Holy Spirit, however, Christian churches should be better prepared.

What happens when people of a different cultural background turn up in "our" church services and congregations? In the following, I will describe three models of how churches deal with cultural diversity:[3]

- *Monocultural*: The church is based mainly on one culture.
- *Intercultural*: The church creates its own mixture of cultures.
- *Multicultural*: The church has culturally diverse groups, but also common programs for all under a common leadership.

These models are not differentiated by the composition of church attendance, but on how a church deals with cultural issues and how much room it grants the original cultures of its members.

Monocultural Churches Appreciate Uniqueness

One option for a church in dealing with the mosaic of cultures around it is to focus on a *single* culture or just a segment of it. This approach can be described as *"mono*-cultural." Consequently, the congregation will attract those who feel comfortable with this specific cultural framework.

Whether a person wants to join a church and become a member depends greatly on the atmosphere the church life conveys. This atmosphere depends significantly on how cultural issues are dealt with. Let me illustrate this in a figurative way. When we book holidays, we intentionally choose a setting in which we are so much at ease that we can relax and unwind. A monocultural church can be compared to holidays in a mountain chalet. A chalet provides warmth in an inhospitable environment and offers a retreat to the personal comfort zone

Monocultural congregations are contextualised for people from the same background, but they feel alien to others. For insiders, however, the congregation offers a safe haven and the feeling of being at home. Preserving their own identity and culture is of greater concern than developing contacts with people of different origin. Most of the time, they are welcome, but are expected to adapt culturally and linguistically. This observa-

---

[3] These models with their strengths and challenges have been presented in the following articles in German and French: Johannes Müller, "Wie gehen Gemeinden in Europa mit kulturellen Unterschieden um?" *Evangelikale Missiologie* 30, 3 (2014), p. 135-153, at www.missiologie.org/mediapool/79/797956/data/em_Archiv/em2014-3.pdf; idem, "Comment les Églises d'Europe peuvent-elles gérer la diversité des cultures?" *Théologie Évangélique* vol. 13, n° 3 (2014), p. 53-83.

tion applies to many indigenous churches, but also, intentionally or not, to several international churches consisting mainly of people from a similar culture and language background.[4]

This focus on a particular cultural mode of operation is an important limitation of the monocultural model. Many people in our Western society no longer define themselves in terms of a single culture, whether they are locals who have lived abroad, or migrants who have resided in the country for some time. It is even more so for the second generation of immigrants. Some of them have grown up in an international church, but they realise that the cultural values of the congregation have very little connection with other aspects of their daily lives, in which they feel just as much at home.

The perception of such a church from within can diverge significantly from the perception from without. Congregations led by African pastors, for example, are very often composed of Christians from various countries and ethnic groups. This can cause cultural tensions within the church, for example, when a particular nationality is overrepresented in the leadership, or when a dish, prepared by a lady of one ethnicity, fails to taste good to other members. Nevertheless, such a congregation, viewed from the outside, may look quite homogeneous. The same applies to many indigenous churches: from the point of view of immigrants, the cultural imprint of the host country can be so strong that they hardly perceive the social diversity and generational differences that might exist in the congregation.

If a monocultural church wants to develop cross-cultural contacts, it will have to connect to people outside the church or to other churches of a different cultural background.

A survey of 370 Catholic, Orthodox, historic and recent Protestant churches planted by migrants in Switzerland differentiates between three different subtypes depending on their perception of themselves:[5]

- *Caring type*: The church conveys a feeling of home to its immigrant members, but it also tries to facilitate the transition process to the new society. The situation of a not fully integrated migrant is per-

---

[4] The designation of churches planted by migrants is very delicate. Terms like "migrant" or "diaspora" church do not reflect the self-perception of many leaders and members. References to ethnicity, minority status or skin colour are not appropriate in several European countries either. In this article, I will purposefully use the very vague term "international church".

[5] Arnd Bünker, "Typen christlicher Migrationsgemeinden und postmigratorischer Perspektiven," in *Kirchen in Bewegung: Christliche Migrationsgemeinden in der Schweiz*, eds. Judith Albisser & Arnd Bünker (St.Gallen: SPI, 2016), p. 118-127.

ceived to be deficient, which can be perceived as shameful and demotivating by the individual.
- *Demarcation type*: The focus is on the preservation of one's own culture and values, which are considered to be strongly linked to faith. Collaboration with other churches is therefore not of primary concern. This attitude of withdrawal is sometimes triggered by the fact that members of the congregation have experienced rejection in the host society.[6] Some churches of the caring type evolve into the demarcation type when they realize that further steps of integration of their members would ultimately lead to the self-dissolution of the church.
- *Mission type*: Some congregations, especially among the newer Protestant churches, have the clear goal of reaching the host society with the Gospel. This orientation increases self-esteem: migrants are not simply seen as deficient (because of their lack of integration) or recipients of help, but on the contrary as having a substantial contribution to make. These churches assume that their programs are open to people of all kinds.[7]

The various monocultural churches in any region form a mosaic in which each church represents a mosaic stone with a specific imprint. Often, however, these mosaic stones are located side by side without much connection between them.

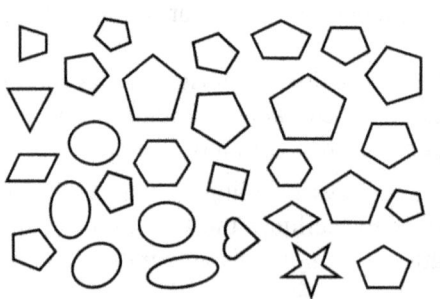 

Fig. 1: Different monocultural churches.
Fig. 2: Detail of a mosaic by Gaudí in Park Güell, Barcelona: Mosaic stones located side by side with little connection between them.

---

[6] A monocultural indigenous church can also develop such a self-image of demarcation from the society around it.

[7] With such an orientation towards society, the mission type approaches the intercultural church model described below, at least to a certain degree.

The second to last chapter of the Bible describes how all ethnic groups appear before the throne of God and bring their treasures and glory to him (Rev 21:24-26). Monocultural congregations prepare this unique contribution of their people and culture to the ultimate glory of God: saved people, a unique praise and sanctified works. The monocultural model develops therefore some characteristics culminating in God's eternal perfection.

Intercultural Churches Live Unity

Some churches try to overcome the limits of their mosaic stone by minimising cultural characteristics.[8] Often this attempt leads to a mixture in which the culture of the leader and that of the host country predominate. Since a position *between* cultures is adopted, this model may be called "*inter*-cultural".

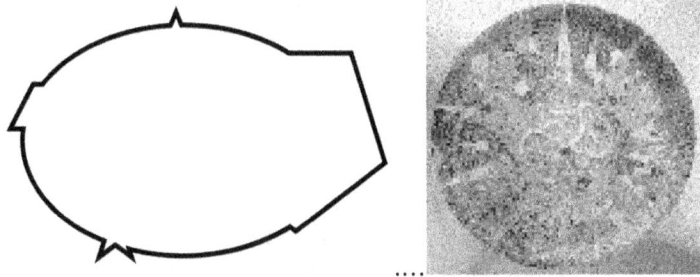

Fig. 3: The intercultural church fits no particular shape as it is a mixture of cultures.

Fig. 4: Mosaic by Gaudi in Park Guëll, Barcelona: an overall picture made up of small multi-coloured pieces.

An intercultural congregation reflects the mosaic of cultures within its own walls. Each member contributes a stone to the church mosaic. Each stone has its own imprint, which, however, has to step back in favour of the effect of the overall picture.

In practice, external observers may sometimes perceive characteristics of a particular culture and get the impression that the church is almost monocultural. Certainly, all transitions between this model and the former are possible, an aspect that we shall discuss later. The real difference from

---

[8] Several pastors have told me that their congregation has only the "Jesus Culture". By using this term, some of them justify their specific expressions of prayer life, music style and leadership, which nevertheless do have cultural characteristics.

the monocultural church model, however, is the vision of the leadership and the highly mixed composition of the assembly. Often, it is also implied that all cell groups are mixed.

Intercultural congregations appeal to people who love a cosmopolitan way of life. In terms of the types of holidays already used as an illustration above, an intercultural church can be compared with a stay in a youth hostel. In a hostel, one meets people from around the world. There is no fear of contact across boundaries, at least in theory. Guests feel part of a larger community, i.e. mankind. The only condition is to adapt to hostel life and its prerequisites.

An intercultural congregation is aimed at a wide audience. It has a missionary orientation because it does not consider cultural barriers. From a practical point of view, it attracts people who are ready to adapt to its style. Due to the church's own cultural mixture, however, each member, no matter the background, at least initially gets the impression of being a stranger. This requires a great willingness to learn and to make compromises. Unity and contacts with people of a different kind are highly valued, the preservation of cultural identity much less.

One of the great advantages of intercultural churches is a common language of communication, often the language of the host country or a widespread international language (mostly English, Spanish, French or Russian). This language prepares the ground for cross-cultural contacts between all members: interculturality is tangible. For this reason, intercultural churches can be very attractive for mixed couples, among others.

At the leadership level, a culturally mixed team is necessary to ensure a balanced development of the congregation, even if discussing topics and reaching decisions turn into time consuming challenges.[9]

One of the Biblical accounts of eternal perfection presents saved humankind as an innumerable multitude of people from all nations, all tribes, all peoples, and all languages. They stand before God's throne, all dressed in white robes which emphasises their unity (Rev 7:9). The intercultural model tries to live this reality as well as possible under the present circumstances.

---

[9] For a vivid description of the dynamics of a mixed leadership team, see Rodrigo Assis da Silva, "From Brazil to multicultural churches in Europe," in Israel Olofinjana, *Turning the Tables on Mission: Stories of Christians from the Global South in the UK* (Watford: Instant Apostle, 2013), p. 59-60.

Multicultural Churches Experience Diversity

Some churches pursue a different approach in order to reflect the mosaic of cultures. They not only receive people of different origins, as in the case of the intercultural model, but also encourage them to live their spirituality in cell groups according to their cultural expression. Such a group takes the place of a mosaic stone in the picture. The church as a whole offers regular joint activities for all members. It opts for a *plurality* of cultures (i.e. at least two) under its roof, thus the term *"multi-*cultural".

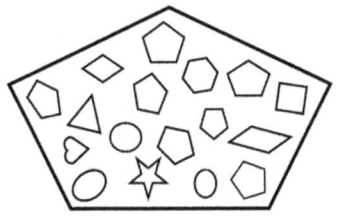 

Fig. 5: Multicultural church with (cell) groups, which are characterized by different cultures.

Fig. 6: Mosaic by Gaudi in Park Guëll, Barcelona: mosaic stones of various kinds contributing to an overall shape.

A multicultural church can have a missionary influence on those segments of society that feel connected to the cultural expression and language of one of its constituting groups. People of the same or similar origin who experience equal integration challenges in the host country are offered a monocultural point of contact.

Multicultural churches attach importance to the fact that its members can preserve their own culture and identity, but at the same time develop contacts with others that are different. In this way, two of the basic needs of migrants are covered, namely to relate to a linguistic and cultural framework considered as home and, on the other hand, to connect with their new society in order to gain opportunities for future life by developing contacts and cross-cultural skills.[10] Cross-cultural contacts are taking place between groups and among individuals, but the latter is limited because not all members of the congregation speak a common language. If somebody, after an integration phase, is looking for a setting closer to the host culture, he or she can find it in a different group inside the same church.

---

[10] Eberhard Werner, "Migration und Flucht – Diaspora als Lebensmitte: Einleitende missiologische Überlegungen," *Evangelische Missiologie* 32, 2 (2016), p. 91.

The framework of the church as a whole often aligns itself with the host culture, because all members have a certain degree of experience in this culture. The movement "MissionMosaik," for example, emphasises this aspect and promotes so called "mono-multicultural" churches. This term describes a variant of the model presented here. "Mono" refers to the host culture which should remain clearly recognisable, and "multi" to the various backgrounds of people the church welcomes and serves.[11]

The atmosphere of a multicultural church can be compared with holidays in a club hotel or holiday resort. The whole family or group spends their holidays in the same facility. Every now and then they meet to spend time together which strengthens their sense of belonging, for example for meals in the large dining room or for special excursions. But most of the time, individuals will split off for activities of their own interest in their favourite setting: different sports and leisure offers, foreign restaurants, etc.

If the overall framework of the church is based on the host culture, the church needs to develop a high degree of sensitivity towards minorities and avoid the impression that the local culture appears superior. Any form of cultural domination undermines the credibility of the Gospel.[12] It is crucial to avoid this danger in joint worship services and in any other aspect of church life. This is especially true in the leadership team of the church, which should be made up of the leaders of the various cultural groups. In addition to his or her responsibility for their own group, every member of the leadership team should also have a role in the church as a whole. This is an important but by far not the only prerequisite for developing a sense of belonging for all members of the church.

Multicultural churches that want to promote cohesion need to deal with possible tensions between the cultural identity of the groups and the profile of the church. Diversity may include theological questions and leadership styles. A healthy way forward is to provide a clear orientation on the one hand, and be ready to learn and to make compromises in non-central issues on the other.

---

[11] Stephen Beck & Frauke Bielefeldt, *Mission Mosaikkirche: Wie Gemeinden sich für Migranten und Flüchtlinge öffnen* (Giessen: Brunnen, 2017), at http://missionmosaik.org/en. The term "mosaic" is applied here primarily to the appearance of the congregation and not so much to the surrounding society.

[12] Frédéric de Coninck, "Confesser Dieu dans une situation de domination culturelle ?" in *L'Église, promesses et passerelles vers l'interculturalité?* ed. Frédéric de Coninck and Jean-Claude Girondin (Charols/Vaux-sur-Seine: Excelsis/Édifac, 2015), p. 119.

One of the greatest strengths of the multicultural model lies in the ministry among children and youths. The programs can be held in the language of the host country by grouping all children and youths together. Yet, families with a migration background receive little help in how to express faith in Jesus in their homes according to their own culture.

In the vision of Revelation 5:9-10, Jesus is presented as the saviour of people of very different origins. The ethnic identity of the individual persists, differences remain visible, but all believers engage in realising the common vision of the church.[13] Multicultural churches already reflect this reality to some degree: diversity is valued, but all members share in the honour of serving God together.[14]

Are Mixed Churches Really Necessary?

Two of the church models are intended for a mixed community. But is that desirable at all? The question is raised by different sides. Some congregations fear losing their identity. This applies equally to indigenous congregations trying to uphold the values of the host country, as well as to international congregations considering themselves as guardians of their ethnic and / or spiritual heritage.

Missionary strategies, which rely on the homogeneous unit principle in order to promote fast-growing church planting movements, are taking the same direction. Initiatives, such as "Fresh Expressions" also encourage the creation of congregations for new, narrowly defined target groups.

Homogeneity or Mixing?

Reservations against building homogeneous churches are raised for theological, strategic and social reasons. In his book on building healthy multi-ethnic churches, Mark DeYmaz writes that the credibility of homogeneous churches is at stake when they preach God's love for all peoples but it cannot be observed in their church life.[15] He refers to the dynamics

---

[13] Roger Standing, "Before the Throne of God: Multicultural Church as Eschatological Anticipation," *Missio Africanus: Journal of African Missiology* 1, 2 (January 2016), p. 24, at http://missioafricanus.org/wp-content/uploads/MAJAM/1-2/Standing_Be fore-the-Throne.pdf.

[14] Jean-Claude Girondin, "Oser l'Église interculturelle," in De Coninck & Girondin, *L'Église, promesses et passerelles vers l'interculturalité?*, p. 18-19.

[15] Mark DeYmaz, *Building a Healthy Multi-ethnic Church: Mandate, Commitments, and Practices of a Diverse Congregation* (San Francisco: Jossey-Bass, 2007), p. 14.

released by the Holy Spirit in the heterogeneous church of Antioch in Acts 11 and 13.[16]

From the letter to the Ephesians DeYmaz develops a theology for mixed churches: "A fresh and more comprehensive look at the letter will challenge popular wisdom concerning church growth and, specifically, the future effectiveness of the homogeneous-unit principle."[17] Why, according to Ephesians, should one prefer intermixing? A mixed church exemplifies that the dividing wall between different people groups has fallen (Eph 2:14), that Jesus created in himself one new man out of them (2:15) and that he reconciled them with one another (2:16). They now share God's household in the Spirit (2:22) and are one body (3:6). Above all, a mixed church better reflects the manifold wisdom of God (3:10).[18]

In practice, it can be observed that a monocultural approach is often better suited for the perceived needs of a target group. Which European pastor would mobilise the prayer group of the church because a member of African descent has been followed by a black cat on his way home, and two days later was attacked by a black bird flying against his window in the middle of the night?[19]

On the other hand, a homogeneous church confines its growth potential to that part of society that corresponds to its cultural framework. Such an assembly, after an initial phase, contributes little to the integration of its members, can even increase the isolation, and, sometimes unconsciously, nurture a certain ethnocentrism, even racism.

Diaspora churches whose membership consists of a relatively homogeneous migrant group are facing a limited future perspective. In his book on the refugee crisis, Patrick Johnstone mentions his broad-based observation that such congregations have a lifespan of only one and a half generations.[20] According to him, the following generations want to assimilate into the new environment.

---

[16] Idem, p. 19-24.

[17] Idem, p. 27. The argument is developed further on pages 27-35.

[18] The original argument of the Apostle Paul refers to the unity between Jews and non-Jews, but it can be applied in a broader sense to other people groups as well.

[19] Example related by Afe Adogame, *The African Christian Diaspora: New Currents and Emerging Trends in World Christianity* (London/New York: Bloomsbury Academics, 2013), p. 91-92.

[20] Patrick Johnstone & Dean Merrill, *Serving God in a Migrant Crisis: Ministry to People on the Move* (Colorado Springs: GMI, 2016), p. 96.

How then should the homogeneous-unit principle be applied? It maintains an important role in evangelism:[21] people who are about to discover what Jesus has done for them, do not immediately develop an understanding of a mixed church that runs against ethnic prejudices. Groups or cells that welcome new people may therefore retain the characteristics of a single culture in order to facilitate the first steps of integration and discipleship. However, the Church as a whole should strive for a heterogeneous composition.[22] Only that way can it express the new identity of believers in Jesus, which ultimately does not depend on skin colour, culture or social class.[23]

On the Move in the Mosaic

Actually, no church completely exemplifies one of the models described above; it normally also draws some elements from another model. All transitions between the models are possible. The three idealised models can be represented as the corners of a triangle (see fig. 7 on the next page). Each church can be located at a certain point inside the triangle, depending on its vision and its history.

If a church has been started in a fairly homogenous environment or targets a particular group, it normally develops a monocultural mode of functioning. In the scheme above, it is situated towards the left-hand corner. If the focus on a homogeneous unit or a specific segment of society is emphasised, the congregation moves further to the left, i.e. towards the monocultural corner of figure 7.

---

[21] Timothy Yates, "David Bosch, South African Context, Universal Missiology: Ecclesiology in the Emerging Missionary Paradigm," *International Bulletin of Missionary Research* vol. 33, n° 2 (April 2009), p. 75, at www.internationalbulletin.org/issues/2009-02/2009-02-072-yates.pdf.

[22] Klaus Schönberg, "Die interkulturelle Gemeinde: Gemeindeaufbau und Evangelisation in der zunehmend multikulturellen Bevölkerung deutscher Ballungsräume," Master thesis, UNISA, 2012, p. 73-74, at http://uir.unisa.ac.za/bitstream/handle/10500/15420/Sch%C3%B6nbergK_MTH_01.2014.pdf.

[23] David Stevens, "God's New Humanity in Diaspora: A Church of the Nations and for the Nations," in *Diaspora Missiology: Reflections on Reaching the Scattered Peoples of the World*, eds. Michael Pocock and Enoch Wan (Pasadena: William Carey Library, 2015), p. 125.

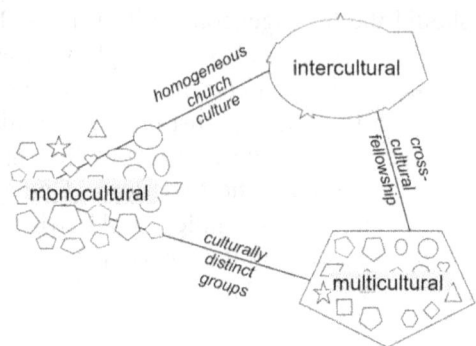

Fig. 7: Transitions between the Different Church Models.

However, when people from a different cultural background (or from other subcultures or social classes) join the church, it will move towards the right corner. A cross-cultural fellowship develops, a feature that characterises both the intercultural and the multicultural models.

At that point, two possibilities open up. If people mainly of diverse origins join the church, it will not be able to consider every cultural feature. The church will tend towards a mixing of cultural elements and therefore move towards the intercultural model (to the upper right corner of the triangle). The characteristics of the original church culture are gradually replaced by a mixed congregation culture, but the way of functioning will remain homogeneous in every part of church life (upper side of the triangle).

If distinct language groups form as part of the church, it develops a multicultural character (towards the lower right corner of the triangle). A similar phenomenon occurs if an indigenous and an international church merge.[24]

Each church, therefore, will follow its own path in the triangle, determined by the vision of the leadership on the one hand and by the background of people joining it on the other. According to my observations, this path is rarely straightforward and requires regular re-evaluation, because the mosaic of cultures inside the church and around it continues to evolve.[25]

---

[24] André Pownall uses the expression "bicultural" for the merge of two churches. André Pownall, "Stratégies pour l'intégration de minorités ethniques dans les Églises évangéliques," in *Vivre la diversité: L'Église dans une société multiculturelle*, ed. Evert van de Poll (Paris: Croire-Publications, 2011), p. 54.

[25] An interesting example of how a church can compare its vision to the different models and reflect on next steps is described by Lukas Etter for the case of GPMC in Thun (Switzerland). Lukas Etter, "Kirche in der multikulturellen Gesellschaft

An important guideline for the orientation of the church in the triangle are the strengths and challenges of the models. Normally the leadership will choose its preferred model depending on the strengths. However, for a healthy development it is essential to face the corresponding challenges and find appropriate solutions. Table 1 at the end of this chapter presents an overview of the strengths and challenges of each model, listed according to cultural and life-related aspects (cultural characteristics, atmosphere and self-understanding, integration and cross-cultural contacts) and important church building features (leadership, younger generation, evangelism).

We Need One Another

Due to the mosaic of cultures in our society, no local church alone can meet the diverse needs of people living in its neighbourhood. This is of course true for monocultural congregations which focus on a specific social segment, but also for the intercultural model (the cultural mixture of the church means an uprooting for all members), as well as for the multicultural model (the languages and cultures covered by the groups in the church will always be outnumbered by the cultural diversity around it). All churches therefore need complementarity.

This also applies to the relationship between indigenous and international churches. Some churches that emerged from recent migrations vividly express their anticipation of Jesus' presence. They often have a more developed prayer life and passion for evangelism. Therefore, joint programs with international churches can bring fresh air to indigenous churches in these and other areas.

On the other hand, several international churches have expressed the desire to cooperate with indigenous ones. In a seminar African pastors living in Switzerland have expressed the desire to receive help for leadership training, legal advice for starting a church and hints for obtaining affordable halls. They also appreciated guidance on how they can evangelise in the language of the host country and with cultural sensitivity.

All churches, both indigenous and international, need to experience cross-cultural fellowship and unity in diversity. Discovering this reality is a key issue for theology: A greater and more balanced understanding of

---

von heute: Eine kontextuelle Evaluation verschiedener Modelle christlicher Gemeinden zum Umgang mit Menschen aus anderen Kulturen," IGW-Abschlussarbeit, 2015, at www.igw.edu/assets/data/Abschlussarbeiten/Kirche_in_ der_multi kulturellen_Gesellschaft_von_heute_Lukas_Etter_2015.pdf.

God's character and plans depends on it. Isolating oneself from the environment is not a permanent solution, although some people would prefer the familiar atmosphere of the church that protects them from the complexity of multicultural society today. Monocultural congregations have two main options for opening up: either to take concrete steps for a greater intermixing of its attendance or to build contacts with other churches from a different background.

Develop Mixing

Building Contacts and Fellowship

How can a church attract people from a different cultural background? An excellent opportunity is provided by multicultural celebrations: the church encourages its members to bring friends, neighbours and work colleagues with them for a relaxed program with music, games, a brief input and a meal. Celebrations are also an excellent way to invite people from the street or from a centre of asylum seekers. Christian feasts are also wonderful occasions. In many other cultures, people speak without shame about religious practices. They are amazed at the silence of Western society in this area. Why not fill this void and offer the opportunity to discover what Christians are celebrating, e.g. at Christmas or Easter? One consequence might be that we will be invited to the religious celebrations of our guests, a wonderful opportunity to further deepen the contact. At other times, a church can organise multicultural events without any reason other than building contacts.

Other opportunities to make contacts are sports or activities with children. A social involvement that addresses the perceived needs of people around the church is another possibility. If such an activity is appropriate and authentic, without hidden intentions, it can also touch people from a different background than the specific target group.

If the church offers translations or small groups in other languages, Christians from other countries can join. A mixed-language approach is a major asset for creating cross-cultural contacts.

As soon as people from different backgrounds feel welcome in the church, they will also invite their friends and a dynamic can develop. For this to happen, visitors should be able to build cross-cultural contacts and friendships with several people. This is only possible if church members show genuine interest in new people.

Hospitality is key, especially if it is not only offered in the church, but also in the homes of the members. Many migrants miss the hospitality they value from their countries. Open houses are particularly precious on occasions like Christmas, when many indigenous families withdraw even more than usual.

Reducing Uneasiness

People arriving in a new environment normally feel insecure. This is the case for migrants visiting an indigenous church, but also for locals who want to discover an international congregation. Therefore, visitors are happy for hints on how to behave. In a mixed audience it is best to offer different options and explain them: during prayer moments, one can pray loudly or quietly; during worship time, people may stand up or remain seated, etc.

In cross-cultural contacts, a few requirements apply to indigenous people and migrants alike: develop a healthy self-image, build cross-cultural skills, dare to talk to other people, show authentic appreciation and live reconciliation. However, since the sensitivities of Western cultures and of relational cultures from the so-called majority world often differ considerably,[26] I would like to give a few hints to indigenous and international churches separately.

Indigenous Churches

How can one engage in conversation with visitors of a different origin? Some Westerners are tempted to ask a whole catalogue of questions, which may remind the visitor of an interview with the immigration officer. Others want to avoid such mistakes and their caution makes them speechless. One possible topic to start a conversation with is to ask what our guests like about our country and what they miss. Some visitors will mention their family, which is highly valued in many cultures. Others, such as war victims, who have painful memories of their lost family, can talk about something else.

As already mentioned, it is important that a new person gets into contact with several church members. New people will only stay if friendships in the church increase their status in the eyes of their present friends and

---

[26] One particularly important issue is the sensitivity of honour-shame oriented cultures on one hand and of justice-guilt oriented cultures on the other. This requires particular attention in the mosaic of culture. See Johannes and Barbara Müller, "Harmonische Beziehungen im Mosaik der Kulturen," in Ruth Lienhard, *Ehre, Scham und Harmonie: Interkulturelle Kontakte und ihre Herausforderungen* (Nürnberg: VTR, 2016), p. 78-101.

family and if they feel accepted, valued and desired.[27] Their self-esteem can be built by offering tasks with real responsibility. For this reason, international congregations often provide their members with a wide range of important tasks.[28] An indigenous church that wants to welcome immigrant Christians should carefully consider which responsibilities it can offer. If someone gets involved, it is important to give helpful feedbacks and communicate genuine appreciation.

International Churches

What should an international church consider if it wants to receive more locals? Westerners usually appreciate a clearly defined framework. It is important that programs start more or less at the indicated time so that visitors will not be confused and not come back. The ushers would normally suggest a seat to an Asian or African visitor, but would rather let Europeans choose themselves in order to avoid the feeling of being boxed in. It can be helpful if a church member of similar age chooses a seat next to the newcomers, welcomes them and discreetly assists them in overcoming uncertainties. If visitors are publicly welcomed, it is worthwhile explaining to them what to expect (e.g. getting up and pronouncing the name) and why ("because we are delighted that you are here and we want to greet you").

To what extent Westerners join a church and participate actively also depends on whether they can build a trustful relationship with the pastor and leaders. Some Western societies have developed hierarchies and titles, but others are used to accessible superiors. In such a setting, a discreet leadership and contacts of the pastor with church members are appreciated. Trust is also built by a transparent financial management, without excessive calls for funds that may be perceived as an attack on personal freedom.

---

[27] David R. Dunaetz, "Three Models of Acculturation: Applications for Developing a Church Planting Strategy among Diaspora Populations," in Pocock and Wan, *Diaspora Missiology*, p. 143, at https://papers.ssrn.com/sol3/papers.cfm?abstract_id=2668916.

[28] Tasks and responsibilities include, among others, ushering, playing in a music group, singing in one of the choirs, joining the prayer warriors, sound and multimedia, leading church service, Sunday school for adults, women's, youth's or children's ministries.

Contacts with Churches of Other Cultures

As the number of international churches is increasing, there are more and more points of contact with indigenous congregations. Sharing the same infrastructure is not sufficient to establish encouraging relationships. On the contrary, if discussions mainly revolve around noise, cleanliness and schedules, frustration is foreseeable on both sides.[29] Intransigence on the part of indigenous Christians can easily be interpreted as an expression of racism.

Therefore, it is important that inter-church contacts do not remain restricted to areas of potential conflict, but include joint activities that will send out constructive signals. I have already mentioned some of the opportunities of multicultural celebrations. If they are to build contacts between churches of different cultures, a few additional points need to be considered. Each participating church should be involved according to its strengths and feel that its contribution is equally appreciated. Only then will the celebration produce mutual stimulations. Significant and visible responsibilities must be evenly distributed. It is important to take enough time for joint preparations, to carefully set the framework and to clarify mutual expectations.

Through programs that consider these points, contacts and confidence will grow deeper. The conviction will increase not to do separately what we can do together, even if multi-cultural cooperation "will always be the harder path, and ... needs a high degree of intentionality and perseverance."[30] Such cooperation will increase the credibility of the participating churches in our present day multicultural societies. Joint evangelism, for example, can benefit from this appreciation. Furthermore, by combining language and culture skills of the involved churches, people of various backgrounds can be reached and invited into a personal relationship with Jesus.

Church unions, composed of indigenous and international congregations, can provide an important framework for cross-cultural inter-church relationships. Within a church union, the member churches share central beliefs and certain forms of organisation. This common foundation promotes cooperation to an extent that is not possible in a loose local network.

---

[29] Johannes Reimer, *Multikultureller Gemeindebau: Versöhnung leben* (Marburg an der Lahn: Francke, 2011), p. 62.

[30] Standing, "Before the Throne of God," p. 26, 27.

Ministry among the Second Generation

A major test for cross-cultural cooperation is the ministry among the second generation. Christian children and youths who experience different cultural standards in their homes and at school must learn to express their faith in both settings. Therefore, in all international churches the youth ministry should have a cross-cultural orientation. A church that is based on the multicultural model provides this under its own roof, because it already lives a cultural diversity.

A church that follows the mono- or intercultural model will have to seek contacts with other churches or Christian organisations if its children and young people should meet Christians of their age from the local culture. Such joint programs are an excellent opportunity for young Christians to learn from one another and grow in faith. This requires a solid foundation of trust on both sides: no one leaves his children to just anybody. Joint activities for young people are a powerful expression of successful cross-cultural relationships between Christians and churches of different backgrounds.

Conclusion

At times, the mosaic of cultures in our societies seems to be chaotic and incoherent. The three basic models presented in this article can provide churches with an orientation and stimulate their reflections about the direction in which they want to develop.

Regardless of the option that is chosen, developing relationships between culturally diverse Christians and churches requires many steps, marked by perseverance, sensitivity and mutual respect. The result of such processes will honour our Lord Jesus until he completes his plan with us. This perspective should encourage us to take the next steps in this direction – whether they are uplifting or sometimes a bit tedious.

Chapter 7 – The Mosaic of Cultures

Summary Table of the Models

Table 1: Strengths (+) and *challenges* (→) of the models

Model	Cultural characteristics	Atmosphere, self-understanding	Integration, cross-cultural contacts
Monocultural	+ One culture clearly put forward + Focus group is consciously chosen + Contextualisation of message and style → *Reflect own cultural characteristics*	+ Offer a home in an environment that feels foreign + Cultivate values of the culture of origin → *Risk of withdrawal to what is known and traditional*	+ Assistance for new members upon arrival in a foreign environment + Often aware of the need for completion → *Risk of isolation within society* → *Cross-cultural fellowship can be experienced only in contact with other churches* → *Building of trustworthy relationships with churches of a different cultural background*
Intercultural	+ Mixture of cultures ideally in all components of church life + Cultural styles remain in the background → *Awareness of cultural characteristics*	+ Cosmopolitan; for everybody; part of something greater + Fellowship across boundaries → *Risk of uprooting because the church specific mixture is alien for everybody*	+ Integration is mutual and towards a common church culture + A common language of communication (occasionally translation from the main church language to the language of the host country) + Attractive for mixed couples → *Cross-cultural fellowship can be experienced between members* → *Contact with churches in the host country of a different cultural background*
Multicultural	+ Several cultures are a part of church life + Diversity through the groups, unity through joint programs → *Realistic view of cultural characteristics*	+ Room for several cultures + Variety; many facets → *Risk of withdrawal to one's own group with well-known framework*	+ Different degrees of integration into the host culture are possible through culturally diverse groups → *Translations are crucial in joint programs due to the absence of a common language* → *Efforts for organisation and communication between the groups* → *Cross-cultural fellowship can be experienced between groups, sometimes between members (depending on language knowledge)*

Model	Leadership	Second generation	Evangelism
Monocultural	+ Leaders with competence in the culture of origin → Leaders with experience in the host culture → Leaders must bridge theological, ethnic, social and political differences in the church	+ Connection to the spirituality of the parents and the country of origin → Learn to live as a Christian in the host country → Bilingual programs for children and young people in the languages of the host country and the country of origin → Joint programs with other churches	+ Primarily people of the same culture as the church who find a safe haven + Discipleship can start with issues relevant in the culture and context → Cross-cultural evangelism remains exceptional
Intercultural	+ Leaders with intercultural competence and sensitivity → Mixed leadership team without cultural predominance → Offer honourable roles for all leaders	+ Grow up in the setting of intercultural fellowship → Learn to understand cultural characteristics → Learn to live as a Christian both in surrounding society and in the culture of the parents → Bilingual programs if the languages of the church and of the host country are different	+ Open intercultural atmosphere + Mixed teams for outreach → Vision for cultural minorities in the neighbourhood of the church → Mixed culture of the church is alien to people around the church
Multicultural	+ Leadership team consisting of the leaders of the cultural groups → Offer honourable roles for all group leaders in the church as a whole → Develop the vision for the church as a whole	+ Grow up in the setting of cultural diversity + Well established programs in the language of the host country for all children and young people together → Learn to live as a Christian in the culture and language of origin of the parents	+ Groups can evangelise and disciple according to their cultural background + Mixed teams for outreach and follow-up in cultural groups are both possible → Contacts with people whose culture is not represented among the groups of the church

Further Reading

Adogame, Afe, *The African Christian Diaspora: New Currents and Emerging Trends in World Christianity* (London/New York: Bloomsbury Academics, 2013).

DeYmaz, Mark, *Building a Healthy Multi-ethnic Church: Mandate, Commitments, and Practices of a Diverse Congregation* (San Francisco: Jossey-Bass, 2007).

Johnstone, Patrick & Merrill, Dean, *Serving God in a Migrant Crisis: Ministry to People on the Move* (Colorado Springs: GMI, 2016).

Pocock, Michael & Wan, Enoch, eds., *Diaspora Missiology: Reflections on Reaching the Scattered Peoples of the World* (Pasadena: William Carey Library, 2015).

Yates, Timothy, "David Bosch, South African Context, Universal Missiology: Ecclesiology in the Emerging Missionary Paradigm," *International Bulletin of Missionary Research* vol. 33, n° 2 (April 2009), p. 75, at www.internationalbulletin.org/issues/2009-02/2009-02-072-yates.pdf.

Sources of Photos

All photos are available on Wikimedia under the Creative Commons license.

Fig. 2: Author: Codex, September 2, 2012, "Gaudi, Parc Güell: Wall covered with trencadis," at https://commons.wikimedia.org/wiki/File:Trencadis-Gaudi-1195.jpg.

Fig. 4: Author: Godmeister, January 22, 2008, "Mosaic on the ceiling of the hypostyle room, Park Güell," at https://commons.wikimedia.org/wiki/File:Barcelona_29-04-2006_11-29-38.jpg.

Fig. 6: Author: Alex Proimos, December 21, 2009, "Mosaic Dragon at the Entrance to Parc Güell," at https://commons.wikimedia.org/wiki/File:Mosaic_Dragon_at_the_Entrance_to_Parc_G%C3%BCell_%28420921 4343%29.jpg.

PART TWO

COMMUNICATING THE GOSPEL

IN EUROPE

Chapter 8
What Is Evangelism?
Biblical Hints for the European Context

Léo Lehmann[1]

Introduction

Whatever the definition of evangelism, it is a practical issue. The biblical and theological conclusions should have a direct influence on the life of the church. And inversely, the practices of a group influence its way of reading the Bible.

But even if the practical considerations are important, our evangelical tradition is firmly rooted in the conviction that Scripture has authority over all matters of faith and life.[2] When defining evangelism, we should therefore refer to the biblical text. However, we should not be blind to the influence of the context on our Bible reading. Our interpretative reflexes, just like our practical habits, are very liable to affect the way we understand the Word of God. They could even falsify our understanding or urge us to an inadequate selection of aspects to be taken into account. How can we arrive then at an adequate biblical understanding of evangelism?

We cannot provide a perfectly neutral interpretation of the biblical text. Probably the most promising way of "neutralising," at least partly, some of the presuppositions of different origins that may disorient our endeavour, is to clarify them. For this reason, we will examine a certain number of problems debated today. Then, being conscious of this context and its influence, we will present what seems to us the main biblical data on evangelism. Finally, we will propose some conclusions about the manner the collected findings should model our way of doing evangelism in Europe.

---

[1] This paper was presented during a Master seminar on evangelism directed by the professors Christophe Paya and Bernard Huck at the *Faculté libre de théologie évangélique de Vaux-sur-Seine* on March 17, 2016.

[2] See for example the Lausanne Covenant (1974), at www.lausanne.org, or the Statement of Faith of the World Evangelical Alliance, at www.worldea.org/who weare/statementoffaith.

What Is Evangelism?

First, we have to define precisely what we understand by "evangelism." This English term is derived from the Greek verb *euangelizô* (54 occurrences in the NT) and its cognates (*euangelion* [76 times] and *euangelistes* [3 times]). Generally, this verb denotes the announcement of good news. In the specific use by several biblical verses it means the proclamation of what we call the Gospel, the Good News. On the basis of this verb, one could define evangelism in summary as verbal proclamation of the Good News.

However, two difficulties arise. The first is biblical: what is exactly the meaning that the biblical text gives to this idea of proclamation of the Good News? How is this concept used? Which other concepts are related to it? It is to this difficulty that we devote the core of this study.

The second difficulty is historical and has to be rapidly examined here. During a certain epoch, the term evangelism denoted a verbal and monocultural communication of the Gospel, as opposed to the concept of mission considered as a cross-cultural communication of the Gospel.[3] When speaking of mission or evangelism one did not distinguish the ministry of individuals but essentially their relationship to the targeted public. This distinction has weakened today as the proclamation of the Gospel spreads from all continents to all continents.

Furthermore, the term mission has the tendency to take on an ever more encompassing meaning today. Shortly after the Lausanne Congress in 1974, John Stott wrote: "The word mission ... is properly a comprehensive word, embracing everything that God sends his people into the world to do."[4] One can find two main reasons for this widening of the meaning of the term mission. The first is that these "far away evangelists," called missionaries, have faced different needs from those at home and have tried to respond to them.[5] Missions have thus been forced to work in response to the social realities of their "mission field."[6] The second reason is related to

---

[3] Hannes Wiher, "Qu'est-ce que la mission?" in *La mission de l'Église au 21ᵉ siècle*, ed. Hannes Wiher (Charols: Excelsis, 2010), p. 18; David J. Bosch, *Transforming Mission: Paradigm Shifts in Theology of Mission* (Maryknoll: Orbis, 1991), p. 409f.

[4] John R.W. Stott, *Christian Mission in the Modern World* (London: Falcon, 1975), p. 58.

[5] The ambiguity of this response resides naturally in the "civilizing" character of certain missionary enterprises which imposed answers to needs that were not those of the targeted populations.

[6] Having said this, many who have practised evangelism in their own context, have also known how to be sensitive to the needs of their contemporaries. The creation of the Salvation Army by William and Catherine Booth is an example.

the contact of the Gospel with other cultures through missions. If in a mono-cultural context the church can sometimes rely on the syntheses that she has made between Gospel and culture, the contact with other cultures does not allow this possibility. Admittedly, there have been attempts to impose a Western Gospel in many places, but where the Gospel has taken root, some recipients question today a mission that has sometimes neglected the implications of the social realities of the Gospel.[7] Today, missions are at the centre of this questioning, which leads them to envisage their role in a more holistic way.

Since the notion of evangelism is linked to that of mission, the evolution of the latter does not leave the former unchanged. Some are calling for a unifying of the two concepts into a concept surpassing the limits imposed so far. In this view, mission and evangelism are considered identical.[8] The new concept would then comprise the preaching of the Gospel, the salvation of souls (or not) and social action. This evolution seems dependent on the first fact that we have indicated, the globalisation of the preaching of the Gospel, a fact that blurs the distinction between what constitutes an "evangelist" as opposed to a "missionary." Mission and evangelism are thus two interchangeable terms. It seems to us a very welcome development that the concept of the mission of the Church should be expanded beyond the verbal proclamation of the Gospel aimed at the conversion of sinners. This evolution opens the way to a greater integration by the totality of Christians of the fact that they are in this world to do or be something in relation to God's project. The Gospel has implications for the whole life of all Christians. We are all in mission. Nevertheless, the biblical text distinguishes different aspects of this sending into the world. The reduction of mission to evangelism or of evangelism to mission seems to give little

---

[7] See for this subject the conclusion of the Lausanne Movement, for example in the Manila Manifesto, which affirms in paragraph 4: "The Gospel and social responsibility:" "We repent that the narrowness of our concerns and vision has often kept us from proclaiming the lordship of Jesus Christ over all of life, private and public, local and global. We determine to obey his command to 'seek first the kingdom of God and his righteousness' (Matt 6:33)." "Manila Manifesto (1989)," at www.lausanne.org. African authors like Barnabé Assohoto are critical of the influence of Western Christianity in Africa, which was more concerned with what one was saved *from* than what one was save *for*, both individually and socially. Barnabé Assohoto, *Le salut en Jésus-Christ dans la théologie africaine. Vol. 3: Le discours africain du salut* (Cotonou: CART, 2002), p. 52-53.

[8] See David J. Bosch, "Evangelism: Currents and Cross-Currents in Theology Today," *International Bulletin of Missionary Research* 11, 3 (1987), p. 98.

expression to this reality. Methodologically, it seems important to us to distinguish between the two things. Evangelism can be seen as the core from where the whole of mission radiates.[9] It can take place in all the dimensions of what the Church does in the world. However, biblically and historically, we believe that the term is related more specifically to a form of initiation into the reality of the kingdom of God.[10] Evangelism concerns the beginning of the pathway of faith. As such, this domain is distinct from mission as a whole and seems to deserve to be studied by itself.

So, in studying evangelism in the Bible, our first question is: How does the Bible speak of the Church's action (within the framework of the Church's mission) for the purpose of enabling new persons to understand and hopefully respond to the Gospel?

Some Questions to Ask

Having said this, we have to present some underlying problems, which feed the debate and which are liable to affect our reading of the biblical text. What, then, are the questions with which we approach the text? Perhaps we cannot give a clear answer to every one of these questions, but in this way we can clarify the alternatives facing us, and requiring us to take up a position, implicitly or explicitly,

The first question is the one about the message we intend to transmit. What is the Gospel? The question is very broad but the answer is important. From what point can we say that the whole Gospel has been announced? Is it sufficient to announce the Cross? Could evangelism be an on-going process during a whole life?

Once the message is established, the following question is about the necessity of its transmission. Do we have to evangelise? Does the message merit being propagated? Are we not daring to proselytise, an activity abhorred by our society? And if we choose to do it anyway, what are the reasons? Are we obeying an order? Do we have other motives?

If we have to evangelise, we can also ask who are the agents of evangelism? Who has to announce the Gospel? Is evangelism the work of some specialists called by God or is it the task of the whole Church? If evangelism depends on the Church, is it the task of all the members or can she delegate it to specialised ministries? And what role does God play in all this?

---

[9] Bosch, "Evangelism: Currents and Cross-Currents," p. 100.

[10] See William J. Abraham, *The Logic of Evangelism* (Grand Rapids: Eerdmans, 1989), p. 13, 55, 69.

Fourthly, who is the target? Does evangelism have to concentrate on unreached peoples? Does it concern people groups or individuals? What do we mean when we talk about making disciples of all nations? We seem to have progressively abandoned the idea of a Christendom that knows the message of Christ, but do we know to what degree our contemporaries need the Gospel?

What, then, is the aim of this evangelism? Are we simply seeking to inform people? Are we aiming to convince, to provoke a change in the person we are facing? From what point on do we consider having finished the task of evangelism?

Finally, we should consider the broad question of the means employed. Which methods seem right and relevant? Which ones are efficient? Do we have to go to the others or do we rather have to attract them to us? What is the place of social action in evangelism? Is it radically distinct from evangelism? And ultimately, is evangelism a matter of doing or being? These are some of the main questions which guide us in our approach to the biblical text.

Biblical Data

Surely, we cannot take into account all biblical findings which might refine our conception of evangelism. Nevertheless, it seems possible to set out some main guidelines of how the Bible speaks about what we call evangelism. We shall tackle the themes mentioned in the order in which they appear in the Bible.

God's Missionary Nature

We have expressed the desire to distinguish between mission and evangelism. However, we believe that we have to start by considering the missionary nature of God in order to be able to define evangelism biblically. Like the mission of the Church, evangelism has its source in God's action in the world. Thus, evangelism has to be situated within the scheme of creation – fall – redemption that many Bible scholars discern in the Bible.

Following the creation of the universe and of man, humanity has separated itself from intimate fellowship with God through the fall. Creator and creation find themselves in rupture (Gen 1-3). But rapidly after this rupture, God seeks the human being and wants to restore the relationship. He makes a covenant with the human race, particularly with Abraham (Gen 12:1-3). Behind this covenant with a man and later a particular people, the whole of humanity is in view. Israel, the people of God, is called to attract all the nations and be a blessing for them. Besides several particular stories (for example Rahab, Ruth, Naaman), the prophets clearly manifest God's concern for the whole of humanity (see for example Isa 45:22, or the book of Jonah).[11]

This process has been described as the mission of God (*missio Dei*), a concept that has been abundantly discussed by missiologists during recent decades.[12] What the Church is going to do in this world, finds its origin in the heart and action of God. Thus, evangelism cannot bypass God's action.[13] We will see it later more deeply through other themes: evangelism is God's work accomplished through individuals.[14] Behind the action of God's people and through his own action in the life of his people, the Creator wants to manifest himself and enter into a relationship with them.

Jesus and the Message of the Gospel

Coming of Jesus Christ

This reality of the prevalence of God's action and his desire to meet human beings reveals itself at its climax in the coming of Jesus Christ on earth. In Jesus Christ God comes personally to meet humanity and takes on himself the human condition (Phil 2:7-8). He meets humanity in all its depth, going as far as to identify himself with it (Heb 2:17).

Jesus carries a message for those who want to hear it. This message, which is usually called the "Gospel" or "Good News," consists of announcing the coming of the kingdom of God.[15] The concept of the kingdom of God (we do not have the space to describe it here in detail), seems to be a central element of the preaching of the Good News by Jesus of Nazareth. This kingdom manifests itself in his preaching and his acts.

---

[11] For a more detailed discussion of the question whether mission exists in the OT, see for example Walter C. Kaiser, Jr., *Mission in the Old Testament: Israel as a Light to the Nations* (Grand Rapids: Baker, 2000); Siegbert Riecker, *Mission im Alten Testament? Ein Forschungsüberblick mit Auswertung* (Frankfurt a.M.: Otto Lembeck, 2008).

[12] See for example Christopher J.H. Wright, *The Mission of God: Unlocking the Bible's Grand Narrative* (Downers Grove: IVP, 2006).

[13] Abraham, *The Logic of Evangelism*, p. 100.

[14] James I. Packer, "What is Evangelism: Evangelism and Theology," in *Theological Perspectives on Church Growth*, ed. Harvie M. Conn (Nutley, NJ: Presbyterian & Reformed, 1976). p. 94.

[15] Abraham, *The Logic of Evangelism*, p. 58, 60, 69. See for example Matt 12:28.

Around him a community of people is formed who accompany him, close by or at a distance. In his teaching, in his relationships with those who are around him, by the miracles that he performs, Jesus announces a new reality. Thus, it is not only a verbal proclamation of a message. This message is incarnated in everything that Jesus is and does. God incarnates in Jesus in order to speak to us, and by this incarnation his message touches all the aspects of life.[16] The life of Jesus Christ is of crucial importance for his message.

However, by his presentation in the Gospels and in the rest of the NT, his death on the cross plays the central role. The last hours of Jesus' life occupy a large space in the Gospel narratives. Jesus had announced it: the Son of Man came to serve, and to give his life a ransom for many (Matt 20:28; Mark 10:45).[17] Beyond the political motives that led to his arrest and execution, the issues are much greater. Jesus accomplished the expiation for the sin that separated man from God. If all the details of this exceptional work were probably not immediately understood by his disciples, his resurrection attests with force that they can place their trust fully in him to seek first the kingdom of God and his righteousness (Matt 6:33). The theological reflections which link the teaching of the OT to the person and work of Jesus Christ are still to come in the epistles. But in Jesus the disciples know that God has come near them and has shown them that they can trust him in all aspects of life. We believe that it is here we find the Gospel.

A Message in a Person

The message is broad and has many implications, to such an extent that its transmission cannot touch all of its aspects, at least in a first approach. This leads to the temptation to choose certain aspects of the Gospel and to make them the core of our proclamation.[18] The tendency that some discern in Protestantism and the evangelical movement has been to concentrate on the proclamation of a Gospel of the Cross offering personal salvation to those who turn to God in repentance.[19] Others today concentrate rather on Jesus' life, seeking to transmit the Gospel by the witness of his acts.

---

[16] See for example John 1:14. The text of Luke 4:18-19 illustrates the global dimension of the Gospel proclaimed.
[17] See also Matt 26:26-29 and parallels.
[18] Abraham, *The Logic of Evangelism*, p. 95.
[19] Idem, p. 58.

Nevertheless, the whole Gospel as it is revealed in the person of Jesus has to be announced. In our European context, where most people hardly know anything about Christianity, this implies that evangelistic preaching has to involve a lot of teaching.[20] The Gospel as Jesus presents it is a message about God's nature, the seriousness of sin, the possibility to repent and to receive a new life, to find a new relationship with our Creator who is our Father. Our understanding of evangelism is too short, if it is reduced to rapidly throwing a message at somebody that tells only a small part of the richness of our faith.[21]

If there has to be proclamation of the Gospel, Jesus Christ in his whole life and his work has to be at the heart of it. Surely, we have to start at some place. However, our presentation of the Gospel should not make people attach themselves to a theological system or a particular formulation of the Christian faith. At the heart of the biblical message we do not just find a system for ascertaining forgiveness of sins and eternal life, no more than we only find an exhortation to act well in order to make God known. At the centre of the Gospel we find Jesus Christ. He is the Gospel. Our faith is linked to a living person whom we cannot confine within our formulations. Evidently, this person gives himself in his presence and his word, and this is the way we can know him. We can establish a coherent discourse about him. However, the reality of this living person whom we confess as God always exceeds what we can say about him. For this reason, caution is necessary before we can conclude that the Gospel has been transmitted. Like Philip, we can say above all: "Come and see" (John 1:46).

A Message that Has to Be Announced

These elements incline us to say that there is surely a message to be announced. If the first century of our era has really been witness to the events that we have described, this message has to be made known. Other elements will add to this necessity, but it seems to us that the message itself is fundamental to the principle of evangelistic proclamation. Even if this always goes beyond our formulations, there is surely a real content, a word that can be transmitted, and its exceptional and revolutionary nature insists that it should not be kept secret. When propagating the Gospel, we do not

---

[20] Packer, "What is Evangelism," p. 100f.

[21] After how much time with Jesus had the disciples been evangelised? Difficult to say. But surely, the process, which the Lord has initiated, has taken time and has not been without problems.

say what we have done or could do. We announce what God has done and continues to do.²² In this, it seems to us, the necessity of verbal witness that directs our acts to God is grounded. It is in the eschatological work of God inaugurated in Jesus Christ that the Church finds the source of evangelism.²³

We conclude here by noting that the life of Jesus reminds us also of the possibility of opposition to the message of the Gospel, of a God who acts in this world by love and truth. The message has to be transmitted, but we do not hold within our hands the nature of the response encountered.²⁴ Our European contemporaries love to study, calculate and refine their methods. For fear of rejection we are sometimes excessively careful. But how ever good our methods and careful our approaches, some prefer the darkness (John 3:19). Certainly we should reflect and act with wisdom, but we should also obey the call to start relying entirely on God.

Jesus Sending the Disciples

The short passage of Matthew 28:18-20 condenses former elements already present in the Gospel of Matthew, particularly in the great sending chapter of Matthew 10.²⁵ However, as regards to evangelism, the end of the Gospel of Matthew is probably the most frequently quoted text today.²⁶ Even when taking into account its parallels (Mark 16:15-18; Luke 24:46-

---

[22] Bosch, "Evangelism: Currents and Cross-Currents," p. 101.

[23] Abraham, *The Logic of Evangelism*, p. 92.

[24] See Christophe Paya, *Pour une Église en mouvement: Lecture du discours d'envoi en mission de Matthieu 9:35-11:1* (Charols: Excelsis, 2010), p. 255.

[25] More precisely Matthew 9:35 to 11:1. Idem, p. 245-246. This book proposes a detailed analysis of the entire discourse with the different conclusions that one can draw for missions. This text, which is more detailed than the end of the Gospel of Matthew, contains many instructive indications.

[26] George Hunsberger estimates that this fact is rather recent. In the course of history, other texts have been used, particularly John 3:16 in the early church period, Luke 14:23 in the medieval Roman Catholic Church, or else Romans 1:16-18 by the early Protestants. George R. Hunsberger, "Is There Biblical Warrant for Evangelism?" in *The Study of Evangelism: Exploring the Missional Practice of the Church*, eds. Paul W. Chilcote et Lacey C. Warner (Grand Rapids, MI: Eerdmans, 2008), p. 62. David Bosch signals that certain portions of the Church estimated for a long time that the program of Matthew 28:18-20 had been accomplished by the first disciples, and that this was no more their responsibility. David J. Bosch, "The Structure of Mission: An Exposition of Matthew 28:16-20," in Chilcote & Warner, *The Study of Evangelism*, p. 73.

49; John 20:21-22; Acts 1:8), it is nevertheless on this passage that we will base our reflection on the sending of Jesus' disciples.

Order or Promise?

Matthew 28:18-20 is usually called the "Great Commission." The propagation of the Gospel would then consist primarily of a command: "Go therefore and make disciples of all nations ..."

Today, some want to put into perspective this grounding of evangelism in a command. For George Hunsberger, it is doubly problematic to give heavy weight to the notion of command.[27] On the one hand, our contemporary society is such that it is often not productive to present a command to get people moving. Moreover the biblical text presents other motives. Surely, Matthew 28:18-20 contains an imperative (*matheteusate* "to make disciples"). Whether this pleases our modern ears or not, the Jesus who presents himself to the disciples is the one who has received all authority on earth and in heaven. He is in the position to give a command to his Church (we will return to its content later). But Jesus does not only give commands.

The text in Matthew contains also the promise of Jesus' presence with his disciples, every day to the end of the age. The promise could be surprising when one considers the narrative of the ascension in the other Gospels and the Acts. The fulfilment of Christ's promise has to be associated with the promise of the Spirit that one finds elsewhere. Luke 24:46-49, Acts 1:8 or John 20:21-22, and Jesus' final discourse to his disciples, during the Passover meal in John 14-16, carry this promise of the coming of the Spirit. From the witness of all these texts, it is the coming of the Spirit, through which Jesus becomes present in his Church, which must make it possible for the Gospel to be carried to the ends of the earth. The Spirit is the power which leads the apostles in the book of Acts (1:8).[28] The Spirit teaches the disciples what they will have to say (Luke 12:11-12).

This brings us back to the idea that God is the first to act in evangelism. It is the Spirit who makes this work possible.[29] God acts primarily, and Jesus sends his disciples whom he reminds that they cannot do anything

---

[27] Hunsberger, "Is There Biblical Warrant for Evangelism?" p. 60-64.

[28] In Acts 14:3, it is interesting to see how Luke, who gives much space to the action of the Holy Spirit, sees also the action of the one whom he calls "the Lord", who renders witness to the preached word.

[29] We should also mention John 6:44, which insists with force that God's action is necessary in order for Jesus to be recognised as who he is.

without him (John 15:5). Although Jesus gives many orders to his disciples, the proclamation of the Gospel rests again primarily on the work of God: work of the missionary God since the beginning, work of the incarnated God in Jesus Christ, and work of God in the Church through his Spirit.[30] This fact motivates Hunsberger and Bosch to suggest that the early church did not engage in mission because of a command, but because of the work of the Spirit.[31] Mission is the result of the successive "Pentecost" experiences in the book of Acts, as described by Luke, in terms of the fulfilment of Jesus' promise, the complete sense of which the Church has progressively understood. Thus, the command at the end of Matthew is probably not the first motivation that has led the disciples into mission. Rather it is reminiscent of the teaching of Jesus validating a posteriori what the Church has experienced by the action of the Spirit, and encouraging subsequent initiatives.[32] The hypothesis seems enriching. It remains to be seen what this teaching tells us about how we are called to participate in the work of God.

Go and Make Disciples of all Nations

Although we translate this passage generally with two imperatives, "go" and "make disciples," the Greek text contains only one. The emphasis is laid on making disciples. Different opinions have been put forward about the emphasis that has to be put on the notion of movement expressed by a participle. Bosch questions the idea of a geographical displacement.[33] Although we may not agree with Bosch to this extent, it seems nevertheless that he is right when saying that mission is not so much qualified in terms of a geographical displacement as by the task given.[34] The geographical displacement is only a means to reach more people.[35]

---

[30] Bosch notes that Jesus' presence with his disciples is the fulfilment of several promises of the OT. Bosch, "The Structure of Mission," p. 87.

[31] Hunsberger, "Is There Biblical Warrant for Evangelism?" p. 60-65; Bosch, "The Structure of Mission," p. 75.

[32] Hunsberger, "Is There Biblical Warrant for Evangelism?" p. 64.

[33] See Bosch, "The Structure of Mission," p. 77; Daniel B. Wallace, *Greek Grammar beyond the Basics: An Exegetical Syntax of the New Testament* (Grand Rapids: Zondervan, 1996), p. 645.

[34] Bosch, "The Structure of Mission," p. 78.

[35] Perhaps this displacement, or this departure, is above all a way of becoming available for the work of God. Thus, the departure could consist more simply of leaving one's habits, one's comfort zone, in order to be able to receive God's calling.

The important aspect is thus to make disciples. Placed at the end of the Gospel of Matthew, this notion is emphasised and vividly coloured by the practice of Jesus himself who made disciples during the whole of his ministry in the Gospels. It would be helpful to highlight the details of his practice, but let us simply focus on the importance of the incarnation of the message and the notion of duration. Jesus has lived with those he trained and has taken time to initiate them progressively in what they needed to understand. In constant dialogue with him, the disciples have been exposed to the practice and teaching of their Lord. This reinforces the importance of an evangelism that takes into account the whole reality of the person.

The concept of discipleship seems to emphasise also what we have said above on the centrality of the person of Christ in the message of evangelism. The context and the call to teach what Christ has taught makes very clear that the disciples are not called to make disciples for themselves. Disciples of Christ have to be trained. Evangelism seeks to lead the person to Christ and not to a system of thought. Christ is a living person with whom the evangelist is in permanent dialogue. He can bring to the other person what results from this dialogue, but he hopes above all that the other person enters into this relationship with Christ who offers forgiveness of sins and a new life. Rather than only an experience of conversion, the aim is an entire life turned to Christ and producing the fruit that he gives.[36]

In this way, we can offer the true Gospel that radiates from Christ to all the nations. When speaking about all the nations, Jesus seems to think rather of all the individuals of all the peoples than of each nation taken as a linguistic or ethnological category.[37] There is thus no more barrier facing the Gospel. Every individual, from wherever it be, is invited to enter into this community that God is building through the disciples. This announcement of an absence of separation by Jesus calls for caution when our projects of evangelism or our ways to conceive church life have a tendency to raise barriers that are hard to cross, be they ethnic, cultural, social or generational.

Baptism and Teaching

Two infinitives qualify the imperative of making disciples: to baptise and to teach. They both specify in what way the disciples have to be introduced into the new community. Baptism and teaching thus go together with discipleship.

---

[36] Packer, "What is Evangelism," p. 105.
[37] Bosch emphasises that the Jews are included in "all the nations." Bosch, "The Structure of Mission," p. 85-88.

Chapter 8 – What Is Evangelism? Biblical Hints for the European Context

The presence of the command to teach in Jesus' sending is very important for our understanding of what we call evangelism. The proclamation of the message of the Gospel implies teaching that is not a distinct entity from making disciples. The idea of a process that will take time is reinforced here. Jesus specifies also the content of the teaching: it is not described in cognitive but in practical terms. The future disciples have to learn to observe all that Jesus has taught. Here again, the teaching transmitted has to affect all of life.[38]

The presence of baptism at the beginning of this work of discipleship has to be emphasised. Let us note that the Trinitarian formula recalls the context of God's work in which the disciples' ministry participates. But beyond this fact, baptism seems to have a crucial role to play in evangelism. It is difficult to know what weight to give to its position before the task of teaching in this text. The data that we have collected so far tend to imply an evangelism that has a certain duration and presents itself like a process of initiation into the knowledge of Christ and his kingdom. A process has the inconvenience of being less tangible than an instant conversion triggered by a vibrant preacher's call. It is difficult to discern its beginning and its end, especially as every Christian knows that he has still to learn many things in order to know his Lord and to live fully the life that is offered to him. Baptism seems here like a means offered to mark the reception of God's grace, the passage from death to life, and the entry into this new walk with Christ. This is how baptism is explained by the apostles: a sign of the reception of grace and a commitment to God (Rom 6:3-5; 1 Peter 3:21). This does not mean that evangelism pertains only to what precedes baptism. In fact, the process of "making disciples" here described comprises a teaching that lasts apparently until after baptism (if one takes into account the order of the words). But if the exact moment of conversion can remain unknown, baptism gives a sign indicating the entry into the community of those who belong to God and walk as his continuously learning disciples. Those who enter into the Christian faith can always ask themselves about the progress in their walk, the depth of their comprehension, the seriousness of their commitment. Baptism gives them a sign that

---

[38] Bosch suggests that this reference to the observation of what has been commanded contains a polemic against those who did not practise the commands of the Law, maintaining however the appearances. On the contrary, the disciples have to practise righteousness and compassion as Jesus has taught particularly in the Sermon on the Mount. The disciple is part of a community that functions according to new principles, in solidarity with the poor and oppressed. Bosch, "The Structure of Mission," p. 83-84.

reminds them that it is by the grace of God that they have entered the Christian community. Thus, baptism has its place in the process of evangelism of the whole person.

Example of the Apostles

After the founding event which we find in the Gospels, the life of the churches develops, during which the Gospel is announced. The most striking examples of the proclamation of the Gospel are the apostles themselves.

From the sending of the Twelve to the sending of the apostle Paul, the NT shows that certain persons are particularly involved in the proclamation of the Gospel, of the person and work of Jesus Christ, of the coming of the kingdom of God, of the possibility of turning towards God and receiving forgiveness and new life. This message is propagated from town to town and across cultural barriers as forecast in Acts 1:8. Many things could be said about the ministry of the apostles but we will limit ourselves to emphasising just two elements.

Firstly, this propagation of the Gospel is very clearly the work of God. The apostles are drawn into a ministry where God precedes them. This is the case for Peter who discovers progressively how God is opening the kingdom to the Samaritans and then to the non-Jews (Acts 8:4-17; 10:1-48).[39] The apostle Paul experiences God's grace in his own life and is then empowered to proclaim it. From journey to journey one sees the Spirit's action leading the apostle and his fellow workers. The propagation of the Gospel finds its grounding in the work of God, and his messengers deepen their understanding of this word progressively as they announce it in all sorts of new situations.[40]

The second important point is that the apostles do not announce their message at random. They have an objective and employ strategies to attain it. Three Greek verbs describe their proclamation: *euangelizô* "tell the good news," *keryssô* "utter an announcement," and *martyreô* "bear witness." The aim of the proclamation is to persuade (Acts 19:8). The apostles have "a communication with a view to conversion."[41] Nothing less than

---

[39] Note in Acts 8:1-4 how the Church seems to be urged unwillingly to go out of Jerusalem and is this way led to proclaim the Gospel in the surroundings.

[40] Hunsberger, "Is There Biblical Warrant for Evangelism?" p. 69-70.

[41] Packer, "What is Evangelism," p. 95f. Even if this does not please our society, we are called to engage into what it calls proselytism, exhorting others to know God and to give him their lives.

eternal life is at stake.[42] Here again, conversion centres on Jesus Christ and his work (Rom 1:1-4; 1 Cor 2:2).[43] And this quest for conversion to Jesus Christ employs multiple strategies: different ways of presenting the Gospel of the Cross, the attitude of the messenger, organisation in networks, search for competent co-workers, and ministry in the church communities.[44] The apostle Paul takes particularly into account cultural, social and relational factors in order to make his message understandable and acceptable for his audiences.[45] Although all are called to make a decision and turn to Christ, the speeches addressed to the Jews are not the same as those targeted at the Greeks, and Christ is not presented the same way (see for example Acts 13:16-41; 17:22-31).

The proclamation of the Gospel is clearly dependent on the work of God. However, those who engage in evangelism are called to a conscious and reflected approach to communicating the Good News of Jesus Christ. We certainly need to draw lessons from these different approaches. The apostle Paul has called the believers to imitate his behaviour as it reflects Christ (1 Cor 4:16; 11:1; Phil 3:17).

One can easily imagine that these exhortations encouraged certain believers to take a more active part in evangelism.[46] Today also we would do well to scrutinise the apostles' attitude in this respect just as in others. We do not mean a servile reproduction of the methods, but an attention to the

---

[42] Bosch discusses the question of the preaching of hell in the context of evangelism. With Newbigin, he thinks that the most serious condemnations and warnings of the NT are generally addressed to those who think they are already saved, and not to the world. Certainly, we do not have to attenuate the menacing reality of hell, but this reality should in fact not be used as the driving force for conversion. It is not fear but love that will keep us attached to Christ. Bosch, "Evangelism," p. 23-24.

[43] See Neal Blough's article "L'évangélisation face au défi de la modernité," *Cahiers de l'École pastorale* 34, 1999, online at www.publicroire.com/cahiers-ecole-pastorale/l-evangelisation/article/l-evangelisation-face-au-defi-de-la-modernite.
There Blough describes the Gospel as the Gospel of the Cross in a way that takes into account several traits of the person and work of Jesus and that offers rich perspectives for evangelism.

[44] On the strategies employed by the apostles, see for example Jacques Buchhold, "Des hommes et des réseaux: la stratégie de Paul," in Wiher, *Bible et mission*, p. 115-134.

[45] Packer, "What is Evangelism," p. 96f.

[46] The idea of imitating the role of apostolic exhortations in the encouragement of communities for evangelism has been suggested to us by Christophe Paya.

underlying principles and a reflection on the way these can be applied today in our different European countries.[47]

Churches of the New Testament

Exhortations to Evangelise?

When observing the example of the apostles and knowing the commission given to the disciples by Jesus as well as the reception of these different elements by the evangelical communities today, one could expect that the believers of the NT churches had been urged to evangelise everywhere where they were. This is however not the case. The pastoral epistles contain appeals to preach the Word (1 Tim 4:13; 2 Tim 4:2; Tit 2:15), but these address servants already committed to this mission. The exhortations to imitate the apostles remain indirect as far as our subject is concerned. Does this mean that the church community has no role to play in evangelism?

The history of the early church suggests that the church community has been widely involved in the proclamation of the Gospel. Hannes Wiher remarks that during the first three centuries a large part of the population of the Roman Empire had been evangelised without any organised strategies of the missionary efforts.[48] The reason for the great success of the Gospel was not charismatic preachers. It was the witness of all sorts of members of the Church, together with all sorts of conditions that have favoured the fact that Jesus Christ has been widely known.[49] And even today, we know that it is through these personal contacts in everyday life that the Gospel is best transmitted.[50]

In fact, this reality seems to be at odds with the absence of commands to evangelise in the epistles of the NT. Although there is no direct order to evangelise, the appeals to be transformed by the Holy Spirit, to put God at

---

[47] This analysis of the methods has to be done in humility without the obligation to reinvent the wheel. We do not have to observe the letter, but the apostles' practices and attitudes could sometimes transmit a wisdom that surpasses the principles set out in our own analysis.

[48] Wiher, "Qu'est-ce que la mission?" p. 10.

[49] See Walter L. Liefeld, "Women and Evangelism in the Early Church," in Chilcote & Warner, *The Study of Evangelism*, p. 93-100. The article emphasises particularly the role of women in evangelism.

[50] Robert E. Coleman, "Evangelism," *Evangelical Dictionary of World Missions*, ed. A. Scott Moreau (Grand Rapids/Carlisle: Baker/Paternoster, 2000), p. 343.

the centre of the different aspects of life, and particularly the relationships between brothers and sisters and with the outside world, play a very important role in evangelism. Just like Israel before, the Church is called to be holy as her Lord is holy (Lev 19:2; 1 Peter 1:15-16). Like the people of the old covenant, the new Israel has collectively the role to be the mediator between God and man (Exod 19:5-6; 1 Peter 2:5,9). This transformation of those whom God calls, affecting progressively all aspects of their lives, can be the best way of speaking about who God is and what he does in this world. A community that "is a radiant manifestation of the Christian faith and has a winsome lifestyle," is a better means to attract people to the Gospel than all the efforts to "push or pull" them into the church.[51] The Christians are the means chosen by God to make himself known to the world.

There is thus no need of the command to evangelise if there is already an appeal to let God sanctify us. It is by observing and listening to Christians that people are led to be touched by God. This mode of action opens up infinitely wider fields than just the few contacts of the church leaders. A transformed life touches many others who are open to reflecting on their lives. And it presents great advantages in terms of contextualisation. In order to accomplish this, every Christian is called to be progressively conformed to the image of Christ.

This interpretation of the Church's mission seems to be supported by the few allusions in the biblical text to the existence of outside witness by the Christians. 1 Peter 3:15-16 mentions particularly that people are likely to ask Christians to justify their faith and hope. Peter recommends that we should be ready to defend this hope – which necessitates continuing training of believers – and to know how to answer in a way that honours Christ, with humility and respect. Colossians 4:5-6 also refers to the attitude of the believers towards "those outside" and speaks of the relevance that one has to show in the answers given to questions asked.

In this way those who do not know Christ are more likely to be attracted to him and to start to walk with those whom he has called. For Christians, this needs a real consistency in their commitment to the faith, a desire to grow in holiness, to conform in every aspect of their lives to what they believe about Jesus Christ, and a great capacity to listen to and reflect on the questions asked in order to give an appropriate answer. Not only should our behaviour not be an obstacle to the Gospel, but our life itself

---

[51] Bosch, "Evangelism: Currents and Cross-Currents," p. 101.

should be a demonstration of what the Gospel is.[52] This pertains to Christians individually and collectively. In fact, "there can be no safer and more natural milieu for evangelism than steady teaching, witnessing and nurturing of the local church."[53] In order to be well understood, the Gospel has to be manifested in the transformation of individuals as well as in social changes.[54] People are by nature relational beings. It is also in this dimension that the relevance of the Gospel has to be shown, in the Church and in the daily life of Christians. In this, everybody has their share and are called to become what God wants them to be. The Gospel announced and applied in the life of believers radiates in a new life that inspires further witness.

Ministry of the Evangelist

Besides apostles already mentioned, the NT also mentions evangelists (Acts 21:8; Eph 4:11; 2 Tim 4:5). Without excluding the common nature of the task, it seems that certain persons have been particularly recognized in their capacity to proclaim the Gospel, as is the case today.

However, we have to restrain from a too narrow conception of this ministry. The diversity of the activities of Philip, who was called an evangelist, leaves open a wide field. Philip is deacon, he proclaims the Gospel, exorcises demons, healings take place, he baptises, welcomes …[55] Timothy is exhorted "to do the work of an evangelist" (2 Tim 4:5), but the letters addressed to him witness to a very diverse activity. Finally, Ephesians 4:11, which mentions the evangelists among the ministries given to the Church, does not specify the nature of their task. Additionally, verse 12 describes the aim of all these ministries as training for those who belong to God.[56]

Without going further here, the evangelist seems to be in continuity with what we have described so far. His ministry is linked to the Church

---

[52] Hunsberger, "Is There Biblical Warrant for Evangelism?" p. 72.

[53] Packer, "What is Evangelism," p. 103. Let us note that 1 Corinthians 14:23-24 allows to suppose that non-Christians had access to at least some meetings of the early church. The worship service was thus a potential place of evangelism.

[54] Bosch cautions against a disincarnated evangelism that calls for changes "in micro-ethical and religio-cultic categories." Bosch, "Evangelism: Currents and Cross-Currents," p. 102.

[55] Abraham, *The Logic of Evangelism*, p. 50.

[56] See Frank Harber, "Evangelist," *Evangelical Dictionary of World Missions*, ed. A. Scott Moreau (Grand Rapids/Carlisle: Baker/Paternoster, 2000), p. 347.

taking into account the whole Gospel and the whole person.[57] Gifted by God for this, he has particular capacities to help people to approach God. In principle nevertheless, his ministry should be supported by the witness of a lively and committed community.[58]

Conclusion

What is evangelism? Now we can ask the question on the basis of some biblical findings, however partial they still may be.

First, at every moment, evangelism is based on the work of God. The work of God is the source and the driving energy of evangelism both by the effective action of God during the process and by the motivation that this work instils in us. God works secretly in the heart of people and opens them to know him. He sends these persons towards us or us towards them and leads us to share with them what he has given to us. The materialism that dominates the worldview of so many Europeans tends to make us lose sight of this reality so that we get caught up in our own enterprises. Yet, God is the first at work in evangelism as in the whole life of the Church. This was true yesterday and is still true today. It is on this action that we have to count primarily and that we are called to solicit by our prayers.

The message that we share is a message that surpasses our understanding. It is given to us in Scripture, but we never grasp it totally. This message rests on a person, Jesus Christ, whom we confess as the living and acting God from eternity to eternity. The work of Christ transforms us and brings about a new life into which we are initiated day after day. From then on we receive forgiveness of our sins and a new relationship with God and our fellow humans. In a postmodern context that doubts the notion of truth but is fond of the relational aspect of life, we should not deprive ourselves of this powerful asset of the Gospel: the truth that we profess is incarnated in a living person today. It is around the living Christ of Matthew 28, almighty and ever-present, that our proclamation has to be constructed.

To share this message exposes ourselves to it. What would I witness of if the relationship which I have with Christ has no effect on my life? At every instant we are called to place ourselves in his light in order to illu-

---

[57] Abraham quotes also Eusebius of Caesarea who describes the ministry of the evangelist as having wider traits than the sole proclamation of a message. Abraham, *The Logic of Evangelism*, p. 54.

[58] In the case of a pioneer ministry, this community can also be at some distance.

minate every sector of our lives. In order to be communicated well, the Gospel has to progressively integrate all our being: words, thoughts, and actions. It must also take the supreme place in our relationships, particularly with those whom God has called like us. This way and by the grace of God, we can present to those around us a Gospel fully incarnated in our human reality. In this way we can also demonstrate the uniqueness and the universal relevance of the message of Jesus Christ who has come to us, has died for our sins and is resurrected for our life. Having evidently a collective dimension, evangelism needs the incarnation of the whole Gospel in men and women who live together the richness and the diversity of the life given by Christ. If history is full of men and women whose individual witness has shone like a lamp in the darkness, the proclamation of the Good News of Jesus Christ is still first based on the church community. Let us learn to think more in terms of community, develop our relationships with each other, and abandon the cult of the leader, in order to see Christ at work in every member: in an individualistic Europe this is a huge project for the Church. But if it progresses in this direction, it will undoubtedly be a lighthouse in the night of loneliness and broken relationships.

In the complexity that we describe, the communication of the Gospel can only be thought of as a process. During this process, God exposes a person progressively to his Word and his Being by employing those whom he has already drawn to him. A walk settles in where individuals are called to surrender completely to God for all their lives. Through the confession of faith and baptism, such people demonstrate their repentance and choice to receive fully the life that is offered to them. This act is not the end of the journey but expresses publicly the attitude in which a person wants to live this walk from now on towards what we call maturity in Christ. Despite the desire for tangible results, let us not be satisfied with a superficial evangelism. Only a patient and in-depth evangelism will produce communities able to radiate Christ. Perhaps we can say that evangelism ends when the individual decides consciously to become God's fellow worker by taking on the task of evangelism himself and reaching out to others.

Let us conclude by saying that we have spoken little about the means of evangelism. It seems to us that the first means of evangelism has to be to align ourselves with what God is doing. When reading his Word, in prayer, in fellowship, we are taking part in a kingdom that God is building and that he wants to be spreading everywhere. From there, from this availability for the work of God that we manifest, we can become aware of gifts, of methods to use and of persons whom he is sending towards us. Evangelism is thus not a supplementary charge put on the Church, but a logical continuity of a life which is receptive for the work of God. By putting together the clear indications that Scripture gives and the silence that it keeps, there is an array of activities that can lead to evangelism and allow us to accomplish our mission.

Further Reading

Abraham, William J., *The Logic of Evangelism* (Grand Rapids: Eerdmans, 1989).

Bosch, David J., "Evangelism: Currents and Cross-Currents in Theology Today," *International Bulletin of Missionary Research* 11, 3 (1987), p. 98-103.

Chilcote, Paul W. & Warner, Lacey C., eds., *The Study of Evangelism: Exploring the Missional Practice of the Church* (Grand Rapids MI: Eerdmans, 2008).

Packer, James I., "What is Evangelism: Evangelism and Theology," in *Theological Perspectives on Church Growth*, ed. Harvie M. Conn (Nutley, NJ: Presbyterian & Reformed, 1976), p. 91-105.

Chapter 9
Cross-Cultural In-Depth Evangelism

Hannes Wiher[1]

The cultural explosion of European societies, the multiplicity of models of socialisation and the presence in Europe of persons from all corners of the world oblige the Christians and the churches (European, African, Korean or Chinese) eager to share the Gospel with their contemporary Europeans to individualise the approach to evangelism to the targeted person or subculture. The trends show an evolution towards more and more relational conscience orientations in young Europeans. This development is growing against the background of a society regulated by efficacy, punctuality and law, all rules-centred characteristics. These are the populations to whom we have to transmit the biblical message. To be interested in the other person requires compassion, and to speak about God in a hostile environment needs a step of faith: a missionary spirituality.

In the following sections, we first reflect on some preliminary questions: what is the Gospel, its relationship with the socio-cultural context, and its communication (evangelism). With regard to witness, we will also study the question of an extroverted rather than introverted spirituality. In a second step we will ask how to communicate the Gospel in Europe, moving towards a concept of evangelism over a period of time (the conversion process), the approach of the early church to evangelism, and finally a collective approach to evangelism in terms of church planting.

Preliminary Considerations

Theology of the Gospel and of Evangelism

"Most evangelists, writes Michael Green, are not very interested in theology; [and] most theologians are not very interested in evangelism."[2] The result is a great loss for both, deplores James Packer, and adds:

---

[1] This chapter is a revised version of the third part of a paper presented at the meeting of the *Réseau de missiologie évangélique pour l'Europe francophone* (REMEEF) on November 20, 2013.

When theology is not held on course by the demands of evangelistic communication, it grows abstract and speculative, wayward in method, theoretical in interest and irresponsible in stance. When evangelism is not fertilized, fed and controlled by theology, it becomes a stylized performance seeking its effect through manipulative skills rather than the power of vision and the force of truth. Both theology and evangelism are then, in one important sense, unreal, false to their own God-given nature; for all true theology has an evangelistic thrust, and all true evangelism is theology in action.[3]

Because of these considerations, it seems important to us to start with a short theological reflection on the Gospel and evangelism.

Etymologically, the term "Gospel" (from Greek *euangelion*) means "good news." In the context of the Roman Empire, the Gospel described good news concerning the emperor: his coming, his victory, the birth of a son, etc. The authors of the NT apply the term to the coming of the Messiah King (Christ) Jesus. In this sense, the term Gospel describes the Good News according to which God has provided for the redemption of humanity in the person of Jesus Christ. This is the good news that God reigns over the universe and that he intervenes in the life of his people. In the NT, the word "Gospel" describes the heart of the promises of salvation in the OT: the coming, suffering and resurrection of Jesus of Nazareth as the foundation of salvation for whoever believes, the proclamation of this event and the literary genre of the gospels.[4] In this vein, Christopher Wright can declare that the Gospel is grounded in the whole Bible:

> Firstly, the Bible as a whole conveys the whole good news. ... Secondly, the Bible as a whole, in all its canonical parts, contributes to the good news. ... Thirdly, the Bible as a whole must function to control the criteria by which we are able to discern what makes the good news truly good.[5]

The fact that God has created the universe and man as its crown and in his image, that right after the fall this God sends his messengers in order to

---

[2] Michael Green, *Evangelism in the Early Church* (London: Hodder & Stoughton, 1970), p. 7.

[3] James I. Packer, "What is Evangelism: Evangelism and Theology," in *Theological Perspectives on Church Growth*, ed. Harvie M. Conn (Nutley, NJ: Presbyterian & Reformed, 1976), p. 91.

[4] Graeme L. Goldsworthy, "Gospel," *New Dictionary of Biblical Theology*, ed. T. Desmond Alexander et al. (Leicester: IVP, 2000), p. 524; Ulrich Becker, "Gospel, Evangelize, Evangelist," *NIDNT*, vol. 2, p. 107-115.

[5] Christopher J.H. Wright, "'According to the Scriptures': The Whole Gospel in Biblical Revelation," *Evangelical Review of Theology* 33, 1 (2009), p. 4.

restore the intimate relationship between Him and man, and that he leads the fallen creation towards a New Creation, all these facts together constitute the Good News. At the favourable time (*kairos*), God sends the announced Messiah King, the Christ, Jesus, Son of God (Mark 1:1; Luke 1:32). This is the Good News that the Gospels talk about particularly, but that the OT has already announced (Luke 24:46). And it is on the OT that the apostle Paul grounds himself (just as Jesus did) to announce the Gospel "according to the Scriptures" (1 Cor 15:3-4). However, Timothy Keller emphasises the fact that not everything that the Bible teaches is the Gospel, that it is not the minimum standard of doctrinal content of Scripture, and that there is no "one size fits all" understanding of the Gospel. In a kind of a slogan he affirms: the Gospel is not everything, it is not a simple thing, but it affects everything.[6]

If the whole Bible speaks about the Gospel, a reflection on the communication (revelation) of the Gospel in the Bible becomes of first importance. In the Septuagint, the Greek translation of the Old Testament, the verb *euangelizomai* is the translation of the Hebrew *bisser* "announce good news." The letter to the Hebrews 1:1 tells us that God has spoken to us "in many and various ways" until he communicated in a definitive way through his Son Jesus Christ. The narratives of the Gospels tell us about the life, passion and resurrection of Jesus Christ. And Jesus has communicated with us through his being, his acts and his words in both a literal and a figurative sense (parables, metaphors and proverbs). Jesus Christ, the "Word" of God, the *Logos* of John 1:1, announces the coming of the Spirit, the second divine mediator and communicator (*parakletos*, John 14:16).[7] The Son and the Spirit are the divine communicators par excellence. The Gospels and the book of Acts witness to this fact.[8] The verbs that describe this both non-verbal and verbal communication are among others: heal (*therapeuô*), cast out demons (*ekballô daimonia*), make disciples (*matheteuô*), witness (*martyreô*), "preach" the Gospel (*keryssô to euangelion*), and "evangelise" (*euangelizomai*), the last a rather generic term.

---

[6] These are the titles of the first three chapters of Keller's book, in which he discusses the theology of the Gospel from a practical and missiological perspective. Timothy Keller, "Gospel Theology," in *Center Church: Doing Balanced, Gospel-Centered Ministry in Your City* (Grand Rapids: Zondervan, 2012), p. 29-53.

[7] *parakletos* "another Counsellor" (NIV), "another Comforter" (KJV), "another Advocate" (NRS) (John 14:16).

[8] From this perspective, the Acts of the Apostles could also be called the "Acts of the Holy Spirit."

The NT usage of the verb "evangelise" (*euangelizomai*) allows two interpretations that are represented in the evangelical movement. On the one hand, evangelism can denote the verbal proclamation of the Gospel.[9] From this point of view, evangelism has priority over social action because it is preoccupied with the eternal destiny of man. In this understanding, evangelism is distinguished from mission, which encompasses all verbal and non-verbal activities linked to the proclamation and presentation of the Gospel. On the other hand, *euangelizomai* can denote all the activities of the ministry of Jesus and the apostles, comprising all the aspects of Gospel communication, including the verbal proclamation.[10] This second interpretation thus encompasses the first one. Conceived in this way, evangelism is synonymous with the notion of "making disciples," "witness" and also of "mission." From this point of view, the eternal destiny of man has priority, independently of whether evangelism is a verbal or non-verbal activity. The first interpretation is the traditional position of Evangelicals, the latter is the position of the Lausanne Movement.[11] It encompasses the first position and leads to the concept of "holistic mission."

---

[9] For the verbal proclamation of the Gospel, see the following occurrences of *euangelizomai* and cognates: Luke 4:43 (parallel to preach in v. 44); Luke 9:6 (evangelise and heal); Luke 20:1 and Acts 5:42 (teach and evangelise); Acts 8:4 and 15:35 ("evangelise" the Word); Acts 8:25 (witness, speak and evangelise); Acts 8:35 (open the mouth and evangelise); Acts 10:36 (proclaim peace); Acts 11:20 (speak and evangelise); Acts 13:32 (proclaim the Gospel of the promise); Acts 17:18 (parallel to speaker); Rom 1:15; 10:15 (parallel to preaching, sending and evangelism); 1 Cor 1:17 (parallel to word); 1 Cor 15:1 (the Gospel that I have taught); Heb 4:2,6 and 1 Peter 1:25 (parallel to the word).

[10] For the whole ministry of Jesus and the apostles, see the following occurrences of *euangelizomai* and cognates: Matt 11:5 and Luke 4:18-19 (if one considers the acts in the following passage as a synonymous parallelism); Luke 16:16; Acts 14:7; 16:10; Rom 10:15 (parallel to preaching, sending and evangelism); Rom 15:20; 1 Cor 9:16,18; 2 Cor 10:16; 11:7; Gal 1:8,11,16,23; 4:13; Eph 2:17; 3:8; 1 Thess 3:6; 1 Peter 1:12. For an argumentation in favour of an interpretation of the notion of "proclamation of the Gospel" in the sense of an integral activity of Jesus and the apostles, see John Stott, *Christian Mission in the Modern World* (London: Falcon, 1975), p. 15-95; Becker, *NIDNT* 2, p. 111, 113. Becker supports this interpretation, in particular concerning the usage of *euangelizomai* by the apostle Paul.

[11] In this vein, the Lausanne Congress (1974) was a congress for "world evangelisation," and the follow up committee was called "Lausanne Committee for World Evangelization" (LCWE). The term evangelisation was preferred to the term mission because it seems less ambiguous and less offensive. See Ralph Winter, "The Highest Priority: Cross-Cultural Evangelism," in *Let the Earth Hear His Voice*, ed. J.D. Douglas (Minneapolis: Worldwide Publications, 1975), p. 213-225.

The expression "to proclaim the Gospel" (Greek *keryssô to euangelion* "preach the Gospel") is used in the majority of occurrences to denote the whole ministry of Jesus and the apostles.[12] In this vein, for example in the Septuagint, *keryssô* is used in Isaiah 61:1 in parallel with *euangelizomai*. Goldsworthy concludes: "This eschatological proclamation is the means by which release and liberty are achieved. This proclamation is an essential part of the ministry of Jesus (Mark 1:38; Luke 4:18-19, which quotes Isaiah 61:1-2; and Luke 4:43-44, and links *euangelizomai* with *keryssein*)."[13] From this perspective, there is no distinction between the notions of mission and evangelism: the disciple is sent to evangelise.

To conclude our short theological reflection on the notion of *euangelizomai* we observe that the two interpretations meet in the fact that Jesus and the apostles have adopted the approach of a holistic communication of the Gospel: the words must explain the life (being and acts) just as the life must confirm the words. One cannot invent the Gospel. It has to be "preached" ("evangelised") and the "preacher" has to be sent, as Romans 10 insist:

> But how are they to call on one in whom they have not believed? And how are they to believe in one of whom they have never heard? And how are they to hear without someone to proclaim him? And how are they to proclaim him unless they are sent? As it is written, "How beautiful are the feet of those who bring good news!" (Rom 10:14-15, NRS).

While adopting a strategy of holistic communication, Jesus and the apostles had the eternal destiny of their contemporaries at the centre of their preoccupations. It is thus important to discern goal and strategy: while salvation remains the ultimate preoccupation of evangelism, the strategy is holistic, both non-verbal and verbal. We do not speak of the priority of evangelism (understood in the Lausanne Covenant and Manilla Manifesto as a verbal act), but of the primacy (or ultimacy) of salvation combined with a holistic approach to witness/mission (as explained in the Cape Town Commitment).[14]

---

[12] See the occurrences of *keryssô to euangelion* in the sense of verbal proclamation of the Gospel: Matt 4:23 (preach the Gospel and heal); 1 Thess 2:2 (tell the Gospel), and in the sense of the whole ministry of Jesus and the apostles: Matt 24:14 par Mark 13:10; Matt 26:13; Mark 1:14; 16:15; Acts 20:24 (witness of the Gospel); Rom 1:1 ("evangelise" the Gospel).

[13] Goldsworthy, "Gospel," *New Dictionary of Biblical Theology*, p. 523.

[14] www.lausanne.org.

Holy Spirit and Missionary Strategies

If the Holy Spirit is the divine communicator par excellence between the two comings of Jesus Christ, how can the human communicator of the Gospel make use of the insights of the science of communication and be at the same time in phase with the Spirit of God? Does he have to choose between listening to the voice of the Holy Spirit and the development of strategies? If this was an exclusive choice, one would have to say: "Trust in the Lord with all your heart, and do not rely on your own insight" (Prov 3:5). But if we look at the apostle Paul's missionary journeys, we note strategic reflections and at the same time God's intervention and direction: God calls Paul to be the apostle of the non-Jews (Acts 9:15), to become together with Barnabas a cross-cultural missionary (Acts 13:2), to cross the Aegean sea towards Europe (Acts 16:9), to witness before Cesar at Rome (Acts 23:11), and he prevents him from preaching the Word in the Roman provinces of Asia and Bithynia (Acts 16:6f). In his own sight, Paul had seen the strategic necessity to go there: he wants "to proclaim the good news, not where Christ has already been named" (Rom 15:20). Following this logic, he wants to go right to the capital of the Roman Empire, and even go beyond it to the Western tip of the Empire, to Spain (Rom 15 :22-24). However, for the apostle Paul it is important "to do the good works, which God prepared in advance for us to do" (Eph 2:10, NIV). We can thus conclude that he has developed his strategic reflection while also seeking the will of God.

The Holy Spirit directs or blocks the missionary strategies and himself conveys divine communication. Paul reflects on strategies, but remains sensitive to the voice of the Holy Spirit in order to be directed and if necessary counteracted in his reflections and strategies.

Evangelism and Transformation of Deep Structures

The analysis of the history of Europe has shown that we are not in the process of the first evangelism. The Europeans think they know the Gospel. They have already tried it and have found that it did not respond to their questions and expectations, that it was not relevant for their daily life. A communication of the Gospel that reaches the deep layers of our contemporaries is primary. How can we evangelise in a way that touches the heart?

We have seen that the biblical notion of the heart has its equivalent in the concept of worldview with its cognitive, affective, evaluative and religious dimensions.[15] Charles Kraft emphasises the importance of communicating

---

[15] See the discussion in chapter 6, and David K. Naugle, *Worldview: The History of a Concept* (Grand Rapids: Eerdmans, 2002), p. 267-274.

the Gospel by targeting the receiver's worldview. He introduces the concept of "receptor-oriented communication."[16] For Paul Hiebert, transformation during conversion should not only change the superficial behavioural forms (not to drink alcohol, not to smoke, go to church, get baptised, memorise the catechism, pray, read the Bible), but also the beliefs (a sincere repentance, follow Jesus, know the Bible), and especially the worldview. The objective is to transform it into a biblical worldview. Additional knowledge of the Bible can imply a transformation of the worldview, but should be completed by approaches to affective and ethical transformation.[17]

In contrast, the philosophical approach to the transformation of man remains essentially a cognitive endeavour. When studying the first evangelisation of Europe during the medieval epoch, James Russell observes that instead of transforming the worldviews of the Germanic peoples it was rather medieval Christianity that accommodated itself to the Germanic worldview.[18] In the next section, we have to ask ourselves how the accommodation to ambient contemporary culture by, for example, the emerging church movement can be linked with the transformation of the worldviews of persons and societies.

Gospel and Culture: Hermeneutic Considerations

The analysis of the European socio-cultural context has shown that the communication of the Gospel in Europe will practically always be cross-cultural. How can today's communicators convey the biblical message to a target person or group, if the biblical message is itself part of the communication between a biblical author and an audience in biblical times and cultures with the aim of generating a response in that time and context? The response which we would like to stimulate is the conversion and the integration of the person or group in a faith community.

The discovery of the meaning of a biblical text has three foci: "author – text – reader."[19] This triangle is itself founded on the principle of the "se-

---

[16] Charles H. Kraft, *Christianity in Culture: A Study in Dynamic Biblical Theologizing in Cross-Cultural Perspective* (rev. ed.; Maryknoll: Orbis, 2005 (1st ed. 1979), p. 147-193.

[17] Paul G. Hiebert, *Transforming Worldviews: An Anthropological Understanding of How People Change* (Grand Rapids: Baker, 2008), p. 314-316.

[18] James C. Russell, *The Germanization of Early Medieval Christianity: A Sociohistorical Approach to Religious Transformation* (New York: Oxford University Press, 1994).

[19] Grant R. Osborne, "The Problem of Meaning: The Issues," in *The Hermeneutical Spiral: A Comprehensive Introduction to Biblical Interpretation* (Downers Grove: Intervarsity, 1991), p. 366-396.

mantic triangle," which includes the symbol (term, sign), the referent (reality) and the sense (mental image or response).[20] In consequence, the meaning of a communication of the Gospel is produced by the *correspondence* between the reality of the Gospel and the mental ideas of the persons who are involved in the communication: the communicator and the receptor(s). The communication of a biblical message thus implies yet another triangle, the one between the Bible, the communicator and the receptor(s).[21] Describing this phenomenon, Eugene Nida introduced the concept of the "cultural triangle."[22] This notion of the "cultural triangle" goes beyond Charles Kraft's concept of "receptor-oriented communication."[23] Cross-cultural evangelism has to be not only receptor-oriented, but also faithful to the Bible. This triangular procedure, which puts Bible and cultural agents in relation, is close to the concept of contextualisation which is a method of cross-cultural communication. The evangelical approach, critical contextualisation, a concept introduced by Paul Hiebert, evaluates every socio-cultural element of personality or society in the light of Scripture.[24] Thus critical contextualisation looks at two angles of the cultural triangle.

Consequently, the cross-cultural communication of the Gospel functions around a triangle: one starts with the analysis of the biblical text by using the four worldview models as tools, particularly analysing the personalities and the socio-cultural context of the passage being studied. Then the disciple studies his own personality and socio-cultural background: European, African, Asian, secular, dichotomist, holistic, rules-centred, relational, etc. This is the second angle of the cultural triangle. Finally, one studies the target personalities and cultures: older or younger generation, intellectual or worker, secular, dichotomist, holistic, rules-centred, relational, etc. If there is correspondence of worldviews around the triangle, that is, if the Bible passage, the communicator and the target are for example relational and holistic, there is no major problem for cross-cultural

---

[20] Osborne, *The Hermeneutical Spiral*, p. 77; Paul G. Hiebert, *Missiological Implications of Epistemological Shifts: Affirming Truth in a Modern/Postmodern World* (Harrisburg, PA: International Trinity Press, 1999), p. 71; David J. Hesselgrave & Edward Rommen, *Contextualization: Meanings, Methods, and Models* (Grand Rapids: Baker, 1989), p. 185.

[21] Hiebert, *Missiological Implications*, p. 71-76, see the synoptic table p. 107.

[22] Eugene Nida, *Message and Mission* (London: Harper & Row, 1960).

[23] Kraft, *Christianity in Culture*, p. 147-193.

[24] Paul G. Hiebert, "Critical Contextualization," in *Anthropological Insights for Missionaries* (Grand Rapids: Baker, 1985), p. 171-192.

evangelism. If there is divergence between the three angles, we have to reflect on how to envisage effective communication faithful to the Bible text and relevant for the audience. Is there a biblical rule to communicate to a relational person by a rules-centred communicator? How can we do it? How to speak of miracles when communicator and target have a secular worldview? How to speak of sin in a society where "everything is permissible"? (1 Cor 6:12; 10:23). Or how to speak of God when God is a non-topic?

It is easy to realise that in Europe there will be many divergences around the cultural triangle. The Bible does not have a secular worldview, even though its first chapters induce already a secularisation of the prevailing animistic worldview. The five basic soteriological concepts of the Bible are different from those of the majority of Europeans. The conscience orientation of persons and cultures in the Bible tends to be balanced but slightly more relational, which does not correspond to the perception of modernity nor to the habitual formulation of Western Christian theology. The biblical conscience orientation corresponds much more to that of Orthodox theology or oriental and traditional religions. Finally, the Bible has no primary concern for efficacy and punctuality like modernity. In fact, the cultures of the Bible are closer to the cultures of postmodernity and the immigrants. But unfortunately, the reflection necessary for good cross-cultural evangelism is too often left undone. In the next section, we ask why, despite efforts at reflection, resulting from a spirit of compassion and humility, this sensitivity is very often absent.

Missionary Spirituality

The missionary drive of the first centuries, that left traces in Patristic theology, has received a heavy blow by the fact that the masses have entered the church without a real conversion, the so called "Constantine paradigm shift." The link between Church and State in the system of Christendom has of course not succeeded in changing the situation. The "discipleship training schools" that produced a missionary drive were from then on in the monasteries. But we note that in several monastic orders spirituality became introverted, rather than turned towards the external non-discipled and non-revived world. Furthermore, the Lutheran Reformation suppressed the monasteries, and with them the missionary monastic orders. That is why Pietism had to reinvent a missionary structure and a missionary spirituality.

The first Protestant missionary movement, the Moravians, recalled the importance of prayer by instituting a daily prayer chain that lasted for a hundred years. It put also a special accent on the discipline of Bible reading by initiating the "Moravian texts," one OT and one NT verse for daily Bible meditation that were sent to all the missionary teams around the world. The Moravians also revived the biblical principle of "mission teams:" missionary teams of two departed to the ends of the world. For the first time in history, these missionaries were non-theologians: farmers, carpenters, masons, and bakers. The concept of "tent maker" was re-actualised by the fact that the missionaries in the Caribbean, for example, worked in the sugar plantations at the side of the slaves in order to gain them for Christ.

The churches often lacked compassion for the masses without Christ, but voluntary orders and societies with this missionary vision were started from the 15th century on in the Roman Catholic Church, and from the 19th century on in the Protestant movement. The missionary society has become the principal missionary structure. Sustained by different revivals, the missionary movement has always been able to recruit disciples in the reservoir of revived churches. But since the end of revivals in the Western Anglo-Saxon world, the Western missionary societies have had problems in finding disciples with a missionary spirituality. We must also remember that the model of the missionary society has only been able to function in a context of economic prosperity during industrialisation. As a result the missionary society became a model of "mission from the centre to the periphery," mission from the rich to the poor.

During the second half of the 20th century, not only has the centre of gravity of Christianity been transferred to the Global South, which is the result of the great missionary movement of the West, but the Global South has also become the main force in the sending of missionaries. Mission is now "from everywhere to everywhere."[25] The reason for this is that the missionaries coming out of the revivals have planted missionary churches

---

[25] Samuel Escobar, "Mission from Latin America," in *Changing Tides: Latin America & World Mission Today* (American Society of Missiology 31; Maryknoll: Orbis, 2002), p. 143-165; Kang San Tan, Jonathan Ingleby, Simon Cozens, eds., *Understanding Asian Mission Movements* (Proceedings of the Asian Mission Consultations 2008-2010; Gloucester: Wide Margin, 2011); Andrew F. Walls, "Christian Mission in a Five-hundred-years Context," in *Mission in the 21st Century: Exploring the Five Marks of Global Mission*, ed. Andrew Walls & Cathy Ross (London: Darton, Longman and Todd, 2008), p. 193-204; Wilbert R. Shenk, *Changing Frontiers of Mission* (Maryknoll: Orbis, 1999), p. 142-185; Patrick Johnstone, "From Everywhere to Everywhere," in *The Future of the Global Church: History, Trends and Possibilites* (Milton Keynes: Authentic, 2011), p. 228-235.

that have produced missionary disciples. Generally speaking, the contemporary West is not capable of producing disciples who have been transformed in their inner being and who are "disciples who make disciples," disciples who are ready to pay the price that witness in a hostile environment can cost: marginalisation, contempt, loss of work, perhaps even persecution.

The main question for the European churches is therefore: "How can we produce disciples with a missionary spirituality?" Our historic study suggests that the response seems to be found in a radical commitment to Christ comprising an intense life of prayer, worship and intercession, together with a discipline in reading the Bible. This radical commitment is grounded in an intimate fellowship with God so that the deep structures of personality are transformed. This intimate life with God has two consequences: first the disciple's personality and life become attractive to nonbelievers. In relation to this observation Lesslie Newbigin tells a story from communist Russia. When he asked the Christians:

> "How is it that in a situation where the church is absolutely forbidden to use any kind of public communication; where printing press, radio and public meetings are forbidden, and where even parents are not allowed to teach religion to their children, the church goes on winning converts?" The answer which I received was "The attractive power of a holy life."[26]

Secondly, God calls and sends, and gives the disciple a task in the kingdom of God. In missiological terms, this means that the disciple allows the missionary God to assign to him a mission in the great mission of God,[27] in other words, to be assigned a task in God's great project for humanity.[28] Filled with the love of the missionary God (John 3:16; 1 John 4:19), in tune with his will (Matt 6:10), sent by Christ (John 17:18; 20:21) and inspired by the Holy Spirit (Acts 4:31), "out of the abundance of the heart the mouth speaks" (Matt 12:34). In this way, the approach to a cross-cultural communication of the Gospel in Europe has more chances to succeed.

---

[26] Lesslie Newbigin, *The Good Shepherd: Meditations on Christian Ministry in Today's World* (Grand Rapids: Eerdmans, 1977), p. 141.

[27] Christopher J.H. Wright, *The Mission of God: Unlocking the Bible's Grand Narrative* (Nottingham, UK: IVP, 2006).

[28] Michael Goheen and Kevin Vanhoozer speak about the "drama" of God that is played in the world. Craig G. Bartholomew & Michael W. Goheen, *The Drama of Scripture: Finding our Place in the Biblical Story* (Grand Rapids: Baker, 2004); Kevin J. Vanhoozer, *The Drama of Doctrine: A Canonical-Linguistic Approach to Christian Theology* (Louisville: John Knox, 2005).

Communication of the Gospel in Europe

After having considered some general requirements for cross-cultural evangelism, we now reflect on the communication of the Gospel in the particular context of Europe. We propose six elements necessary for a successful communication (one could add others): in approaching the person or group in front of us we have to rethink our language, adopt a holistic communication and choose intentionally between oral and written presentation of Scripture. Then we have to identify the stage of the conversion process relevant to our person or group, think of the lessons drawn from the early church, and include a reflection on the Church as collective witness, the concept of the Church as "hermeneutic community" introduced by Lesslie Newbigin.

A New Language

After the long history of Christianity in Europe, the terms for the basic soteriological concepts like sin, repentance, redemption and atonement are in a first approach difficult to understand, and secondly loaded with a long history of misunderstandings. Almost the only meaning of the word "sin" that has resisted the secularisation and de-Christianisation process in Europe is the concept of one's "little weaknesses." In order to make more sense in communicating with our contemporaries, it can be useful to first understand the etymology of the terms, secondly go back to the images of the biblical terms, and thirdly use figurative language like the biblical prophets.

To understand the etymology of these terms may help to use them better: sin comes from Old English *syn(n)* "offence, wrong-doing, misdeed," which may be related to Latin *sons* "guilty." The Old English use can be seen both as rules-centred concept or a relational one. Repentance from Latin *repentare* "pay, repair," and redemption from Latin *redemptio* "repurchase," are both rules-centred concepts. Atonement from old English at-one-ment "being at one, in harmony with someone," that is forgiveness through the blood of sacrifice, has been interpreted by the animistic Anglo-Saxons through a relational filter as reconciliation. The interpretation of salvation (from Latin *salus*), depends largely on the concept of forgiveness in view, reparation or repayment being rules-centred, whereas reconciliation is a relational concept.[29]

---

[29] The five theories of forgiveness (atonement) are 1) the *Christus Victor* theory, 2) the ransom theory, 3) the satisfaction theory, 4) the penal substitution theory, and 5)

Biblical languages use images to express meaning. As a second step these images can be an additional help in understanding the abstract terms in our European languages. The Hebrew and Greek terms for sin mean literally "miss the mark" (*hata'* and *hamartia*) or "deviate (from the road)" (*'awon* and *parabasis*) or "transgress (the edge of the road)" (*paraptoma*). In order to correct the deviation one has to change direction (*shub* and *epistrephô* "turn") and transform one's thought and behavioural patterns (*metanoia* "reorientation"). Forgiveness is attained through the mediation of the priest or the high-priest, in the NT Jesus Christ. This is the relational dimension of forgiveness which is easy to explain in a relational society. Through this mediation a repurchase is made. This is the legal dimension which is well understandable for a rules-centred segment of the population. Finally, for this repurchase one needs a "means of repurchase," the redemption price or ransom: in the OT it is a sacrificial animal; in the NT the death of Jesus Christ on the cross is considered as the necessary blood sacrifice for redemption (repurchase). In Romans 3:24-26, the apostle Paul makes use of the OT imagery by indicating that the cross is the "means of atonement (repurchase)," that is the place where the priest sprinkled the blood with the hyssop branch: the horns of the altar or the cover of the covenant ark (Hebrew *kapporet* and Greek *hylasterion*). The way Paul uses this picture makes the event of the cross much more easily understandable for the Jews and the already encultured proselyte non-Jews of his time. For contemporary English speaking Europeans the English translation of the terms can help: the cross is the means of "at-one-ment," of reconciliation, in the relational perspective, and the means of repurchase in the legal perspective. The fact that a blood sacrifice is needed for forgiveness (Lev 17:11; Heb 9:22) is much more difficult to explain to secular Europeans. For many, this fact takes us back to the barbarian Dark Middle Ages, before the progress made during the Enlightenment. The idea of a blood sacrifice is thus inacceptable for many Europeans. Consequently, we have to explain the reason why a blood sacrifice is needed in the logical progression of ideas in the OT. Missiology calls this pedagogical development of a concept "chronological evangelism." We will come back to this problem below, when we present this concept in the section on the "conversion process."

---

the moral transformation theory. The first two are the Patristic or "classical" theories, the second two "scholastic" theories. The penal substitution theory was emphasised during Protestant Reformation. The last is the "subjective" or "humanist" view. In relation to conscience orientation, the ransom and the penal substitution theory are rules-centred views, the *Christus Victor*, the satisfaction and the transformation theory are relational views.

A third step includes the use of figurative language. Already the prophets had used images in their communication. The prophet Amos uses the image of funerals (5:1-2), of lamentation (5:18; 6:1), proverbs (3:3-6) and riddles (2:9; 3:12; 5:2, 7, 19, 24) to explain his message. The prophet Hosea uses symbolic names to make God's message understandable (Hos 1:3-9) and communicates through the marriage with a prostitute (a relational non-verbal communication). The prophet Ezekiel describes the relationship between God, Judah and Israel through the metaphor of two sisters: Jerusalem and Samaria (Ezek 16). Figurative language is part of non-verbal communication and thus of relational conscience orientation. Since the second half of the 20th century, that is, in the current of postmodernity, and with the influx of migrant workers, relational conscience orientation becomes more and more frequent. Consequently, figurative language becomes a very appropriate communication style.

How can we speak about the five basic soteriological concepts to contemporary Europeans? Beyond the original meaning of English, Hebrew and Greek terms the concepts have a relational and a legal aspect that can be appropriate when talking to relational or rules-centred persons. Salvation can be conceived in a relational perspective as harmony, honour, well-being and prosperity. The Hebrew term *shalom* translates a notion of integral well-being. Salvation can become practical for relational persons when they are on the side of the greater and more powerful God (Ps 96:4; Col 1:13-20). For rules-centred persons, it is more important to believe in the right and true God (John 14:6). Sin can mean to bring disharmony into a relationship (with God or humans, the relational component) or to violate God's law (the judicial dimension). We see the relational aspect of grace and forgiveness for example in the parable of the prodigal son (Luke 15:11-32), and the judicial dimension in the parable of the unmerciful servant (Matt 18:23-35).

How can we speak about God in a secular society where the biblical God is no longer familiar and well known, but rather strange and unknown, and where God and Jesus Christ are rarely present in daily conversation, and seldom part of people's understanding of life? This fact implies at the same time a difficulty and an opportunity: a difficulty because biblical knowledge is greatly or totally absent. It is necessary to transmit this knowledge during a long and patient process through conversations with interested persons, debates and, toward the end of the conversion process, possibly systematic and chronological Bible studies.[30] It is also an oppor-

---

[30] For chronological Bible studies, see the section "Conversion Process" below.

tunity because this unknown God is always surprising, a God of the paradox who transforms a failure into a victory, death into life, wisdom into folly and folly into wisdom, the one who "makes all things new." This mysterious God can become the point of departure for evangelism.[31]

Holistic Communication of the Gospel

The Protestant Reformers, especially the German ones, emphasised the communication of the Gospel through the *kerygma*, the "ministry of the Word". Relying on the efficacy of the Word, they can be regarded as continuing the Hebrew concept of *dabar*, the acting Word of God. God's efficient Word becomes visible in his acts of creation and redemption, particularly in Jesus Christ, the Word of God. Through their great insistence on verbal communication, the Reformers, and the Protestant and evangelical theologians after them, neglected the non-verbal communication. However, the prophets, Jesus and the apostles made ample use of non-verbal communication in their transmission of God's message. As shown above, the prophets Hosea and Ezekiel had to transmit the message they had received from God through symbolic acts (Hos 1:2-3; 3:1-2; Ezek 4; 12:-20). Jesus and the apostles healed sick persons and cast out demons. In order to "lead the Gentiles to obey God," the apostle Paul communicates "by word and deed, by the power of signs and wonders, by the power of the Spirit of God" (Rom 15.18f).

We find we have to return to the debate on the meaning of *euangelizomai* and cognate terms. Does the verb denote only the verbal ministry of Jesus and the apostles or their whole ministry? Theologians with a rules-centred conscience orientation emphasise the verbal ministry, whereas those with a relational conscience opt for the whole ministry.

The science of communication maintains the second option which encompasses the first. The specialists of communication attribute the main transmission of the message to non-verbal communication, that is, 50 % or more of the transmitted message. Additionally, they demonstrate that only an integral communication is efficient: life must confirm the words, and the words must explain the presence and the acts.[32] In the Roman Catholic and Orthodox Churches biblical teaching is very much via non-verbal

---

[31] See Thomáš Halik, "The Soul of Europe: An Altar to the Unknown God," *International Review of Mission* vol. 95, n° 378-379 (July-October 2006), p. 265-270.

[32] See for example Paul Watzlawick, Janet H. Beavin, Don D. Jackson, *Pragmatics of Human Communication: A Study of Interactional Patterns, Pathologies and Paradoxes* (New York: Norton, 1967).

means of communication: through the painted images on the walls of the church buildings. In former days this was the approach to the relational and illiterate populations. The iconoclastic movements like the Protestant Reformation suppressed this approach. One discerns in this period a rules-centred conscience that promotes verbal communication. During the last fifty years, besides the preaching ministry, pieces of theatre, pantomimes, dramas, films and videos have become more and more important means to transmit the biblical message.[33] In this vein, Jean-Georges Gantenbein proposes an "aesthetic missiology" for contemporary Europe.[34] Are television and the Internet the appropriate media for populations with a relational conscience? The exchange of SMS and the chat on the Internet introduce a new phenomenon: digital orality. Literate persons write short messages that correspond rather to an oral communication style. Orality and literacy will be the subject for our reflection in the next section.

The Bible exhorts us to be witnesses (Luke 24:48; Acts 1:8). To witness through the whole life is a challenge that is much greater than to transmit the message by words alone. Often, Evangelicals with a rules-centred conscience orientation have understood this challenge in the second sense. Lesslie Newbigin remarks in this regard:

> In our evangelism, we have departed from Christ's own way – the way of the incarnation. Jesus became man – completely one among those for whom he came. We do not. We remain at a distance. I am thinking from time to time: We go to a village, stand in the street, sing a few lyrics, perhaps shout a few texts through a loud-speaker, deliver a message and go home to supper. We do not become really involved with the people. We do not sit down beside them and listen to their thoughts, their problems, their hopes. ... Our model is not the incarnation of the Word of God, but the methods of a modern commercial or political advertiser.[35]

Newbigin follows here the apostle Paul who made himself a slave to everyone to win as many as possible (1 Cor 9:22). In particular the emerging church movement tries to follow this maxim by adopting more holistic

---

[33] The discipline of missiology that studies these approaches is called "ethnodoxology." See James R. Krabill et al. (eds.), *Worship and Mission for the Global Church: An Ethnodoxology Handbook* (Pasadena: William Carey Library, 2012); www.ethnodoxology.org.

[34] Jean-Georges Gantenbein, *Mission en Europe: Une étude missiologique pour le 21ᵉ siècle* (Ph.D. thesis at the Faculté de théologie protestante de Strasbourg; Studia Œcumenica Friburgensia 72; Münster: Aschendorff, 2016).

[35] Lesslie Newbigin, *The Good Shepherd: Meditations on Christian Ministry in Today's World* (Madras: Christian Literature Society in India, 1978), p. 60.

and relational approaches towards our contemporaries: they have developed "messy churches," "liquid churches," "café churches," "cyber churches," churches that are specialised for certain segments of society: bikers, motorcyclists, marginalised, Caribbean, etc.[36] However, it is deplorable that these attempts to contextualise the church, which are by the way very welcome in view of the failure of many churches to come to terms with our transformed European context, are unfortunately very often without any theological reflection.

In recent years missiologists have observed a great increase in the popularity of old church buildings in town centres. Cathedrals, which may only have an attendance of fifty people at their worship service on Sunday, attract several thousand people during the week: regular church goers, visitors, and tourists. What do they come to such traditional religious buildings for? These persons' concern is to approach God, to bathe in a spiritual ambiance, to be imbued by a sacred place. These are phenomena of non-verbal communication to which relational persons and cultures are very sensitive. In thinking about how to balance non-verbal communication with verbal communication, missiologists are asking to what degree buildings can favour or hinder the communication of the Gospel.[37]

Linked to such spatial non-verbal communication is communication through music. Since people's consciences have started to become more relational and given that non-verbal communication has assumed greater importance (in the West since the second half of the 20th century), the notion of worship has progressively been emphasised and has been given more time during Sunday worship services and in the life of churches. The missiological reflection on the subject has developed in consequence. In the Orthodox Church, mission has been defined as "liturgy after the litur-

---

[36] For European studies on the emerging church, see for example: Graham Cray, *Mission-Shaped Church: Church Planting and Fresh Expressions in Changing Contexts* (London: Church House Publishing, 2004); Mike Breen & Alex Absalom, *Launching Missional Communities: A Field Guide* (London: 3DM Press, 2010); "Bibliography on Mission Studies," *International Review of Mission* vol. 95, n° 378-379 (July-October 2006), p. 419-443; Gabriel Monet, *L'Église émergente: Être et faire Église en postchrétienité* (Berlin: LIT, 2014). For American studies, see for example: Eddie Gibbs & Ryan K. Bolger, *Emerging Churches: Creating Christian Community in Postmodern Cultures* (Pasadena: William Carey Library, 2005); Donald A. Carson, *Becoming Conversant with the Emerging Church* (Grand Rapids: Zondervan, 2005).

[37] See Marc Spindler, *Pour une théologie de l'espace* (Neuchâtel: Delachaux et Niestlé, 1968).

gy."[38] No wonder that the Orthodox Church and its theology are relational. In evangelical circles, a new discipline that is called ethno-doxology has developed since: the scientific study of worship and liturgy in different cultures.[39]

Another aspect of the holistic communication of the Gospel is the participation of Christians in social life and in the public ongoing debates, particularly through active engagement in social issues, membership of charitable associations, etc. During the period of the "ideological crisis" after the 1960s, questions of economic, social, medical, and scientific ethics, of genetic manipulation and ecological problems have priority in public interest. It seems that Christians could contribute positively in these public domains. Additionally, Christians could be precursors in engaging in the integration of immigrants, the first weeks in the welcoming country being a very fragile period for the refugees. Personal coaching, gestures of friendship and strategic guidance during this phase could open doors.

Europe being a cultural and social mosaic, the challenge consists of using diversified approaches towards our contemporaries, including traditional churches, new expressions of churches and approaches without church.[40] The objective is a creative and original mix like the one Jesus offered: mingling with our fellow human beings without withdrawal or break (except for times of prayer), provoking in their minds questions and curiosity about who we are. This corresponds to a continuous non-verbal communication. Second, a sensitivity to the needs of our neighbours with responses as signs. And finally, a verbal communication in response to situations that need an explanation or to questions asked (event-speech), and short interventions touching deep layers at fruitful (*kairos*) moments.

Oral and Written Presentation of the Bible

The traditional approach to the presentation of the biblical message was to motivate people to reading the Bible and to teach people to read. In the Global South missionary societies have organised large literacy programs. This was a rules-centred approach. As a reaction to it, a reflection on the oral functioning of the majority of the world population has started, initiated by the International Orality Network, a working group of both the Lau-

---

[38] Ion Bria, *The Liturgy after the Liturgy: Mission and Witness from an Orthodox Perspective* (Geneva: WCC, 1996).
[39] Krabill, *Worship and Mission*; www.ethnodoxology.org.
[40] This reflection will follow in the section "Church Planting" below.

sanne Movement and of the World Evangelical Alliance.[41] Its main approach to the presentation of the Bible is to tell biblical stories in a way that is appropriate for oral cultures. These efforts were accompanied by the development of pieces of theatre, drama, pantomime, films and art, according to the perspective of the Ethno-doxology Network.

These two networks take into account the oral functioning of relational persons and cultures. The recent integration of the model of conscience orientation into the Orality and the Ethno-doxology Networks has helped to realise that the two modes of functioning (oral and literate) can be combined in one and the same person just as the profile of values can contain the two conscience orientations:[42] this is for example the case for young people in their communication with SMS and in the chat on Internet which one can call "digital orality."[43] Every one of us, even a literate person, can prefer following the news on radio or television instead of reading a newspaper, or listen to books, for example the audio Bible, instead of reading it. It is necessary to analyse the preferred functioning of a person, a subculture or a segment of society in order to better choose the appropriate approach to evangelism.[44]

Conversion Process

The immediate goal of the communication of the Gospel is the conversion of persons who are around us: our families, friends, and colleagues. From a biblical perspective, conversion is the work of the Holy Spirit who "convicts" (*elenghô*) the conscience of a person (John 14:6; 16:8; Rom 3:23; 6:23; 10:9f).[45] The target of evangelism is thus the conscience of a

---

[41] Its website: www.orality.net. The publications of the network including the digital journal *Orality Journal* are downloadable from this site. See Grant Lovejoy, ed., *Making Disciples of Oral Learners* (Lausanne Occasional Paper No. 54; Lima, NY/Bangalore: Lausanne Committee on World Evangelization/International Orality Network, 2005), at http://orality.net/resources/docs/Making_Disciples_of_Oral_Lea rners-126469 1848.pdf.

[42] See the section "Conscience and Personality" in chapter 6 of this book.

[43] See Samuel E. Chiang, "Three Worlds Converged: Living in an Oral, Literate, and Digital Culture," in Krabill, *Worship and Mission*, p. 179-183.

[44] See Hannes Wiher, "Worldview and Oral Preference Learners and Leaders," in *Beyond Literate Western Practices: Continuing Conversations in Orality and Theological Education*, ed. Samuel E. Chiang and Grant Lovejoy (Hong Kong: Capstone Enterprises, 2014), p. 109-125.

[45] On the basis of the Greek term *elenghô* "convict," the study of the human conscience is called "elenctics." The term has been introduced by Johan Bavinck. This

person. A biblical understanding of sin ("miss the mark") opens the door for the Gospel. The change of direction in conversion (Hebrew *shub* and Greek *epistrephô* "turn") corrects the false direction of journeying without God towards the true target who is God. The false targets are the other gods, idols, and the self. Thus, conversion consists of turning away from evil, from idols and the domination of Satan, and turning towards God (Acts 26:18; 1 Thess 1:9; 2 Tim 2:19).[46]

The way which leads to salvation has been opened by the expiatory sacrifice of Jesus Christ on the cross that provides forgiveness of sins. In the NT, the apostle Paul uses the OT notions of justification, redemption and sanctification for forgiveness (Rom 3:21-26; 5:1-5; 1 Cor 1:30). On this basis, he introduces new metaphors like regeneration, new creation, reconciliation and adoption (2 Cor 5:17-20; Rom 8:14-17). These different representations illustrate the different aspects of forgiveness, and thus of conversion. Their intentional use in relation to the conscience orientation of our conversation partner can enhance understanding of the conversion process and open doors: reconciliation as a relational concept is the appropriate term for relational persons, and justification as a legal term is best reserved for rules-centred persons. It is interesting to note that southern relational theologians speak either about salvation by grace through faith or reconciliation, but almost never about justification by faith, a legal concept.

From the biblical perspective, conversion is an event of instantaneous renewal of the deep structures of man: the regeneration of the "inner man," of the "heart," the "new birth." By contrast, from the anthropological perspective, conversion is understood as a process that can last a long time. The disciplines of the natural and social sciences illuminate different aspects of this process. From the psychological perspective, conversion is part of the maturation process of a person. Conversion fills the void that a person feels, and calms the feeling that something is lacking in life. In this way, religion strengthens personality. From the sociological perspective, conversion is seen as part of the socialisation process: to adopt a certain conviction can facilitate the integration in a social group. In this line of thought, for Clifford Geertz, religion is "a historically created system of

---

new sub-discipline is a fundamental element of the studies of evangelism. See Johan H. Bavinck, "Elenctics," in *An Introduction to the Science of Missions* (Grand Rapids: Baker, 1960), p. 221-275.

[46] For a more detailed treatment of conversion, see Hans Kasdorf, *Christian Conversion in Context* (Scottdale: Herald Press, 1980); Reinhold Strähler, *Coming to Faith in Christ: Understanding Conversion* (Nairobi: Life Challenge, 2010).

meanings available in a society."[47] Presented negatively, conversion can be the consequence of social pressure. The decision can be individual or collective. From the physiological perspective, a decision can be facilitated through overstimulation of the nervous system, for example by accelerated rhythms, mystical mediation, lack of sleep, hunger, drugs and other techniques.

From the perspective of the science of communication, conversion is a communication process that implies several stages and a progressive transformation of the recipient. This process of conversion is influenced by two agents: the sovereign God and his human envoy. It sees as one process the two traditionally separated phases of evangelism and discipleship, the former understood as the period before, the latter after conversion. From the communication perspective, one can also call the conversion process "discipleship process." It runs through different stages with one or several themes. On the basis of these data, James Engel, an evangelical specialist in communication, has conceived the so called "Engel scale." We have adapted it for the purposes of cross-cultural evangelism and present it on the next page.[48]

God's Role	Role of the Communicator	Scale	Theme
General Revelation	Information	-9	Is there a God?
General Revelation	Information	-8	Who is God?
Conviction	Information	-7 - -5	Know the Bible
Conviction	Call	-4 - -3	A choice to make
Conviction	Call	-2	Decision
Conviction	Follow up	-1	Evaluate decision
Regeneration	Follow up	0	New creation
Sanctification	Edification	+1	Become a disciple
Sanctification	Edification	+2	Discipleship
Sanctification	Edification	+3	Make disciples

---

[47] Geertz, *The Interpretation of Cultures*, p. 52, 125.
[48] James F. Engel, *Contemporary Christian Communication: Its Theory and Practice* (Nashville: Nelson, 1979); see also "The Engel Scale Explained," www.gospelcom.net/guide/resources/tellitoften.php.

It is important to realise that the Engel scale is a model: it does not represent all of reality or a personal situation. In particular, it only renders visible the cognitive dimension of the conversion process. The relational and affective dimension, which are of capital importance, are not represented. Instead of a vertical movement on the cognitive axis, a person travels on a diagonal line (if the affective axis is thought to be horizontal). We have to reduce the negative feelings towards the Christian faith and replace them by positive feelings, a movement on the horizontal affective axis. At the same time, we have to increase Bible knowledge. The potential moment for conversion arrives when this process is sufficiently advanced, meaning that the person has enough positive feelings towards the Christian faith and enough Bible knowledge.[49] According to the progress in the conversion process, activities that target the affective or the cognitive axis will be offered. In the beginning of the process, interventions will target predominantly the affective dimension. During this essentially relational phase (-9 to -8), non-verbal communication is primary. We pass time together, talk about everything and nothing, and become friends (*friendship evangelism*). Later in the process (-7 to -3), we put the accent on increasing Bible knowledge, that means motivating our friend to study the Bible with us. Let us note that the moment of decision does not coincide necessarily with regeneration. The former is a human act, while the latter is a divine act. The first 48 hours after the decision are very sensitive and fragile because the decision can be cancelled due to outside pressure. During this phase, the convert needs follow-up and coaching by a close friend or a counsellor. Regeneration is followed by the process of edification with the goal that the person becomes a disciple who makes disciples (Matt 28:19).

As an illustration we can ask why Billy Graham succeeded in his evangelistic campaigns in the past, and how he would do in contemporary Europe? As the Engel scale shows, an evangelistic call addresses the persons in stages -4 to -2. When Graham made his appeals from the 1950s to the 1980s, the majority of his audiences in North America and Europe had passed through Sunday school and consequently disposed of sufficient Bible knowledge to realise that there was a decision to make. These persons in the stages -4 to -2 were then able to respond to Graham's call. They were usually in the hundreds. Today, Graham would find few persons with sufficient Bible knowledge. Most persons would find themselves in the stages -9 to -5 unable to make a decision. Consequently, most evangelistic campaigns address

---

[49] Viggo Søgaard has added the affective dimension to the Engel's scale, on the basis of which Frank Gray has developed a matrix: http://thegraymatrix.org.

their message to "Christians" who are already somewhat discipled, but are not attractive to non-Christians. Considering, however, the desire of relational persons with a strong group identity to gather in order to have a group feeling, large events have a useful function in encouraging Christians to witness. Besides large events relational Christians like the intimate relationship in small groups, for example house church networks.

For Paul Hiebert, it is important to discern three levels of conversion: change of behaviour, of beliefs and of worldview.[50] The Roman Catholic missions from the 16th century on, and the Protestant missions from the 19th century on, insisted on behavioural change. They looked for evidence of conversion at this superficial level. The converts had to stop drinking alcohol and smoking; the polygamists had to send back the extra wives. Francis Xavier baptised the converts who could recite the Lord's Prayer, the twelve articles of the abridged Catholic Symbol and the Ten Commandments. But a change in behaviour does not necessarily mean that the underlying beliefs have also been transformed. In the 19th century, the Protestant missionaries started to insist on the transformation of beliefs. They required a sincere repentance and the confession of sins. A baptismal formula had to give evidence of this. But if the beliefs change without behavioural change, James 2 tells us that this is hypocrisy. And if the worldview is not transformed, belief will be perverted in the long run and syncretism will result, or "Christopaganism" as Hiebert calls it.[51] A good example of the reinterpretation of an act of faith from the perspective of a cultural (animistic) worldview is Simon's misunderstanding of the prayer of Peter and John in Acts 8 (v. 14-24). Let us recall the fact that in Europe conversion implies almost always a change of worldview, a secular worldview having to be transformed into a Hebrew (or biblical) worldview. This fact represents a serious obstacle to conversion.

As indicated above, during the process of conversion, the objective is to study the Bible with the person or the group. In practice this is achieved in the nowadays very popular Alpha Course schemes, a relational approach including fellowship during and outside meal times.[52] In missiological terms, a comparative study of the five basic soteriological concepts in the

---

[50] Hiebert, *Transforming Worldviews*, p. 10-12, 314-316.

[51] Hiebert, *Anthropological Insights for Missionaries*, p. 184f.

[52] Nicky Gumbel, *How to Run the Alpha Course* (new ed.; Eastbourne: Kingsway, 2004), at www.alphacourse.org/itv/nickygumbel. Alpha explained: A: anyone interested in finding out more about the Christian faith; L: learning and laughter; P: pasta; H: helping one another; A: asking anything.

Chapter 9 – Cross-Cultural In-Depth Evangelism

culture and the Bible has to be done. A method which recognises that conversion is a process and which gives a framework for a comparative study of Bible and culture is "chronological evangelism" or chronological Bible teaching. It starts with the creation accounts in Genesis, works through the fall and presents the offer of a saviour through selected stories. In this way it respects the rule of cross-cultural communication: to present the discontinuities between two thought systems (cultures or religions) in a progressive way in order to avoid the breaking of the relationship and misunderstandings, especially of the person of Christ. The five basic soteriological concepts (God, man, evil, sin, and salvation) are taught through selected biblical stories, before and after conversion. This is at the same time a relational and rules-centred procedure: to tell stories is the relational aspect while transmitting Bible knowledge is the rules-centred aspect. During the process of conversion, which is the framework of chronological evangelism, the comparative study will be covered in a way which evaluates the cultural concepts in the light of Scripture. In this way, the cultural worldview will progressively be transformed into a biblical worldview.

The pioneer book of chronological evangelism is *Building on Firm Foundations* by Trevor McIlwain with sixty lessons (Bible stories).[53] On the basis of Luke 24:44-46 where Jesus explains the messianic prophecies of the OT to the two disciples of Emmaus, a shortened version with fourteen lessons of Bible stories has been produced: *The Stranger on the Road to Emmaus* by John R. Cross (pseudonym). Later on, adaptations for several contexts have been developed: for a secular context *By This Name* (with the Gospel of John as a template), and for a Muslim context *All that the Prophets Have Spoken* by Yehia Sa'a (with minor modifications of *The Stranger*).[54] For oral or "digit-oral"[55] cultures this teaching has to be transmitted in a narrative form. The chronological Bible teaching in oral form, called Chronological Bible Storying (CBS), was originally developed by the Southern Baptists (USA). It uses a set of narrative techniques. Recently, the International Orality Network (ION)[56] has begun to develop the concept further in a great variety of presentations and training schemes.[57] Al Massira,

---

[53] Trevor McIlwain, *Building on Firm Foundations* (9 vol.; Sanford: NTM, 1991).
[54] These texts are produced by Goodseed and available on www.goodseed.com in English, French, German, Arab, Chinese, Korean, Russian, and other languages.
[55] For the concept of "digit-orality," see Chiang, "Three Worlds Converged," in Krabill, *Worship and Mission*, p. 179-183.
[56] www.orality.net.
[57] For example: "Storying: Training for Trainers," www.st4t.org.

for example, is a scheme that combines the relational approach of the Alpha Course with the concept of chronological evangelism adapted to an oral narrative approach and a Muslim context.[58] It presents selected stories with informal discussions on a series of twelve DVDs.

Learning from the Early Church: A Relational Approach

Several historians and sociologists of religion have undertaken studies of the early church in order to inspire contemporary evangelism. We mention only three of them: *Evangelism in the Early Church* (1979) by the historian Michael Green, *The Rise of Christianity* (1996) by the sociologist of religion Rodney Stark, and *Worship and Evangelism in Pre-Christendom* (1995) by Alan Kreider.[59] All of them show how we can learn from the early church, Green and Kreider through a historic-analytic approach, and Stark through a comparative sociological study. Several historians, sociologists and missiologists have observed that the multicultural and multi-religious postmodern societies of Europe have many similarities with Mediterranean societies during the first centuries of the Christian era.[60] Green, Kreider and Stark compare the expansion of Christianity during the first centuries with contemporary approaches to evangelism.

Based on the fact (among others) that half of the Ethiopian population was Jewish and that most of them converted to Christianity, Stark concludes that cultural continuity between the religious group and the context favours conversion. In the same vein, Stark thinks that Christianity started as a Jewish heresy and that its initial attraction concerned the culturally related Jews, especially the proselytes. Later on, Gnosticism started as a Christian heresy attracting mainly Christians (because of its anti-Judaic content). Evangelistic approaches in continuity with the socio-cultural context like those of the emerging church movement are more likely to appeal than traditional endeavours. There remains the question of how faithful they are to the Bible, a question that critical contextualisation would ask. Stark's data about religious scepticism towards classical religions indicate that it is highest among

---

[58] www.almassira.org.
[59] Michael Green, *Evangelism in the Early Church* (rev. ed.; Eastbourne: Kingsway, 2003; 1st ed.: Grand Rapids: Eerdmans, 1970); Rodney Stark, *The Rise of Christianity: A Sociologist Reconsiders History* (Princeton, NJ: Princeton University Press, 1996); Alan Kreider, *Worship and Evangelism in Pre-Christendom* (Joint Liturgical Studies, 32; Cambridge: Grove Books Limited, 1995).
[60] For example Wayne A. Meeks, *The First Urban Christians: The Social World of the Apostle Paul* (New Haven, Conn.: Yale University Press, 1983).

the educated. They are attracted to religions that are new to contemporary Europe like the oriental and traditional religions or new sects. Stark observes that the New Religious Movements recruit their converts mainly among the religiously inactive and unsatisfied population groups and among those who are affiliated to religious communities in cultural continuity with the cultural context, i.e. ordinary everyday communities.

Concerning the motivation for conversion, Stark aims to demonstrate that conversion does not consist of searching for an ideology and adhering to it (a rules-centred dimension), but rather of aligning one's religious behaviour to that of one's family and friends (a relational dimension). Thus, conversion tends to function on the basis of social networks built on interpersonal attachments. When Mormon missionaries make door-to-door evangelism of persons they do not know, they will see one conversion per a thousand solicitations. However, when the missionaries enter the first time into contact with a person who is a friend or a relative of a Mormon, it results in one conversion per two contacts. Furthermore, socially marginal individuals will be more inclined to conversion in order to escape their marginal position. Kreider emphasises the influence of acts of mercy, miracles and exorcism as factors in conversion.

Additionally, Green stresses the importance of personal evangelism in the early church, especially evangelism in people's homes. The Gospel generally entered new households through the slaves, the children or the spouse to finally reach the family chief. Personal visits and spontaneous encounters were the usual means. Kreider speaks of the attractiveness of "peace making relationships" and the "Jesus-shaped distinctiveness" of early Christians in everyday life.

The lesson that we can draw from these studies is that most of the mentioned factors that favour successful evangelism can be reduced to an initial relational approach to evangelism. This lesson from the early church is in line with our insight that a first approach to our contemporary postmodern Europeans has to be primarily relational if it should have some chance to succeed. However, let me nuance this statement somewhat: in terms of conscience orientation, we find all sorts of persons in our late modern European societies, also more rules-centred individuals. And in terms of Heinzpeter Hempelmann's basic mentalities, we will also want to communicate the Gospel to premodern and modern persons.[61] We will thus

---

[61] Heinzpeter Hempelmann, *Prämodern, Modern, Postmodern: Warum „ticken" Menschen so unterschiedlich? Basismentalitäten und ihre Bedeutung für Mission, Gemeindearbeit und Kirchenleitung* (Neukirchen-Vluyn: Neukirchener Verl., 2013).

have to individualise our approach to Europeans. Secondly, when we stress the relational approach of the early church, this does not mean that the rules-centred aspect did not exist in their evangelism. We know that the access to Holy Communion was not easy for non-believers and that church discipline was pursued harshly. In the multicultural and multi-religious society of the first century, a holy life increased the attractiveness of the early church. Let us also repeat that chronological evangelism, a rules-centred dimension of the discipleship process, is absolutely indispensable. On the negative side of the balance, Kreider mentions the fact that with the transition to Christendom the church leaders centred their attention on doctrine and orthodoxy, thus a change in emphasis from relationships to rules.[62]

Church Planting

Beyond individual factors, the community of the believers (Hebrew *qahal*, Greek *ekklesia*) plays an important role in Christian witness. In this vein, Lesslie Newbigin has introduced the concept of the church as a "hermeneutic community" of the Gospel. This means that it is the community of the believers that interprets through its life and witnessing the biblical message for the people in the urban district or the village.[63]

The discipleship (or conversion) process can be practised in an individual approach or can naturally extend into a church planting effort if the approach includes a vision of the community. Since the fall God's deep desire is to create an alternative humanity that is formed in his image (Gen 1:26f), a people that belongs to him (Exod 6:7; Lev 26:12; Jer 31:33) and is devoted to him (Exod 9:5f; 1 Peter 2:9; Titus 2:14). Jesus Christ has come to build his Church, and nothing will be able to destroy it (Matt 16:18). It will be good to remember these biblical foundations when we discuss sociological, anthropological and strategic aspects of church planting.

The subject of church planting has mobilised many missiological reflections during the last fifty years and has generated a lively debate. The following movements have been inspired by it: the church growth movement initiated by Donald McGavran, also founder of the School of World

---

[62] Kreider, *Worship and Evangelism in Pre-Christendom*, p. 40-45.
[63] In this section, we do not intend to treat the subject of church planting in an exhaustive way. For more details, we refer the reader to the manual by Timothy Keller, *Center Church*; or Craig Ott & Gene Wilson, *Global Church Planting: Biblical Principles and Best Practices for Multiplication* (Grand Rapids: Baker, 2011).

Missions at the Fuller Seminary,[64] the church planting movement, with David Garrison as pioneer,[65] the emerging church movement,[66] a movement of church planters with a desire to experiment practically in contextualising the church for Western culture. Moving in the same direction there is the theological reflection on the missional church initiated by Lesslie Newbigin, and structured in the 1980s in the Gospel and Our Culture Network (GOCN), which expanded later in the broadly based American missional church and church planting networks and into the European leadership and church planting network.[67] In France all these initiatives are reflected in the movement "One church for a thousand inhabitants,"[68] and in French-speaking Switzerland "M4 Suisse," a branch of "M4 Europe."[69]

The thesis which underlies this current is that the best evangelism for each segment of the population is through church planting.[70] The impact of this strategy has been demonstrated in many regions of the world.[71] In France, the recent development of evangelical churches confirms the thesis, even if one takes into account the influence of immigration on its evo-

---

[64] Donald A. McGavran, *Understanding Church Growth* (Grand Rapids: Eerdmans, 1980); see also C. Peter Wagner, *Church Growth and the Whole Gospel: A Biblical mandate* (New York/San Francisco: Harper & Row, 1981). For an evaluation of the church growth movement, see Gary L. McIntosh, ed., *Evaluating the Church Growth Movement: Five Views* (Grand Rapids: Zondervan, 2004).

[65] David Garrison, *Church Planting Movements: How God Is Redeeming a Lost World* (Midliothan, VA: WIG Take Resources, 2004).

[66] See for example Graham Cray, *Mission-Shaped Church: Church Planting and Fresh Expressions in Changing Contexts* (London: Church House Publishing, 2004); Mike Breen & Alex Absalom, *Launching Missional Communities: A Field Guide* (London: 3DM Press, 2010); Gabriel Monet, *L'Église émergente: Être et faire Église en postchrétienté* (Berlin: LIT, 2014).

[67] See for example Darrell L. Guder & Lois Barrett, *Missional Church: A Vision for the Sending of the Church in North America* (Gospel and Our Culture; Grand Rapids: Eerdmans, 1998). For the GOCN publications, see www.gocn.org, and also www.missionalchurchnetwork.com; www.churchplantingnetwork.com; www.leadnet.org/category/european_church_planting.

[68] www.1pour10000.fr.

[69] The four Ms are: Master, Mission, Multiplication, Movement: http://m4europe.com.

[70] See Daniel Liechti, "La meilleure évangélisation de l'Europe francophone: l'implantation et le développement d'Églises centrées sur l'Évangile, au service de leur ville," in Keller, *Une Église centrée sur l'Évangile*, p. 603-623.

[71] Garrison, *Church Planting Movements*.

lution.[72] However, the thesis is questioned by several missiologists.[73] Additionally, after this long history of Christendom and while the section of the population with a relational conscience is growing, the church as an institution is for many contemporary Europeans a repellent rather than attractive idea. Consequently, two alternatives have developed.

On the one hand, movements of house churches have developed without any institutional barriers. The chronological Bible study group, or the one that follows the Alpha Course scheme (the "Beta group"), can be naturally transformed into a house church. In the meantime, several large networks of house churches exist in the different corners of the world, equally in Europe. This option, which prefers the intimacy of the small group, corresponds to the relational conscience which is dominant in the global South and progresses steadily in Europe.

On the other hand, a reflection on the believers outside the church has been initiated. This has especially developed after the famous survey of the British sociologist of religion Grace Davie in Liverpool published in 1994.[74] The result of this survey was summed up in the catchphrase *"believing without belonging:"* many believers prefer to stay outside the church and live a Christian life by themselves. This attitude corresponds to European individualism which is a product of modernity, schematically a rules-centred system. Later on, Grace Davie's survey has been extended to the whole of Europe.[75] Of course, a solitary Christian life can have harmful spiritual and theological consequences. It is generally looked upon with suspicion by Evangelicals.[76] This individualism, which has developed during the period of modernity, continues during postmodernity as "soft individualism." This variety of individualism, for whom the group becomes

---

[72] André Pownall, "Un demi-siècle d'implantation d'Églises évangéliques en région parisienne (1950-2000)," *Théologie Évangélique* 4, 1 (2005), p. 47-80.

[73] See for example Stefan Paas & Alrik Vos, "Church Planting and Church Growth in Western Europe: An Analysis," *International Bulletin of Missionary Research* 40, 3 (2016), p. 243-252.

[74] Grace Davie, *Religion in Britain since 1945: Believing without Belonging* (Oxford: Blackwell, 1994); idem, "Believing without Belonging: A Liverpool Case Study," *Archives de sciences sociales des religions* 81 (1993).

[75] Grace Davie, *Religion in Modern Europe: A Memory Mutates* (Oxford: Oxford University Press, 2000).

[76] Wilbert Shenk, "Believing Without Belonging? Reflections on the Consultation," *International Review of Mission* 92, 365 (2003), p. 231-239; Timothy C. Tennent, "The Challenge of Churchless Christianity: An Evangelical Assessment," *International Bulletin of Missionary Research* 29, 4 (2005), p. 171-177.

important besides individual decision making, is due to the relational dimension of the conscience in the young generation.

Another face of the transformation of the conscience orientation in Europe can be expressed by a variant of Grace Davie's catchphrase: *"believing after belonging."* In former days, a person had to first understand the basis of faith before entering the church: *"belonging after believing."* This corresponds to a rules-centred approach: one must first accept the rules before belonging to the group. Today, relational persons are invited into an attractive community by their friends. It is later that these persons will understand what the Christian faith is all about. This is Grace Davie's famous option: *"believing after belonging"*. This second approach corresponds to a relational conscience orientation. The relationships with friends attract to the church. The relational ambiance at the church makes people stay and come back another time. The rules lose their importance and will (perhaps) be followed later. The so-called emerging churches, which experiment with the new expressions mentioned above, try to create an attractive atmosphere for non-Christians invited by their Christian friends in the community. A church can also become attractive by serving the surrounding population.[77] However, the chronological Bible teaching, that is the rules-centred aspect which is so necessary for the transformation of the worldview, is often lacking in these pragmatic relational approaches during discipleship.

The challenge in contemporary Europe consists of offering attractive expressions of church for a vertiginous diversity of personalities and subcultures. The spectrum will range from traditional evangelical churches to house churches and informal meetings in bar-café churches as far as the structural aspect is concerned. Concerning conscience orientation, the spectrum will cover churches with a well-structured worship service, a three-point sermon and good doctrine at the centre, that is rules-centred communities, as well as unstructured, informal "liquid" or "fluid" churches.[78]

In a relational perspective, the emerging church movement proposes to plant and model "missional, incarnational and experiential" (that is partici-

---

[77] Michael Moynagh, *Church for Every Context* (London: SCM, 2012), p. 283-299: "Action-based Learning."

[78] See McIntosh, *Make Room for the Boom... or Bust: Six Church Models for Reaching Three Generations* (Grand Rapids: Revell, 1997), p. 14-15, 18-21; Zygmunt Bauman, *Liquid Modernity* (New York: John Wiley & Sons, 2013); Pete Ward, *Liquid Church* (Exeter: Paternoster, 2002).

pative) churches.[79] These incarnational churches will be, according to Gabriel Monet, at the same time transcultural, contextual, counter-cultural and intercultural:

> The church ... will be transcultural by discerning in the Gospel that which is not dependent on times and places, ... contextual by taking seriously into account the world in which it is called to radiate, in a mutually nourishing dialogue, ... counter-cultural by being faithful to its Christian identity by challenging that which is not conforming to Jesus' spirit, ... [and] intercultural by being proactive and empathetic towards all those who live their faith in different ways.[80]

Conclusion

The drive for evangelism is one of four characteristics of Evangelicals proposed by David Bebbington.[81] After all these centuries of the simultaneous presence of a revived Christianity that induced a European Christian culture, and the Enlightenment philosophy that induced scientific and technological development, Europe has been de-Christianised during one century so that it has become a "mission-field." Schematically and in relation to conscience orientation, after several centuries of a predominantly rules-centred functioning that has largely imbued European popular and theological cultures during modernity, the transformations during the second half of the 20th century that favour a relational functioning have changed the situation for evangelism in Europe during postmodernity.

Following the massive immigration of predominantly relational persons, life in Europe has become multicultural and multi-religious. Consequently, evangelism in Europe will be cross-cultural. If a reflection on cross-cultural evangelism in the Europe of the 21st century does not want to repeat the current and past errors, it has to be first interdisciplinary, founded on an analysis which at the same time takes into account theology, history, philosophy, psychology, sociology and anthropology, to mention just these components. In addition, it has to be an in-depth analysis on the level of subconscious deep reflexes, as well as those on the level of worldview. Four worldview models have been presented in order to make this concept practical: the stratigraphic model of creation, the five basic

---

[79] Monet, *L'Église émergente*, p. 189-380.
[80] Idem, p. 309.
[81] The four characteristics are: biblicism, crucicentrism, conversionism and missionary activism. David Bebbington, *Evangelicalism in Modern Britain: A History from 1730 to the 1980s* (London: Unwin Hyman, 1989), p. 2-3.

soteriological concepts, conscience orientation and the time concept. The conscience orientation model is particularly fruitful to orient an approach to evangelism after having analysed persons, subcultures and segments of European societies.

Further Reading

Breen, Mike & Absalom, Alex, *Launching Missional Communities: A Field Guide* (London: 3DM Press, 2010).

Chilcote, Paul W. & Warner, Lacey C., *The Study of Evangelism: Exploring the Missional Practice of the Church* (Grand Rapids: Eerdmans, 2008).

Cray, Graham, *Mission-Shaped Church: Church Planting and Fresh Expressions in Changing Contexts* (London: Church House Publishing, 2004).

Cross, John R., *The Stranger on the Emmaus Road* (Gatineau: Goodseed, 2000), www.goodseed.com/thestranger.aspx.

Engel, James F., "The Engel Scale Explained," www.gospelcom.net/guide/resources/tellitoften.php.

Gray, Frank, « Engel Scale or Gray Matrix? », http://thegraymatrix.org/?p=211.

Green, Michael, *Evangelism in the Early Church* (rev. ed.; Eastbourne: Kingsway, 2003; 1st ed.: Grand Rapids: Eerdmans, 1970).

Keller, Timothy, *Center Church: Doing Balanced, Gospel-Centered Ministry in Your City* (Grand Rapids: Zondervan, 2012)

Krabill, James R. et al. (eds.), *Worship and Mission for the Global Church: An Ethnodoxology Handbook* (Pasadena: William Carey Library, 2012).

Lovejoy, Grant, ed., *Making Disciples of Oral Learners* (Lausanne Occasional Paper No. 54; Lima, NY/Bangalore: Lausanne Committee on World Evangelization/International Orality Network, 2005). http://orality.net/resources/docs/Making_Disciples_of_Oral_Learners-1264691848.pdf.

Ott, Craig & Wilson, Gene, *Global Church Planting: Biblical Principles and Best Practices for Multiplication* (Grand Rapids: Baker, 2011).

Sa'a, Yehia, *All that the Prophets Have Spoken* (Gatineau: Goodseed, 2000), www.goodseed.com/theprophets.aspx.

Stark, Rodney, *The Rise of Christianity: A Sociologist Reconsiders History* (Princeton, NJ: Princeton University Press, 1996).

Strähler, Reinhold, *Coming to Faith in Christ: Understanding Conversion* (Nairobi: Life Challenge, 2010).

Ward, Pete, *Liquid Church* (Exeter: Paternoster, 2002).

Wiher, Hannes, *Shame and Guilt: A Key to Cross-Cultural Ministry* (Bonn: VKW, 2003).

Wiher, Hannes, "Worldview and Oral Preference Learners and Leaders," in *Beyond Literate Western Practices: Continuing Conversations in Orality and Theological Education*, ed. Samuel E. Chiang and Grant Lovejoy (Hong Kong: Capstone Enterprises, 2014), p. 109-125.

Chapter 10
Outreach amongst African-Led Churches in Switzerland: A Case Study

Johannes Müller

The Lord's Hand Was with Them

A great number of people of many nations believing and turning to God. That is the desire and prayer of Christians today. This already happened, almost 2000 years ago, in the ancient city of Antioch. Refugees persecuted for their faith arrived in this city bringing with them their belief in Jesus Christ. Like many refugees today, they spread their faith amongst people of their own culture and origin. As the saying goes, "charity begins at home." With positive experiences from their kin, they continued spreading their faith. But the real breakthrough came when some of the migrants started to use their cross-cultural experience and spoke to people of a different culture and language background. "The two key attributes that these accidental church planters had from the Jerusalem experience was a passion for Jesus and the fire of evangelism – missional zeal!"[1] The account in Acts 11:19-21 makes it clear that, as soon as evangelism became cross-cultural, the Lord's hand was with them and great numbers came to Christ.

In present day Europe, among many other refugees and migrants, fervent believers in Jesus Christ are arriving from distant countries of Latin America, Africa and Asia. Many of them are highly motivated to communicate the Gospel in their host countries. As they share their faith, can the Lord's hand be seen in action as during the times of Acts?

In this study we will narrow the scope down to a case study of African initiated evangelism in Switzerland. As part of the activities of "African Link," a ministry alongside African church leaders in Switzerland, we have interviewed several pastors and elders about the evangelism of their

---

[1] Anderson Moyo, "Missional Strategies from Antioch: Lessons for African Missionaries in Britain," *Missio Africanus* vol. 1, No. 2 (January 2016), p. 43.

churches. Before presenting the survey, I will briefly sum up a few observations made by other authors on evangelism and church planting in Europe through Christians from other continents and more specifically from Africa.

Role of African Christians in the West

"African Christians and African-led churches in Europe interpret their presence in terms of a call to mission and evangelism," as Kwabena Asamoah-Gyadu expresses it.[2] The understanding is that the Holy Spirit brought them to Europe to evangelise both fellow Africans and Europeans.[3] A fast-growing number of churches have been planted that "have provided a space for black people to develop their complex identity and feel included in a country that often excludes them."[4] Thus they contribute to the renewal and preservation of Christianity in the Western world. This missionary role is being more and more acknowledged by traditional churches in Europe, including in Switzerland.[5]

What do African Christians bring to the West? Cathy Ross puts it like this: "Africans offer a focus on spiritual power, a strong belief in the supernatural, a moral and ethical conservatism, a clear belief in the authority of the Scriptures, a sensibility towards injustice and a communal apprehension and realisation of the Christian faith."[6]

---

[2] Kwabena Asamoah-Gyadu, "African-Led Christianity in Europe: Migration and Diaspora Evangelism," *Lausanne World Pulse* (July 2008), p. 11, at www.lausanne worldpulse.com/pdf/issues/LWPJuly2008PDF.pdf (accessed on July 24, 2017).

[3] Johannes Müller, "Afrikanische Diaspora in der Schweiz," *Evangelikale Missiologie* 25, 3 (2009), p. 138, at www.missiologie.org/mediapool/79/797956/data/em_Archiv/em2009-3.pdf (accessed on July 24, 2017).

[4] Israel Olofinjana, *Reverse in Ministry and Missions: Africans in the Dark Continent of Europe* (Milton Keynes: Author House, 2010), p. 48.

[5] See e.g. studies sponsored by the Catholic and Protestant churches, respectively: Arnd Bünker, "Typen christlicher Migrationsgemeinden und postmigratorischer Perspektiven," in *Kirchen in Bewegung: Christliche Migrationsgemeinden in der Schweiz*, ed. Judith Albisser & Arnd Bünker (St.Gallen: SPI, 2016), p. 123-127; Simon Röthlisberger & Matthias Wüthrich, *Neue Migrationskirchen in der Schweiz* (Bern: Schweizerischer Evangelischer Kirchenbund, 2009), p. 43-44, at www.migrationskirchen.ch/resources/Neue_Migrationskirchen_in_CHSEKStudie1.pdf (accessed July 26, 2017).

[6] Cathy Ross, "Mission in a Strange Land," *Missio Africanus: Journal of African Missiology*, vol. 1, No. 2 (January 2016), p. 32.

This is a reviving wind of an authentic faith in Jesus Christ that Western societies have been missing for a while already. Therefore, a majority of members of African-led churches in the United States interviewed by Jehu Hanciles are very much in favour of more cross-cultural outreach, but they are also ambivalent about how the "Africanness" of their church life influences the fruit of their efforts.[7] Harvey Kwiyani observes the same evangelistic zeal, but also points to the fact that very often methods from Africa are being used.[8] It may be due to this fact that some authors question the effectiveness of evangelism among the indigenous population, at least in Germany.[9]

Nonetheless, Africans have brought some of the fastest growing church movements to Europe. The Redeemed Christian Church of God (RCCG) has initiated a bold vision and strategy for a Nigeria sponsored *reverse mission*, i.e. the initiative to bring back faith in Christ to the countries that sowed it in Africa in the past.[10] This strategy is bearing fruit: RCCG is spreading to more and more countries and in some of them, they multiply fast.

Africans have also started and continue to lead the largest churches in Europe. The largest church in Western Europe, Kingsway International Christian Centre (KICC) in London, has reached an attendance of at least 12 000 people.[11] However, they seem to mainly attract and cater for immigrants.[12] According to Harvey Kwiyani's observation, 97 % of the 16 000

---

[7] Jehu J. Hanciles, *Beyond Christendom: Globalization, African Migration, and the Transformation of the West* (Maryknoll: Orbis Books, 2008), p. 366.

[8] Harvey Kwiyani, "Blessed Reflex: African Christians in Europe," *Missio Africanus* vol. 3, No. 1, 2017, p. 46-47.

[9] Samuel D. Johnson, "Europa im Visier afrikanischer Missionare," in *Missionare aus der Zweidrittel-Welt für Europa*, ed. Klaus W. Müller (Nürnberg: VTR, 2004), p. 71; Claudia Währisch-Oblau, "Getting Ready to Receive? German Churches and the 'New Mission' from the South," in *Lausanne World Pulse* (July 2008), p. 18, at www.lausanneworldpulse.com/pdf/issues/LWPJuly2008PDF.pdf (accessed on July 24, 2017).

[10] Afe Adogame, *The African Christian Diaspora: New Currents and Emerging Trends in World Christianity* (London/New York: Bloomsbury, 2013), p. 182-184.

[11] Israel Olofinjana has dedicated a very inspiring chapter of his book to a description of KICC. Olofinjana, *Reverse in Ministry and Missions*, p. 58-72.

[12] Jehu J. Hanciles, "Migration and Mission: The Religious Significance of the North South Divide," in *Mission in The Twenty-First Century: Exploring the Five Marks of Global Mission*, ed. Andrew F. Walls & Cathy Ross (Maryknoll: Orbis Books, 2008), p. 128.

members of the Church of Pentecost in the UK in 2015 were Ghanaian and over 90 % of the 150 000 members of RCCG Nigerian.[13]

The largest church in all of Europe, the Embassy of God Church in Kiev, Ukraine, planted by Sunday Adelaja from Nigeria, shows a different picture. It claims to have a membership of up to 25 000 and has reached masses of Ukrainians from various strata of society. In his portrait of the church, Afe Adogame points to a key element for its success: "Adelaja weaves elements of indigenous African cosmology to appeal to the spiritual sensibilities of Ukrainians."[14] The African cosmology translates for example into fervent spiritual warfare.

Doubtlessly, African-led churches in Europe are growing and multiplying, often very fast. Several are struggling to connect to the indigenous European population. However, some churches are reaching nationals, such as Sunday Adelaja's church in Ukraine exemplifies.

Most authors present the vision and calling of African church leaders. When it comes to results, they mention a few large churches, but there is little insight into the evangelism of average African-led churches that are much smaller. For this reason, we wanted to discover more about the experience of African-led churches in Switzerland.

Survey among African Church Leaders in Switzerland

Between 2013 and 2016, "African Link" conducted 28 structured qualitative interviews with African church leaders. It covered the three major language groups among African-led evangelical and charismatic/Pentecostal churches in Switzerland.

Ten interviews were done with leaders of English speaking churches. They represent foreigners of the most widely spread international language. Eleven interviews were conducted with French speaking leaders. The ministry of five of them is based in the French speaking part of the country. Their churches use the same language as the society around them, but the cultural expression is very different. The remaining seven interviews were with leaders of Eritrean and Ethiopian churches. Two of them have an almost entirely Eritrean membership, the others are a mix of migrants from the two neighbouring countries. These churches represent the situation of churches from a specific ethnolinguistic region whose language is not easily accessible for people of the host country.

---

[13] Kwiyani, "Blessed Reflex: African Christians in Europe," p. 45.
[14] Adogame, *The African Christian Diaspora*, p. 188.

On average, the Sunday services of the churches covered by the survey are attended by 70 adults and young people, plus about 20 children, mostly taken care of in special programs. The largest church counts about 200 adults and teens, plus 50 children. In eight of the surveyed churches, the programs are either conducted in or interpreted into the language of the respective host region.[15] In six more churches, a translation was available upon request. The rest of the churches, i.e. half of them, used a language different from the one spoken in society around it.

The oldest church in the survey was founded in 1990, the youngest in 2012. The average age of the churches was 14 years. Thus, African-led churches in Switzerland are young, as are several of their leaders. Only few had received pastoral training before arriving in Switzerland, while others were trained in Swiss institutions, through their movements or by informal channels.

Over the past ten years, I have visited a considerable number of African church leaders and their churches in Switzerland. Regularly, the calling of the church, testimonies from evangelistic outreach and conversion stories of new members were related. Some of these observations and reports will be used to exemplify the findings of the survey.

Evangelism through African-led Churches

A remarkable finding of the survey is that about half of the present members of the surveyed churches came to a living faith in Jesus Christ through the ministry of the respective church. The evangelism of African-led churches in Switzerland bears fruit. Several of the new believers had been nominal protestant Christians before, others were members of the orthodox or other traditional churches, or of no church at all.

There is, however, a notable difference between the language groups in the sample. The English-speaking churches claimed about a third of their present membership who had come to faith in Jesus Christ through their own ministry. This proportion rises to slightly over a half for the French-speaking and close to 60% for the Tigrinya/Amharic-speaking churches.

The actual number of conversions is higher than these figures indicate. Most churches mention that they regularly lose members due to departures to other countries. Unless international churches find new members, the

---

[15] German or French, depending on the part of the country. No leaders of churches in the much smaller Italian speaking south of Switzerland were interviewed.

participation in their programs invariably decreases. Therefore, evangelism is critical for their survival, not just an option.

Approaches to Evangelism

The most extensive part of the interviews was about the methods for evangelism the churches used, what kind of results they experienced and which approaches they expected to be effective. Most frequently, the leaders mentioned evangelism in public places, big events, church programs and personal evangelism.

Outreach to the Public Place

Several of the interviewed leaders first mentioned evangelism in the street with music, preaching and talking to people. They noted that they could relatively easily contact people of a similar cultural and linguistic background, explain the Gospel and invite them to visit their church.

Most leaders, however, doubted the effectiveness of evangelism in public places to reach the local population. Swiss people do not seem to have time nor are they open for contacts with people they are not acquainted with. Therefore, several church leaders didn't feel encouraged by their experiences, but nevertheless said that they should do outreach in the streets more frequently.

Reaching out to fellow Africans can take on a special form, namely through contacts with new arrivals in waiting halls of migration offices or visits in centres for asylum seekers. One of the churches participating in the survey was even started as a prayer group in such a centre, but became a regular church a long time ago; at present, it does not have any attendees in the asylum process any more.

A few years ago, Ethiopian and Eritrean Evangelical/Pentecostal Christians were the only ones to visit their newly arrived countrymen in these centres, and they could easily invite them to their churches. With Eritrea currently having been among the top two countries of origin of asylum seekers in Switzerland for more than ten years, the community has grown considerably and continues to do so. Other programs for Eritreans have multiplied, and Evangelical or Pentecostal churches cannot rely solely on the attraction of providing the feeling of home anymore.

One of the pastors also visits Africans who are in detention pending repatriation back to their countries of origin. If such detainees have managed to stay in Switzerland, they are highly motivated to join their visitor's church after release from detention. Tangible signs of love such as visiting detainees make a church attractive.

Jointly Organised Big Events

A common expectation of several interview partners was that more partnerships of churches in the area of evangelism would produce better results. Some anticipated that intercultural collaboration between African-led and Swiss churches would broaden the scope of evangelistic outreach and make it more relevant for the Swiss population.

It is the hope of some of the pastors that events on such a broad basis would produce more effect: the higher the number of involved churches, the bigger the campaign, which would attract a larger audience and have a stronger impact on public visibility and results. In a Swiss city, a small African-led association that has the objective to evangelise through African Christian music stimulated the local section of the Swiss Evangelical Alliance to organise major international church services together. The events were a multicultural highlight drawing as many as 2500 people in the peak year. They were a major success in the networking of the body of Christ, but the evangelistic impact was difficult to determine.

What should the main thrust of joint evangelistic programs be? An African pastor expressed his vision in this way: "We believe that all human beings, irrespective of their background or nationality, are looking for the supernatural. That's why I think that if we do our evangelism with the power of the supernatural, it will be much easier." Another pastor also encouraged joint evangelism based on healing, miracles and preaching of salvation, but he was much more sceptical about potential results. According to him, Swiss people are rather closed and not even miracles change that. Unlike one would expect from this opinion, this pastor is actually experiencing miracles in his ministry. After a car accident, he was confined to a wheel chair. In the centre for paraplegia patients, he started to pray for people who shared his condition and some started walking. However, he himself remained in the wheel chair. He himself was not healed until two years later. His healing ministry continued and he receives invitations for campaigns in several countries. Nevertheless, he is still unconvinced that miracles contribute substantially to open the Swiss public for the Gospel.

African pastors seem to notice the difficulty in mobilising big crowds for evangelistic programs in today's Switzerland. One interview partner also noticed that big churches were reluctant to participate in joint activities, because – in his understanding – they wanted to protect what they have.

Some African-led churches are seeking new channels to reach larger audiences and stream their programs on the internet, but they realise that there also, they have to compete with many other Christian offers. As a result, some of my interview partners mentioned their dream to get access to nationwide media for broadcasting Christian programs, a dream not yet materialised.

Church Programs

Since joint programs are rare, almost all African-led churches rely on their own programs to attract new visitors. Some encourage their members to invite friends, family and neighbours for normal Sunday services or for special family events such as child dedications. One church gives special attention to such events by providing an important time slot during the worship service and inviting family members and friends for snacks afterwards.

Other churches organise conferences with special speakers and spread invitations as broadly as possible in the church's social networks. The more church members identify with these programs and the more personal contacts they have, the greater is the likelihood of bringing new people to the church through such programs.

A particularly important contact format are food parties. They express African hospitality and are a special attraction for two diverse groups: people of the same origin who want to reconnect with the taste of their homeland, culinarily and otherwise, and for other people on the quest of an exotic flavour.

Interestingly French speaking African-led churches in the French speaking part of Switzerland do not seem to have an advantage in inviting Swiss people compared to their sister churches in a German-speaking environment. Although they share the language of the surrounding community, the cultural difference is so visible that only Swiss people searching for a cross-cultural experience would accept an invitation to such an African-led church.

Once visitors have turned up, much depends on how they are received. One pastor explained his strategy: "We focus on a conducive atmosphere. When people are in the atmosphere, they find themselves quickly participating in church activities. When they are involved, they want to know more, how to do it better, and they are discipled through it. We bring them to a life style, and finally they come to Jesus."

Cultural and linguistic proximity, however, do not guarantee a good contact. An Eritrean church leader told me that Orthodox countrymen are highly suspicious towards their Pentecostal group and would not easily accept an invitation to one of their programs or worship services. He had better contacts at a multicultural celebration organised by a Swiss church where he could translate for Orthodox Eritreans who were invited by his Swiss friends and explain the Gospel to them.

One of my interview partners stressed that his main strategy was to start new branches in other towns. Through this method, his church could multiply the relational networks of the members and get access to new communities at the new locations.

International, African-initiated denominations pursue a similar goal.[16] In Switzerland, the multiplication of their branches has so far been relatively slow, probably because immigration from their countries of origin is almost impossible via legal channels.

Personal and Relational Evangelism

Most respondents agreed that the main channel to get in contact with new people are personal networks. This applies primarily to reaching fellow Africans. Up to now, the African community in the country is relatively small (less than 1.5 %) and scattered throughout Swiss cities and towns. Attracting crowds just by offering an African style program hardly produces significant results.

Therefore, several pastors put an emphasis on training: "It is the key. When people know why they do what they do, they can come to another level." This also applies to inviting their acquaintances to church events. Some pay special attention to strengthening new believers and encouraging them to use their contacts for spreading the Gospel.

Many leaders presume that relational evangelism is most promising, but not straightforward in practice. As one pastor explained, it requires showing interest in the other person's life and developing friendships. But many of his church members, due to the requirements of everyday life in Switzerland, do not have enough time for contacts with new people.

Relational evangelism will only become cross-cultural if Christians build cross-cultural contacts. Africans are known for their hospitality, but many find it hard to offer it to Swiss people or other immigrants. Language is an important obstacle, bridging the cultural gap another. Harvey Kwiyani sums it up: "Many say it is too difficult to reach out to Europeans. Many have told me, 'It forces us to do things differently, and that is too uncomfortable.' By 'doing things differently,' they mean such things as

---

[16] Some of the most active denominations in Switzerland are: "Lighthouse Chapel International" (LCI) from Ghana, "Redeemed Christian Church of God" (RCCG) from Nigeria, and "L'Éternel est bon" from Congo.

having shorter worship services or having to embrace relational evangelism."[17]

Despite such challenges, some Africans find paths to communicate the Gospel even where they are not supposed to. A lady from Congo told us: "I really love my job at the retirement home. Sometimes, I offer to pray for the elderly and they gladly accept. Or I sing for them in French. Several asked me for a Bible and one lady accepted Jesus Christ as her Lord and Saviour. Recently, my superior, a Muslim immigrant from south-eastern Europe, rebuked me and told me not to sing Christian songs at work. I think that he is jealous because many of the elderly ask me to look after them. The chief of the nursing service, a Swiss lady, also called for me. She told me that, when she is, she would love to be taken care of by someone like me. Nevertheless, the home did not permit religious propaganda at work, and therefore I should stop telling people about my faith. But I found the solution: now I sing when I wash an elderly person in the shower – no one else hears me."

Summary and Complementary Observations

In summary, what are the approaches that most of the interviewed African leaders felt were essential? Many mentioned the need for intensive and ongoing prayer, often combined with fasting and spiritual warfare. One pastor puts it like this: "It is impossible to plant a church without all nights," referring to a monthly all night's prayer meeting. These are frequent in African-led churches, either during the first or the last Friday to Saturday night of each month.

The second emphasis, as the discussion of the different approaches above has shown, was on using the relational networks of the members. They are encouraged to invite their family, friends, neighbours, and work colleagues for family events at church, conferences, or worship services. Or to build friendships and evangelise them in their context.

Beyond the above approaches used by most churches, further methods that were quoted are diverse and seem to depend largely on the vision and the personal gifting of the pastor or evangelist. A few mentioned encouraging responses to their ministry among young Africans born in Switzerland. A few others related experiences of healings and miracles. Some rely on African style worship, music and hospitality to attract new people. Others promote church multiplication as a means to draw more attendants.

---

[17] Kwiyani, "Blessed Reflex: African Christians in Europe," p. 45.

The communities that see an important inflow of asylum seekers are also the ones who reach out specifically to this group. In Switzerland, in recent years, by far the most numerous African refugees came from Eritrea. Almost all Eritrean churches mentioned that they do visits in asylum centres and other locations set aside for refugees.

Many of the interviewed African leaders were not aware of any evangelistic efforts by Swiss churches. Only a few had observed Swiss Christians distributing tracts or reaching out in the streets, sometimes together with specialised ministries or regional networks. None of them mentioned Swiss-initiated church plants or Alpha sessions.[18] These courses that present Christian faith to interested people have produced an encouraging response in Swiss churches over the last twenty years. African church leaders do not seem to be aware of these activities. This exemplifies that there is very little exchange between African and Swiss church leaders about evangelism and about approaches each side considers to be most effective. Their perception that Swiss churches are not active in evangelism will not encourage African leaders to deepen cross-cultural collaboration in this area.

Who Is Being Reached?

The qualitative survey has shown that one out of two current members of African-led churches have come to an authentic faith in Jesus Christ through the ministry of the church. But which backgrounds do the new members come from?

Fellow Africans

By far the largest part of the church attendants are of African origin. All surveyed English and French speaking churches have a mix of different African nationalities and different language groups within the countries. However, Ghanaian and Nigerian pastors respectively seem to attract more of their own countrymen. In the French speaking churches, people from Congo or Angola predominate. Eritrean led churches seem to be quite homogeneous, Ethiopian-led churches more often also have a partially Eritrean membership.

---

[18] These courses are promoted in Switzerland under the name of "Alphalive" in the languages of the country (www.alphalive.ch). Only recently, a few multicultural churches started courses in a multilingual setting.

African-led churches attract new arrivals from the continent by offering them a feeling of home. One pastor emphasised that a particular appeal of his church to fellow Africans are transformed lives: former prostitutes or thieves having changed due to the action of the Holy Spirit in their hearts and turning into models for others.

Several churches, many of them Eritrean led, grow due to the number of children. However, this only partially compensates for departures due to migration dynamics and lack of residency status.

Only very few pastors mentioned having one or two Muslim background believers who attend their churches. Some of the countries of origin such as Eritrea, Nigeria and Ghana, have significant Muslim populations, but Christians constitute an overwhelming majority of the immigrants to Switzerland. Churches led by pastors from these countries seem to reach out more effectively to nominal Christian than to Muslim countrymen. Contacts with Muslims from other countries are no more frequent.

Swiss People

Only one of the African initiated churches has a significant Swiss membership. In this case, Swiss people even constitute the larger part of the church. Most other churches have only won a very small number of Swiss people, if any at all. In some churches, most Swiss are spouses of African members.

Many Swiss who have joined an African-led church have initially been invited either for church conferences or, often more effectively, for food parties. African relational culture and hospitality combined with the exotic flavour of new dishes are attractive to some. In order to get beyond mere curiosity, the church needs to involve visitors in practical activities as quickly as possible. At least this is the procedure of the church with the most significant Swiss membership. By active participation, new people build friendships with church members and finally start inquiring about the source of the authentic love they experience.

However, language constitutes a major barrier. In the above-mentioned example, the church translates all activities from English into both German and French, since it is located in a bilingual city. Translations of programs are not sufficient, it is equally important that newcomers can communicate with church members after the service. This is a major obstacle for French language churches in the German-speaking part of the country: there are not many Swiss around feeling comfortable in the language of the other part of the country. And it definitely applies to the Tigrinya and Amharic speaking churches. However, at least in two of these churches, a Swiss person has joined, learned the language and now serves as a bridge person for outside contacts.

A different phenomenon are a few Swiss churches in the French-speaking part of the country that have engaged an African pastor. One of the interviewed pastors leads two churches. The church he planted himself consists mainly of Africans. The other one was entirely Swiss when it invited him to become their pastor, but it has gained some African members since. The present survey did not cover any other Swiss churches led by African pastors. Additional interviews are needed to discover what can be learned from their experience.

Other Immigrant Minorities

Interestingly, immigrant groups other than Africans were not mentioned in any interview. This is very astonishing since about 36 % of the residential population of Switzerland have a migration background.[19] In a few churches, some isolated immigrants from non-African countries attend the service. But most African-led churches do not seem to be aware that reaching out to other immigrant groups may be a special opportunity. At least, they share similar migration experiences and integration challenges. Theoretically, this constitutes a common basis for African Christians to share how they experienced the love and power of Jesus in this situation.

Why does evangelising other immigrant groups not seem be a focus of African-led Churches? Building contacts with people of a higher social position increases one's status in the eyes of one's friends and family.[20] However, evangelising immigrants who struggle with Swiss life will not produce that type of esteem. This could also be a reason why there are only very small numbers of Muslim background believers in African-led churches, as already mentioned.

---

[19] www.bfs.admin.ch/bfs/en/home/statistics/population/migration-integration/by-migra tion-status.html (accessed on July 24, 2017).

[20] David R. Dunaetz, "Three Models of Acculturation: Applications for Developing a Church Planting Strategy among Diaspora Populations," in *Diaspora Missiology: Reflections on Reaching the Scattered Peoples of the World*, ed. Michael Pocock & Enoch Wan (Pasadena: William Carey Library, 2015), p. 143, at https://papers.ssrn.com/sol3/papers.cfm?abstract_id=2668916 (accessed on April 29, 2017).

International Outreach

About two thirds of the interviewed church leaders are involved in various types of international outreach.[21] Three churches are planting branches in neighbouring European countries, at least five in the leader's country of origin and two in new African countries. One of these church plants took off when the member of an African-led church moved to Mauritius and invited her former pastor to start a church in her new host country.

Several pastors regularly receive invitations for ministry in other countries, some as far as South and North America, or South and East Asia. At least one is involved in a global internet ministry. Three of the interviewed pastors are part of African denominations that are active worldwide.

The Eritrean churches have the fewest opportunities for international ministry, mostly due to travel restrictions and lack of religious freedom in their home country. However, at least one is actively supporting suffering brothers and sisters in faith in their home country.

In summary, African-led churches in Switzerland are actively involved in missions that the Global Diaspora Network of the Lausanne Movement calls "through" and "beyond" the diasporas, i.e. to people of the same origin, and other populations on a worldwide scale.[22]

Perspectives for Cross-Cultural Outreach

In the near future, public awareness of African-led churches will rise in Switzerland and in Europe. On one hand, more refugees and migrants will come and the number of Africans, i.e. the number of potential church members, will grow. As the survey has shown, the African-led churches will not miss the opportunity. On the other hand, Swiss-led churches, in particular the state churches, face ongoing decline. Therefore, the proportion of churches with an African, Latin American and Asian background will significantly grow in Switzerland and other European countries.

With time and intensifying contacts, African-led churches will become better aware of how to build bridges to the European population and more and more Europeans will join these churches.

What can be done to increase this impact? During a seminar, several African church leaders in Switzerland compiled a list of the needs of their

---

[21] Jehu Hanciles mentions that more than half of the African pastors in the US are engaged in international ministry. Hanciles, *Beyond Christendom*, p. 364.

[22] Lausanne Committee of World Evangelization, *Scattered to Gather: Embracing the Global Trend of Diaspora* (Manila: LifeChange, 2010), p. 28-29.

churches.²³ In first place, they mentioned leadership training, followed by finance. This second issue is particularly critical for churches composed of a high proportion of asylum seekers. Other challenges listed were building intercultural bridges, collaboration between churches and questions about children and the second generation.

We will look at these challenges from the perspective of their relevance for evangelism.

Readiness to Learn

Israel Olofinjana has published an eye-opening book with stories of missionaries from Asia, Latin America and Africa to the United Kingdom. In the concluding chapter, he explains that all the self-portrayed ministers, and many others, learned on the job how to be a missionary.²⁴ He also relates his own decision to join an existing British church because he noted that "many Nigerian churches had not managed to attract white British indigenes [and] did not know how to engage in cross-cultural missions."²⁵ His desire to learn was so intense, that he was prepared to sacrifice part of his identity in order to gain new perspectives – an attitude he challenges others to adopt.²⁶

The learning may also include language. Olofinjana encourages migration background churches in Britain to speak English during church services, even if it requires that some members and leaders get enrolled in language classes. According to him, using the language of the country is not only important to attract people from other cultures, but also to retain their second and third generations.²⁷

Contextualisation of Message and Style

Language constitutes a formidable obstacle,²⁸ but cultural expression and style sometimes even more. Therefore, every preacher of the Gospel

---

²³ Müller, "Afrikanische Diaspora in der Schweiz," p. 140-143.
²⁴ Israel Olofinjana, *Turning the Tables on Mission: Stories of Christians from the Global South in the UK* (Watford: Instant Apostle, 2013), p. 226.
²⁵ Idem, p. 225.
²⁶ Idem, p. 230.
²⁷ Idem, p. 230.
²⁸ In a country like Switzerland, the obstacle is big indeed. Each region has a different official language. Furthermore, in the German speaking part, people use a very strong dialect in social contacts, even in church programs.

should question himself, as Olofinjana puts it: "Am I communicating to anyone?"[29]

This is the challenge of contextualising message and style. Harvey Kwiyani presses the point:

> African Christians want to reach out to Westerners, but they find it hard to make congregational cultures open to Westerners. ... Many African immigrant ministers preach their long sermons in a very African style – spiced with vernacular jokes and delivered with shouting and sweating. Most Westerners who appreciate shorter, well-prepared sermons delivered in a talk/presentation style find these African tendencies off-putting. Africans end up raising barriers to their own effectiveness – barriers that separate insiders from outsiders, consequently discouraging outsiders from joining their congregations.[30]

Joint efforts are an ideal framework for learning how to contextualise message and style in evangelism.

Strategic Partnerships

Joint evangelistic programs and, even more so, strategic partnerships with churches that are different in terms of culture require building good relationships and mutual trust.[31] An important starting point is an open attitude on both sides. Moyo Anderson expresses it as follows: "In order to become cross-culturally appealing, the diaspora church in the Western world needs to develop strategic partnerships without the colonial paternalistic tendencies of the traditional mission models."[32] He challenges mother churches in Africa to allow their overseas branches to develop in tune with their new context and milieu.

Well established intercultural partnerships will allow each side to contribute its best: African Christians will bring their irresistible zeal to pray and evangelise, European Christians their grasp of the cultural gap that needs to be bridged to connect with people.[33] Thus, the partnership will turn into a platform of mutual stimulation and learning from one another. And the joint evangelism will generate more public awareness and, above

---

[29] Idem, p. 229.
[30] Harvey C. Kwiyani, *Sent Forth: African Missionary Work in the West* (Maryknoll: Orbis, 2014), p. 151.
[31] For more hints on intercultural collaboration between churches, see also chapter 7: "The Mosaic of Cultures: A Challenge for European and International Churches," by the present author in this volume.
[32] Moyo, "Missional Strategies from Antioch," p. 47-48.
[33] Kwiyani, "Blessed Reflex: African Christians in Europe," p. 47.

all, result in more effectiveness.[34] The faith of Africans is perceived as more authentic and credible. And Africans and Europeans sharing their faith together is seen as even more authentic and credible.

Such intercultural collaboration will have to get over some hurdles. Which church shall people who are interested be encouraged to join? The church that reflects their culture more closely? Or the church of the Christian who established the contact? If the involved churches have a trusting relationship and are open for the leading of the Holy Spirit, they will find the best solution.

Another critical issue is the cost of joint programs. As a few leaders expressed in the above-mentioned seminar, finance can constitute a major obstacle for some African-led churches, but not for all. Again, trusting relationships between the leaders will open the path for a solution in which each church contributes as it can. It is important not to see only the financial part of the partnership, but also the human involvement and gifting. This will give a more balanced picture of the role of each church.

A Key: The Second Generation

The potentially largest impact of African Christianity on Switzerland and Europe is still underway: the second-generation Christians of African descent. Afe Adogame describes his hope:

> The second and third generation immigrant youth might be the most versatile missionaries for the mission field of Europe and North America, if they are well harnessed and empowered.[35]

This "harnessing" will start at a young age and include bilingual Sunday school programs for children in the languages of the host country and of the church, as well as joint programs with young Christians of the host country, not forgetting a close follow-up of this young generation growing up between cultures. Some of them will be called by the Holy Spirit and realise how God has prepared them for a missionary service. They need to be linked up with training institutions in the host country and with sources for special funding.

---

[34] Siegfried Winkler, "Miteinander und / oder nebeneinander evangelisieren," Runder Tisch Evangelisation 2006, at www.lausannerbewegung.de/data/files/content.runde rtisch/102.pdf (accessed on July 25, 2017).

[35] Adogame, *The African Christian Diaspora*, p. 208.

What Can Swiss and European Churches Learn?

Swiss churches need to acknowledge that more than a third of the country's residents have a migration background. This is a too important part of the population to be ignored. And they need to acknowledge that they cannot do the job by themselves. It would even be a sign of ethnocentrism to try to do so. They don't even need to. God has sent a new harvest force to join indigenous churches in this harvest field: Christians from Africa, Latin America and Asia.

In this new community of Christians from various backgrounds, all sides are learners. Indigenous churches are not simply senior partners. They can learn from the African community-oriented culture – a big need in today's Western individualistic societies where many people are becoming lonely – and from the African zeal for Jesus, for prayer and for evangelism. Joint efforts and strategic partnerships for evangelism are wonderful opportunities for Swiss and European churches to serve their African-led counterparts through their experience of the local culture. But even there, indigenous churches need the new look of African immigrant Christians to help them avoid their weaknesses. And last, but not least, indigenous Christians have an important role to play in empowering the second-generation African young people.

Conclusion

The qualitative survey of 28 African-led churches in Switzerland has revealed a steady, but not yet spectacular growth. In the context of stagnating indigenous churches, any progress is a special grace operated by the Holy Spirit.

This picture matches the account of evangelism and church growth in the ancient city of Antioch in Acts 11. The biblical text does not present a success method, but it shows God's hand at work when interculturally experienced Christians share their faith. Part of this is already under way, more is to come when the young second-generation Africans will be fully released.

The Antioch experience also stresses the role of interculturally experienced leaders and partners.[36] The arrival of Barnabas, this "good man, full of the Holy Spirit and of faith" (Acts 11:24), was instrumental in furthering the impact of evangelism in the city. Barnabas was able to see the

---

[36] See Anderson Moyo's insightful description of the role of Barnabas and Paul: Moyo, "Missional Strategies from Antioch," p. 45-47.

grace of God in these possibly chaotic beginnings of intercultural outreach. He could foster the new plant by seeking more cross-culturally experienced partners such as Paul and others (Acts 11:25-26; 13:1) and by training the new church. Finally, the church sent a missionary team to his home region, Cyprus, and to new regions beyond (Acts 13:4-9 and following).

The present survey has unveiled all these aspects in the life of African-led churches in Switzerland, sometimes only to a limited extent. May we develop Barnabas' discernment of the grace of God and imitate his sensitive implication alongside what God is planning.

Further Reading

Adogame, Afe, *The African Christian Diaspora: New Currents and Emerging Trends in World Christianity* (London/New York: Bloomsbury, 2013).

Asamoah-Gyadu, Kwabena, "African-Led Christianity in Europe: Migration and Diaspora Evangelism," *Lausanne World Pulse* (July 2008), at www.lausanneworldpulse.com/pdf/issues/LWPJuly2008PDF.pdf.

Hanciles, Jehu J., *Beyond Christendom: Globalization, African Migration, and the Transformation of the West* (Maryknoll: Orbis Books, 2008).

Kwiyani, Harvey C., *Sent Forth: African Missionary Work in the West* (Maryknoll: Orbis, 2014).

Kwiyani, Harvey, "Blessed Reflex: African Christians in Europe," *Missio Africanus: Journal of African Missiology* vol. 3, No. 1 (2017), p. 46-47, at http://missioafricanus.org/wp-content/uploads/MAJAM/3-1/Harvey_Kwiyani_Blessed-Reflex-African-Christians-in-Europe.pdf.

Missio Africanus: Journal of African Missiology vol. 1, No. 2 (January 2016), at http://missioafricanus.org/wp-content/uploads/MAJAM/1-2/Missio-Africanus-Journal-Vol-1.-Iss-2.pdf.

Olofinjana, Israel, *Reverse in Ministry and Missions: Africans in the Dark Continent of Europe* (Milton Keynes: Author House, 2010).

Olofinjana, Israel, *Turning the Tables on Mission: Stories of Christians from the Global South in the UK* (Watford: Instant Apostle, 2013).

Pocock, Michael & Wan, Enoch, eds., *Diaspora Missiology: Reflections on Reaching the Scattered Peoples of the World* (Pasadena: William Carey Library, 2015).

Chapter 11
Demonology:
A Forgotten Dimension

Hannes Wiher[1]

In post-Enlightenment Western Europe demons are a largely unknown subject. In evangelical circles, one talks about "occult" phenomena or "occultism," literally "hidden" things. Many specialists in counselling have hardly had any experiences of the demonic world. In theological books, the subject has found little space and attention. While the Church remains perplexed and ignorant, there is a resurgence of interest in these phenomena in certain segments of European society.

This chapter approaches this neglected subject of demonology in a general manner and gives some missiological guidelines. First, we will reflect on the relationship between the biblical God and the other divinities. Then we will study the concept of demons in the Bible. Third, we try a transfer of the biblical data to our European context and our contemporary epoch, and conclude with a reflection on the antagonistic dimension of mission.

God and Gods

In this section we ask how the Bible sees the biblical God and the other divinities, and what is the relationship between them.

Relationship between the Biblical God and the Other Gods

When talking about the biblical God in comparison with the other divinities, the apostle Paul affirms the uniqueness of God the Father and of the Lord Jesus Christ:

> Indeed, even though there may be so-called gods in heaven or on earth – as in fact there are many gods and many lords – yet for us there is one God, the Fa-

---

[1] This text is a revised and enlarged version of a paper presented at the meeting of the Réseau de missiologie évangélique pour l'Europe francophone (REMEEF) on November 19, 2014.

ther, from whom are all things and for whom we exist, and one Lord, Jesus Christ, through whom are all things and through whom we exist (1 Cor 8:5-6).

The apostle Paul says that there are seemingly many divinities but in fact there is only one: the biblical God. The other divinities exist and at the same time do not really exist. Jesus Christ illuminates another dimension of this relationship between the biblical God and the other divinities when he talks about the good shepherd in comparison with the other shepherds. His statement is surprising and challenging:

> Very truly, I tell you, anyone who does not enter the sheepfold by the gate but climbs in by another way is a thief and a bandit. The one who enters by the gate is the shepherd of the sheep. The gatekeeper opens the gate for him, and the sheep hear his voice. He calls his own sheep by name and leads them out. When he has brought out all his own, he goes ahead of them, and the sheep follow him because they know his voice. ... Very truly, I tell you, I am the gate for the sheep. All who came before me are thieves and bandits; but the sheep did not listen to them. ... The thief comes only to steal and kill and destroy. I came that they may have life, and have it abundantly (John 10:1-10).

Jesus Christ says here that he is the only good shepherd; all the other "shepherds" are thieves who come to steal, kill and destroy, not to give life but to take it away. The destructive character is an important sign that indicates the demonic character of divinities. Or else, if the other gods, the state or the ego are perceived as the "good shepherd" who cares, Jesus becomes irrelevant.[2]

Uniqueness of the Biblical God

The Bible affirms that God is unique as Creator, Sovereign and Redeemer. Many times God is presented to us as the creator of the universe (Gen 1-2; Job 40-41; Ps 19; 93; 103:19-22). God is sovereign in history; he directs the life of his people with providence and loving-kindness.[3] The biblical God is not only the Creator, but also the Redeemer after humanity became bogged down in the rut of sin.[4] The people of God who have experienced God's sovereign and redemptive interventions in their lives are called to account for them: "To you it was shown so that you would acknowledge that the Lord is God (*ha'elohim*); there is no other besides

---

[2] Philip Jenkins, *God's Continent: Christianity, Islam, and Europe's Religious Crisis* (Oxford: Oxford University Press, 2007), p. 43.
[3] See Gen; Exod; Josh; 1 & 2 Sam; 1 & 2 Kgs; Ps 105; 106; 136.
[4] See Ruth; Job 19:25; Isa 40ff.

him (*'ein 'od milbado*)" (Deut 4:35).[5] Thus, it is not sufficient to recognise the fact that God is unique. His people are called to witness to this fact.

Uniqueness of Jesus Christ

The uniqueness of Jesus Christ is based on several facts: first it is founded on the uniqueness of YHWH, the "I am" of Exodus 3:14. Jesus presents himself through a series of metaphors from daily life and nature as the "I am" of the OT. In the Gospel of John he says: "I am ...:" the light of the world (John 1:4; 8:12), the bread of life (6:35), the gate (10:9), the good shepherd (10:11), the resurrection and the life (11:25), the way, the truth and the life (14:6), and the vine (15:1). His uniqueness is also founded on the uniqueness of his person (Col 2:9). Christ has come to us (John 1), his life was without sin (Heb 4:15), and he has been announced many times by the patriarchs and the prophets.[6] Not only the patriarchs and the prophets have announced particular details of the life of Jesus, Jesus himself has announced his death and his resurrection (Matt 12:38-42; 16:1-4, 21-23; 17:22f; 20:17-19). Jesus Christ is also unique because of his work of redemption (John 1:9; 1 Tim 2:5). Being truly God and man, only Jesus could be the expiatory sacrifice necessary for the forgiveness of the sins of humanity (Acts 4:12). Finally, Jesus Christ is also unique because of his relationship with the believer through the Holy Spirit (John 14:16). When acknowledging this fact, the apostle Paul talks about "Christ in us" (Col 1:27), and the Catholic dogma describes it in terms of the "inhabitation of the soul" by the Son of God.

As in the OT, where God calls his people to witness to the exploits they have experienced, Jesus exhorts his disciples to witness:

> And he said to them: "Thus it is written, that the Messiah is to suffer and to rise from the dead on the third day, and that repentance and forgiveness of sins is to be proclaimed in his name to all nations, beginning from Jerusalem. You are witnesses of these things (Luke 24:46-48).

Biblical monotheism implies a missionary dimension. If God and Jesus are unique, let us confess it!

---

[5] See also 1 Sam 2:2; 1 Kgs 8:60; Joel 2:27; Isa 45:5.
[6] See for example Gen 3:15; 22:8; Exod 12:5; Deut 18:15; Ps 2:7; 110:4; Isa 52:13-53:12.

Other Divinities

The two Testaments insist on the fact that God is unique. If the proper name of YHWH ("I am") is significant, the names of the other divinities are too. The first name that the Bible gives to them is "image" (Hebrew *'etseb*, Greek *eidolon*, Ps 115:4; 135:15; Isa 46:1f; Hos 13:2; 1 Cor 8:4). Our word "idol" is derived from this Greek word, as used in Psalm 115:

> Their idols are silver and gold, the work of human hands.
> They have mouths, but do not speak; eyes, but do not see.
> They have ears, but do not hear; noses, but do not smell.
> They have hands, but do not feel; feet, but do not walk.
> They make no sound in their throats (Ps 115:4-8; see Ps 135:15-18).

The author of the Psalm remarks that the idols are the "work of human hands" (*ma'aseh yedei 'adam*). In Revelation 9:20 the equivalent Greek term *ergon anthropon* is used. Despite the fact that they have all that a human being can have (a mouth, eyes, ears, etc.), they do not see nor hear nor speak nor walk. Consequently, they can neither help nor save. Habakkuk qualifies the images: a "graven image" (*pesel*, in stone, silver or wood) and a "molten image" (*maseka*, in metal).

> What use is an idol [graven image, KJV] once its maker has shaped it, a cast image [molten image, KJV], a teacher of lies? For its maker trusts in what has been made, though the product is only an idol [*'elil*] that cannot speak! Alas for you who say to the wood, "Wake up!" to silent stone, "Rouse yourself!" Can it teach? See, it is gold and silver plated, and there is no breath in it at all [*ruah*] (Hab 2:18-19).

These idols are simply created beings; they are "profane"; they do not have life in themselves; they are "not God" (*lo 'el*, Deut 32:21; Hos 8:4-6). Being the "work of human hands," they are situated at a different ontological level than the biblical God who is the creator of the universe. In relation to the Creator God, they are "zeros" or "nothings." The name *'elil* "small god" ridicules them (Hab 2:18). Psalm 96 makes a word play out of it: "For all the gods of the nations [*'elohei ha'amim*] are idols [*'elil*]: but the Lord made the heavens (Ps 96:5). Of the 2570 occurrences of the term *'elohim*, the great majority refer to the Creator God, the God of Israel. But in some cases, the same term can equally denote the other divinities, as Psalm 96 has already shown[7]. To avoid this problem, the Septuagint[8] trans-

---

[7] See also Exod 18:11; 20:3; Ps 97:7. Terence E. Fretheim, "*'elohim*," *NIDOTTE*, vol. 1 (Carlisle, UK: Paternoster, 1996), p. 405f.

[8] The Greek translation of the OT during the 3rd and 2nd century BC.

lates *'elohim* in these cases by *angeloi* "angels" (Ps 8:6; 97:7; 138:1).[9] When the sorcerer of Endor calls Samuel, it is also a *'elohim* who appears (1 Sam 28:13).

The book of Samuel picks up the term "chaos" (*tohu*) from Genesis 1:2 to denote the idols: "And do not turn aside after useless things [*tohu*] that cannot profit or save, for they are useless [*tohu*] (1 Sam 12:21). And Isaiah says: "You, indeed, are nothing [*me'ain* "less than nothing"] and your work is nothing [*'epa*] at all; whoever chooses you is an abomination [*to'ébah*]" (Isa 41:24). The prophet Jeremiah calls the idols "vanity" or "breath" (*hebel*, Jer 10:15; 16:19; 51:18). For example: "Goldsmiths are all put to shame by their idols [graven images, KJV]; for their [molten] images are false, and there is no breath [*ruah*] in them. They are vanity [*hebel*], and the work of errors" (Jer 10:14f; see Jon 2:9).

Nevertheless, the idols exist materially, they are visibly active in history and today. They can represent evil spiritual powers, the "demons" (Hebrew *shed*, Greek *daimonion*, Deut 32:16; Ps 106:37; 1 Cor 10:20; Rev 9:20). The NT speaks also of an "impure spirit" (*to akatharton pneuma*) or even an "impure demon" (Matt 12:43; Mark 1:26; Luke 4:33). The OT mentions an "evil spirit" (*ruah ra'ah*) which has come on King Saul (1 Sam 16-19). The author of Deuteronomy mentions the regrettable fact that the Israelites adore strange gods who are demons:

> They made him jealous with strange gods [*zarim*], with abhorrent things [*to'ébot* "abominations"] they provoked him. They sacrificed to demons [*shed*], [who are] not God [*lo 'eloha*], to deities [*'elohim*] they had never known, to new ones recently arrived, whom your ancestors had not feared (Deut 32:16f).

So are idols to be identified with demons? The position taken by the apostle Paul about meat sacrificed to idols could give an indication:

> What do I imply then? That food sacrificed to idols [*eidolothyton*, literally "that which belongs to idols"] is anything, or that an idol [*eidolon*] is anything? No, I imply that what pagans sacrifice, they sacrifice to demons [*daimoniois*] and not to God. I do not want you to be partners with demons. You cannot drink the cup of the Lord and the cup of demons. You cannot partake of the table of the Lord and the table of demons (1 Cor 10:19-21).

When describing the plagues of the sixth trumpet, the apostle John seems to take the same position:

---

[9] G.H. Twelftree, "Spiritual Powers," *New Dictionary of Biblical Theology*, ed. T. Desmond Alexander & Brian S. Rosner (Leicester: IVP, 2000), p. 796.

By these three plagues a third of humankind was killed, by the fire and smoke and sulphur coming out of their [the horses'] mouths. ... The rest of humankind, who were not killed by these plagues, did not repent of the works of their hands [*ergon ton cheiron autou*, that is the idols] or give up worshiping demons [*daimonia*] and idols [*eidola*] of gold and silver and bronze and stone and wood, which cannot see or hear or walk. And they did not repent of their murders or their sorceries or their fornication or their thefts (Rev 9:18-21).

According to the position of Deuteronomy, Paul and John, idols are demons. But why does John mention both of them in Revelation 9:20? Are they still different entities?

Two Paradoxes

Here we are facing the dilemma that Christopher Wright calls "the two paradoxes."[10] Despite the fact that the other divinities exist, they do not really exist, but rather represent powers.

The first paradox consists in the fact that the idols are the "work of human hands." They are part of creation. They have eyes that do not see, ears that do not hear, mouths that do not speak, and they have no breath. They have not life in themselves, and cannot be compared with the God who is the creator of the universe and who is himself the source of life. In relation to this Creator God they are "nothings." From an ontological point of view they do not really exist. But visibly and materially they still exist, in history and today.

The second paradox describes the fact that the idols do not seem to exist ontologically, but can at the same time represent demonic powers. The apostle Paul for example exhorts us not to take part in common meals in the temple of an idol because this could mean to be in fellowship with a demon (1 Cor 10:18-20).

In conclusion, even though the gods exist in the Bible and today, they are infinitely inferior to the biblical God, creator of the universe, and can represent demons.

Tripolar Perspective of Religions

Another evangelical approach to this complex phenomenon is the concept of the "tripolar perspective of religions" introduced by Peter Beyer-

---

[10] Christopher J.H. Wright, *The Mission of God: Unlocking the Bible's Grand Narrative* (Downers Grove: IVP, 2006), p. 136-188, summary p. 187f.

haus.[11] This tripolar scheme proposes that the non-Christian religions have a divine, human and demonic imprint. The divine imprint refers to general revelation and signifies that every culture and religion contains, just like every human being created in the image of God, elements "in the image of God" (Acts 14:17; Rom 1:19f). The human imprint is displayed in obedience or resistance of the human being to God's will. Since the fall, "the inclination of the human heart is evil" (Gen 8:21).[12] It implies that every culture and religion contains sinful elements (Isa 53:6a). Finally, according to Beyerhaus, every culture and religion has a demonic imprint: the demons take advantage of the human being's openness to the invisible world and attempt to manipulate and destroy it (Eph 2:1f). This openness is particularly present in adherents to Animism and to similar religious systems with a holistic worldview like Esotericism. The Lausanne Covenant takes up the tripolar perspective of religions in its tenth paragraph on "Evangelism and culture" when it says:

> Culture must always be tested and judged by Scripture. Because men and women are God's creatures, some of their culture is rich in beauty and goodness. Because they are fallen, all of it is tainted with sin and some of it is demonic.[13]

The concept of the "tripolar perspective of religions" is so far the only model of the theology and philosophy of religions that integrates the notion of demon. As Timothy Tennent and Marc Spindler have well observed, the secular worldview of the Enlightenment is determinative for the positions taken in Western Europe, especially in its academic, theological and philosophical culture.[14] The model of the tripolar perspective of religions is a commendable exception. Spindler formulates his view of religions in relation to our subject like this:

> We have the conviction that the religions demonstrate a satanic stronghold in their religious aim (independently of the social, economic, political and cultural functions that they fulfil). In their religions men are victims of diabolic alienation.[15]

---

[11] Peter Beyerhaus, "Theologisches Verstehen nichtchristlicher Religionen," *Kerygma und Dogma* 35, n° 2 (1989), p. 106-127.

[12] See also Matt 15:18f; Acts 17:27f; Eph 2:3.

[13] www.lausanne.org/content/covenant/lausanne-covenant.

[14] Timothy C. Tennent, *Invitation to World Missions: A Trinitarian Missiology for the Twenty-first Century* (Grand Rapids: Zondervan, 2010), p. 214f; Marc Spindler, *La mission: Combat pour le salut du monde* (Paris: Delachaux et Niestlé, 1967), p. 181.

[15] Spindler, *La mission*, p. 181.

Demons in the Bible

After having introduced the concepts of the two paradoxes and the tripolar perspective of religions, we still have to clarify the biblical notion of "demon." We do this by selective studies in both Testaments.

Demons in the Old Testament

The OT mentions the presence of diviners, magicians and sorcerers in the Ancient Near East. The Egyptian magicians, for example, performed on the order of Pharaoh as many miracles as Moses (Exod 7-9). We should also mention the seer Balaam from Mesopotamia, a specialist in the matter, who was called by the Moabite king Balak to curse the people of Israel (Num 22-24). In order to distinguish his people from these prevailing practices, God forbids, at the heart of the book Leviticus, in the Holiness Code, child sacrifice to Molech and contact with the spirits of the dead (Lev 20:2, 6, 27). In the "second law," Deuteronomy, God reiterates the prohibition to contact the invisible world in the law on the diviners (Deut 18:9-22):

> No one shall be found among you who makes a son or daughter pass through fire, or who practices divination, or is a soothsayer, or an augur, or a sorcerer, or one who casts spells, or who consults ghosts or spirits, or who seeks oracles from the dead. For whoever does these things is abhorrent to the Lord; it is because of such abhorrent practices [*to'ébah*, "abomination"] that the Lord your God is driving them out before you (Deut 18:10-12; see Isa 8:19).

In the Animism of the Ancient Near East, this prohibition is a difficult one. Everybody has contacts with the invisible world through mediums. Contacts with ancestors are welcomed and very common. Why not have contact with the invisible world apart from the living God? Why not call the ancestors? Because it is impossible to know the spirit who presents himself. Is it really the father or grand-father, or does a demon mimic his face and voice in order to manipulate and destroy the family?

Despite the animistic context, in Israel serious efforts were undertaken to satisfy God's requirements. This is demonstrated by the narrative of the meeting between King Saul and the sorcerer of Endor. It starts with these words: "Saul had expelled the mediums [*'ob*, 'one who evokes the dead, a necromancer'] and the wizards [*idoni*, 'one who possesses a spirit of the dead, a soothsayer'] from the land" (1 Sam 28:3). In fact, these two Hebrew terms can denote at the same time the spirits of the dead and those who contact them. But when God does "not answer him, not by dreams, or by Urim, or by prophets" (v.6), Saul says to his servants: "Seek out for me a woman who is a medium [*ba'alat 'ob* 'a master of the spirits of the dead']" (v.7). Despite the fear of transgressing the prohibition, the woman of Endor calls up Samuel for King Saul. The text describes the scene like this: the king asks the woman: "What do you see?" The woman says to Saul, "I see a divine being [*'elohim*] coming up out of the ground" (v.13). Then, according to the text, Samuel addresses King Saul. The question is whether this was really the prophet Samuel or a spirit of the dead who tricks Saul in order to manipulate him? Half of the commentators are favourable to the first option, the second half to the second option.[16] It is very significant that the answer to the question is divided and open. One cannot know it. The law that prohibits contacts with spirits of the dead has exactly this aim: to avoid being deceived by the demonic world. A passage which complicates the situation even further is Genesis 6:

> When people began to multiply on the face of the ground, and daughters were born to them, the sons of God [*bnei ha'elohim*] saw that they were fair; and they took wives for themselves of all that they chose. Then the Lord said, "My spirit shall not abide in mortals forever, for they are flesh; their days shall be one hundred twenty years." The Nephilim were on the earth in those days – and also afterward – when the sons of God went in to the daughters of humans, who bore children to them. These were the heroes that were of old, warriors of renown (Gen 6:1-4).

Three questions arise: does this text speak of the "sons of God" or the "sons of the gods"? And who are these "sons of God (of the gods)"? Are they demons who present themselves to human daughters? Does the formula "and also afterward" refer to the time of Israel or equally to our epoch? The Hebrew words *bnei ha'elohim* allow both meanings: "the sons of God" (Job 1:6; 2:1) or "the sons of the gods" (Ps 29:1; 89:7). And who are these sons of God (of the gods)? The exegetes propose three interpretations: 1) angels, demons or spirits, 2) kings (see 2 Sam 7:14; Ps 2:7), and 3) "men of God" like Seth's descendants opposed to Cain's descendants (see Exod 4:22; Deut 14:1). The first interpretation is at the same time the older and the more recent. The NT (2 Pet 2:4; Jude 6f) and the majority of the Church Fathers adopt it.[17] In Job 1-2, the formula "sons of the gods" seems to indicate the divine council and in the Ugaritic literature the members of the divine pantheon. And the last question: does the formula "and also afterward" refer to the time of Israel or equally to our epoch? The

---

[16] Laurent Clémenceau, "Saül et la nécromancienne: Étude exégétique de 1 Samuel 28.3-25," Master thesis, Vaux-sur-Seine, 1995.

[17] For example Justin Martyr, Irenaeus of Lyon, Clement of Alexandria, Tertullian, Origen.

Chapter 11 – Demonology: A Forgotten Dimension 243

introduction *waihi ki* (Gen 6:1; see also 26:8; 27:1; Exod 1:21; 13:15) seems to indicate the background of the multiplication of the human race and its expansion on the earth after God's order to be fertile and to multiply (Gen 1:28).[18] As this process still continues, these phenomena can refer to the period before or after the flood "in those days – and also afterward," and perhaps even the contemporary epoch.

Demons and Jesus

During his ministry, Jesus Christ had many encounters with demons, in areas inhabited by both Jews and non-Jews. We mention the man possessed by an impure spirit in the synagogue at Capernaum,[19] the Gadarenes,[20] the dumb man (Matt 9:32-34), Mary Magdalene (Luke 8:42), another dumb man,[21] a crippled woman in the synagogue (Luke 13:10-13), the daughter of the Canaanite woman,[22] and a lunatic boy.[23] Even Jesus himself is often accused of being possessed by a demon.[24] The people said: "He is mad! He performs miracles by demonic power." In his speeches, Jesus includes teaching on demons (Matt 12:43-45). The question of demons was present in the minds of the inhabitants of Palestine at the time of Jesus. Is it not surprising that after so many centuries of walking with the biblical God there were so many demons who came to encounter Jesus and the apostles, even right in the synagogue?

Demons and the Apostle Paul

In the beginning of the apostle Paul's ministry, the book of Acts reports the encounter at Cyprus between Paul and Bar Jesus, the magician and false prophet in the service of the proconsul Sergius Paulus. The exorcism is accompanied by the blinding of the one who wanted to oppose the faith (Acts 13:6-12). At Philippi, Paul had an encounter with a female slave with a spirit of divination (Acts 16:16-24). Her liberation caused a great

---

[18] Gordon J. Wenham, *Genesis 1-15* (WBC 1; Waco, TX: Word Books, 1987), p. 138-143.

[19] Mark 1:21-28 par Luke 4:31-37.

[20] Matt 8:28-34 par Mark 5:1-20; Luke 8:26-39.

[21] Matt 12:22-32 par Mark 3:22-30; Luke 11:14-23.

[22] Matt 15:21-28 par Mark 7:24-30.

[23] Matt 17:14-20 par Mark 9:14-29; Luke 9:37-43. See a similar list in Fred Dickason, *Demon Possession and the Christian* (Wheaton: Crossway, 1987), p. 35-36.

[24] Matt 9:34; Mark 3:30; John 7:20; 8:48, 52; 10:20.

financial loss to her master, which led to riots and to Paul's imprisonment. At Ephesus, "God did extraordinary miracles through Paul, so that when the handkerchiefs or aprons that had touched his skin were brought to the sick, their diseases left them, and the evil spirits [*pneumata ta ponera*] came out of them" (Acts 19:11f). The attempts of some itinerant Jewish exorcists had a disastrous end for them through a violent attack by the possessed man so that "many of those who became believers confessed and disclosed their practices. A number of those who practised magic collected their books and burned them publicly" (Acts 19:18f). In the letter to the Ephesians, the apostle Paul mentions several varieties of celestial powers:

> What is the immeasurable greatness of his power for us who believe, ... God put this power to work in Christ when he ... seated him at his right hand in the heavenly places, far above all rule [*arche*] and authority [*exousia*] and power [*dynamis*] and dominion [*kyriotes*], and above every name that is named, not only in this age but also in the age to come (Eph 1:19-21).[25]

In the letter to the Romans, the apostle Paul adds "the angels" to this list of terms, which can be disconcerting for some (Rom 8:38f). In summary, in the ministry of the apostle Paul as it is related in the book of Acts, the encounters with demons seem to be less frequent and less in view than those of Jesus, but this dimension is nevertheless well present in his ministry just as in Jesus' ministry.

Demons and the European Christian

Following this analysis of the notion of demon in the Bible, we will now attempt to transpose the biblical data to our contemporary epoch. But before doing this, we will look at the early church and Saint Anthony's life in the 3rd and 4th century. Then we will try to make the jump to contemporary Europe where we will study the non-Christian and Christian settings separately.

Demons and the Early Church

Everett Ferguson observes that "an important factor in the Christian success in the Roman world was the promise which it made of deliverance

---

[25] The more familiar terms in the KJV translation are: "Far above all principality [*arche*], and power [*exousia*], and might [*dynamis*], and dominion [*kyriotes*]" (Eph 1:21).

from demons."[26] Athenagoras writes that by offering the services of exorcists, Christians could help free people from the "delusions" and "illusions" of demonic forces.[27] Alan Kreider has established a firm link between exorcism and conversion and cites several passages of early Christian writers confirming this.[28] These data may suffice to conclude that dealing with demons played a significant role in evangelism beyond the biblical period. In the next section we shall devote more detail to an outstanding figure at the transition of the pre-Christendom to the Christendom period who has influenced Western Christians from the medieval epoch to the modern times.

Demons and Anthony the Great

Anthony the Great (251-356) is considered to be the "father of monasticism." Born in Kome in Middle Egypt, Anthony was the son of wealthy Christian parents. At the age of about twenty, he was challenged by Matthew 19:21: "If you wish to be perfect, go, sell your possessions, and give the money to the poor, and you will have treasure in heaven; then come, follow me." In response, he started an ascetic life, first in the proximity of his home village, then in the desert as a hermit. Thus, shortly before 300, he initiated the individual form of monasticism (eremitic monasticism).[29] From there, Anthony's influence spread through counselling, healing, deliverances and correspondence with important personalities. In so doing he also experienced great temptations and terrible struggles with Satan and the demons. These struggles have become the subject of popular artistic representations, for example the altar of Issenheim at Colmar (France). Anthony's life was popularised through the biography written by Athana-

---

[26] Everett Ferguson, *Demonology in the Early Christian World* (Symposium Series, 12; New York: Mellen, 1984), p. 129.

[27] Athenagoras, *Legatio*, 23, quoted by Alan Kreider, *Worship and Evangelism in Pre-Christendom* (Joint Liturgical Studies, 32; Cambridge: Grove Books Limited, 1995), p. 14.

[28] Kreider, *Worship and Evangelism*, p. 14, quoting Irenaeus, *Adversus Haereses* 2,32,4; Tertullian, *Ad Scapulam*, 4; idem, *Apol* 23,18; Origen, *Homilies on Samuel*, 1,10; idem, *Contra Celsum*, 7,18.

[29] The individual (or eremitic) form of monasticism (life in solitude: anachoretism [from Greek *anachôreô* "retreat"] or eremitism [from Greek *eremos* "desert"]) is to be distinguished from the collective (or cenobitic) form of monasticism (life in community: cenobitism [from Greek *koinos* "communal" and *bios* "life"]) of which Pachomius is the initiator around 320.

sius of Alexandria shortly after his death in 356.[30] Through the *Life of Saint Anthony*, Athanasius wanted to render fruitful the experiences of the desert monks for the life of the Church. Shortly afterwards it was translated into Latin by Evagrius, bishop of Antioch (388-392). The Latin book, by the way one of the first hagiographies,[31] had a great impact on Western monasticism.

In the *Life of Saint Anthony*, paragraphs 22-43, comprising almost a quarter of the book, are dedicated to Anthony's encounter with demons. He observes that a Christian who prays and practises an ascetic life style receives first the discernment of spirits, enabling one to distinguish the Holy Spirit from deceiving spirits which want to lure Christians away from God. Such Christians, living in an intimate relationship with God, will be protected from evil spirits. These spirits, says Anthony, can produce manifestations and take the appearance of wild animals and serpents or transform themselves into immense corpses or into legions of soldiers with the aim to intimidate, or appear as women to seduce (§ 23).

Anthony insists on the fact that all these impressing behaviours and words fade away like smoke before those who fear God. As the Lord says to Job: "Look on all who are proud, and bring them low; tread down the wicked where they stand" (Job 40:12). And as Jesus told his disciples: "I watched Satan fall from heaven like a flash of lightning. See, I have given you authority to tread on snakes and scorpions, and over all the power of the enemy; and nothing will hurt you" (Luke 10:18f) (§ 24). For Christ has "disarmed the rulers and authorities and made a public example of them, triumphing over them in it" (Col 2:15) (§ 35). The name of Christ dispels them (§ 40).

Demons and Western Europe

In the medieval epoch, the artistic tables representing Anthony with the demons were very popular. One could find them on many altars in churches and monasteries. With the movements of the Renaissance, the Reform and the Enlightenment, secularisation has increased in European societies. This process continues to the present day. Today, the realm of the demonic

---

[30] Athanasius of Alexandria, *Life of Saint Anthony* (Ancient Christian Writers: the Works of the Fathers 10; transl. and annotated Robert T. Meyer; New York: Paulist, 1950). The biographical data are drawn from this book. The paragraphs are referred to in the text.

[31] A hagiography (from Greek *hagios* "saint" and *graphe* "writing") is a biography of a saint.

world is relegated to the "supernatural," which according to science is not relevant for everyday life. One talks about "occultism," hidden phenomena that one knows little about, as the term indicates. A holistic worldview has been transformed into a secular worldview. However, theology maintains the scholastic dichotomist worldview that confines the spirit realm to the margins of its reflections. Thus, the subject of demons is hardly brought into discussion by theologians nor clarified by the churches.

Another aspect of this "hidden" reality is the proposition that the phenomena that are attributed to the demonic world have diminished or even disappeared with the Christianisation of Europe (this is at least what people believe), or have withdrawn to remote areas, to the countryside or to the mountains. A similar phenomenon is observed in Rwanda, a thoroughly Christianised country, where demonic manifestations are infrequent as opposed to Benin where Voodoo is prevalent. The belief that they have retreated to the mountains seems to be confirmed by the report of a student of the author originating from a mountainous region of Switzerland.[32] The house where an evangelical community has been meeting for more than a century is visited almost every night by a person who enters through the main door, climbs the stairs, enters the room which is significantly the visitors' room, opens the window, looks outside, returns to the door of the room, closes it and goes down the stairs in order to leave the house. If a believer is sleeping in this room, still according to my student, the person contemplates the facts with a certain emotional distance. If a non-believer is sleeping in the room, the person is terrified by the events.

In contrast, the observation of the marginalisation of "occult" phenomena seems to be contradicted by the presence in our societies of long-standing esoteric movements like the Free Masons and Rosicrucians, but also of modern esoteric movements like Druidism and New Age, to mention only these. Parapsychology has seen an enormous rise in interest in recent decades and seers and healers offer their services in magazines, on television and the internet. An edition of the magazine of a Swiss supermarket chain read by the author in June 2005 was entirely filled with anonymous accounts of bizarre nocturnal experiences in one district of Bern: shadows that slid along the bed, thoracic oppressions, black cats that lay on the eiderdown, etc. In conclusion, it is not only in remote mountainous regions or in the countryside that we find these phenomena in contemporary Europe, but in all of society up to the leaders' and academicians' level.

---

[32] Personal Communication by Lukas Wäfler in October 2010.

How can we explain these facts? And how can we explain that these phenomena are present in Europe after so many centuries of Christian presence? A first explanatory approach is based on the link between worldview and Animism. Animism can be defined as a holistic worldview incorporating the visible and invisible world, and seeking harmony between the two.[33] If modernity has induced the transformation of a holistic (or dichotomist) worldview into a secular worldview, the emergence of a counter movement to modernity could be interpreted as a process of transformation of a secular into a holistic worldview. The latter favours the adoption of points of view that are familiar to the holistic worldview of Animism like the concepts of spirit doubles, both of persons and of objects in the natural world, of the quest for harmony in the universe, etc. This phenomenon expresses itself in Esotericism and New Age.

A second explanatory approach is based on the link between Animism and the demonic world. Animism and Esotericism imply a holistic worldview with a great openness to the invisible world. In the demonic world, profiting from this openness in non-Christian or Christian segments of populations with a holistic worldview, "occult" manifestations could multiply. This is the author's experience when he gives lectures on Animism in Europe. Questions on the interpretation of "occult" phenomena abound. This is also the experience of the Roman Catholic Church which has instituted exorcists in all its European dioceses.

Demons and Western Christians

"Can a Christian be possessed?" This was the research question of a Master thesis defended at the evangelical seminary of Paris[34] in January 2013.[35] It is rare to find such a subject for a master's thesis at a theological faculty in Europe. Richard Morris, the author of this thesis, observes that the Bible does not give clear answers to this question. In this case, he infers, one has to find a balance that takes into account both biblical teaching and personal experience. Henri Blocher gives us guidelines how to link Scripture and experience. He warns us to be cautious:

---

[33] See Lothar Käser, "Concepts of Man in Different Societies," and "Concepts of the World in Different Societies," and "Man and his Spirit-Double," in *Animism: A Cognitive Approach* (Nürnberg: VTR, 2014), p. 40-55, 56-65, 158-185.

[34] Faculté libre de théologie évangélique de Vaux-sur-Seine.

[35] Richard Morris, "La démonisation des chrétiens selon le Nouveau Testament," Master thesis, Vaux-sur-Seine, 2013.

1) No matter how impressive the experience may be, Blocher says, it is never sufficient to confer the authority of a doctrine on a thesis: *Sola Scriptura!*
2) The lack of biblical evidence is also not sufficient to condemn an opinion accredited by experience, if it does not contradict Scripture: in fact, the Bible does not pretend to say everything about all matters.
3) The experience rarely allows a univocal verdict: the same facts are susceptible to very diverse interpretations; for example we know little about the enormous efficacy of unconscious mechanisms of the human psyche, with their collective dimension – they could explain in certain cases what one may attribute to spiritual warfare.
4) Experience is not only difficult to interpret in retrospect, but it is determined and fashioned to a large extent by prior expectations and opinions [the worldview].[36]

Drawing on experience, Morris answers positively the question whether a Christian can be subject to demonic influence. With Saint Anthony he affirms that

> the believers who maintain a pure and just relationship with the Lord Jesus have nothing to fear from demons. It is sufficient to confess one's sins to God (1 John 1:9), to keep from idols (5:21), and to walk in purity and worship of the true God (5:19-20). In contrast, those who do not walk in obedience, holiness and truth, risk finding themselves under the influence of demons.[37]

After having studied the occurrences of *daimonizomai* "tormented by a demon" and *echein daimonion* "to have a demon," Morris concludes that it is necessary and useful to distinguish several degrees of the intensity of demonic influence: in ascending order, "spiritual disturbance," "spiritual oppression," "obsession" and "possession."[38] Regarding the issue from a slightly different angle, Alain Nisus proposes a distinction between an external "demonic influence" (an oppression that can be very intense) and "demonisation" as the internal influence of a demon. In Nisus' distinction, the difference is not so much the intensity of the demonic influence, but the internal or external presence of the demon.[39]

Morris' and Nisus' conviction that the believer can be subject to a demonic influence is apparently confirmed by the stories of Job and King

---

[36] Henri Blocher, "Démonologie," *Fac-réflexion* n° 31, June 1995, p. 29.
[37] Morris, "La démonisation des chrétiens," p. 94.
[38] Idem, p. 24-27.
[39] Alain Nisus, *Mais délivre-nous du mal* (Romanel-sur-Lausanne: La Maison de la Bible, 2016), p. 125-194, particularly p. 157-160.

Saul (Job 2:6f; 1 Sam 15-31), and by the witnesses of Jesus (Matt 12:43-45) and the apostle Paul (2 Cor 12:7). God had sent an evil spirit to King Saul after his disobedience. This spirit was the source of his choleric attacks and of his melancholic disposition (1 Sam 16:14-23; 18:10; 19:9). Experiential data confirm this equally. Anthony's experiences have already been mentioned above. Relative to our epoch, we select a case from Western Europe and another from Western Africa. In Europe, Gottliebin Dittus' case (1842-1843), followed by Johann-Christoph Blumhardt (1805-1880), has become very famous during the first half of the 20th century.[40] This Lutheran pastor of Möttlingen in Wurttemberg, shaped by theological studies imbued by German rationalism, discovered with surprise that one of the members of his church suffered seriously from demonic attacks. In a spiritual struggle that lasted two years he encountered bizarre phenomena like, for example, the release of a great number of needles from her body.

The African experience was reported to the author by one of his students in the Republic of Guinea, a mainly Muslim country.[41] This student was then chaplain of an evangelical school in the capital Conakry.[42] In this school, which covers courses from kindergarten to grammar school, there were around a thousand students comprising 300 girls and 700 boys. According to my student, among the 300 girls there were an average of thirty who would regularly faint and wake up after prayer. Many other girls and boys had character traits outside of the norm. We recall that King Saul's evil spirit was the source of a choleric character. Among the thirty girls that fainted regularly, an average of twenty were Muslim, five Catholic and five evangelical. According to the witness of my student, the girls lived in a sort of marital relationship with nocturnal male visitors, a union which was the source of these phenomena. Is this a re-enactment of Genesis 6, the union of the "sons of God" with the "daughters of humans"? Many questions remain open. Concerning our subject, it suffices to conclude that Christian girls have been subject to demonic influence. Biblical and extra-biblical data confirm this fact.

---

[40] Johann Christoph Blumhardt, *Krankheitsgeschichte der Gottliebin Dittus: Ausführlicher originaler Bericht* (Neu durchgesehen von E. Zuber; Basel: Brunnen, 1943).

[41] In the Republic of Guinea around 80 % of the inhabitants declare themselves to be Muslims, 15 % Animists and 5 % Christians. Islam is a folk Islam imbued by the (animistic, holistic) worldview of the country.

[42] Personal Communication in December 2008. For security reasons the name of the student cannot be disclosed.

Modern Idols

How about idols in contemporary Europe? In his book *Gods That Fail: Modern Idolatry and Christian Mission* (1996),[43] Vinoth Ramachandra, a Sri Lankan consultant of the International Fellowship of Evangelical Students (IFES), gives the following definition of a modern idol:

> When human beings give to any aspect of God's creation (for instance sexuality and/or fertility) or to the works of their hands (e.g. science, the nation-state, the market mechanism) the worship that is due to the Creator alone, they call up invisible forces that eventually dominate them. When what is meant to be a servant is treated as a master, it quickly becomes a tyrant. ... This is seen in every human project: once a project acquires a certain size and becomes invested with human dreams of "progress" or of "liberation," it attains a life of its own, dragging human beings and societies in its wake.[44]

Idols are thus aspects of God's creation and "works of our hands" that take away the worship due to our Creator. They call up invisible forces that finally dominate and enslave us. Ramachandra's definition reminds us of Jesus' presentation of the other shepherds in comparison with the good shepherd in John 10:1-10 mentioned at the beginning of this chapter. The influence of the latter is destructive, an enemy of life. We find a similar concept in the apostle Paul's "principalities and powers" (*archai kai exousiai*) that can be interpreted either as spiritual or earthly powers, or, in the logical development of our discussion, as both.[45] The same logic refers to Paul's "elements of the universe" (*stoicheia tou kosmou*, Col 2:8,20; Gal 4:3,9), which can be interpreted as the four basic material elements of the Greek worldview i.e. earth, air, water and fire, or as destructive spiritual powers. Within the perspective of our discussion, it can also be seen as spiritual powers corresponding to earthly powers. Paul's concept of "principalities and powers" or the "elements" and Ramachandra's definition of idols remind us of the animistic notion of the "spirit double." It implies that, in the animistic worldview, every material subject or object has an

---

[43] Vinoth Ramachandra, *Gods That Fail: Modern Idolatry and Christian Mission* (rev. ed.; Eugene, OR: Wipf & Stock, 2016 [1st ed. 1996]).

[44] Idem, p. 109.

[45] 1 Cor 15:24; Eph 1:21; 3:10; 6:12; Col 1:16; 2:10. See John H. Yoder, "How H. Richard Niebuhr Reasoned: A Critique of *Christ and Culture* », in *Authentic Transformation: A New Vision of Christ and Culture*, eds. G.H. Stassen, D.M. Yeager, John H. Yoder (Nashville: Abingdon, 1996), p. 54-61; Donald A. Carson, *Christ and Culture Revisited* (Grand Rapids: Eerdmans, 2008).

immaterial corresponding subject or object, a spirit double.[46] The underlying concepts are those of correspondence and harmony, expressions of a relational conscious orientation, and of holism, in the sense of a holistic worldview. The demonic world can profit from the openness of human beings to the invisible world in order to manipulate and destroy them. Taking this thought to its logical conclusion, Ramachandra links idols and demons to ideologies:

> Having surrendered our hearts, individually and collectively, to idols, we become enslaved by demons. Such demons always demand human sacrifices. The cult of idolatry leads to the sacrifice of the weak and apparently useless members of society (from foetuses to other ethnic groups, to the infirm or the mentally handicapped), to the destruction of the earth's ecosystems and the abdication of human responsibility for the planet. ... Idols are sustained and animated by belief-systems which disguise their role in human affairs. These belief-systems (or ideologies ...) lend an air of legitimacy to every idol.[47]

Idols are thus at the basis of ideologies, which are actually belief systems. Ramachandra enumerates the following main ideologies of modernity: Scientism (based on reason, science, technology, promoting the ideologies of progress and development), Marxism, Capitalism (implying the free market mechanism), Sexism (based on certain concepts of the role of women connected to or disconnected from fertility), and Nationalism (promoting the nation-state as the "good shepherd who cares for us"). He calls these ideologies the "new demons."[48] In the prophetic mockery of idols and idolatry, attention is often drawn to the dehumanising effects of such false worship on individuals and societies. So says Psalm 115 at the end of the mockery of the idols: "Those who make them will be like them" (Ps 115:8). This logic follows from the biblical doctrine of man. As we are created in God's image, whose true likeness is disclosed in Jesus Christ, worship involves a restoration of our fallen humanity to Christ-like humanness (1 Cor 3:18). Likewise when we worship idols and ideologies, it will show in the way we treat ourselves and our fellow humans. Consequently, it is not surprising that those who adhere to technology eventually develop machine-like personalities. Those who worship sex are incapable

---

[46] See Lothar Käser, "Concepts of Man in Different Societies," "Concepts of the World in Different Societies," and "Man and his Spirit-Double," in *Animism*, p. 40-55, 56-65, 158-185.

[47] Ramachandra, *Gods That Fail*, p. 109.

[48] For the following development, we are indebted to Ramachandra, *Gods That Fail*, p. 111f.

of trust and commitment in their human relationships and hide a lonely existence behind a mask of a sociable person. Those who desire power live in a constant climate of suspicion, insecurity and fear. Consequently, the underlying causes of apparently this-worldly secular phenomena have to be looked for in the invisible world, sometimes the demonic world.

Antagonistic Dimension of Mission

The Christian Church in the West must thus rediscover the dimension of the invisible world and be able to give a valuable response to the problems of contemporary Europeans. One of the four missionary models proposed by the missiologist Peter Beyerhaus, the antagonistic model of mission, can help to do this:[49] God wants to destroy evil (Gen 3:15; Exod 4-15; 1 Kgs 17-18; 1 John 3:8). The aim of mission, which conforms to the logic of this model, is to see men engaged in the struggle against evil and for the salvation of humanity. The antagonistic model of mission affirms that Christ is victor over the powers of darkness (Col 2:15). For the Church Fathers just as for many churches of the Global South operating in animistic contexts, and also for many Pentecostal and charismatic churches in the West, the concept of *Christ Victor* has been and still is an important theme. The logical theological consequence is a "theology (or missiology) of spiritual warfare."

The missiologist Marc Spindler has developed this theme in his thesis *La mission: Combat pour le salut du monde* (Mission: Struggle for the Salvation of the World, 1967).[50] He introduces the section on the "Struggle of Mission" by an affirmation that is as much astonishing as avant-garde for the 1960s: "Let us insist on the fact that the struggle of mission is neither a political nor a military war, and that the Enemy to combat is not a man or a group of men, but the Devil."[51] Spindler links the theme of the missionary struggle with the doctrine of the three offices of Christ, principally with the royal office. Question 32 of the *Heidelberg Catechism* makes spiritual warfare part of the Christian's royal ministry: "I am a member of Christ ... to fight during this life ... against sin and against the

---

[49] The four models are: the soteriological, antagonistic, eschatological and doxological model. Peter Beyerhaus, *Er sandte sein Wort: Theologie der christlichen Mission*, vol. 1: *Die Bibel in der Mission* (Wuppertal/Bad Liebenzell: Brockhaus/VLM, 1996).

[50] Spindler, *La mission: Combat pour le salut du monde*, p. 165-209.

[51] Idem, p. 165.

Devil, and to reign finally with him [Christ] over all creatures."[52] The sacerdotal office integrates warfare through the concepts of sacrifice, holiness, intercession and martyrdom. Finally, the prophetic office implies, according to Spindler, "a struggle in the truth and for truth."[53] Another aspect of this thought is represented in the three relationships of Christ: "Christ's relationship with God, with the anti-God, and with the world, a triple relationship characterised by the terms doxology, antagonism and soteriology."[54] Here Spindler comes close to Beyerhaus' missionary models. From a practical point of view, he says, the point of departure of the struggle is missionary failure because of resistance to the Gospel. He remarks that modern authors have proceeded to a "demythologisation" in the analysis of failure by drawing from psychological, sociological, anthropological and strategic explanations."[55] David Powlison calls this attitude "practical atheism."[56] It originates from an uncritical integration of the social scientific data into our missiological analysis without considering the discontinuities between the secular and the biblical worldview.

How does the antagonistic dimension of mission express itself in daily life? Anthony and Morris agree that it is embodied by an intimate life with God imbued by prayer, intercession, repentance and confession of sins. Strauss and Moreau talk about *Christlikeness*, a progressive transformation of the disciple into the image of Christ (Rom 12:1f; 2 Cor 3:18).[57] A missionary spirituality should integrate the request of the Our Father: "Deliver us from evil [the Evil]," and also that of God's protection in our struggle. This is true all the more as our Master Jesus Christ prayed in this sense in his sacerdotal prayer: "I am not asking you to take them out of the world, but I ask you to protect them from the evil one" (John 17:15). The apostle Paul develops the theme of warfare in more detail in the famous passage of Ephesians 6:

> Put on the whole armour of God, so that you may be able to stand against the wiles of the devil. For our struggle is not against enemies of flesh and blood,

---

[52] Quoted in idem, p. 170.
[53] Idem, p. 173.
[54] Idem, p. 101.
[55] See for example Maurice Leenhardt, *Les propos missionnaires* n° 16 (Feb. 1930).
[56] David Powlison, *Power Encounter: Reclaiming Spiritual Warfare* (Grand Rapids: Baker, 1995), p. 21, 36, 37.
[57] Stephen J. Strauss, "Spiritual Dynamics and Mission," in *Encountering Theology of Mission. Biblical Foundations, Historical Developments, and Contemporary Issues*, ed. Craig Ott et al. (Grand Rapids: Baker, 2010), p. 247; A. Scott Moreau, *Essentials of Spiritual Warfare* (Wheaton: Shaw, 1997).

but against the rulers, against the authorities, against the cosmic powers of this present darkness, against the spiritual forces of evil in the heavenly places. Therefore take up the whole armour of God, so that you may be able to withstand on that evil day, and having done everything, to stand firm. Stand therefore, and fasten the belt of truth around your waist, and put on the breastplate of righteousness. As shoes for your feet put on whatever will make you ready to proclaim the gospel of peace. With all of these, take the shield of faith, with which you will be able to quench all the flaming arrows of the evil one. Take the helmet of salvation, and the sword of the Spirit, which is the word of God. Pray in the Spirit at all times in every prayer and supplication. To that end keep alert and always persevere in supplication for all the saints (Eph 6:11-18).

In order to avoid surprises during the Christian life, Morris recommends the teaching of this subject during baptism preparation courses.[58] Moreover, it is important to maintain a certain balance: to discern the physical, psychic, social and demonic causes of observed phenomena, and to recognise on the one hand the reality of the invisible world, of Satan and his demons, and on the other hand to avoid interpreting all the phenomena in this perspective and thus integrate animistic elements into the life of the Church without realising it. However, it is not always easy to discern the underlying causes of empirical phenomena, especially concerning the influence of ideologies.

For the Roman Catholic Church, exorcism dates from the time of the early Church, following the example of Christ[59] and the order of the first popes:

> When the Church asks publicly and authoritatively in the name of Jesus Christ that a person or object be protected against the power of the Evil One and withdrawn from his dominion, it is called exorcism. Jesus performed exorcisms and from him the Church has received the power and office of exorcizing (Mark 1:25-26; 3:15; 6:7, 13; 16:17).[60]

After the Second Vatican Council, the Roman Catholic Church revised the ritual of exorcism and instituted exorcists in all the dioceses. According to Canon Law, the bishop as successor to the apostles receives the authority from the Roman Catholic Church to practise exorcisms.[61] Most

---

[58] Morris, "La démonisation des chrétiens," p. 94.
[59] Matt 8:28-34; 9:32-34; 12:22-24; 15:21-28; Mark 1:23-28; 5:1-20; Luke 4:33-36; 13:10-17.
[60] *Catechism of the Catholic Church* (rev. in accordance with the official Latin text promulgated by Pope John Paul II; Vatican City: Vatican Press, 1997), no. 1673.
[61] *Canon Law*, can. 1167-1172.

often, he delegates this authority to an exorcist: "a presbyter who has piety, knowledge, prudence, and integrity of life."[62]

The 54-page ritual book was published on January 26, 1999, making it the last liturgical book to be revised following the Second Vatican Council of 1962-1965. It replaces chapter XII of the Roman Ritual of 1614 established by Pope Paul V during the reform of the Catholic liturgy after the Council of Trent (1545-1563).[63] The new document advises exorcists to be aware of imaginative persons who may think that they are a prey of demons. It invites exorcists and candidates for exorcism to allow for an examination by a medical doctor and a psychiatrist before exorcism:

> Regarding the necessity of using the Rite of Exorcism, the Exorcist will make a prudent judgment after diligent inquiry, always preserving the seal of confession, having consulted, to the extent possible, experts in spiritual matters and, if necessary, in the science of medicine and psychiatry, who have a sense of spiritual realities.[64]

The Roman Catholic Church thus affirms the possibility of demonic influence on Christians. The new ritual is simplified and no longer makes any distinction between "major exorcism," the ritual that included interpellations to Satan, and "minor exorcism," a prayer for deliverance.

The ritual starts with a prayer, the blessing of the water and the sprinkling of the possessed. The litany of supplication, the recitation of the Psalm and the reading of the Gospel follow. The priest lays hands on the head of the possessed, then all present recite the Credo and renounce Satan. After the Lord's Prayer, the exorcist presents the Cross to the possessed and commands the evil spirits to depart, before breathing on the face of the person. The rite of exorcism itself comprises a prayer of supplication for protection addressed to God (deprecative formula) and three interpellations to Satan to depart (imperative formula). It ends with the Magnificat and the final blessing. Here is a schematic presentation of the ritual in eleven steps:[65]

---

[62] Idem, can. 1172, § 2.

[63] *De exorcismis et supplicationibus quibusdam*, ex decreto Sacrosancti Oecumenici Concilii Vaticani II instauratum auctoritate Ioannis Pauli PP. II promulgatum (Città del Vaticano: Tipografia poliglotta vaticana, 1999 (Of Exorcisms and Certain Supplications). A slightly amended edition was issued in 2004. The document was originally issued only in Latin, but some versions in the vernacular are extant.

[64] Idem, Praenotanda no. 17.

[65] Idem, no. 39-66.

1. Recitation of the litany of supplication by the priest with a violet stole that encircles the neck of the possessed, accompanied by the aspersion with holy water.
2. Recitation of Psalm 54.
3. Adjuration of the divinity and interrogation of the demon's name and provenance (repeatedly the in case of several demons).
4. Recitation of certain passages of the Gospels (John 1; Luke 10-11; Mark 16).
5. Pronunciation of the first exorcism against the demon by the priest laying his right hand on the head of the possessed.
6. Preparatory prayer.
7. Prayer accompanied by several presentations of the Cross to the possessed person.
8. Second exorcism pronounced with a certain violence.
9. New prayer.
10. Third and last exorcism.
11. Thanksgiving songs, recitation of Psalms and final prayers.

The real cases of possession seem to be rare. However, according to the testimony of the exorcist of Rome, Father Gabriele Amorth, several youths have been liberated by exorcism or deliverance prayer. According to him, it can take two to three years of prayer sessions every two or three weeks until a person is totally delivered, this under the condition that the person adopts a life of prayer and stays away from risky practices.[66]

Apart from exorcism of persons under demonic influence, a prayer of exorcism (or "prayer for the protection from evil") remains an element of the Catholic rite of child baptism to this day.

> Since Baptism signifies liberation from sin and from its instigator the devil, one or more exorcisms are pronounced over the candidate. The celebrant then anoints him with the oil of catechumens, or lays his hands on him, and he explicitly renounces Satan. Thus prepared, he is able to confess the faith of the Church, to which he will be "entrusted" by Baptism (Rom 6:17).[67]

It is evident that baptismal exorcism has its roots in the early Church when adult candidates were prepared for baptism. Until the medieval epoch it was progressively enlarged and precedes child baptism since the

---

[66] Gabriele Amorth, *Un exorciste raconte* (Paris: Guibert, 1993).
[67] *Catechism of the Catholic Church*, no. 1237.

introduction of this practice. In the abridged form of the baptismal rite, the prayer of exorcism is omitted.

In 2004, the first international meeting of Catholic exorcists took place in Mexico, and in July 2014 Pope Francis I officially recognized the International Association of Exorcists (IAE).

The Orthodox Churches have their own exorcism rite. In contrast, the Protestant churches do not practice exorcism rites. They seem to be influenced much more by Enlightenment philosophy than the former two churches. The situation is very different in the Pentecostal and charismatic churches. They are generally very open for the activity of the Holy Spirit and the invisible world. Their approach is very simple: generally it consists of a shorter or longer prayer with or without laying on of hands. In certain churches one can find regular or irregular sessions that can last a whole day or night, with or without fasting.

In Pentecostal and charismatic churches another feature has developed during these last years. Several activities have been initiated that can be classified under the category of "spiritual warfare:" the "warfare prayer," the "prayer walk" with "identificational repentance" also called "strategic prayer," the "strategic level spiritual warfare" and "spiritual mapping."[68] The accent that is usually put on "warfare techniques"[69] in this discourse recalls the importance of exact formulations and procedures in magic rites. Following the logic of this interpretation, certain missiologists classify these approaches as "Christianised Animism."[70] However, in missionary ministry, prayer is strongly recommended.[71] One should not ignore Satan's projects (2 Cor 2:11). On the other hand, we do not need to know everything and pray at precise locations or bind spiritual powers at specific places like certain people do by invoking some biblical passages (Deut 32:17; 1 Kgs 20:23; 2 Kgs 5:17; 17:24-31; Dan 10; Matt 12:29; Luke 7:1-10; John 4:19-24).

---

[68] Strauss, "Spiritual Dynamics and Mission," p. 248f, 257f.

[69] See for example Charles Kraft & Mark White (ed.), *Behind Enemy Lines: An Advanced Guide to Spiritual Warfare* (Ann Arbor, MI: Servant, 1994); C. Peter Wagner (ed.), *Engaging the Enemy: How to Fight and Defeat Territorial Spirits* (Ventura, CA: Regal, 1991).

[70] See for example Robert J. Priest, Thomas Campbell, Bradford A. Mullen, "Missiological Syncretism: The New Animistic Paradigm," in *Spiritual Power and Missions: Raising the Issues*, ed. Edward Rommen (Pasadena: William Carey Library, 1995), p. 11-12.

[71] Matt 9:38; Rom 15:31f; Eph 6:18-20; Col 4:3f, 12; 1 Thess 3:1f.

In this respect, we have to be able to distinguish between searching God's face sincerely and identifying with his projects on the one hand, and our desire to control the evil forces on the other hand. Paul Hiebert sums up this challenge in the following way:

> We need to center our theology on God and his acts and not, as modern secularism and animism do, on human beings and their desires. We need to focus on worship and our relationship to God, and not on ways to control God for our own purposes through chants and formulas. ... It is all too easy to make Christianity a new magic in which we as gods can make God do our bidding.[72]

Secondly, we have to seek a balance between power encounter (spiritual warfare) and truth encounter (the apologetic approach).[73]

Conclusion

Concerning demonology, European Christians can learn a lot from Christians from the Global South. They usually have a lot of experience in this subject. European Christians will want to respect the biblical basis that acknowledges demons and at the same time be conscious of the influence of world views on the position taken by different Christians. We have to maintain a certain balance. According to Powlison, the two mismatches are equally false: the disenchanted world of modern rationalism and the enchanted world of premodern and postmodern Animism.[74] C.S. Lewis expresses this idea in the preface to the *Screwtape Letters*:

> There are two equal and opposite errors into which our race can fall about the devils. One is to disbelieve in their existence. The other is to believe, and to feel an excessive and unhealthy interest in them. They themselves [human beings] are equally pleased by both errors and hail a materialist or a magician with the same delight.[75]

If sufficient knowledge of the subject is acquired and balance in the analysis is achieved, balance has also to be found in the practical approach

---

[72] Paul G. Hiebert, "The Flaw of the Excluded Middle," in *Anthropological Reflections on Missiological Issues* (Grand Rapids: Baker, 1994), p. 200f.

[73] For an evaluation of the concept of "spiritual warfare" in evangelical perspective, see Strauss, "Spiritual Dynamics and Mission," p. 255; Hiebert, "Biblical Perspectives on Spiritual Warfare," in *Anthropological Reflections on Missiological Issues*, p. 203-215.

[74] Powlison, *Power Encounter*, p. 25.

[75] C.S. Lewis, *The Screwtape Letters* (London: Bles, 1946), preface.

to persons seeking a solution to their problems. The Church in Europe is called to manage this question with competence, prudence and wisdom.

Further Reading

Beyerhaus, Peter, "Theologisches Verstehen nichtchristlicher Religionen," *Kerygma und Dogma* 35, n° 2 (1989), p. 106-127.

Dickason, Fred, *Demon Possession and the Christian* (Wheaton: Crossway, 1987).

Powlison, David, *Power Encounter: Reclaiming Spiritual Warfare* (Grand Rapids: Baker, 1995).

Moreau, A. Scott, *Essentials of Spiritual Warfare* (Wheaton: Shaw, 1997).

Rommen, Edward, ed., *Spiritual Power and Missions: Raising the Issues* (Pasadena: William Carey Library, 1995).

Strauss, Stephen J., "Spiritual Dynamics and Mission," in *Encountering Theology of Mission: Biblical Foundations, Historical Developments, and Contemporary Issues*, ed. Craig Ott et al. (Grand Rapids: Baker, 2010), p. 238-262.

Wright, Christopher J.H., "The Living God Confronts Idolatry," in *The Mission of God: Unlocking the Bible's Grand Narrative* (Downers Grove: IVP, 2006), p. 136-188.

Chapter 12
What Kind of Church for Postmodern Europeans?

David Brown[1]

Introduction

A former Canadian ice-hockey player, Wayne Gretzky, used to explain his goal scoring ability by saying: "I skate to where the puck is going to, not where it has been." Steve Jobs loved this quotation as an explanation of the success of Apple. Does it have any relevance to us as Christians?

As a convinced conservative Evangelical, I firmly hold to the fundamental doctrines of the authority of Scripture and God's grace to sinners and salvation received through repentance and faith. But how should we live this out as churches today? In the course of my life, I have already seen two styles of church life:
- A rather formal approach, with the men in suits and ties and the women in dresses, observing silence in the sanctuary before the service started. The hymn sandwich was the standard order of service, with the use of an organ (or harmonium) for the music. Most of the meetings were held on church premises and led by the minister. This lasted as the normal type of church life through to the early seventies.
- Then followed a more informal, Californian hippy inspired approach with "praise" as the main aspect of Sunday services (often led by a worship leader) with a guitar backing, although a wider range of instruments were included as the years went by. Casual clothing is the norm, and group leadership is often the preferred style of church structure, so we have seen a considerable development of home groups led by lay people.

---

[1] An earlier version of this chapter was published in *Church Planting in Europe*, eds. Evert van de Poll & Joanne Appleton (Eugene, OR: Wipf & Stock, 2015), chapter 10, p. 137-147.

Today this style is in turn being challenged by an approach which goes under several names, such as "emerging church," "fresh expressions of church" or "messy church." There has been some resistance to the ideas coming out of these movements: their theology has sometimes been doubtful, their thinking has too often focused on a style of meetings rather than on the whole life of a church, and their approach has often been inspired by a reaction to the church situation in North America, which is not the same as in Europe. But the questions asked are extremely relevant.

My feeling is that the first two styles of church I have described have something in common. In both cases, but in different ways, they encouraged the believer, directly and indirectly, to come out of the world and to move into a Christian "bubble" in order to live the Christian life. The so-called emerging church is trying to do the exact opposite by reducing the gap between what Christians are experiencing when they meet together and what they are living out in the world. In other words, the aim of the meeting is to help them live everywhere and all times with their Christian identity.

So the question we are facing is: where do we go from here in considering what kind of church for postmodern Europeans? Most of my books are about cultural trends in the particular French context. However I believe that the thinking I have developed will be applicable in a wider European perspective because I am not talking about short-term tactics but rather longer-term strategy. I'm trying to see the main thrust of the New Testament as compared to what seems normal because it's in widespread usage.

In fact, this rethink must also concern every church, not just those planting new churches. Existing churches need to adapt to the surrounding culture. Some statistics from the USA will help us to focus our minds on this aspect of church for postmodern Europeans. Estimates from the United States show that three quarters of all evangelical churches are plateauing or slowly declining, and as many as 15% are at risk of simply disappearing.[2]

State of the Church in the USA	Proportion
Healthy churches, growing and multiplying	10-15 %
Churches which are plateauing or slowly declining	70-75 %
Churches in danger of disappearing	10-15 %

When I discovered these figures from across the Atlantic, I contacted the denominations affiliated to the National Council of French Evangeli-

---

[2] Source: North American Mission Board of Southern Baptists, at www.namb.net (accessed on February 4, 2016).

cals (CNEF) in order to make a comparison with these findings from North America. This wasn't a rigorously academic study since I asked the leaders to tell me intuitively how many of their churches would fall into these three categories. The results show that we in France need to rethink our strategy as at least half of our churches need action to be taken, even those planted as recently as in the last quarter of the 20th century.

State of the Church in France	Proportion
Healthy churches, growing and multiplying	51 %
Churches which are plateauing or slowly declining	38 %
Churches in danger of disappearing	11 %

Faced with this reality, I am not going to suggest a pragmatic process to arrive at the "ideal church" for postmodern Europeans. Firstly, because this may vary enormously from one country to another, and from one context to another. But also because our contemporaries would not be open to such an approach: they like to look at life in all its complexity and anything looking like an ideology or an "-ism" would be rejected as an attempt to manipulate the general public. But I hasten to add that they are not always very consistent in this and all too easily adopt self-help miracle solutions. But we as Christians must not fall into this trap. I like to recall the famous dictum of T.R. Glover of Oxford University which is often quoted in books on missiology. In order to explain the rapid spread of the Christian faith in the decades following the life of Jesus on earth, Glover stated that the Gospel spread throughout the Mediterranean world because the first Christians out-lived and out-thought their contemporaries.[3]

I would like to suggest four areas which a church for postmodern Europeans must address: the human condition, the church as the new humanity, true spirituality, and the story line of human history. As a bonus we'll find that each component doubles up as being relevant in evangelism. That means that we don't have to choose between evangelism and edification since each bridge to unbelievers is at the same time a basic part of Christian life! I have developed these ideas further in my book *Passerelles* ("Bridges").[4]

---

[3] Terrot R. Glover, *The Jesus of History* (Calcutta: Association Press, 1917), chapter 9: "The Christian Church in the Roman Empire."

[4] David Brown, *Passerelles: Entre l'Évangile et nos contemporains* (Marne-la-Vallée: Farel, 2005).

Four Bridges

1) The Human Condition

One obvious thing that Christians and non-Christians have in common is our humanity. Believers face the same questions and challenges as every human being on earth, albeit with a different perspective. So how does this become an important part of our church life? I would like to suggest that this should be in three ways.

Our Human Solidarity

Jesus made it very clear that after our love for God, the greatest commandment is to love our neighbour as ourselves (Matt 22:39). This can be simply helping in our neighbourhood or at work, or it may involve a more structured approach, when money is involved, to help the poor. In the case of our church in Paris, situated in a fairly affluent district of the city, we have opened a Fair Trade shop so that our fellow citizens can help developing countries by purchasing their produce – the food they have grown or the handicrafts they have made – in such a way that the producers receive a decent income for their work. And of course, the shop brings us in contact with non-Christians as a bonus!

Our Human Identity

In postmodern Europe, identity questions are everywhere. Christians can help people to see their value as we proclaim and live out the fundamental truth that we have been created in the image of God (Gen 1:27). Rather than being obliged to construct our own identity, which is quite unnerving once people start to really think about it, we can find our true identity and tell people that "you can become the sort of person you really want to be," confident that the image of God in them is really pulling them towards Biblical truth.

The core issue is this: is there such a thing as human nature? Now it is true that Plato held to the idea that everything has an "essence" which is not dependant on our senses, and that neo-Platonic thought infiltrated Christin theology, particularly after Augustine. But I think that Christians really are "essentialists," since we believe in the fundamental essence or nature of human beings given us by a Creator God. However, postmodern thinkers follow the classical statement of the existential philosopher Jean-Paul Sartre: "Existence precedes essence." His partner Simone de Beauvoir affirmed in similar terms (back in 1949!): *On ne naît pas femme, on le devient* ("You aren't born as a woman, you become one"). So postmodernists are trying to construct their own identity since nothing is predetermined. That is what is at stake, and Christians can bring a real feeling of relief into this situation: we really do have value and values. We do not deny the complexity of a world which is broken and twisted since the fall, but we must fight the temptation to restrict humanity to an amalgam of personal choices. As Christians we strive to live out our calling to be human, created in God's image. We do have a heavenly Father. We are not alone. We do not have to carry the burden of constructing ourselves by our own efforts and intuitions.

Our Human Conduct (Being True to Our Human Condition)

The New Testament makes it clear that our conversion means the restoration of our relationship with God (John 17:3). But that is only half the story, since conversion starts a process of the restoration of God's image in us so that we become like His Son, Jesus, the perfect man (Rom 8:29; 2 Cor 3:18). In other words, Christians should become the most human of all humans, and avoid false triumphalism. I believe that non-Christians would rather hear how we cope with our problems and difficulties with God's help than listen to implausible testimonies of complete and instantaneous deliverance.

2) The Church Is the New Humanity

This leads on from the previous point. Christians are to become like Christ in their humanity, but it doesn't stop there. Our Trinitarian God is a God of relationships. The two greatest commandments exhort us to love God and to love others, both Christians and non-Christians (1 Thess 3:12; 5.15). But the church is God's letter that anyone can read (2 Cor 3:3), and it is most visible when there is a genuine love between the members of a church fellowship: "By this all men will know that you are my disciples, if you love one another" (John 13:35). Two New Testament texts beginning with the same words illustrate this well: "No-one has ever seen God." In John 1:18: "No-one has ever seen God," but He is made visible by the incarnation of Jesus. In 1 John 4:12: "No-one has ever seen God," but He is made visible when Christians have real love for each other, in other words, an unselfish interest in each other's good in a spirit of practical service. The incarnation in the strictest theological sense is that of Jesus, but there is an incarnation in a secondary sense since Christians are the body of Christ (1 Cor 12:12ff; Eph 4:15-16). We are members of that body, and the main visible revelation of God in the midst of unbelievers.

Ephesians 2 starts with salvation by grace (v. 8-9) to affirm that we are God's workmanship (v. 10) and the new humanity (v. 11-18) – this is explicitly stated in verse 15. And yet the apostle has to exhort Christians to live out this fact. Just as Jewish and Gentile believers didn't find it easy in the early church, Christians today also have to make the effort to really form this new humanity by accepting our differences (of temperament, age gender, culture and so on) on God's basis: "Accept one another, then, just as Christ accepted you, in order to bring praise to God" (Rom 15:7).

3) True Spirituality

Surprisingly, in the postmodern world, there has been a resurgence of spirituality, the need for something to re-enchant the world. Some 21st century atheist philosophers in France have even written about the way in which they are attracted to spirituality. However, this postmodern spirituality is more concerned with immediate feelings of individual well-being (and not with God or eternity). "Living fully the here and now" is the most often quoted definition of this return to "spiritual life." In this context, it has even been suggested that a synonym for evangelism could be "initiation into true biblical spirituality"! This spirituality puts God's eternal salvation at the centre, which we have already seen is first and foremost relational (with God, within the church, with non-Christians), refusing the sacred/secular divide (since we are Christians 24 hours a day, 7 days a week).

How can we live this out? One analysis of the chronology of culture goes as follows. Pre-modernity is turned towards the past (traditions), modernity is turned towards the future (the idea of progress), but postmodernity is focused on the present. However this isn't a problem for Christians because the Bible repeatedly uses the word "today" (well over 200 times in fact) and exhorts us to live in the present – albeit in the light of eternity, *sub specie aeternitatis* (Ecc 11:9-10). In other words, God wants us to live seamlessly, not with two or more different identities according to the group of people we are with, as many Postmoderns do without even realizing it. I suggest that there are four main aspects of the life of a disciple (worship, trust, obedience, loving people), and that each one can be summarised by the word "today."

Worship

"The living, the living — they praise you, as I am doing *today*" (Isa 38:19). Our deepest desire is to worship and glorify God day by day: "Your name be hallowed," that God should be recognised, respected, worshipped by the whole world ... starting with me. The expression "living *coram Deo*" has even come into contemporary evangelical language: a sense of God's presence and a sense of wonder about life where God is never absent from anything we do. How else can postmodern men and women understand the importance of faith in God as compared to a "lifestyle choice," which is a purely personal decision, and only applies to our lives when we feel like it?

Trust

"So that your trust may be in the Lord, I teach you *today*, even you" (Prov 22:19). A large part of our Christian walk is to learn to depend on God in all circumstances. "Give us *today* our daily bread" (Matt 6:11). Bread is a very real and concrete example. But as disciples of Jesus, trust is a characteristic attitude in every area of our life. A great many of the Psalms dwell on trust in God when everything seems hopeless. And the New Testament teaching on prayer comes back repeatedly to the fact that Christians need not be anxious about anything but "in everything, by prayer and petition, with thanksgiving, present your requests to God. And the peace of God, which transcends all understanding, will guard your hearts and your minds in Christ Jesus" (Phil 4:6-7).

Obedience: Fighting the Good Fight, Day by Day

This is the bravery of down to earth sanctification: this is our Christian "fight club." "But encourage one another daily, as long as it is called *today*, so that none of you may be hardened by sin's deceitfulness" (Heb 3:13). The model of Alcoholics Anonymous (AA) is very useful here:

> A member of AA never promises that he will never again drink alcohol. His biggest problem is to abstain today – those 24 hours are the only ones when he can act. Yesterday has gone. Tomorrow never comes. But he can decide not to drink today.

The same principle applies to the Christian in his daily fight to please God and resist temptation. It is heroic to live in the present, since most people prefer to wallow in nostalgia ("things were better in the past") or to live in a hypothetical future ("everything will be fine when … I pass my exams, I get a job, I find a husband, I can buy a nice house, I'm retired"). I believe that this concept of heroism is a particularly good approach for men who are often in short numbers in our churches.

Loving People

The Christian life isn't only heroic; it's also a daily adventure. Each day we can ask God to put people on our path and for him to help us to recognise them when they appear: people whom we can care for and love and with whom we can share the good news.

> *Devote yourselves* to prayer, being watchful and thankful. And pray for us, too, that God may open a door for our message, so that we may proclaim the mystery of Christ, for which I am in chains. Pray that I may proclaim it clearly, as I should. Be wise in the way you act toward outsiders; make the most of *every opportunity*. Let your conversation be always full of grace, seasoned with salt, so that you may know how to answer everyone (Col 4:2-6).

I love a sentence from a recent book, explaining the situation of women in the early church:

> In a world where the majority of people were suffering poverty, illness or abuse, a woman would have countless opportunities to help where help was desperately needed. She would then naturally explain how she had learned this happy way of life from Jesus who had done so much for her.[5]

Yes indeed! The best evangelism is each Christian's daily life, but too often churches feel the need for a "campaign" to mobilise the troops (in the same way that we say that a trade union in France needs to organise the occasional strike to remain plausible for its members!). But compared to the proven way of spreading the Gospel – through relationships – I have the impression that this can be counter-productive.

This was confirmed in my view by the results of a questionnaire organised in France in 2013 by the Evangelism Commission of the National Council of French Evangelicals (CNEF). In answer to the question: "What is the best form of evangelism today?" a massive 87.6 % of pastors chose: "Encouraging church members to build relationships with non-Christians." Unsurprisingly, the type of training most requested in the contemporary context was how to successfully build such relationships in order to share the Gospel (75.3 % of respondents)!

4) The Story Line of Human History

For most Postmoderns, history is going nowhere. There is no meaning, no direction, no goal. Just a whole population that wants to make their own choices and feels in need of protection from society in order to keep this freedom. Thus, the only widely accepted value is the concept of tolerance. But the Bible does provide a story line for human history, which allows us

---

[5] Robin Daniel, *Missionary Strategies Then and Now* (Chester, UK: Tamarisk Publications, 2012); see also Graham Orr, *Not So Secret: Being Contemporary Agents for Mission* (Nottingham: Inter-Varsity Press, 2012).

to make sense of what's going on around us in the world. The outline the Bible presents is in five stages: creation – fall – redemption – the present age ("already but not yet") – eternity.

The very fact that Christians think that history is neither circular nor meaningless, but moving towards a goal (when God will be all in all), can be seen as a shocking claim in today's world – it seems arrogant and intolerant. But there is a French proverb: *chassez le naturel, il revient au galop* ("If you drive out what is natural, it will only come galloping back"). We believe that humans are made in the image of God and will respond to the truth. And one of these truths is that we live in an abnormal world since the fall. The 17th century French scientist and philosopher Blaise Pascal became a Christian at the age of 31 and wrote in his *Pensées*: "No other religion has taught that man is born in sin. No philosophers have affirmed it, so none of them have spoken truly."

This means that we can call our contemporaries to repentance in the deepest sense of the word: to change their way of thinking and their mental constructions (their picture of reality, their worldview). This is so important today! And in fact the process of transformation continues as we grow in the faith: "Do not conform any longer to the pattern of this world, but be transformed by the renewing of your mind. Then you will be able to test and approve what God's will – his good and pleasing and perfect will" (Rom 12:2).

As Christians we have the privilege of taking our place in the unfolding of history, seeking to do God's will and seeing his eternal plans come to fruition in Christ in our local churches and worldwide. And since God is our creator as well as our redeemer, the story line of history helps us get the right balance in our life and witness, namely that the spiritual is not more important than the material, but that the eternal is more important than the temporal.

Practical Ways towards the Outworking of These Four Bridges

To conclude this chapter, I would like to suggest four ways in which all this can work out as we look at the form of church, which will be plausible, relevant and biblical in the 21st century.

1) As we meet together as churches, we must consciously aim at being the people of God who know each other and care for one another. Small groups are one way to do this but I would also plead for the weekly service to be more like a "gathering" with (a) worship that is both festive and med-

itative (and adapted to each culture), (b) teaching which engages with an intergenerational church, and (c) space for fellowship (we have a meal together practically every week in our church in Paris). This enables us to encourage real face to face relationships ... and to provide a useful counterbalance to the more impersonal side of social networks!

2) In the city, the best strategy could well be to multiply progressively the number of services and meetings at various times in the week to meet the diverse needs of people in this context. Hours of work can be very varied, but the cost of property might well make constant growth prohibitively expensive if the aim is to bring all the members of the church together at the same time. "Micro" churches help people to really get to know each other, but all these congregations make up just one church in fact, since they share the same premises, the same website, and the same overall leadership group.

3) We need to ensure that we give space to people to travel towards faith at their speed within the Christian community. This does not mean that we will lose our Christian identity, since baptism and church membership will continue to keep our churches functioning as "confessing churches." But people do need time in today's context to understand what it means to become a Christian. Society has moved so far from our European Christian roots that we must extend a welcome to people and let them see our day in, day out, week in, week out way of life, so that they can move beyond the two big barriers to faith:
- Ignorance of what the Bible says
- Christianity's lack of plausibility.

The question each Christian then has to ask is: Would I be happy to invite someone to my church who is not yet started on the journey to faith? Will they understand what is going on? Will they see that the Christians are really interested in the whole of life? And that applies not just to the individual Christian: each church should be looking at itself and asking the same questions.

4) But at the same time, it is not enough to be plausible within the four walls of our church building. Churches need to have visibility in the community. They need to be seen as partners (at least in some sense) with the local authorities, and to be present in the municipal magazine and on the town's website. A humanitarian project involving non-Christians may well be another bridge towards the community.

Conclusion

Coming back to my original question: What type of church for postmodern Europeans? I am aware that the cultural forms of the past also contain elements which are important to remember. In the first church style I mentioned, there is the notion of respect for the majesty of God ("You would put on your best clothes to meet the President of the Republic"). In the second church style, there is the recognition that God is present and sees the heart, so the outer surface of our being is not so important ("Come as you are").

However, I contend that what we should be aiming at today is simple, no-frills Christianity which in postmodern society is the new radical. Therefore, a church for postmodern Europeans will be integrated into culture (and so not a sub-culture), but vitally different, because the Christians will be living out "today" the basics of discipleship. And we will find that this is also the best form of evangelism.

So to come back to our initial question: Where is the puck going to be? What kind of church for postmodern Europeans? Of course, it is not at all necessary to deny the past. The two types of church which I described both enshrined important aspects of biblical truth which we must never forget. The first style reminds us that we must respect the majesty of God: "Fear the Lord, you his saints" (Psalm 34:10). And the second style reminds us that God looks at our heart, not our outside appearance (1 Sam 16:7). But the type of church I am pleading for in this chapter is simple, relational, with no frills, but that is to be truly radical in today's context. A church for postmodern Europeans will be integrated into our culture (it will not be a sub-culture), but it will be different precisely because of what is truly basic for Christians: the love of God and the love of our fellow humans. And that in itself is the best form of evangelism I know.

Conclusion

Hannes Wiher

At the end of this reflection on evangelism in Europe, we present some salient features collected from the different authors of this book. In this summary, we follow the missiological procedure proposed in the introduction: first a historical review of evangelism in Europe, then a socio-cultural analysis, third a concise reflection on the theology of the Gospel and of evangelism, and fourth on the communication of the Gospel and church planting in the European context.

We have noted that the definitions of both evangelism and Europe are not clear. Evangelism can be understood as a whole spectrum of concepts ranging from verbal proclamation as the core of mission to the totality of the ministry of Jesus, the apostles and today's disciples. Europe is not only a geographical entity, however fuzzy its eastern limits may be, but also a cultural expression taking different forms during the two thousand years of its Christian history.[1] The modelling through the Enlightenment and modernity has been of particular importance for today's cultural expressions.

As far as Europe's history is concerned, the Christianisation was, to say the least, questionable. Then followed around a thousand years of history, during which Christianity accommodated itself to European cultures and the Church became closely linked to the nation states, a condition that is called Christendom.[2] Today, under the influence of Enlightenment philosophy, many contemporary Europeans conclude that Christianity in the form of Christendom has rather been part of the European problem than of its solution. They have the tendency to say: "We have already tried it and it has not worked." According to Neal Blough, it is the social and political dysfunction of "premodern" Christian Europe that is largely responsible

---

[1] See Philip Jenkins, *God's Continent: Christianity, Islam, and Europe's Religious Crisis* (Oxford: Oxford University Press, 2007), p. 260.

[2] For a detailed analysis of this process, see for example James C. Russell, *The Germanization of Early Medieval Christianity: A Sociohistorical Approach to Religious Transformation* (New York: Oxford University Press, 1994); Anton Wessels, *Europe: Was It Ever Really Christian? The Interaction between Gospel and Culture* (London: SCM, 1994).

for the rejection of Christianity by modernity.[3] The French historian Jean Delumeau summarises this fact well when he writes: "As a constituted body, Christendom has constantly disclaimed itself ..."[4] During the postmodern period (also called late modernity), the offer of Christianity as a premodern system seems to many Europeans ridiculous and obsolete, and as a desperate attempt to bring Europe back to the barbarian darkness before the Enlightenment. This situation can cause concern to committed Christians. "Does the Gospel today still offer salvation to a Europe open to the world, and if so, under what conditions?" asks Jean-Marie Aubert.[5] "Of course, old-stock Europeans might continue their progress toward secularism, with Christian practice declining virtually to nothing, observes Philip Jenkins, but the contact with Islam could also inspire a rethinking of Christian roots and identity."[6] Moreover, remarks Jürgen Habermas, "recognising our Judaeo-Christian roots ... not only does not impair intercultural understanding, it is what makes it possible."[7]

Evert Van de Poll, Hannes Wiher, David Brown and Julien Coffinet (who presents a summary of Jean-Georges Gantenbein's and Van de Poll's books), have analysed the European context today. According to James O'Connell, Europe is built on three constitutive pillars: Judeo-Christian monotheism, Greek rationalism and Roman organisation.[8] Among these three, Christianity represents for many the "soul of Europe." For them, Europe is a Christian continent. However, in the 21st century, Europe presents a paradox: it is the continent of our planet that has been exposed to the Gospel the longest and most deeply. The Christian faith has pressed its imprint on European culture and worldview and has left many marks in the visible and invisible aspects of European culture. These are more easily noted by an external observer (Asian, African or American) than by Europeans who often perceive Europe as post-Christian. During the epoch of the Enlightenment, and particularly during the 20th century, we note a rapid

---

[3] See chapter 1 of this book: Neal Blough, "Evangelism in Europe: Historical Background."

[4] Jean Delumeau, *Le christianisme va-t-il mourir?* (Paris: Hachette, 1977), p. 40.

[5] "A note from Jean-Marie Aubert," *International Review of Mission* vol. 95, n° 378-379 (July-October 2006), p. 230.

[6] Jenkins, *God's Continent*, p. 261.

[7] Jürgen Habermas, *Time of Transitions* (New York: Polity Press, 2006).

[8] James O'Connell, *The Making of Modern Europe. Strengths, Constraints and Resolutions* (University of Bradford Peace Research Report n° 26; Bradford: University Press, 1991).

decline of the Christian faith. In contrast, its effects on the European culture and worldview retreat much more slowly. In this sense, one can see Europe as Christian and post-Christian at the same time.

In our secular societies, the biblical God is no longer a known and familiar God, but rather an "unknown god" (see Acts 17:23).[9] Moreover, the concept of a god is rather absent from the daily interrogations and interpretations of Europeans. Consequently, some would say that Europe is not only post-Christian, but also post-religious. This statement needs to be nuanced. If religion is defined as "a collection of state-sanctioned symbols and rituals," this definition of *religio* introduced by Cicero was appropriate during the epoch of the Roman imperial cult and also of Christendom. According to this definition, which implies that religion is the symbolic expression of a shared identity and a "common language" of a society, "Christianity is not the religion of present-day Europe and European Christianity no longer a religion."[10]

The de-Christianisation of Europe has led to a deconstruction of the religion as fact, and secondly to an individualised recomposition of the religious phenomena through a "patchwork of religious convictions."[11] Contemporary Europeans seek to satisfy their religious needs through all sorts of offers, which seem at first sight secular but entail religious elements. They find them in the entertainment that society offers: film, sport, music, and Internet, to mention only a few. Although the interest in the invisible world is maintained, a relational "default" spirituality regulates everyday life: on the one hand, there are oriental religions and a pre-Christian European spirituality, the famous "mystical esoteric nebula,"[12] which present themselves in a relational manner to a society that has an increasingly rela-

---

[9] See Thomáš Halik, "The Soul of Europe: An Altar to the Unknown God," *International Review of Mission* vol. 95, n° 378-379 (July-October 2006), p. 265-270.

[10] "It took several centuries before Christianity assumed the form of a 'religion' in the ancient sense, and played that political role not only in Rome after Constantine but also throughout practically all of the Middle Ages. On the threshold of the modern age, Christianity began to lose that role and in a certain sense science was to become the *religio* of the West. Christianity was assigned the status of a 'philosophy of life' (*Weltanschauung*) and gradually came to be regarded as another ideology." Halik, "The Soul of Europe," p. 266f.

[11] Danièle Hervieu-Léger speaks of a "*bricolage de croyances*" in *La religion pour mémoire* (Paris: Cerf, 1993).

[12] A concept introduced by Françoise Champion in her article "Les sociologues de la post-modernité religieuse et la nébuleuse mystique ésotérique," *Archives de sciences sociales des religions* 67, 1, 1989, p. 155-169.

tional functioning. It is this fact and the novelty of these religions which is at the basis of their attractiveness. On the other hand, Islam proposes a very simple and practical grid of orientation at a time when all the points of reference seem to be falling apart. In this way, Islam succeeds in providing security and identity to persons in quest of existential values. Nevertheless, only a minority of Europeans seem to opt for another religion. They are mostly the religions of the migrants and much less of old-stock Europeans who have gone through a sort of "conversion."

However, many migrants are Christians. So far we may have simply perceived "migrant" or "ethnic churches" from the outside, and have not realised the complexity of the mix *within* the churches. Johannes Müller helps us to better understand this mosaic of mono-cultural, intercultural and multicultural churches, showing that European Christianity itself forms a very diversely coloured mosaic.

Within the context of secular and individualistic societies, European Christianity is characterised by the formula "believing without belonging," a catch-phrase introduced by Grace Davie.[13] The decline of the Church, the loss of credibility of science and contemporary individualism often induce the European Christian to opt for a solitary life. Yet, the variations of the above formula are also valid: "belonging without believing" for the Christians of the mainline churches, and "belonging before believing" for the relational persons on a journey towards the Christian faith. Despite all this, Christianity remains the "default religion" of Europeans. They tend to need it for the rites of passage (baptisms, weddings, funerals). Even though practised only by a small minority, according to Grace Davie, Christianity remains also the "vicarious religion." By this, Davie means "the notion of religion performed by an active minority but on behalf of a much larger number, who (by implication at least) not only understand, but, quite clearly, approve of what the minority is doing."[14] Concerning religious behaviour, Grace Davie notes also the change "from a culture of obligation or duty to a culture of consumerism or choice."[15] One does not go regularly to church. If one has other obligations or is tired, one stays away. Or if the offer in another community seems better, one changes.

---

[13] Grace Davie, *Religion in Britain since 1945: Believing without Belonging* (Oxford: Blackwell, 1996).

[14] Grace Davie, "Is Europe an Exceptional Case?" *International Review of Mission* vol. 95, n° 378-379 (July-October 2006), p. 248.

[15] Davie, "Is Europe an Exceptional Case?" p. 251.

Consequently, in Europe we have to deal with multicultural and multi-religious societies, for some even post-religious societies. What are then the particular difficulties that our contemporaries have in understanding and accepting the Gospel? According to David Brown, it is the vocabulary of the Christians, the ignorance of the Bible and of its message and the secular worldview that constitute the main problem. The "premodern" message of the Gospel is simply not plausible any more for "post-modern" Europeans. Facing this plausibility shift, Marie-Hélène Robert encourages the disciple of Christ "not to be ashamed of being a Christian [and] not to be afraid of its unpopularity, but to listen, question and hear the critics. This is the price of proclaiming the Saviour," she says.[16]

Evangelism in Europe should be in tune with the plausibility structure of European societies. In order to evangelise well, the disciple of Christ needs a burning heart with a missionary spirituality and competence in theology, communication and contextualisation. The main theological questions are: What is the Gospel, and what is evangelism? We have defined the Gospel as the Good News according to which God has provided for the redemption of humanity in the person of Jesus Christ. According to Timothy Keller, the Gospel has to answer the questions a worldview is supposed to answer: Where did we come from? Why did things go wrong? What is the solution? How can I myself profit from this solution?[17] The answers to these questions are found in the biblical concepts of God, man, sin, evil and salvation, the five basic soteriological concepts.[18] The science of religion teaches us that men develop their religions with the aim of answering their questions and satisfying their needs. If Christianity succeeds in answering the questions of Europeans and satisfying their needs, the Gospel of Jesus Christ will again become relevant for them, despite the heavy baggage of a compromising history.

In evangelism, David Brown and Léo Lehmann emphasise the importance of living examples (of Jesus, the apostles and the disciples today). In this way the message becomes embodied: personal, relational and holistic, characteristics in tune with "postmodern" culture. The NT demon-

---

[16] Marie-Hélène Robert, *"Pour que le monde croie:"* Approches théologiques de l'évangélisation (Lyon: Profac-Théo, 2014), p. 294.

[17] Timothy Keller, *Center Church: Doing Balanced, Gospel-Centered Ministry in Your City* (Grand Rapids: Zondervan, 2012), p. 29-37, formulated by Keller in a rules-centred perspective: "Where did we come from? Why did things go so wrong? What will put things right? How can I be put right?"

[18] For a discussion, see the section "Five basic soteriological concepts" in chapter 6.

strates these models in a context which is becoming increasingly similar to ours in terms of its pluralism and multiculturalism, but which is also infinitely different compared with the two thousand years of Christian history between them. Although the Gospel is communicated by "a life that speaks," we should nevertheless not neglect its verbal proclamation. For, "how are they to call on one in whom they have not believed? And how are they to believe in one of whom they have never heard? And how are they to hear without someone to proclaim him?" (Rom 10.14). One cannot invent the Gospel. One has to hear it, and we have to proclaim it. But how can we speak about God in a society where he is absent, where one does not know him anymore? We cannot presuppose biblical knowledge like Billy Graham could during his evangelistic campaigns. We have to patiently proceed with interested persons: become their friend, motivate them to become interested in the Bible and pass through the important stages of the conversion process with them. We find ourselves presenting an unknown, unfathomable and ever surprising God, the God of the paradox who transforms failure into victory, death into life, wisdom into folly, and folly into wisdom, the one who "makes all things new."

Consequently, if evangelism in Europe is to have a chance of succeeding, it should present an authentic Christian faith with a deep and attractive spirituality, and at the same time individualise its approaches to each member of the society. Christ's disciples have to present and proclaim the Gospel by a convincing life, an understandable new language and a relevant message for Europeans.

In this communication of the Gospel in the European context, we are living in the tension between faithfulness to the Bible and relevance for our contemporaries. Among the attempts to contextualise the Gospel in Europe, we observe with interest the "emerging conversation" and the reflections on the "missional church." Unfortunately, they are mostly accommodating themselves to the "postmodern culture" without a great concern for faithfulness to Scripture. Substantial theological reflections on the "emerging church" and the "missional church" are rare but enlightening. With equal interest we follow the attempts at church planting here and there. To demonstrate the Gospel under the eyes of our contemporaries in the urban district and the village, twenty-four hours a day and seven days a week, individually and collectively, and explain to them the deep motivations of our life, remains one of the best approaches to evangelism and church planting. In a relational setting with a group identity, the communal approach becomes ever more important. In this vein, Lesslie Newbigin speaks of the church as a "hermeneutic community," a community that "interprets" and demonstrates Christ and the Christian faith.

What will be the contribution of migrant churches to evangelism in Europe? Bernard Coyault remarks: "I take the train in from the suburbs every day, and I have plenty of stories of Caribbean or African preachers, men and women, getting up to preach or sing or testify to their neighbours."[19] According to Jean-Claude Girondin, the process of integrating migrant churches starts with the recognition of their presence and their rapid growth by old-stock Europeans. Jean-Georges Gantenbein writes in the same vein:

> This learning process is only possible in the measure that Western Christians are ready to humble themselves by an in-depth analysis of their own mission history, by the acceptance of the critic of Western culture expressed by the Christians from the Global South, by the acknowledgement of our spiritual poverty and of the need for help in the "new" evangelism of the West.[20]

On the positive side of the balance, the conviviality of migrant churches in the suburbs allows a natural proximity to non-Christian populations, whom old-stock Europeans have more difficulty in approaching. Secondly, the fact that the immigrant populations are less affected by Enlightenment philosophy renders their worldview closer to certain segments of our populations. Additionally, their holistic approach to the Christian faith is more in tune with the postmodern worldview.[21] However, efforts to train them in cross-cultural communication are essential for giving their approach to secular Europeans a chance. In many cases this effort will however not be sufficient to achieve positive results. We may have to wait for the second and third generation immigrants whose worldview will have made the necessary adaptations to the European context. They may well be the future missionaries of Europe.

While secular European culture is largely ignorant of demonology, these phenomena are more familiar to immigrant populations than to old-stock Europeans. The demonic world profits from the openness of a holis-

---

[19] Bernard Coyault, "Christianisme : radioscopie des Églises d'expression africaine en France," at www.bethel-fr.com/afficher_info.php?id=12897.72.

[20] Jean-Georges Gantenbein, "*La France, pays de mission?* La définition de la mission et les critères d'une missiologie de la culture occidentale," Master thesis, University Marc Bloch, Strasbourg, 2006, p. 98.

[21] See Majagira Bulangalire, "The Consequences of the Englightenment: A Point of View from the Churches of African Expression in France," *International Review of Mission* vol. 95, n° 378-379 (July-October 2006), p. 293-296; Léonard Santedi Kinkupu, "Reflections from an African Theologian," *International Review of Mission* vol. 95, n° 378-379 (July-October 2006), p. 390-400.

tic worldview toward the invisible world, facilitating their contact with humans in order to deceive, manipulate, and finally destroy them. Lately, the Roman Catholic Church has instituted exorcists in every diocese. Christ's disciples have to be informed and at the same time cautious in this area.

Finally, what "new expressions" of church will attract contemporary Europeans? According to David Brown, convincing churches are those which demonstrate the love of God and neighbour in everyday life. Christians will be able to convince by an authentic spirituality and everyday practical application of Christian ethics. Concerning church life, David Brown proposes to move away from the model of "worship service" and to adopt a relational "meeting" model. By multiplying the places and times of meeting with fellow Europeans, Christians will be able to join their contemporaries in their demanding professional life and their free-time activities. Brown insists that we do not only have to be plausible inside the four walls of our church, but also in our town, district, or village. Participating in associative life, political parties or sports clubs, will bring us closer to our friends. Christianity being little known and having scant plausibility in the contemporary European culture, we have to reserve enough time for our contact persons' walk toward faith, each at their own pace.

The subject of evangelism in Europe is interdisciplinary and broad. Wanting to respond to such a challenge in a book like this would be pretentious. However, we hope these essays on the subject, from an evangelical perspective, offer a treasury of ideas. Yet, each theme could and should be examined more deeply. It is important and urgent that evangelism in Europe becomes a priority subject of reflection. Other deeper and more complete treatments should follow.

Appendix

Hannes Wiher

Appendix 1: European Statistics

Note: any statistical evaluation of religious convictions in relation to religious affiliation and practice is very delicate. Among believers there are non-practising and practising members. Non-practising Christians are also called "nominal" Christians. Jenkins calls non-practising Muslims "potential" Muslims. In some statistics practising Christians are called "born-again" or "Great Commission" Christians (each term having its particular connotation). Here we adopt the term chosen by *Operation World*: Evangelicals. All the terms are questionable, and the classification of Christians within these labels even more. One can find practising Christians not only among Evangelicals but in every Christian denomination. On the other hand, there are also non-practising Christians among Evangelicals. For Muslims, there are no European statistics with the distinction between practising and non-practising Muslims available.

Religions

Note: for the sake of coherence, we present all the figures on religion and Christianity from Jason Mandryk, *Operation World* (Colorado Springs: Biblica, 2010), p. 73, 75. Figures below include the Russian Federation.

Religions	Population	Pop %	Annual Growth
Christian	552 017 165	71.34	- 0.3 %
Non-religious	156 917 869	21.45	1.1 %
Muslim	44 381 426	6.07	1.7 %
Buddhist	2 539 523	0.35	1.9 %
Jew	2 126 325	0.29	- 1.3 %
Other	1 403 686	0.19	1.4 %
Hindu	1 054 915	0.14	2.3 %
Animist	579 375	0.08	- 0.4 %
Sikh	498 474	0.07	2.1 %
Baha'i	101 002	0.01	0.2 %
Chinese	68 197	0.01	1.0 %

Appendix

Christianity

Christian Confessions

Source: Mandryk, *Operation World* (2010), p. 75.

Confession	Affiliates	Pop %	Annual Growth
Catholic	245 192 242	33.51	- 0.5 %
Orthodox	176 662 319	24.14	- 0.2 %
Protestant	66 680 808	9.11	- 0.1 %
Anglican	22 835 894	3.12	- 0.8 %
Evangelical	5 492 468	0.75	1.0 %
Marginal	3 918 130	0.54	0.4 %
Unaffiliated	10 051 449	1.37	- 1.1 %
Doubly affiliated	- 8 934 950	- 1.22	1.3 %

Evangelicals

Note: only countries with a population of 100 000 or more figure in the tables below.

Source: Mandryk, *Operation World* (2010), p. 73.

Country	Population (millions) 2010	Christians (% of tot. pop.)	Evangelicals (% of tot. pop.)	Evangelicals (in 1000) 2010
Albania	3.17	30.5	0.5	16
Austria	8.39	82.6	0.5	42
Belarus	9.59	70.5	1.3	125
Belgium	10.7	62.7	1.2	128
Bosnia	3.76	41.0	0.1	4
Bulgaria	7.50	79.9	1.9	143
Croatia	4.41	92.0	0.4	18
Cyprus	0.88	72.4	0.8	7
Czech Republic	10.41	25.9	0.7	73
Denmark	5.48	85.3	3.5	192
Estonia	1.34	45.3	4.9	66
Finland	5.35	83.8	12.1	647
France	62.64	61.1	1.0	626
Germany	82.06	64.3	2.1	1 723
Greece	11.18	91.5	0.4	45

Country	Population (millions) 2010	Christians (% of tot. pop.)	Evangelicals (% of tot. pop.)	Evangelicals (in 1000) 2010
Hungary	9.97	88.0	2.8	279
Iceland	0.33	90.6	3.8	13
Ireland	4.59	91.7	1.6	73
Italy	60.10	82.4	1.1	661
Latvia	2.24	60.0	7.0	157
Lithuania	3.26	85.4	1.1	36
Luxembourg	0.49	81.6	0.5	3
Macedonia	2.04	65.5	0.2	4
Malta	0.41	96.8	1.3	5
Moldova	3.58	73.4	3.7	132
Montenegro	0.63	77.1	0.1	0.6
Netherlands	16.65	46.6	4.3	716
Norway	4.86	91.1	8.4	408
Poland	38.04	89.6	0.3	114
Portugal	10.73	91.4	3.0	322
Romania	21.19	97.0	5.4	1 144
Russia	140.37	66.9	1.2	1 684
Serbia	7.77	80.4	0.6	47
Slovakia	5.41	93.3	1.2	65
Slovenia	2.02	54.2	0.1	1
Spain	45.45	77.1	1.0	454
Sweden	9.29	57.2	6.9	641
Switzerland	7.59	75.8	4.4	333
Ukraine	45.43	79.0	3.8	1 726
United Kingdom	62.13	59.7	8.8	5 467
TOTAL	731.69	71.3	2.5	18 292

British Megachurches

Note: churches with average weekly attendance of two thousand or more.
Source: Andy Peck, "What the Mega Church Can Teach You," *Christianity Magazine* (August 2006), at www.christianitymagazine.co-uk/engine.cfm?i=92&id=7423&arch=1, quoted in Philip Jenkins, *God's Continent: Christianity, Islam, and Europe's Religious Crisis* (Oxford: Oxford University Press, 2007), p. 92.

Megachurch	Attendance claimed (2006)
Kingsway International Christian Centre	10 000 - 12 000
Kensington Temple (Elim Pentecostal Church)	5 500
Hillsong Church	5 000
Ruach Ministries	4 000
Glory House	3 000
Jesus House	2 500
St. Thomas's, Sheffield	2 500
Holy Trinity, Brompton	2 500
New Wine Ministries	2 100

Islam

Note: The countries of the former Soviet Union are excluded from this table.
Source: Adapted from Jenkins, *God's Continent* (2007), p. 16.

Country	Population (millions) 2007	Muslims (millions) 2007	Muslims (% of pop.)
Northern, Western & Southern Europe			
Austria	8.1	0.35	4.4
Belgium	10.2	0.4	3.9
France	60.4	5	8.3
Germany	82	3.5	4.3
Denmark	5.3	0.27	5
Finland	5.2	0	
Ireland	3.7	0	
Italy	57.6	1	1.8
Luxembourg	0.4	0	

Country	Population (millions) 2007	Muslims (millions) 2007	Muslims (% of pop.)
Malta	0.4	0	
Netherlands	15.8	1	6.3
Norway	4.6	0.08	1.8
Portugal	10.8	0	
Spain	39.4	1	2.4
Sweden	8.9	0.4	4.4
Switzerland	7.2	0.31	4.3
United Kingdom	58.6	1.6	2.7
TOTAL	378.6	14.91	3.9
Eastern Europe			
Czech Republic	10.3	0	
Estonia	1.4	0	
Hungary	10.1	0	
Latvia	2.4	0	
Lithuania	3.7	0	
Poland	38.7	0	
Slovakia	5.4	0	
TOTAL	72.0	0	
South Eastern Europe			
Albania	3.6	2.5	70
Bosnia	4.1	1.6	40
Bulgaria	7.5	0.9	12.2
Croatia	4.5	0.2	4.4
Cyprus	0.9	0.16	18
Greece	10.6	0.14	1.3
Macedonia	2.1	0.6	17
Romania	22.3	0.2	0.8
Serbia & Montenegro	10.8	2.2	19
Slovenia	22.2	0.05	2.5
TOTAL	88.6	7.83	8.8

There are no European statistics with the distinction between practising and non-practising Muslims available. For a country like France, Jenkins estimates that in 2007 approximately 5 % of Muslims attend mosques with some degree of regularity (Jenkins, *God's Continent*, p. 122).

Appendix

Two Religious Minorities in Europe 1900-2025

Note: Population numbers are in millions and include Russia.
Source: David B. Barrett, George T. Kurian, Todd M. Johnson, *World Christian Encyclopedia* (2nd ed.; New York: Oxford University Press, 2001), p. 12-15, quoted by Jenkins, *God's Continent*, p. 75.

(in millions)	**1900**	**1920**	**2000**	**2025**
Muslims	9 (2.3 %)	18 (2.7 %)	32 (4.3 %)	36 (5.1%)
Evangelicals	32 (8 %)	30 (4.6%)	59 (8.2%)	69 (9.8 %)

Appendix 2: Literature Review

This literature review[1] of research in the different disciplines does not claim to be complete or exhaustive. It will be necessarily selective and partial. Its particular objective is to present research that tackles new aspects of evangelism in Europe. It follows the classical steps of a missiological approach designed in the introduction: a history of evangelism in Europe, an analysis of the socio-cultural context, a theology of the Gospel and of evangelism, and a reflection on the communication of the Gospel and church planting in the European context. There is an outstanding work that has already followed this procedure: it is Urs von Balthasar's Trilogy. Karl Barth's Catholic colleague in Basel has followed in his triptych the missiological approach indicated above: a history and analysis of European philosophical thought, a fundamental theology, and in the last part of his triptych a reflection on theologising in the European context, a theo-logic.[2]

History of Evangelism in Europe

During the first three centuries Christianity was naturally attractive. Despite the fact that it did not have an explicit strategy for evangelism and despite the persecutions in the Roman Empire, it grew until it had reached between 5 % and 25 % of the general population by the beginning of the 4th century. In addition to Eckhard Schnabel's reference work *Early Christian Mission* (2004),[3] it is Michael Green who analyses this period in his book *Evangelism in the Early Church* (2003),[4] and Roland Allen in *Missionary Methods. St. Paul's or Ours?* (1912/1962), and in *Spontaneous Expansion of the Church* (1927/1962).[5]

---

[1] This literature review is a revised version of the first part of a paper presented by Hannes Wiher at the meeting of the *Réseau de missiologie évangélique pour l'Europe francophone* (REMEEF) on November 20, 2013.

[2] Hans Urs von Balthasar, *The Glory of the Lord: a Theological Aesthetics* (ed. Joseph Fessio and John Riches; Edinburgh: T. & T. Clark, 1982-1991); idem, *Theodrama* (transl. Graham Harrison; San Francisco: Ignatius Press, 1988-2000); idem, *Theo-logic* (transl. Adrian J. Walker; San Francisco: Ignatius Press, 2000-2005).

[3] Eckhard J. Schnabel, *Early Christian Mission*, 2 vol. (Downers Grove: IVP, 2004).

[4] Michael Green, *Evangelism in the Early Church* (rev. ed.; Eastbourne: Kingsway, 2003; 1st ed.: Grand Rapids: Eerdmans, 1970).

[5] Roland Allen, *Missionary Methods. St. Paul's or Ours?* (Grand Rapids: Eerdmans, 1962; 1st ed. 1912); idem, *Spontaneous Expansion of the Church* (Grand Rapids: Eerdmans, 1962; 1st ed. 1927).

Rodney Stark's comparative historical-sociological approach in *The Rise of Christianity* (1996)[6] is particularly interesting for our reflection. He compares Christianity during the first centuries and today. According to him, all religions emerge in reaction to crises. In the case of Christianity, the epidemics of smallpox, measles and plague submerged the capacities of paganism and Hellenistic philosophies to offer explanation and comfort. Conversion is seen among the inactive and unsatisfied population group. Based on the fact that half of the Ethiopian population was Jewish and that most of them converted to Christianity, Stark concludes that cultural continuity between the religious group and the context favours conversion. He insists on the fact that conversion does not consist in searching for an ideology and adhering to it, but in aligning one's religious behaviour with that of one's family and friends. Thus, conversion tends to function on the basis of social networks built on interpersonal attachments. When Mormon missionaries carry out door to door evangelism of persons they do not know, they will see one conversion per a thousand solicitations. However, when the missionaries enter the first time into contact with a person who is a friend or a relative of a Mormon, it will result in one conversion per two contacts. His insights about religious scepticism indicate that it is highest among the educated.

After the "Constantine paradigm change" and during the medieval epoch, the European regions integrated into the Roman Empire evolved like the Mediterranean region towards the system of "Christendom": the Church was linked to the State and the Christian faith assimilated to the ambient culture. In his book *The Germanization of Early Medieval Christianity* (1994),[7] James Russell undertakes a study of this period. He remarks that during this process of Christianisation the Christian faith accommodated itself strongly to the Germanic worldview. However, parallel to "top down" efforts of Christianisation through marriages, alliances and conquests, monastic communities undertook patient "bottom up" efforts at evangelism. We find descriptions of both of them in major history books like Kenneth Latourette's seven-volume *magnum opus*: *A History of the Expansion of Christianity* (1937-1939).[8] Specific to Latourette's presenta-

---

[6] Rodney Stark, *The Rise of Christianity: A Sociologist Reconsiders History* (Princeton, NJ: Princeton University Press, 1996).

[7] James C. Russell, *The Germanization of Early Medieval Christianity: A Sociohistorical Approach to Religious Transformation* (New York: Oxford University Press, 1994).

[8] Kenneth S. Latourette, *A History of the Expansion of Christianity* (7 vol.; New York & London: Harper & Bros., 1937-1939).

tion is his thesis that new church denominations and new missionary movements have been initiated by spiritual revivals. Another specific historical approach is presented by Stephen Bevans and Roger Schroeder in *Constants in Context* (2004),[9] where they investigate missionary models and mission theologies (constants) applied in the different epochs (contexts). A cross-cultural historical approach is proposed by Andrew Walls in his two major books, *The Missionary Movement in Christian History: Studies on the Transmission of Faith* (1996), and *The Cross-Cultural Process in Christian History* (2002).[10]

The medieval epoch was followed by the Reformation, the wars of religion, Pietism and the revivals. Culturally this period was influenced by the philosophy of the Enlightenment and the industrial and technological revolution. Together they constitute the framework of modernity. This epoch has marked Europe strongly and separates it from other continents which have not undergone these two influences. The Enlightenment affected Protestantism more than Roman Catholicism.

For the mainly Roman Catholic country of France it is the historian of religion Sébastien Fath who has done research on the evangelical movement in France between 1800 and today. He has synthesised his results in *Du ghetto au réseau* (From the ghetto to the network, 2003)[11]. In an article on the French Baptists and evangelism, Fath observes three major obstacles to evangelism in France: first a French universalistic mentality for which a missionary Christianity would be a factor of alienation; second the French pride in their historical and cultural roots; and third the fear of foreigners. Concerning the obstacles of evangelism in France, he sums his findings as: "we find the main keys in history and culture."[12]

A colleague in our REMEEF network, Neal Blough, professor of church history at the evangelical seminary of Vaux-sur-Seine (Paris)

---

[9] Stephen B. Bevans & Roger P. Schroeder, *Constants in Context: A Theology of Mission for Today* (Maryknoll: Orbis, 2004).

[10] Andrew F. Walls, *The Missionary Movement in Christian History: Studies on the Transmission of Faith* (Maryknoll: Orbis, 1996); idem, *The Cross-Cultural Process in Christian History* (Maryknoll: Orbis, 2002).

[11] Sébastien Fath, *Du ghetto au réseau: Le protestantisme évangélique en France 1800-2005* (Genève: Labor et Fides, 2003). See the summary in idem, "Evangelical Protestantism in France: An Example of Denominational Recomposition?" *Sociology of Religion* 66, 4 (2005), p. 399-418.

[12] Sébastien FATH, "Les baptistes français et l'évangélisation: Enseignement de l'histoire" (The French Baptists and Evangelism: What History Teaches), *Cahiers de l'école pastorale* 45 (Sept. 2002).

makes the same observation. He shows clearly and in several publications that it is impossible to ignore two thousand years of Christian history if we want to do a good job today.[13] His article "Pluralism and Truth: Can the Church Still Be Missionary in the West?"[14] inspired by Lesslie Newbigin's famous question,[15] reflects on the same problem more specifically.

Evert Van de Poll, professor of missiology at the Evangelical Theological Faculty in Heverlee, Belgium, chooses in his book *Europe and the Gospel: Past Influences, Current Developments, Mission Challenges* (2013)[16] a historical, economic and political approach. By tracing the Christian history of Europe and the development of the European Union, he puts special emphasis on the Christian cultural heritage of Europe. At the same time, and justly, he indicates that after several centuries under the influence of Enlightenment philosophy, certain Europeans estimate that it is no longer relevant to ask the question whether there is a god. After twenty centuries of Christianity in Europe it seems that Europeans have forgotten God.

Analysis of the European Context

After the book *La France, pays de mission?* (France: A Mission Field? 1943)[17] by Henri Godin and Yvan Daniel, which was like a trumpet blast for a "missionary-sending" continent, a great number of research has been done on the European context.

One enterprise on the European level was the *European Values Study*[18]. A group that started in the 1970s has carried out between 1981 and 2008,

---

[13] Neal Blough, "Mission in Europe," in *Evangelical, Ecumenical and Anabaptist Missiologies in Conversation*, ed. James R. Krabill, Walter Sawatsky & Charles van Engen (Maryknoll: Orbis, 2006), p. 216-222. See also idem, "Évangéliser la France. Une expression à clarifier" (Evanglise France: An expression to be clarified), *Perspectives missionnaires* 33 (1997), p. 40-52; idem, "Évangéliser en France. Regards en arrière" (Evangelise France: A glance backward), in *La mission de l'Église au 21ᵉ siècle: Les nouveaux défis* (The mission of the Church: The new challenges), ed. Hannes Wiher (Charols: Excelsis, 2010), p. 35-47.

[14] Neal Blough, "Pluralisme et vérité. L'Église peut-elle encore être missionnaire en Occident?" *Perspectives missionnaires* 39, 1 (2000), p. 5-18.

[15] Lesslie Newbigin, "Can the West Be Converted?" *Princeton Seminary Review* 6, 1 (1985), p. 25-37. Reprint: *International Bulletin of Missionary Research* 11, 1 (1987), p. 2-7.

[16] (London: de Gruyter/Versita, 2013).

[17] Henri Godin & Yvan Daniel, *La France, pays de mission?* (Paris: L'Abeille, 1943).

[18] http://www.europeanvaluesstudy.eu.

at regular intervals and in an increasing number of countries, surveys on the moral and social values of Europeans. In their last survey they covered 47 countries, almost the whole of Europe. The main questions ask whether the Europeans have common values, whether these values are changing in Europe, and if yes, in which direction? Publications that summarise the findings of this research are *European Values at the Turn of the Millennium* (2004), and the *Atlas of European Values* (2005).[19] The European group collaborates with the *World Values Survey*[20] and coordinates the values studied and the methods used with the latter. The surveys indicate clearly that life satisfaction does not depend on income. They show also that a "post-materialist" attitude is becoming more frequent among the younger generations and particularly among intellectuals. Young and intellectual Europeans are more open to non-material aspects of life. They are searching for identity and spirituality.

We also have to mention the Sinus analyses in fifteen countries of Europe.[21] The Sinus-Milieus® are a sociological instrument developed in the world of public relations for the definition of the target clientele with regard to the planning of marketing and integrated communication. They visualise the life style of the inhabitants of a region or a country. The worldview and the values are part of the analysis of every milieu. The "Sinus" milieus developed at the Heidelberg research institute are derived from a holistic approach and reflect individual worlds. On the horizontal coordinate they range from traditionalism to postmodernism, for example from the traditional conservative, through the popular, bourgeois, quiet, consumer, intellectual, new rich, to the experimentalist and frustrated milieu. The milieus differ in number for a particular country.[22]

The sociologists of religion have reflected on the phenomenon of religion in a secular society, about its fall and its reappearance under new forms. The British sociologist of religion Grace Davie has greatly influenced the research on the continent through her innovative approach. Among her multiple publications we will only mention the most important

---

[19] Wil Arts & Loek Halman, eds., *European Values at the Turn of the Millennium* (Leiden: Brill, 2004); Loek Halman, Ruud Luijkx, Marga van Zundert, eds., *Atlas of European Values* (Leiden: Tilburg University, 2005).

[20] http://www.worldvaluessurvey.org.

[21] Austria, Bulgaria, Croatia, France, Germany, UK, Hungary, Italy, Poland, Czech Republic, Russia, Slovakia, Slovenia, Spain, Switzerland.

[22] For example, ten in Germany, eight in Russia, nine in France. See e.g. www.sinus-sociovision.de; www.levidepoches.fr; www.marketopedia.ru.

ones: *Religion in Britain since 1945: Believing without Belonging* (1993);²³ the subtitle introduced a catchphrase for being a Christian, for evangelism and discipleship in a postmodern society; three years later *Identités religieuses en Europe* (Religious Identities in Europe, 1996), edited together with Danièle Hervieu-Léger;²⁴ then *Europe, the Exceptional Case* (2002),²⁵ where she defends the thesis that the influence of the Enlightenment and the industrial revolution make Europe an exception among world cultures; then *Religion in Modern Europe: A Memory Mutates* (2005),²⁶ where she talks about the paradox of Europe where secularisation and de-secularisation can be observed at the same time. Grace Davie has also introduced other innovative concepts as "vicarious religion" and "default religion."

Rather than speaking of a religion as an isolated fact, its elements are sought for in apparently secular events. This is Danielle Hervieu-Léger's approach. She introduced the notions of "lost religion" and "the religious everywhere." For her, the religious is not only defined through the religions, but it is a horizontal dimension of the human phenomenon. Among her books we will mention the very instructive research *Vers un nouveau christianisme? Introduction à la sociologie du christianisme occidental* (Towards a New Christianity? Introduction to the Sociology of Western Christianity, 1986) by the two French sociologists Danielle Hervieu-Léger and Françoise Champion;²⁷ *De l'émotion en religion: Renouveaux et traditions* (From Emotion in Religion: Renewal and Traditions, 1990)²⁸, *La religion pour mémoire* (Religion as a Memory, 1993)²⁹, and *La religion en mouvement: Le pèlerin et le converti* (Religion in Movement: The Pilgrim

---

²³ Grace Davie, *Religion in Britain since 1945: Believing without Belonging* (Oxford: Blackwell, 1996).

²⁴ Grace Davie & Danièle Hervieu-Léger, eds., *Identités religieuses en Europe* (Paris: La Découverte, 1996).

²⁵ Grace Davie, *Europe, the Exceptional Case: Parameters of Faith in the Modern World* (London: Darton, Longman & Todd, 2002).

²⁶ Grace Davie, *Religion in Modern Europe: A Memory Mutates* (New York: Oxford University Press, 2005).

²⁷ Danièle Hervieu-Léger & Françoise Champion, *Vers un nouveau christianisme? Introduction à la sociologie du christianisme occidental* (Paris: Cerf, 1986).

²⁸ Françoise Champion & Danièle Hervieu-Léger, eds., *De l'émotion en religion: Renouveaux et traditions* (Paris: Centurion, 1990).

²⁹ Danièle Hervieu-Léger, *La religion pour mémoire* (Paris: Cerf, 1993).

and the Convert, 1999)[30], the last two published by Danièle Hervieu-Léger. In the latter she designs a threefold typology of contemporary Christians: the stable "practitioner," the mobile "pilgrim" and the "convert" who is open to new forms of faith, changes religion and finds a new identity. In her contribution to the collective book *La globalisation du religieux* (2001),[31] she observes the contemporary trends in religion and makes three interesting statements: the more belief individualises, the more it homogenises; the more belief homogenises, the more the believers circulate; the more the beliefs circulate, the less they determine and respond to practical belonging, and the more they favour a communitarian voluntarism susceptible to evolve towards sectarian forms.

From Great Britain come two interesting contemporary research endeavours: Philip Jenkins' *God's Continent* (2007),[32] and the research on the European context by the very dynamic missiology department of Redcliffe College. It edits the digital journal *Vista*.[33] Jean-Georges Gantenbein, president of Vision France and missiology professor at the Bible institute of Chrischona (Basel), chooses a sociological approach in his thesis *Mission en Europe: Une étude missiologique pour le 21e siècle* (Mission in Europe: A Missiological Study for the 21st Century, 2010).[34] In his reflection on the correlation between the Gospel and the sociological context of Europe, starting from a cultural esthetical sensitivity and an opening for spirituality, he proposes an esthetical and pneumatological missiology.[35]

We will also want to mention the European missiological conferences in collaboration with the International Association for Mission Studies (IAMS). The first European conference was held at Stavanger (Norway) in 1998 under the organisational leadership of the Nordic Institute of Mission and Ecumenical Research (NIME) with the theme: "Christianity in multi-

---

[30] Danièle Hervieu-Léger, *La religion en mouvement: Le pèlerin et le converti* (Paris: Flammarion, 1999).

[31] Danièle Hervieu-Léger, "Crise de l'universel et planétarisation culturelle: les paradoxes de la 'mondialisation' religieuse," in *La globalisation du religieux*, ed. Jean-Pierre Bastian, Françoise Champion, Kathy Rousselet (Paris: Harmattan, 2001), p. 87-96.

[32] Philip Jenkins, *God's Continent: Christianity, Islam, and Europe's Religious Crisis* (Oxford: Oxford University Press, 2007).

[33] https://europeanmission.redcliffe.ac.uk.

[34] Münster: Aschendorff, 2016.

[35] Cf. the German missiologist Peter Beyerhaus who proposes a pneumatological hermeneutics. Peter Beyerhaus, *Er sandte sein Wort: Die Bibel in der Mission*, vol. 1 (Wuppertal: Brockhaus, 1996).

religious societies: Missiological perspectives." The second conference held in Halle (Germany) under the auspices of the *Deutsche Gesellschaft für Missionswissenschaft* (DGMW) in 2002 had as its theme: "Postmodern Europe: Context and Mission".[36] The third conference was organised in Paris in 2006 under the auspices of the *Association francophone œcuménique de missiologie* (AFOM) and had the following theme: "Europe after the Enlightenment: To dare to evangelise in a Europe in construction."[37]

On the evangelical German speaking side, the *Arbeitskreis für evangelikale Missiologie* (AfeM), recently renamed *Evangelisches Forum für Mission, Kultur und Religion* which edits the journal *Missiotop* organised its annual meeting 2008 around the theme of "Mission in postmodern Europe."[38] Wilhelm Faix, professor at the theological seminary of Adelshofen, presented several models of sociological analysis: the European metamilieus and the Sinus-Milieus including the migrant milieus in Germany.[39] His results are partly congruent with those of the European Values Study and show the complexity of the European landscape often uniting paradoxes, as for example atheism and religion, experience and achievement orientations, globalisation and fragmentation, and consumerism and asceticism. Consequently, after a thorough analysis, the evangelistic approach will have to be individualised.

Another German contribution are the two books by Markus Müller, former director of Chrischona international, on the trends in the European context (*Trends* 2016 and 2021).[40] Müller presents the developments in Europe and the world, then exposes the defaults of European Christians

---

[36] The papers of the two conferences are published in *Swedish Missiological Themes* vol. 86, n° 4 (1998), and vol. 90, n° 4 (2002).

[37] Published in English in *International Review of Mission* vol. 95, n° 378-379 (July-October 2006), p. 229-443; published in French in *Perspectives missionnaires* 52, 2 (2006), and *Spiritus* 185 (2006).

[38] Klaus W. Müller, ed., *Mission im postmodernen Europa* (Referate der Jahrestagung 2008 des Arbeitskreises für evangelikale Missiologie (AfeM); Nürnberg/Bonn: VTR/VKW, 2008).

[39] Wilhelm Faix, "Gesellschaftsanalyse Europa," in Müller, *Mission im postmodernen Europa*, p. 10-45. For migrant milieus in Germany, see www.sinus-sociovision.de/Download/Navigator/2_2007_Insight_Migranten-Milieus-in-Deutschland.pdf See also Wilhelm Faix et al., *Theologie im Kontext von Biographie und Weltbild* (Marburg a. Lahn: Francke, 2011).

[40] Markus Müller, *Trends 2016: Die Zukunft lieben* (2nd ed.; Basel/Giessen: Brunnen, 2011; 1st ed. 2009); idem, *Trends 2021: Es wird anders werden* (Basel: Brunnen, 2012).

and finishes with today's challenges and the Christian response. According to Müller, world developments show the following trends: from industry to information, from technology to communication, from national economy to world economy, from long term to short term, from centralised to decentralised, from hierarchy to network, from North to South, and from a logic "or-or" to a logic "and-and." In Europe we find, according to Müller, a loss of meaning and of hope, individualism, materialism, consumerism and secularism, with the consequence that religion in its classical form becomes a non-topic. On the other hand, Islam is making its presence felt and esotericism is a growing force. Müller observes the following defaults in evangelical European Christians: a lack of historical perspective, a withdrawal from the world, the role of arbiter instead of engagement in society, an anthropocentric and achievement-oriented thinking, Christian faith perceived as private and as theory (geared to doctrine) rather than as a practice.

Theology of Evangelism

Since the decision of the Second Vatican Council to conceive of the Church as intrinsically missionary (especially *Ad Gentes* and *Lumen Gentium*), missiological reflection has been stimulated in the Roman Catholic Church. In 1975 the encyclical *Evangelii nuntiandi* by Paul VI followed, and in 1990 *Redemptoris missio* by John-Paul II, and the missiological texts *Dialogue and Mission* (1984) and *Dialogue and Proclamation* (1991) by the Pontifical Council for Interreligious Dialogue. In 1979 the expression "new evangelisation" was initiated by John-Paul II and appeared in 1988 in *Christifideles laici*. On September 21, 2010, Benedict XVI even instituted a new dicastery: the Pontifical council for the promotion of the new evangelisation. The text of his motu proprio *Ubicumque et semper* insists on the fact that "the Church has the duty to proclaim the Gospel everywhere and always [*ubicumque et semper*]." The cycle is concluded by the apostolic exhortation *Evangelii gaudium* promulgated on November 24, 2013, by Francis I. His concern is to not dissociate the new evangelisation from the involvement with the poor and the marginalised, a holistic concern.

Being unable to follow this new enthusiasm the missiologist René Luneau, in his book *Le rêve de Compostelle: Vers la restauration d'une Europe chrétienne?* (The Dream of Compostela: Towards the Restoration of a Christian Europe? 1989),[41] expresses the impression that the concept of

---

[41] Paris: Centurion, 1989.

"new evangelisation" translates a simple nostalgia of European Christendom as it was before the Enlightenment. In the same vein, Marie-Hélène Robert, professor of missiology at the Catholic University of Lyon, invites missiologists to engage in a reflection on the concept. In her article "Orientations de Vatican II, la nouvelle évangélisation et Édimbourg 2010" (Orientations from Vatican II: The New Evangelisation and Edinborough 2010),[42] she deplores the lack of reflection on evangelism in Europe. This is surely the reason why she started an investigative study on "Evangelisation in the European context: Interdisciplinary research" at the Catholic University of Lyon. The fruit of this reflection is a new book with the title *"Pour que le monde croie": Approches théologiques de l'évangélisation* (That the World May Believe: Theological Approaches to Evangelisation, 2014).[43] In theological, historical and contextual reflections Marie-Hélène Robert nuances and differentiates the concept of "new evangelisation" through considerations based on apostolic preaching, missiological paradigms and different approaches to cultures and religions, in order to arrive at a new concept of evangelism in the context of postmodernity.

From Scandinavia we want to mention the book *Mission in the New Millennium* (2000)[44] by Risto Ahonen, professor of missiology at the University of Helsinki (Finland), and the articles "Three Missiological Perspectives: What Testimony?" and "Mission, Evangelism and Evangelization: From the Perspective of the Lausanne Movement,"[45] by Tormod Engelsviken, professor of missiology at the Lutheran School of Theology in Oslo (Norway), and member of the WCC Commission on World Mission and Evangelism and of the WEA Missions Commission.

In the Netherlands, Stefan Paas, J.H. Bavinck professor of church planting and church renewal at the Free University of Amsterdam, and lecturer in missiology at the Theological University of Kampen, has published together with Gerrit Noort and Kyriaki Avtzi a *Handbook of Evangelism in Europe* (2017) in the WCC series. In a paper presented at the European

---

[42] *Perspectives missionnaires* 60, 2 (2010), p. 38-49.

[43] Marie-Hélène Robert, *"Pour que le monde croie": Approches théologiques de l'évangélisation* (Lyon: Profac-Théo, 2014).

[44] Risto A. Ahonen, *Mission in the New Millennium: Theological Grounds for World Mission* (Helsinki: Finnish Evangelical Lutheran Mission, 2000).

[45] Tormod Engelsviken, "Three Missiological Perspectives: What Testimony?" *International Review of Mission* vol. 95, n° 378-379 (July-October 2006), p. 329-333; idem, "Mission, Evangelism and Evangelization: From the Perspective of the Lausanne Movement," *International Review of Mission* vol. 96, n° 382-383 (July-October 2007), p. 204-209.

Conference of Reformed Churches in 2011, he also reflected on the "Missionary Ministry in 21st Century Europe."[46]

In the German linguistic zone, Friedemann Walldorf, professor of missiology at the Freie Theologische Hochschule Giessen (Germany), presented three traditional models of mission theologies from which, according to him, a new model will erupt by incorporating the three former models.[47] He distinguishes the ecclesiocentric model of inculturation that perceives the Church as "soul of Europe" (the Catholic model); the cosomocentric dialogical model that seeks to discover God in Europe (the ecumenical model); and the bibliocentric model of translation that wants to present Christ to the Europeans (the evangelical model). The new model will be, according to Walldorf, more Christo- and ecclesiocentric (Benedict XVI), will include dialogue and mission, the latter conceived as holistic mission (ecumenical contribution), and will value biblical faith and experience (evangelical contribution).

Very interesting reflections on evangelism in the Western context were made by Lesslie Newbigin, a missionary theologian returning to Europe after a long ministry in India. His publications include an article asking the famous question: "Can the West be converted?" but started actually with a reflection on *Honest Religion for Secular Man* (1966), followed by *Foolishness to the Greeks: The Gospel and Western Culture* (1986), and *The Gospel in a Pluralist Society* (1989).[48] His publications had a great impact on many European theologians' and missiologists' thinking about evangelism in Europe. He initiated the network "Mission-shaped Church" in the United Kingdom, which later became the Gospel and Our Culture Network

---

[46] Gerrit Noort, Kyriaki Avtzi and Stefan Paas, eds., *Sharing Good News: Handbook of Evangelism in Europe* (Geneva: World Council of Churches, 2017); Stefan Paas, "Prepared for a Missionary Ministry in 21st Century Europe," Opening Paper for the European Conference of Reformed Churches (EuCRC), Kampen (Netherlands), March 22, 2011.

[47] Friedemann Walldorf, "Kontextuelle Missionstheologien für das postmoderne Europa," in *Mission im postmodernen Europa*, ed. Klaus W. Müller (Nürnberg/Bonn: VTR/VKW, 2008), p. 46-66. See also his Ph.D. thesis *Die Neuevangelisierung Europas: Missionstheologien im europäischen Kontext* (Giessen: Brunnen, 2002).

[48] Lesslie Newbigin, "Can the West Be Converted?" *Princeton Seminary Review* 6, 1 (1985), p. 25-37; reprint: *International Bulletin of Missionary Research* 11, 1 (1987), p. 2-7; idem, *Honest Religion for Secular Man* (London: SCM, 1966); *Foolishness to the Greeks: The Gospel and Western Culture* (London: SPCK, 1986); idem, *The Gospel in a Pluralist Society* (Grand Rapids: Eerdmans, 1989).

(GOCN),[49] with a very dynamic branch in the United States.[50] The resulting Gospel and Our Culture Series was published by Eerdmans.[51] The first publication, Darrell Guder's *Missional Church* (1998), which targeted North America, also had a great impact on European theological thinking on Church and Mission.[52] The last two productions are Michael Goheen's *Reading the Bible Missionally* (2017) and Stefan Paas' *Church Planting in the Secular West* (2016).[53] During the last ten years, under the initiative of George Hunsberger, the Gospel and Our Culture Network started joint meetings between the Society of Biblical Literature and the American Academy of Religion on the theme of a missiological hermeneutic of Scripture.[54]

In line with Newbigin's reflections, N.T. Wright,[55] former Anglican bishop of Durham (Scotland), now Research Professor of New Testament and Early Christianity at the University of St. Andrews (Scotland), developed a biblical theology with implications for mission in the contemporary European context. To mention just one of his books with a special importance for our topic: *Surprised by Hope: Rethinking Heaven, the Resurrection, and the Mission of the Church* (2008).[56]

On the basis of Newbigin's and N.T. Wright's reflections, Kevin Vanhoozer, Research Professor of Systematic Theology at Trinity Evangelical Divinity School, Deerfield (Illinois), continues missional reflection in the light of the postmodern culture. He uses the metaphor of theatre to proceed from hermeneutics via systematic theology to missional practice. His main work on this topic is *The Drama of Doctrine* (2005).[57] Thus, during recent years, support in thinking about a theology of evangelism

---

[49] www.gospel-culture.org.uk.

[50] www.gocn.org.

[51] www.eerdmans.com/Products/CategoryCenter.aspx?CategoryId=SE!GOCS.

[52] Darrell L. Guder & Lois Barrett, *Missional Church: A Vision for the Sending of the Church in North America* (Grand Rapids: Eerdmans, 1998).

[53] Michael Goheen, ed., *Reading the Bible Missionally* (Grand Rapids: Eerdmans, 2016); Stefan Paas, *Church Planting in the Secular West: Learning from the European Experience* (Grand Rapids: Eerdmans, 2016).

[54] See for example George R. Hunsberger, "Proposals for a Missional Hermeneutic: Mapping a Conversation," *Missiology* 39, 3 (2011), p. 309-321.

[55] http://ntwrightpage.com.

[56] N.T. Wright, *Surprised By Hope: Rethinking Heaven, the Resurrection, and the Mission of the Church* (New York: HarperCollins, 2008).

[57] Kevin J. Vanhoozer, *The Drama of Doctrine: A Canonical-Linguistic Approach to Christian Theology* (Louisville: John Knox, 2005).

has been coming from biblical and systematic theologians rather than from missiologists.

In the German linguistic sphere, Roland Hardmeier makes two important contributions to mission theology: with his doctoral thesis *Kirche ist Mission: Auf dem Weg zu einem ganzheitlichen Missionsverständnis* (2009),[58] he promotes a holistic concept of mission with regard to a missional church. In his second book, *Missionale Theologie: Evangelikale auf dem Weg zur Weltverantwortung* (2015),[59] he makes, from the perspective of "radical Christianity", a plea for a concept of mission embedded in a Missio-Dei theology that leads to Christian responsibility for the people in the immediate and larger context.

Communication of the Gospel

Among the theological and missiological reflections on evangelism few authors think about the question how an inward-looking Christian or church can be motivated to witness to a hostile neighbourhood. How is it possible to get interested in our contemporaries and dare to talk to them about God? The question of a missional spirituality remains fundamental. Actually, the Bible gives us the answer: "Out of the abundance of the heart the mouth speaks" (Mt 12:34; Lk 6:45).

Two evangelical contributions should be mentioned: the first one is a biblical and theological reflection by Christophe Paya, *Pour une Église en mouvement* (Towards a Church in Movement, 2010)[60], an exegesis of the sending of the disciples in the Gospel of Matthew (9:35-11:1). The second by Hannes Wiher is a historical and practical reflection entitled "Une spiritualité missionnaire" (A Missional Spirituality, 2012)[61]. In this article, Wiher forwards the hypothesis that a missional rather than introverted spirituality is the result of a discipleship process oriented towards mission.[62] Formerly, discipleship was practised mainly in Roman Catholic monasteries. Today one can find "schools of discipleship training" in some missionary movements of young people and student movements, as for

---

[58] Roland Hardmeier, *Kirche ist Mission: Auf dem Weg zu einem ganzheitlichen Missionsverständnis* (D.Th. thesis UNISA; Schwarzenfeld: Neufeld, 2009).
[59] Roland Hardmeier, *Missionale Theologie: Evangelikale auf dem Weg zur Weltverantwortung* (edition IGW Bd. 7; Schwarzenburg: Neufeld, 2015).
[60] Charols: Excelsis, 2010.
[61] In Hannes Wiher, ed., *Bible et mission, vol. 2: Vers une pratique évangélique de la mission* (Charols: Excelsis, 2012), p. 75-100.
[62] See Simon Pierre Gatera, *Le discipulat axé sur la mission* (Nürnberg: VTR, 2009).

example the Intervarsity Fellowship of Evangelical Students (IFES), Youth for Christ (YFC), Youth with a Mission (YWAM) and Operation Mobilisation (OM), as well as in the neo-monastic wing of the emerging church movement.[63]

When we start thinking about the communication of the Gospel, we have a whole wealth of literature coming from the United States. Widely circulating is the popular biblical approach by Robert Coleman, *The Master Plan of Evangelism* (1972).[64] After the so called "cultural turn" of missiology in the 1970s, much of the literature from the United States is building on communication theory much more than on biblical exegesis. This is typical of the literature published from the late 1970s to the early 1990s. We think of classics like *Contemporary Christian Communication* (1979) by James F. Engel[65] who has switched from a public relations department of a large American enterprise to a mission society. He schematises the conversion process in the famous "Engel's scale."[66] There followed the classics by David Hesselgrave, *Communicating Christ Cross-Culturally* (1980), and Charles Kraft, *Communication Theory for Christian Witness* (1983).[67] Daniel Shaw and Viggo Sogaard of Fuller Seminary later supplemented the "Engel's scale" with an affective dimension creating a matrix.[68] The resulting publications were: *Transculturation: The Cultural Factor in Translation and Other Communication Tasks* (1988) by Daniel Shaw, *Media in Church and Mission* (1993) by Viggo Sogaard, and *Communicating God's Word in a Complex World* (2003) by Daniel Shaw and Charles van Engen.[69] In 2003, Robert Frykenberg produced a historical

---

[63] See for example Rutba House, ed., *School(s) for Conversion: 12 Marks of a New Monasticism* (Eugene, OR: Cascade Books, 2005); Gabriel Monet, *L'Église émergente. Être et faire Église en postchrétienté* (Berlin: LIT, 2014), p. 64.

[64] Robert E. Coleman, *The Master Plan of Evangelism* (Grand Rapids: Revell, 1972).

[65] James F. Engel, *Contemporary Christian Communication: Its Theory and Practice* (Nashville/New York: Thomas Nelson, 1979).

[66] James F. Engel, "An Interpersonal Communication Model: The Engel Scale Explained," at www.gospelcom.net/guide/resources/tellitoften.php.

[67] David J. Hesselgrave, *Communicating Christ Cross-Culturally* (Grand Rapids: Zondervan, 1980); Charles H. Kraft, *Communication Theory for Christian Witness* (Nashville: Abingdon, 1983).

[68] For a concise summary, see Frank Gray, « Engel Scale or Gray Matrix? », http://thegraymatrix.org/?p=211.

[69] R. Daniel Shaw, *Transculturation: The Cultural Factor in Translation and Other Communication Tasks* (Pasadena: William Carey Library, 1988); Viggo Sogaard, *Media in Church and Mission. Communicating the Gospel* (Pasadena: William Car-

overview of the different approaches to the cross-cultural communication of the Gospel.[70] The more recent combined biblical and practical approaches *The Logic of Evangelism* (1989) by William Abraham, and *The Study of Evangelism: Exploring the Missional Practice of the Church* (2008) by Paul Chilcote & Lacey Warner, are much less known than the old classics.[71] Lately, two books on the communication of the Gospel more geared to theological reflection have been published by the Gospel and Our Culture Network: Michael Gorman's *Becoming the Gospel* (2015), and Darrell Guder's *Called to Witness* (2015).[72]

But what about European contributions to a theological reflection about the communication of the Gospel? As far as my experience goes, most communicative attempts in Europe build on American social scientific and pragmatic models. Exceptions are Markus Müller's two books on the contemporary challenges in Europe and the Christian response they require (*Trends* 2016 and 2021),[73] and Deborah Meroff's *Europe: Restoring Hope* (2011)[74] that we have briefly presented in the Introduction. Another happy exception are the efforts in the French speaking region of Western Europe. For several years David Brown, president of the *Groupes bibliques universitaires* (GBU-IFES), France, has been thinking about new approaches which could respond to the aspirations and the worldview of French people. Since the beginning of the new century, he has published a series of books: *Une Église pour aujourd'hui* (A Church for Today, 2001), *Passerelles: Entre l'Évangile et nos contemporains* (Bridges: Between the Gospel and our Contemporaries, 2003), and *"Servir à nos Français:" Le défi de l'Église émergente: Bien vivre notre foi et la communiquer à nos*

---

ey Library, 1993); R. Daniel Shaw & Charles E. van Engen, *Communicating God's Word in a Complex World: God's Truth or Hocus Pocus?* (Lanham, MD: Rowman and Littlefield, 2003).

[70] Robert E. Frykenberg, ed., *Christians and Missionaries: Cross-Cultural Communication since 1500* (Grand Rapids: Eerdmans, 2003).

[71] William J. Abraham, *The Logic of Evangelism* (Grand Rapids: Eerdmans, 1989); Paul W. Chilcote & Lacey C. Warner, *The Study of Evangelism: Exploring the Missional Practice of the Church* (Grand Rapids: Eerdmans, 2008).

[72] Michael J. Gorman, *Becoming the Gospel: Paul, Participation, and Mission* (Gospel and Our Culture; Grand Rapids: Eerdmans, 2015); Darrell C. Guder, *Called to Witness* (Gospel and Our Culture; Grand Rapids: Eerdmans, 2015).

[73] Markus Müller, *Trends 2016: Die Zukunft lieben* (2nd ed.; Basel/Giessen: Brunnen, 2011; 1st ed. 2009); idem, *Trends 2021: Es wird anders werden* (Basel: Brunnen, 2012).

[74] Deborah Meroff, *Europe: Restoring Hope* (Nürnberg/Linz: VTR/OM Books, 2011).

contemporains (Serve the French: Live Our Faith and Communicate it to our Contemporaries, 2009). The article "Une apologétique plausible pour la culture contemporaine" (A Plausible Apologetic for Contemporary Culture, 2010)[75], is a brief summary of his approach *Passerelles* "bridges."[76]

Raphael Anzenberger, general secretary of France Evangelisation and coordinator of the Forum of evangelists[77] in the French speaking world, presents an apologetic approach in his book, *Moi aussi je voudrais croire, mais ...* (Me Too, I Would Like to Believe But ..., 2010), and describes the ministry of an evangelist in *L'évangéliste sous toutes ses formes* (The Evangelist in All His Forms, 2012)[78]. He starts from the idea that many think that religion belongs to the Middle Ages, a time when it was possible to believe in just about anything and that we live in a context which is hostile to the idea of God. This is the reason, according to him, why many break with their religion and try other ways.

Yannick Imbert, professor of apologetics and history at the evangelical-reformed seminary of Aix-en-Provence (France),[79] asks in his book, *Croire, expliquer, vivre* (Believe, Explain, Live, 2014),[80] whether apologetics is a philosophical exercise, a form of pre-evangelism or rather a way of life that requires a daily commitment. Imbert proposes returning to a biblical consideration of apologetics in order to better discern its definition and practice.

In German we have the publications of the *Arbeitskreis für evangelikale Missiologie* (renamed *Evangelisches Forum für Mission, Kultur und Religion*) on the topic of their annual meeting *Gott zur Sprache bringen* (Talk about God, 2003), and the commemorative publication for Ursula Wiesemann, a German pioneer in Bible translation, *Mission als Kommunikation* (Mission as Communication, 2007).[81]

---

[75] Published in Wiher, ed., *La mission de l'Église au 21e siècle*, p. 145-153.

[76] For a summary of the concept of *Passerelles*, see chapter 12. *Passerelles* goes together with a manual, a moderator's guide and a DVD.

[77] http://globalevangelistsforum.org.

[78] Raphaël Anzenberger, *Moi aussi je voudrais croire, mais...* (Marpent: BLF, 2010); idem, *L'évangéliste sous toutes ses formes* (Marpent: BLF, 2012).

[79] Faculté Jean Calvin (FJC).

[80] Yannick Imbert, *Croire, expliquer, vivre: Introduction à l'apologétique* (Charols: Excelsis, 2014).

[81] Klaus W. Müller, ed., *Gott zur Sprache bringen*, afem mission reports 11 (Nürnberg: VTR, 2003); Klaus W. Müller, ed., *Mission als Kommunikation: Die christliche Botschaft verstehen*, Festschrift für Ursula Wiesemann (Nürnberg: VTR, 2007).

Church Planting

Moving from the individual to a collective approach with the view to presenting the Gospel efficiently to our contemporaries, we want to mention the multiple reflections and attempts at church planting in postmodern Europe, particularly the emerging church movement. An older European proposal comes from Johan Lukasse from the Netherlands, *Churches with Roots* (1990), which was originally published in Dutch (1989), but has been translated into English and French.[82] Recently, Evert van de Poll and Stefan Paas, also from the Netherlands, have published three reference works. Evert van de Poll, professor of the science of religions and of missiology at the Free Evangelical Faculty of Heverlee (Leiden), has published, together with Joanne Appleton, *Church Planting in Europe* (2015).[83] Stefan Paas, J.H. Bavinck professor of church planting and church renewal at the Free University of Amsterdam, published *Church Planting in the Secular West: Learning from the European Experience* (2016) in the Gospel and Our Culture Series, and *Sharing Good News: Handbook of Evangelism in Europe* (2017) in the World Council of Churches Series, together with Gerrit Noort and Kyriaki Avtzi.[84]

Of course, the classics of the North American church growth movement have also been circulating in Europe: *Understanding Church Growth* (1980) by Donald McGavran, and *Church Growth and the Whole Gospel* (1981) by Peter Wagner, together with the classic of the more recent concept of "church planting movement": *Church Planting Movements* (2004) by David Garrison, evaluated by Gary McIntosh and others in *Evaluating the Church Growth Movement: Five Views* (2004).[85] The publications de-

---

[82] Johan Lukasse, *Churches with Roots* (London: STL, 1990); French translation: *Mission Possible! Implantation d'églises dans une Europe post-chrétienne* (Bruxelles/St Légier: Le Bon Livre/Emmaüs, 1993).

[83] Evert van de Poll & Joanne Appleton, eds., *Church Planting in Europe* (Eugene, OR: Wipf & Stock, 2015).

[84] Stefan Paas, *Church Planting in the Secular West: Learning from the European Experience* (Grand Rapids: Eerdmans, 2016); see the summary in: Stefan Paas & Alrik Vos, "Church Planting and Church Growth in Western Europe: An Analysis," *International Bulletin of Missionary Research* 40, 3 (2016), p. 243-252; Gerrit Noort, Kyriaki Avtzi and Stefan Paas, eds., *Sharing Good News: Handbook of Evangelism in Europe* (Geneva: World Council of Churches, 2017).

[85] Donald A. McGavran, *Understanding Church Growth* (Grand Rapids: Eerdmans, 1980); C. Peter Wagner, *Church Growth and the Whole Gospel: A Biblical Mandate* (New York/San Francisco: Harper & Row, 1981); David Garrison, *Church Planting Movements. How God is Redeeming a Lost World* (Midliothan, VA: WIG

scribing the experiences of "seeker-friendly" megachurches like Willow Creek found a large following in Europe.[86] They represent again the pragmatic American approach.

More recently, two North American approaches combining biblical perspectives and best practices have been published: the first by Craig Ott and Gene Wilson, *Global Church Planting: Biblical Principles and Best Practices for Multiplication* (2011);[87] the second *Center Church: Doing Balanced, Gospel-Centered Ministry in Your City* (2012) by Timothy Keller. Well known through the popularity of the author, the latter has already become a benchmark and has also been applied widely in Europe. Lately, it has been translated in French.[88]

Recent initiatives are choosing to develop networks on the internet: some years ago the Eurochurch network tried to assemble church planters throughout Europe. Today Acts29 initiative, the continuation of the book of Acts, the Europe Christian Mission and M4 Europe are very active.[89] The four Ms represent the basic concepts of the M4 Movement: Master, Mission, Multiplication, and Movement. We have already mentioned the Global Forum of Evangelists.[90] An interesting initiative of the Association of Evangelicals in Africa (AEA) is the Gift from Africa to Europe (GATE) network, which tries to assemble European and African church planters in Europe.[91] On the American side, we have to mention the broadly based Missional Church Network.[92]

In French it is Gabriel Monet who has published *L'Église émergente: Être et faire Église en postchrétienté* (Emerging Church: Being and Doing

---

Take Resources, 2004); Gary L. McIntosh, ed., *Evaluating the Church Growth Movement: Five Views* (Grand Rapids: Zondervan, 2004).

[86] Among many others see for example, Lynne Hybels & Bill Hybels, *Rediscovering Church: The Story and Vision of Willow Creek Community Church* (Grand Rapids: Zondervan, 2016).

[87] Craig Ott & Gene Wilson, *Global Church Planting: Biblical Principles and Best Practices for Multiplication* (Grand Rapids: Baker, 2011).

[88] Timothy Keller, *Center Church: Doing Balanced, Gospel-Centered Ministry in Your City* (Grand Rapids: Zondervan, 2012). French translation: *Une Église centrée sur l'Évangile* (Charols: Excelsis, 2015).

[89] www.acts29.com/network/europe; www.ecmi.org/discipleship-and-planting-churches; https://m4europe.com.

[90] http://globalevangelistsforum.org.

[91] www.gate-mission.org/index_en.html.

[92] www.missionalchurchnetwork.com.

Church in Post-Christendom, 2014),[93] and the practical manual by David Brown, *L'implantation d'une Église racontée à mon stagiaire* (An Effort of Church Planting Explained to my Trainee, 2013).[94] Among other efforts we would like to mention the French campaign "A church for 10 000 inhabitants,"[95] initiated by the Church Planting Commission of the National Council of Evangelicals of France (CNEF[96]).

In German we have to mention the reflections of Johannes Reimer, who is professor of missiology at the University of South Africa (UNISA), Pretoria, and at the *Theologischen Hochschule* of the Free Evangelical Churches (FEG) at Ewersbach (Germany), and President of the *Gesellschaft für Bildung und Forschung in Europa* (GBFE), in collaboration with UNISA. His publications comprise a whole program for the creation of a missional and multicultural church: *Die Welt umarmen: Theologie des gesellschaftsrelevanten Gemeindebaus* (Embrace the World: Theology of Church Planting that Is Relevant for Society, 2009), *Gott in der Welt feiern: Auf dem Weg zum missionalen Gottesdienst* (Celebrate God in the World: Towards a Missional Worship, 2010), *Multikultureller Gemeindebau: Versöhnung leben* (Multicultural Church Planting: To Live Reconciliation, 2011).[97]

---

[93] Gabriel Monet, *L'Église émergente: Être et faire Église en postchrétienté* (Ph.D. thesis, Faculté de théologie protestante, Strasbourg; Berlin, Lit, 2014).

[94] Lyon: CLÉ, 2013.

[95] www.1pour10000.fr.

[96] *Conseil national des évangéliques de France* (CNEF).

[97] Johannes Reimer, *Die Welt umarmen: Theologie des gesellschaftsrelevanten Gemeindebaus* (Marburg a. Lahn: Francke, 2009); idem, *Gott in der Welt feiern: Auf dem Weg zum missionalen Gottesdienst* (Schwarzenfeld: Neufeld, 2010), *Multikultureller Gemeindebau: Versöhnung leben* (Marburg a. Lahn: Francke, 2011).

List of Authors

Neal BLOUGH is professor of Church History at the *Faculté libre de théologie évangélique* (FLTE) at Vaux-sur-Seine (Paris region), visiting professor at the Theological Seminary Bienenberg (TSB) at Liestal (Switzerland), and Director of the Mennonite Centre in Paris.

David BROWN has planted three churches in France (two at Nancy and one in the Paris region) and is pastor of an evangelical church in Paris. He has been working for thirteen years in the *Groupes Bibliques Universitaires* (GBU-IFES) in France, first as general secretary, then as president. He is coordinator of the Evangelism Commission of the *Conseil national des évangéliques de France* (CNEF; equivalent of the Evangelical Alliance), and has published several books on church planting in the contemporary context of France.

Julien COFFINET studied theology at the University of Strasbourg, then at the *Institut protestant de théologie* at Montpellier where he obtained his professional Master's degree. Today, he is pastor of the United Protestant Church of France (*Église protestante unie de France*, EPUF) at Saint-Germain-en-Laye in the Paris region, and student for a research Master's degree at the *Faculté libre de théologie évangélique* (FLTE) at Vaux-sur-Seine.

Léo LEHMANN obtained a research Master's degree at the *Faculté libre de théologie évangélique* (FLTE) at Vaux-sur-Seine. He and his wife are pastors of the *Église protestante évangélique* at Ganshoren, in the north of Brussels (Belgium).

Johannes MÜLLER is the director of African Link, a ministry working alongside African church leaders in Switzerland, which is associated with MEOS and relates to the Intercultural Working Group of the Swiss Evangelical Alliance. He teaches on migration and mission in different training institutions.

Evert VAN DE POLL is professor of the science of religions and missiology at the Evangelical Theological Faculty (ETF) at Leuven (Belgium), and pastor in the Baptist Federation of France (*Fédération des Églises évangéliques baptistes de France*).

Hannes WIHER is a doctor in theology and medicine. He is associate professor of missiology at the *Faculté libre de théologie évangélique* (FLTE) at Vaux-sur-Seine, and at the *Faculté Jean Calvin* (FJC) at Aix-en-Provence (France), and visiting professor at the *Faculté de théologie évangélique de Bangui* (FATEB), extension of Yaoundé (Cameroon), and at the University Shalom at Bunia (Congo DRC). He is the president of the *Réseau de missiologie évangélique pour l'Europe francophone* (REMEEF).

Bibliography

Abraham, William J., *The Logic of Evangelism* (Grand Rapids MI: Eerdmans, 1989).

"Acts of the First European Conference of Missiology, Stavanger, August 1998," *Swedish Missiological Themes* vol. 86, n° 4 (1998).

"Acts of the Second European Conference of Missiology, Halle, August 2002," *Swedish Missiological Themes* vol. 90, n° 4 (2002).

"Acts of the Third European Conference of Missiology, Paris 24-28 August 2006," *International Review of Mission* vol. 95, n° 378-379 (July-October 2006). French edition: *Perspectives missionnaires* n° 52, 2 (2006); and *Spiritus* 185 (2006).

Adogame, Afe, *The African Christian Diaspora: New Currents and Emerging Trends in World Christianity* (London/New York: Bloomsbury Academics, 2013).

Agier, Michel, *La condition cosmopolite: L'anthropologie à l'épreuve du piège identitaire* (Paris: La Découverte, 2013).

Ahonen, Risto A., *Mission in the New Millennium: Theological Grounds for World Mission* (Helsinki: Finnish Evangelical Lutheran Mission, 2000).

Ahrweiler, Hélène & Aymard, Maurice, ed., *Les Européens* (Paris: Hermann, 2000).

Albisser, Judith & Bünker, Arnd, eds., *Kirchen in Bewegung: Christliche Migrationsgemeinden in der Schweiz* (St.Gallen: SPI, 2016).

Allen, Roland, *Missionary Methods: St. Paul's or Ours?* (Grand Rapids: Eerdmans, 1962; 1st ed. 1912).

Allen, Roland, *Spontaneous Expansion of the Church* (Grand Rapids: Eerdmans, 1962; 1st ed. 1927).

Altermatt, Urs, Delgado, Mariano, Vergauwen, Guide, eds., *Europa, ein christliches Projekt? Beiträge zum Verhältnis von Religion und europäischer Identität* (Stuttgart: Kohlhammer, 2008).

Amorth, Gabriele, *Un exorciste raconte* (Paris: Guibert, 1993).

Anderson, Allen, "Pentecostalism, the Enlightenment and Christian Mission in Europe," *International Review of Mission* vol. 95, n° 378-379 (July-October 2006), p. 276-281.

Anzenberger, Raphaël, *Moi aussi je voudrais croire, mais...* (Marpent: BLF, 2010).

Anzenberger, Raphaël, *L'évangéliste sous toutes ses formes* (Marpent: BLF, 2012).

Appadurai, Arjun, *Après le colonialisme: Les conséquences de la globalisation* (Paris: Payot, 2006).

Asamoah-Gyadu, J. Kwabena, "African-led Christianity in Europe: Migration and Diaspora Evangelism," *Lausanne World Pulse* (July 2008), at www.lausanneworldpulse.com/pdf/issues/LWPJuly2008PDF.pdf.

Asamoah-Gyadu, J. Kwabena, "Migration, Diaspora Mission, and Religious Others in World Christianity: An African Perspective," *International Bulletin of Missionary Research* 39, 4 (2015), p. 189-192.

Assohoto, Barnabé, *Le discours africain du salut* (3 vol.; Cotonou: CART, 2002).

Athanasius of Alexandria, *Life of Saint Anthony* (Ancient Christian Writers: the Works of the Fathers 10; transl. and annotated Robert T. Meyer; New York: Paulist, 1950).

Barrett, David B., Kurian, George T., Johnson, Todd M., *World Christian Encyclopedia* (2nd ed.; New York: Oxford University Press, 2001).

Bartholomew, Craig G. & Goheen, Michael W., *The Drama of Scripture: Finding our Place in the Biblical Story* (Grand Rapids: Baker, 2004).

Bastenier, Albert, *Qu'est-ce qu'une société ethnique? Ethnicité et racisme dans les sociétés européennes d'immigration* (Paris: PUF, 2004).

Bastian, Jean-Pierre, Champion, Françoise & Rousselet, Kathy, eds., *La globalisation du religieux* (Paris: L'Harmattan, 2001).

Bauman, Zygmunt, *Liquid Modernity* (New York: John Wiley & Sons, 2013).

Bavinck, Johan H., "Elenctics," in *An Introduction to the Science of Missions* (Grand Rapids: Baker, 1960), p. 221-275.

Bebbington, David, *Evangelicalism in Modern Britain: A History from 1730 to the 1980s* (London: Unwin Hyman, 1989).

Berger, Peter L., *The Sacred Canopy: Elements of a Sociological Theory of Religion* (New York: Doubleday, 1967).

Berger, Peter L. & Luckmann, Thomas L., *The Social Construction of Reality: A Treatise in the Sociology of Knowledge* (Harmondsworth: Penguin, 1967).

Besse, Jean-Pierre, *Des cellules de maisons pour l'Église en mission* (Vennes: Ligue pour la Lecture de la Bible, 1996).

Bevans, Stephen B. & Schroeder, Roger P., *Constants in Context: A Theology of Mission for Today* (Maryknoll: Orbis, 2004).

Beyerhaus, Peter, "Theologisches Verstehen nichtchristlicher Religionen," *Kerygma und Dogma* 35, n° 2 (1989), p. 106-127.

Beyerhaus, Peter, *Er sandte sein Wort: Die Bibel in der Mission*, vol. 1 (Wuppertal: Brockhaus, 1996).

Billings, Alan, *Secular Lives, Sacred Hearts: The Role of the Church in a Time of no Religion* (London: SPCK, 2004).

Blocher, Henri, "Démonologie," *Fac-réflexion* n° 31 (juin 1995), p. 29.

Blocher, Henri, "Le contexte européen de notre théologie," *Hokhma* 98 (2010), p. 3-20.

Blough, Neal, "Évangéliser la France: Une expression à clarifier," *Perspectives missionnaires* 33 (1997), p. 40-52.

Blough, Neal, "L'évangélisation face au défi de la modernité," *Cahiers de l'École pastorale* 34 (1999).

Blough, Neal, "Pluralisme et vérité: L'Église peut-elle encore être missionnaire en Occident?" *Perspectives missionnaires* 39, 1 (2000), p. 5-18.

Blough, Neal, "Mission in Europe," in *Evangelical, Ecumenical and Anabaptist Missiologies in Conversation*, eds. James R. Krabill, Walter Sawatsky, Charles van Engen (Maryknoll: Orbis, 2006), p. 216-222.

Blough, Neal, "Réveil ou *ecclesia semper reformanda*?" *Théologie Évangélique* 7, 1 (2008), p. 31-39.

Blough, Neal, "Évangéliser en France: Regards en arrière," in *La mission de l'Église au 21ᵉ siècle: Les nouveaux défis*, ed. Hannes Wiher (Charols: Excelsis, 2010), p. 35-47.

Blumhardt, Johann Christoph, *Krankheitsgeschichte der Gottliebin Dittus: Ausführlicher originaler Bericht* (Neu durchgesehen von E. Zuber; Basel: Brunnen, 1943).

Bonny, Yves, *Sociologie du temps present: Modernité avancée ou postmodernité?* (Paris: Armand Colin, 2004).

Bosch, David J., "Evangelism: Currents and Cross-Currents in Theology Today," *International Bulletin of Missionary Research* 11, 3, 1987, p. 98-103.

Bosch, David J., *Transforming Mission: Paradigm Shifts in Theology of Mission* (Maryknoll: Orbis, 1991).

Bosch, David J., "Croire en l'avenir: Vers une missiologie de la culture occidentale," *Lettre interéglises du Centre de recherche théologique missionnaire* n° 69-70, vol. 2 (1995), p. 1-49.

Bosch, David J., "The Structure of Mission: An Exposition of Matthew 28:16-20," in *The Study of Evangelism: Exploring the Missional Practice of the Church*, eds. Paul W. Chilcote et Lacey C. Warner (Grand Rapids, MI: Eerdmans, 2008), p. 73-92.

Bousquet, François, "The Englightenment, the Foundation of Modern Europe," *International Review of Mission* vol. 95, n° 378-379 (July-October 2006), p. 236-246.

Bria, Ion, *The Liturgy after the Liturgy: Mission and Witness from an Orthodox Perspective* (Geneva: WCC, 1996).

Breen, Mike & Absalom, Alex, *Launching Missional Communities: A Field Guide* (London: 3DM Press, 2010).

Brown, David, *Une Église pour aujourd'hui* (Marne-la-Vallée: Farel, 2001).

Brown, David, *Passerelles: Entre l'Évangile et nos contemporains* (Marne-la-Vallée: Farel, 2003).

Brown, David, *"Servir à nos Français" Le défi de l'Église émergente: Bien vivre notre foi et la communiquer à nos contemporains* (Marne-la-Vallée: Farel, 2009).

Brown, David, "Mission dans la (post)modernité," in *Bible et mission, vol. 2: Vers une pratique évangélique de la mission*, ed. Hannes Wiher (Charols: Excelsis, 2012), p. 219-230.

Brown, David, *Disciple 24/24* (Marne-la-Vallée: Farel, 2015).

Buchhold, Jacques, "Des hommes et des réseaux: la stratégie de Paul," in *Bible et mission. Vers une théologie évangélique de la mission*, ed. Hannes Wiher (Charols: Excelsis, 2011), p. 115-134.

Bulangalire, Majagira, "The Consequences of the Englightenment: A Point of View from the Churches of African Expression in France," *International Review of Mission* vol. 95, n° 378-379 (July-October 2006), p. 293-296.

Bühler, Pierre et al., *Humain à l'image de Dieu. La théologie et les sciences humaines face au problème de l'anthropologie* (Lieux théologiques 15; Genève: Labor et Fides, 1989).

Bünker, Arnd, "Typen christlicher Migrationsgemeinden und postmigratorischer Perspektiven," in *Kirchen in Bewegung: Christliche Migrationsgemeinden in der Schweiz*, ed. Judith Albisser & Arnd Bünker (St.Gallen: SPI, 2016), p. 123-127.

Cai, Zong-Qi, "Synthetic Parallelism as a Cultural Expression: A Cross-Cultural and Cross-Disciplinary Study," *Tamking Review* 20, 2 (1989), p. 151-167.

Carson, Donald A., *Becoming Conversant with the Emerging Church* (Grand Rapids: Zondervan, 2005).
Carson, Donald A., *Christ and Culture Revisited* (Grand Rapids: Eerdmans, 2008).
Césaire, Aimé, *Discours sur le colonialisme: Suivi du discours sur la négritude* (Paris: Présence africaine, 2004).
Chai, Henri, "La vocation des Églises multiculturelles: Perspectives missiologiques et interculturelles," in *L'Église, promesses et passerelles vers l'interculturalité*, ed. Jean-Claude Girondin & Frédéric de Coninck (Charols: Excelsis, 2013), p. 39-46.
Champion, Françoise, "Les sociologues de la post-modernité religieuse et la nébuleuse mystique ésotérique," *Archives de sciences sociales des religions* 67, 1 (1989), p. 155-169.
Champion, Françoise, "L'univers mystique-ésotérique et croyances parallèles," *Futuribles* n° 260 (January 2001), p. 49-59.
Champion, Françoise & Hervieu-Léger, Danièle, eds., *De l'émotion en religion: Renouveaux et traditions* (Paris: Centurion, 1990).
Chiang, Samuel E., "Three Worlds Converged: Living in an Oral, Literate, and Digital Culture," in *Worship and Mission for the Global Church: An Ethnodoxology Handbook*, ed. James R. Krabill et al. (Pasadena: William Carey Library, 2012), p. 179-183.
Chilcote, Paul W. & Warner, Lacey C., eds., *The Study of Evangelism: Exploring the Missional Practice of the Church* (Grand Rapids, MI: Eerdmans, 2008).
Cholvy, Gérard & Hilaire, Yves-Marie, *Le fait religieux aujourd'hui en France: Les trente dernières années (1974-2004)* (Paris: Cerf, 2004).
De Clermont, Jean-Arnold, "Une présence humble et ferme dans l'espace public," *Perspectives missionnaires* 52, 2 (2006), p. 201-203. English version: *International Review of Mission* vol. 95, n° 378-379 (July-October 2006), p. 301-304.
Clémenceau, Laurent, "Saül et la nécromancienne: Étude exégétique de 1 Samuel 28.3-25," Master thesis, Vaux-sur-Seine, 1995.
Clouser, Roy, "A Blueprint for a Non-Reductionist Theory of Reality," *Contact* 19, 2 (December 2007).
Coleman, Robert E., *The Master Plan of Evangelism* (Grand Rapids: Revell, 1972).
Cook, Matthew, Haskell, Rob, Julian, Ruth, Tanchanpongs, Natee, eds., *Local Theology for the Global Church: Principles for an Evangelical*

Approach to Contextualization (Pasadena: William Carey Library, 2010).

Cray, Graham, *Mission-Shaped Church: Church Planting and Fresh Expressions in Changing Contexts* (London: Church House Publishing, 2004).

Cross, John R., *The Stranger on the Road to Emmaus* (Gatineau: Goodseed, 2000), at www.goodseed.com/thestranger.aspx.

Cross, John R., *By This Name* (Gatineau: Goodseed, 2000), at www.good seed.com/thename.aspx.

Cullmann, Oscar, *Christ and Time: The Primitive Christian Conception of Time and History* (London: SCM, 1951).

Cullmann, Oscar, *Salvation in History* (New York: Harper, 1967).

Daniel, Robin, *Missionary Strategies Then and Now* (Chester, UK: Tamarisk Publications, 2012).

Davie, Grace, "Believing without Belonging: A Liverpool Case Study," *Archives de sciences sociales des religions* 81 (1993).

Davie, Grace, *Religion in Britain since 1945: Believing without Belonging* (Oxford: Blackwell, 1996).

Davie, Grace & Hervieu-Léger, Danièle, eds., *Identités religieuses en Europe* (coll. Recherches; Paris: La Découverte, 1996).

Davie, Grace, *Religion in Modern Europe: A Memory Mutates* (New York: Oxford University Press, 2005).

Davie, Grace, "Is Europe an Exceptional Case?" *International Review of Mission* vol. 95, n° 378-379 (July-October 2006), p. 247-258.

Davie, Grace, *Europe, the Exceptional Case: Parameters of Faith in the Modern World* (London: Darton, Longman & Todd, 2007).

Davies, Norman, *Europe: A History* (Oxford: Oxford University Press, 1996).

De Coninck, Frédéric & Girondin, Jean-Claude, eds., *L'Église, promesses et passerelles vers l'interculturalité?* (Charols: Excelsis, 2013).

Delumeau, Jean, *Le christianisme va-t-il mourir?* (Paris: Hachette, 1977).

Demorgon, Jacques, *L'interculturation du monde* (Paris: Anthropos, 2000).

DeYmaz, Mark, *Building a Healthy Multi-ethnic Church: Mandate, Commitments, and Practices of a Diverse Congregation* (San Francisco: Jossey-Bass, 2007).

Dickason, C. Fred, *Demon Possession and the Christian* (Wheaton: Crossway, 1987).

Donovan, Kath & Myors, Ruth, "A Generational Perspective into the Future," in *Too Valuable to Lose: Exploring the Causes and Cures of Missionary Attrition*, ed. William D. Taylor (Pasadena: William Carey Library, 1997), p. 41-73.

Dooyeweerd, Herman, *A New Critique of Theoretical Thought*, vol. 1 (transl. David H. Freeman, William S. Young, et H. de Jongste; Jordan Station, Ont.: Paideia Press, 1984).

Douglas, Mary, *Leviticus as Literature* (New York: Oxford University Press, 1999).

Dunaetz, David R., "Three Models of Acculturation: Applications for Developing a Church Planting Strategy among Diaspora Populations," in *Diaspora Missiology: Reflections on Reaching the Scattered Peoples of the World*, ed. Michael Pocock & Enoch Wan (Pasadena: William Carey Library, 2015).

Engel, James F., *Contemporary Christian Communication: Its Theory and Practice* (Nashville/New York: Thomas Nelson, 1979).

Engel, James F., "An Interpersonal Communication Model: The Engel Scale Explained," at www.gospelcom.net/guide/resources/tellitoften.php.

Engelsviken, Tormod, "Three Missiological Perspectives: What Testimony?" *International Review of Mission* vol. 95, n° 378-379 (July-October 2006), p. 329-33.

Engelsviken, Tormod, "Mission, Evangelism and Evangelization – from the Perspective of the Lausanne Movement," *International Review of Mission* vol. 96, Nos. 382/383 (July-October 2007), p. 204-209.

Escobar, Samuel, *Changing Tides: Latin America & World Mission Today* (American Society of Missiology 31; Maryknoll: Orbis, 2002).

Escobar, Samuel, *A Time for Mission* (Leicester: IVP, 2003).

Faivre, Antoine, *Accès de l'ésotérisme occidental* (Paris: Gallimard, 1986).

Faix, Wilhelm et al., *Theologie im Kontext von Biographie und Weltbild* (Marburg a. Lahn: Francke, 2011).

Fancello, Sandra & Mary, André, eds., *Chrétiens africains en Europe: Prophétisme, pentecôtisme et politique des nations* (coll. Religions contemporaines; Paris: Karthala, 2010).

Fath, Sébastien, "Les Français et l'évangélisation: Enseignement de l'histoire," *Cahiers de l'École pastorale* 45 (sept. 2002).

Fath, Sébastien, *Du ghetto au réseau: Le protestantisme évangélique en France 1800-2005* (Genève: Labor et Fides, 2003).

Fath, Sébastien, "Evangelical Protestantism in France: An Example of Denominational Recomposition?" *Sociology of Religion* 66, 4 (2005), p. 399-418.

Fath, Sébastien & Willaime, Jean-Paul, *La nouvelle France protestante: Essor et recomposition au 21ᵉ siècle* (Genève: Labor et Fides, 2011).

Ferry, Luc, *La révolution de l'amour* (Paris: Plon, 2010).

Flemming, Dean, *Contextualization in the New Testament: Patterns for Theology and Mission* (Leicester: Intervarsity Press, 2005).

Fondja, Patrice, "La mission africaine dans un contexte non africain," *Perspectives missionnaires* n° 65, 1 (2013), p. 30-40.

Fox, James, "Roman Jakobson and the Comparative Study of Parallelism," in *Roman Jakobson: Echoes of His Scholarship* (PdR Press Publications on Roman Jakobson; Lisse: Peter de Ridder Press, 1977).

Frykenberg, Robert E., ed., *Christians and Missionaries: Cross-Cultural Communication since 1500* (Grand Rapids: Eerdmans, 2003).

Gantenbein, Jean-Georges, "La France, pays de mission? La définition de la mission et les critères d'une missiologie de la culture occidentale," Master thesis, University Marc Bloch, Strasbourg, 2006.

Gantenbein, Jean-Georges, "Inventer une missiologie pour le contexte européen: Un pari risqué, une exigence de première importance," *Perspectives missionnaires* 61, 1 (2011), p. 29-39.

Gantenbein, Jean-Georges, "Mission en Europe," in *Bible et mission, vol. 2: Vers une pratique évangélique de la mission*, ed. Hannes Wiher (Charols: Excelsis, 2012), p. 203-218.

Gantenbein, Jean-Georges, *Mission en Europe: Une étude sociomissiologique pour le 21ᵉ siècle* (Ph.D. thesis, Faculté de théologie protestante Strasbourg, Université Marc Bloch, 2010; Studia Œcumenica Friburgensia 72; Münster: Aschendorff, 2016).

Garrison, David, *Church Planting Movements: How God Is Redeeming a Lost World* (Midliothan, VA: WIG Take Resources, 2004).

Gatera, Simon Pierre, *Le discipulat axé sur la mission* (Nürnberg: VTR, 2009).

Groupes Bibliques Universitaires de France, *Questions autour de Dieu: Les sept questions le plus fréquemment posées sur la foi* (Marne-la-Vallée: Farel/GBU, 2009).

Geertz, Clifford, *The Interpretation of Cultures* (New York: Basic Books, 1973).

Gibbs, Eddie & Bolger, Ryan K., *Emerging Churches: Creating Christian Community in Postmodern Cultures* (Pasadena: William Carey Library, 2005).

Gilliland, Dean S., "The Incarnation as Matrix for Appropriate Theologies," in *Appropriate Christianity*, ed. Charles H. Kraft (Pasadena: William Carey Library, 2005), p. 493-520.

Girondin, Jean-Claude, *Religion, ethnicité et intégration parmi les Protestants évangéliques en région parisienne: La dynamique interculturelle d'un protestantisme aux prises avec la créolité* (thèse de doctorat; Paris: École pratique des hautes études de la Sorbonne, 2003).

Girondin, Jean-Claude, "Les défis de l'évangélisation dans une société multiculturelle," *Perspectives missionnaires* n° 65, 1 (2013), p. 7-21.

Girondin, Jean-Claude, "Églises de migrants et la mission en Europe francophone," in *L'Église locale en mission interculturelle: Communiquer l'Évangile au près et au loin*, ed. Evert van de Poll (Charols: Exclesis, 2015), p. 177-195.

Glover, Terrot R., *The Jesus of History* (Calcutta: Association Press, 1917).

Godin, Henri & Daniel, Yvan, *La France, pays de mission?* (Paris: L'Abeille, 1943).

Goheen, Michael, ed., *Reading the Bible Missionally* (Grand Rapids: Eerdmans, 2016).

Gorman, Michael J., *Becoming the Gospel: Paul, Participation, and Mission* (Gospel and Our Culture; Grand Rapids: Eerdmans, 2015).

Gray, Frank, « Engel Scale or Gray Matrix? », http://thegraymatrix.org/?p=211.

Green, Michael, *Evangelism in the Early Church* (rev. ed.; Eastbourne: Kingsway, 2003; 1st ed.: Grand Rapids: Eerdmans, 1970).

Grellier, Isabelle, "Les démarches de théologie pratique," in *Introduction à la théologie pratique*, ed. Bernard Kaempf (Strasbourg: Presses Universitaires, 1997).

Guder, Darrell L. & Barrett, Lois, *Missional Church: A Vision for the Sending of the Church in North America* (Grand Rapids: Eerdmans, 1998).

Guder, Darrell C., *Called to Witness* (Gospel and Our Culture; Grand Rapids: Eerdmans, 2015).

Guéroult, Marianne, "Les Églises issues de l'immigration: de quoi parlons-nous ?" in *L'Église, promesses et passerelles vers l'interculturalité?*

eds. Frédéric de Coninck & Jean-Claude Girondin (Charols: Excelsis, 2013), p. 21-33.

Guillebaud, Jean-Claude, *La refondation du monde* (Paris: Seuil, 1999).

Guillebaud, Jean-Claude, *Le commencement d'un monde: Vers une modernité métisse* (Paris: Seuil, 2008).

Gumbel, Nicky, *How to Run the Alpha Course* (new ed.; Eastbourne: Kingsway, 2004; 1st ed.: *The Alpha Course*, London: HTB Publications, 1995).

Halik, Thomáš, "The Soul of Europe: An Altar to the Unknown God," *International Review of Mission* vol. 95, n° 378-379 (July-October 2006), p. 265-270.

Hall, Edward T. & Hall, Mildred R., *Understanding Cultural Differences* (Yarmouth, MA: Intercultural Press, 1990).

Hanciles, Jehu J., *Beyond Christendom: Globalization, African Migration, and the Transformation of the West* (Maryknoll: Orbis, 2008).

Hanciles, Jehu J., "Migration and Mission: The Religious Significance of the North South Divide," in *Mission in The Twenty-First Century: Exploring the Five Marks of Global Mission*, ed. Andrew F. Walls & Cathy Ross (Maryknoll: Orbis Books, 2008), p. 118-129.

Hardmeier, Roland, *Kirche ist Mission: Auf dem Weg zu einem ganzheitlichen Missionsverständnis* (D.Th. thesis UNISA; Schwarzenfeld: Neufeld, 2009).

Hardmeier, Roland, *Missionale Theologie: Evangelikale auf dem Weg zur Weltverantwortung* (edition IGW 7; Schwarzenburg: Neufeld, 2015).

Hempelmann, Heinzpeter, *Prämodern, Modern, Postmodern: Warum „tikken" Menschen so unterschiedlich? Basismentalitäten und ihre Bedeutung für Mission, Gemeindearbeit und Kirchenleitung* (Neukirchen-Vluyn: Neukirchener Verl., 2013).

Hervieu-Léger, Danièle, *La religion pour mémoire* (Paris: Cerf, 1993).

Hervieu-Léger, Danièle, *Le pèlerin et le converti: La religion en mouvement* (Paris: Flammarion, 1999).

Hervieu-Léger, Danièle & Champion, Françoise, *Vers un nouveau christianisme? Introduction à la sociologie du christianisme occidental* (Paris: Cerf, 1986).

Hesselgrave, David J., *Communicating Christ Cross-Culturally* (Grand Rapids: Zondervan, 1980).

Hesselgrave, David J., *Planting Churches Cross-Culturally: A Guide for Home and Foreign Missions* (5th pr.; Grand Rapids: Baker, 1986).

Hesselgrave, David J. & Rommen, Edward, *Contextualization: Meanings, Methods and Models* (Grand Rapids: Baker, 1989).

Hiebert, Paul G., Critical Contextualization», *Missiology* 12 (1984), p. 287-296. Reprints: *International Bulletin of Missionary Research* 11 (1987), p. 104-112; *Anthropological Insights for Missionaries* (Grand Rapids: Baker, 1985), p. 171-192; *Anthropological Reflections on Missiological Issues* (Grand Rapids: Baker, 1994), p. 75-92.

Hiebert, Paul G., "The Flaw of the Excluded Middle," *Missiology: An International Review* 10, 1 (1982), p. 35-47; reprint in *Anthropological Reflections on Missiological Issues* (Grand Rapids: Baker, 1994), p. 189-201.

Hiebert, Paul G., *Missiological Implications of Epistemological Shifts: Affirming Truth in a Modern/Postmodern World* (Harrisburg, PA: International Trinity Press, 1999).

Hiebert, Paul G., *Transforming Worldviews: An Anthropological Understanding of How People Change* (Grand Rapids: Baker, 2008).

Hiebert, Paul G., Shaw, Daniel R., Tiénou, Tite, *Understanding Folk Religion: A Christian Response to Popular Beliefs and Practices* (Grand Rapids: Baker, 1999).

Hillion, Daniel, "Does Integral Mission Include Everything that God Requires of us and Does God Require of us Everything Included in Integral Mission?" at http://www.micahnetwork.org/sites/default/files/doc/page/does_im_include_everything_that_god_requires_of_us_daniel_hillion.pdf.

House, Rutba, ed., *School(s) for Conversion: 12 Marks of a New Monasticism* (Eugene, OR: Cascade Books, 2005).

Hunsberger, George R., "Is There Biblical Warrant for Evangelism?" in *The Study of Evangelism: Exploring the Missional Practice of the Church*, eds. Paul W. Chilcote & Lacey C. Warner (Grand Rapids, MI: Eerdmans, 2008), p. 59-72.

Hunsberger, George R., "Proposals for a Missional Hermeneutic: Mapping a Conversation," *Missiology* 39, 3 (2011), p. 309-321.

Hybels, Lynne & Hybels, Bill, *Rediscovering Church: The Story and Vision of Willow Creek Community Church* (Grand Rapids: Zondervan, 2016).

Imbert, Yannick, *Croire, expliquer, vivre: Introduction à l'apologétique* (Charols: Excelsis, 2014).

Jackson, Darrell, "'Mission-Shaped Presence' in Europe," *International Review of Mission* vol. 95, n° 378-379 (July-October 2006), p. 341-351.

Jacques, Francis, ed., *Les racines culturelles et spirituelles de l'Europe: Trois questions sur la place de la source chrétienne* (Paris: Parole et Silence, 2008).

Jenkins, Philip, *God's Continent: Christianity, Islam, and Europe's Religious Crisis* (Oxford: Oxford University Press, 2007).

Jenkins, Philip, "Godless Europe?" *International Bulletin of Missionary Research*, 31, 3 (2007), p. 115-120.

Johnson, Samuel D., "Europa im Visier afrikanischer Missionare," in *Missionare aus der Zweidrittel-Welt für Europa*, ed. Klaus W. Müller (Nürnberg: VTR, 2004), p. 61-78.

Joncheray, Jean, "Théologie et sciences humaines," in *Précis de théologie pratique*, eds. Gilles Routhier & Marcel Viau (Bruxelles/Montréal: Lumen Vitae/Novalis, 2004).

Johnstone, Patrick, *The Future of the Global Church: History, Trends and Possibilities* (Milton Keynes: Authentic, 2011).

Kaiser, Walter C., Jr., *Mission in the Old Testament: Israel as a Light to the Nations* (Grand Rapids: Baker, 2000).

Kasdorf, Hans, *Christian Conversion in Context* (Scottdale: Herald Press, 1980).

Käser, Lothar, *Foreign Cultures* (Nürnberg: VTR, 2014; German ed. 1997).

Käser, Lothar, *Animism: A Cognitive Approach* (Nürnberg: VTR, 2014; German ed. 2004).

Kearney, Michael, *Worldview* (Novato, CA: Chandler and Sharp, 1984).

Keller, Timothy, *Center Church: Doing Balanced, Gospel-Centered Ministry in Your City* (Grand Rapids: Zondervan, 2012).

Kim, Kirsteen, "The Potential of Pneumatology for Mission in Contemporary Europe," *International Review of Mission* vol. 95, n° 378-379 (July-October 2006), p. 334-340.

Kirk, J. Andrew, *The Future of Reason, Science and Faith: Following Modernity and Post-Modernity* (Aldershot: Ashgate, 2007).

Kirk, J. Andrew & Vanhoozer, Kevin, eds., *To Stake a Claim: Mission and the Western Crisis of Knowledge* (Acts of a Conference in Paris of the Epistemology Group of the Missiology of Western Culture Project; Maryknoll: Orbis, 1999).

Krabill, James R. et al., ed., *Worship and Mission for the Global Church: An Ethnodoxology Handbook* (Pasadena, CA: William Carey Library, 2012).

Kraft, Charles H., *Communication Theory for Christian Witness* (Nashville: Abingdon, 1983).
Kraft, Charles H., "'Christian Animism' or God-given Authority?" in *Spiritual Power and Missions: Raising the Issues*, ed. Edward Rommen (Pasadena: William Carey Library, 1995), p. 88-136.
Kraft, Charles H., *Christianity in Culture: A Study in Dynamic Biblical Theologizing in Cross-Cultural Perspective* (rev. ed.; Maryknoll: Orbis, 2005; 1st ed. 1979).
Kraft, Charles H. & White, Mark, ed., *Behind Enemy Lines: An Advanced Guide to Spiritual Warfare* (Ann Arbor, MI: Servant, 1994).
Kreider, Alan, *Worship and Evangelism in Pre-Christendom* (Joint Liturgical Studies, 32; Cambridge: Grove Books Limited, 1995).
Kwiyani, Harvey C., *Sent Forth: African Missionary Work in the West* (Maryknoll: Orbis, 2014).
Kwiyani, Harvey C., "Blessed Reflex: African Christians in Europe," *Missio Africanus* vol. 3, No. 1, 2017, p. 40-49. http://missioafricanus.org/wp-content/uploads/MAJAM/3-1/Harvey_Kwiyani_Blessed-Reflex-African-Christians-in-Europe.pdf
Latourette, Kenneth S., *A History of the Expansion of Christianity* (7 vol.; New York & London: Harper & Bros., 1937-1939).
Lausanne Committee of World Evangelization, *Christian Witness to Secularized People* (Lausanne Occasional Paper No. 8: Thailand Report; Wheaton, IL: LCWE, 1980).
Lausanne Committee of World Evangelization, *Christian Witness to Large Cities* (Lausanne Occasional Paper No. 9: Thailand Report; Charlotte, NC: LCWE, 1980).
Lausanne Committee of World Evangelization, *Christian Witness to Nominal Christians among Roman Catholics* (Lausanne Occasional Paper No. 10; Charlotte, NC: LCWE, 1980).
Lausanne Committee of World Evangelization, *Christian Witness to Nominal Christians among the Orthodox* (Lausanne Occasional Paper No. 19: Thailand Report; Charlotte, NC: LCWE, 1980).
Lausanne Committee of World Evangelization, *An Evangelical Commitment to a Simple Life-style* (Lausanne Occasional Paper No. 20; Wheaton, IL: LCWE, 1980).
Lausanne Committee of World Evangelization, *Evangelism and Social Responsibility: An Evangelical Commitment* (Lausanne Occasional Paper No. 21: Grand Rapids Report; Wheaton, IL: LCWE, 1982).

Lausanne Committee of World Evangelization, *Christian Witness to Nominal Christians among Protestants* (Lausanne Occasional Paper No. 23: Thailand Report; Wheaton, IL: LCWE, 1980).

Lausanne Committee of World Evangelization, *Holistic Mission* (Lausanne Occasional Paper No. 33: 2004 Forum; Wheaton, IL: LCWE, 2004).

Lausanne Committee of World Evangelization, *The Local Church in Mission: Becoming a Missional Congregation in the Twenty-first Century Global Context and the Opportunities Offered through Tentmaking Ministry* (Lausanne Occasional Paper No. 39: 2004 Forum; Wheaton, IL: LCWE, 2004).

Lausanne Committee of World Evangelization, *Scattered to Gather: Embracing the Global Trend of Diaspora* (Manila: LifeChange, 2010).

Lenoir, Frédéric, "Vers un catholicisme minoritaire?" *Le monde des religions* n° 21 (jan.-fév. 2007).

Lenoir, Frédéric, *Le Christ philosophe* (Paris: Plon, 2007).

Lewis, C.S., *The Screwtape Letters* (London: Bles, 1946).

Liechti, Daniel, "Bâtir des Églises majeures: Un défi à relever," *Fac-réflexion* 45 (1998), p. 18-32.

Liechti, Daniel, "Un défi missionnaire pour les Églises de France: Implanter de nouvelles Églises," in *La mission de l'Église au 21ᵉ siècle: Les nouveaux défis*, ed. Hannes Wiher (Charols: Excelsis, 2010), p. 155-164.

Liechti, Daniel, "La meilleure évangélisation de l'Europe francophone: l'implantation et le développement d'Églises centrées sur l'Évangile, au service de leur ville," Supplément B in Keller, Timothy, *Une Église centrée sur l'Évangile: La dynamique d'un ministère équilibré au cœur des villes d'aujourd'hui* (Charols: Excelsis, 2015), p. 603-623.

Liefeld, Walter L., "Women and Evangelism in the Early Church," in *The Study of Evangelism: Exploring the Missional Practice of the Church*, eds. Paul W. Chilcote & Lacey C. Warner (Grand Rapids, MI: Eerdmans, 2008), p. 93-100.

Lingenfelter, Sherwood G. & Mayers, Marvin K., *Ministering Cross-Culturally: An Incarnational Model for Personal Relationships* (Grand Rapids: Baker, 1986).

Lodberg, Peter, "Ministries in Post-Enlightenment Europe," *International Review of Mission* vol. 95, n° 378-379 (July-October 2006), p. 359-364.

Lovejoy, Grant, ed., *Making Disciples of Oral Learners* (Lausanne Occasional Paper No. 54; Lima, NY/Bangalore: Lausanne Committee on World Evangelization/International Orality Network, 2005). http://orali ty.net/resources/docs/Making_Disciples_of_Oral_Learners-12646918 48.pdf.

Luneau, René, *Le rêve de Compostelle: Vers la restauration d'une Europe chrétienne?* (Paris: Centurion, 1989).

Lukasse, Johan, *Churches with Roots* (London: STL, 1990).

Lyotard, Jean-François, *The Postmodern Condition: A Report on Knowledge* (transl. from the French by Geoff Bennington and Brian Massumi; Minneapolis, MN: University of Minnesota Press, 1993; French version 1979):

Mandryk, Jason, *Operation World* (Colorado Springs: Biblica, 2010).

Mangalwadi, Vishal, Vishal Mangalwadi, *The Book that Made your World. How the Bible Created the Soul of Western Civilization* (New York: Thomas Nelson, 2011).

Marshall, Paul A., Griffioen, Sander, Mouw, Richard J., ed., *Stained Glass: Worldviews and Social Science* (Christian Studies Today; Lanham, MD: University Press of America, 1989).

Matthey, Jacques, "La liturgie au cœur de la mission: un point de vue protestant," *Perspectives missionnaires* 45-46 (2003), p. 87-114.

Mbiti, John S., *New Testament Eschatology in an African Background* (London: SPCK, 1969).

Mbiti, John S., "The Concept of Time as a Key to the Understanding and Interpretation of African Religions and Philosophy," in *African Religions and Philosophy* (London: Heinemann, 1969), p. 15-28.

McGavran, Donald A., *Understanding Church Growth* (Grand Rapids: Eerdmans, 1980).

McIlwain, Trevor, *Building on Firm Foundations* (9 vol.; 5th pr.; Sanford: New Tribes Mission, 1991).

McIntosh, Gary L., *Make Room for the Boom... or Bust: Six Church Models for Reaching Three Generations* (Grand Rapids: Revell, 1997).

McIntosh, Gary L., ed., *Evaluating the Church Growth Movement: Five Views* (Grand Rapids: Zondervan, 2004).

Meeks, Wayne A., *The First Urban Christians: The Social World of the Apostle Paul* (New Haven, Conn.: Yale University Press, 1983).

Mermet, Gérard, *Francoscopie 1985: Qui sont les Français? Faits, analyses, tendances, comparaisons, 10 000 chiffres* (Paris: Larousse, 1984).

Meroff, Deborah, *Europe: Restoring Hope* (Nürnberg/Linz: VTR/OM, 2011).

Micklethwait, John & Wooldridge, Adrian, *God is Back: How the Global Revival of Faith is Changing the World* (New York: Penguin Press, 2009).

Monet, Gabriel, *L'Église émergente: Être et faire Église en postchrétienté* (Berlin: Lit, 2014).

Moreau, A. Scott, *Essentials of Spiritual Warfare* (Wheaton: Shaw, 1997).

Moreau, A. Scott, *Contextualization in World Missions: Mapping and Assessing Evangelical Models* (Grand Rapids: Kregel, 2012).

Moreau, A. Scott, Adeyemo, Tokunboh, Burnett, David G., Myers, Bryant L., Yung, Hwa, eds., *Deliver Us from Evil: An Uneasy Frontier in Christian Mission* (Monrovia, CA: MARC, 2002).

Morris, Richard, "La démonisation des chrétiens selon le Nouveau Testament," Master thesis, Vaux-sur-Seine, 2013.

Moser, Felix, *Les croyants non pratiquants* (Genève: Labor et Fides, 1994).

Moynagh, Michael, *Church for Every Context* (London: SCM, 2012).

Moyo, Anderson, "Missional Strategies from Antioch: Lessons for African Missionaries in Britain," *Missio Africanus* vol. 1, No. 2 (January 2016), p. 40-58. http://missioafricanus.org/wp-content/uploads/MAJAM/1-2/Moyo_Missional-Strategies-from-Antioch.pdf

Murray, Stuart, *Post-Christendom: Church and Mission in a Strange New World* (Milton Keynes: Paternoster, 2004).

Müller, Johannes, "Afrikanische Diaspora in der Schweiz," *Evangelikale Missiologie* 25, 3 (2009), p. 136-143.

Müller, Klaus W., ed., *Gott zur Sprache bringen* (afem mission reports 11; Nürnberg: VTR, 2003).

Müller, Klaus W., ed., *Mission als Kommunikation: Die christliche Botschaft verstehen* (Festschrift für Ursula Wiesemann; Nürnberg: VTR, 2007).

Müller, Klaus W., ed., *Mission im postmodernen Europa* (Referate der Jahrestagung 2008 des Arbeitskreises für evangelikale Missiologie (AfeM); edition afem mission reports 16; Nürnberg/Bonn: VTR/VKW, 2008).

Müller, Markus, *Trends 2016: Die Zukunft lieben* (2nd ed.; Basel/Giessen: Brunnen, 2011; 1st ed. 2009).

Müller, Markus, *Trends 2021: Es wird anders werden* (Basel: Brunnen, 2012).

Naugle, David, *Worldview: The History of a Concept* (Grand Rapids: Eerdmans, 2002).

Naugle, David, "The Educational Power of Great Tradition Christianity," *Contact* 22, 1 (September 2010).

Newbigin, Lesslie, *Honest Religion for Secular Man* (London: SCM, 1966).

Newbigin, Lesslie, "Can the West Be Converted?" *Princeton Seminary Review* 6, 1 (1985), p. 25-37. Reprint: *International Bulletin of Missionary Research* 11, 1 (1987), p. 2-7.

Newbigin, Lesslie, *Foolishness to the Greeks: The Gospel and Western Culture* (London: SPCK, 1986).

Newbigin, Lesslie, *The Gospel in a Pluralist Society* (Grand Rapids: Eerdmans, 1989).

Nida, Eugene, *Message and Mission* (London: Harper & Row, 1960).

Nisus, Alain, *Mais délivre-nous du mal: Traité de démonologie biblique* (Romanel-sur-Lausanne: La Maison de la Bible, 2016).

Noort, Gerrit, Avtzi, Kyriaki, Paas, Stefan, eds., *Sharing Good News: Handbook of Evangelism in Europe* (Geneva: World Council of Churches, 2017).

Nyirongo, Leonard, "The African and Biblical View of Time, History and Progress," in *The Gods of Africa or The God of the Bible?* (Potchefstroom: Potchefstroom University, 1997), p. 89-98.

O'Connell, James, *The Making of Modern Europe: Strengths, Constraints and Resolutions* (University of Bradford Peace Research Report n° 26; Bradford: University Press, 1991).

Olofinjana, Israel, *Reverse in Ministry and Missions: Africans in the Dark Continent of Europe* (Milton Keynes: Author House, 2010).

Olofinjana, Israel, *Turning the Tables on Mission: Stories of Christians from the Global South in the UK* (Watford: Instant Apostle, 2013).

Ong, Walter J., *Orality and Literacy* (London/New York: Routledge, 1982).

Orr, Graham, *Not So Secret: Being Contemporary Agents for Mission* (Nottingham: Inter-Varsity Press, 2012).

Osborne, Grant R., *The Hermeneutical Spiral: A Comprehensive Introduction to Biblical Interpretation* (Downers Grove: Intervarsity, 1991).

Ott, Bernhard, *Shalom: Le projet de Dieu* (Montbéliard: Éditions Mennonites, 2003).

Ott, Craig & Wilson, Gene, *Global Church Planting: Biblical Principles and Best Practices for Multiplication* (Grand Rapids: Baker, 2011).

Paas, Stefan, "Prepared for a Missionary Ministry in 21st Century Europe," Opening Paper for the European Conference of Reformed Churches (EuCRC), Kampen (Netherlands), March 22, 2011.

Paas, Stefan, *Church Planting in the Secular West: Learning from the European Experience* (Grand Rapids: Eerdmans, 2016).

Paas, Stefan & Vos, Alrik, "Church Planting and Church Growth in Western Europe: An Analysis," *International Bulletin of Missionary Research* 40, 3 (2016), p. 243-252.

Packer, James I., "What is Evangelism: Evangelism and Theology," in *Theological Perspectives on Church Growth*, ed. Harvie M. Conn (Nutley: Presbyterian & Reformed, 1976), p. 91-105.

Paya, Christophe, *Pour une Église en mouvement: Lecture du discours d'envoi en mission de Matthieu 9:35-11:1* (Charols: Excelsis, 2010).

Pfister, Jürg, *Motivating the Generation X: The Potential of Generation X as a Challenge for Christians and for Missions* (Nürnberg: VTR, 2004).

Pocock, Michael & Wan, Enoch, eds., *Diaspora Missiology: Reflections on Reaching the Scattered Peoples of the World* (Pasadena: William Carey Library, 2015).

Pope Jean-Paul II, *Ecclesia in Europa* (Post-Synodic Apostolic Exhortation; Rome: Vatican Press, 2003).

Poulat, Émile, *Église contre bourgeoisie: Introduction au devenir du catholicisme actuel* (Tournai: Castermann, 1977).

Powlison, David, *Power Encounter: Reclaiming Spiritual Warfare* (Grand Rapids: Baker, 1995).

Pownall, André, "Un demi-siècle d'implantation d'Églises évangéliques en région parisienne (1950-2000)," *Théologie Évangélique* 4, 1 (2005), p. 47-80.

Pownall, André, "Stratégies pour l'intégration de minorités ethniques dans les Églises évangéliques," in *Vivre la diversité: L'Église dans une société multiculturelle*, ed. Evert van de Poll (Paris: Croire-Publications, 2011), p. 37-60.

Priest, Robert J., Campbell, Thomas, Mullen, Bradford A., "Missiological Syncretism: The New Animistic Paradigm," in *Spiritual Power and*

Missions: Raising the Issues, ed. Edward Rommen (Pasadena: William Carey Library, 1995), p. 9-87.

Ramachandra, Vinoth, *Gods That Fail: Modern Idolatry and Christian Mission* (rev. ed.; Eugene, OR: Wipf & Stock, 2016; 1st ed. 1996).

Reimer, Johannes, *Die Welt umarmen: Theologie des gesellschaftsrelevanten Gemeindebaus* (Marburg a. Lahn: Francke, 2009).

Reimer, Johannes, *Gott in der Welt feiern: Auf dem Weg zum missionalen Gottesdienst* (Schwarzenfeld: Neufeld, 2010).

Reimer, Johannes, *Multikultureller Gemeindebau: Versöhnung leben* (Marburg a. Lahn: Francke, 2011).

Riecker, Siegbert, *Mission im Alten Testament? Ein Forschungsüberblick mit Auswertung* (Frankfurt a.M.: Otto Lembeck, 2008).

Robert, Marie-Hélène, "Orientations de Vatican II, la nouvelle évangélisation et Édimbourg 2010: Mise en perspective," *Perspectives missionnaires* 60, 2 (2010), p. 38-49.

Robert, Marie-Hélène, *"Pour que le monde croie:" Approches théologiques de l'évangélisation* (Lyon: Profac-Théo, 2014).

Rommen, Edward & Corwin, Gary, eds., *Missiology and the Social Sciences: Contributions, Cautions and Conclusions* (Evangelical Missiological Society Series No. 4; Pasadena: William Carey Library, 1996).

Ross, Cathy, "Mission in a Strange Land," *Missio Africanus: Journal of African Missiology*, vol. 1, No. 2 (January 2016), p. 28-39. http://missioafricanus.org/wp-content/uploads/MAJAM/1-2/Ross_Mission-in-a-Strange-Land.pdf

Röthlisberger, Simon & Wüthrich, Matthias, *Neue Migrationskirchen in der Schweiz* (Bern: Schweizerischer Evangelischer Kirchenbund, 2009), p. 43-44.

Russell, James C., *The Germanization of Early Medieval Christianity: A Sociohistorical Approach to Religious Transformation* (New York: Oxford University Press, 1994).

Sa'a, Yehia, *All that the Prophets Have Spoken* (Gatineau: Goodseed, 2000). Text available at www.goodseed.com/theprophets.aspx.

Santedi, Kinkupu Léonard, "Reflections from an African Theologian," *International Review of Mission* vol. 95, n° 378-379 (July-October 2006), p. 390-400.

Schnabel, Eckhard J., *Early Christian Mission* (2 vol.; Downers Grove: IVP, 2004).

Shaw, R. Daniel, *Transculturation: The Cultural Factor in Translation and Other Communication Tasks* (Pasadena: William Carey Library, 1988).

Shaw, R. Daniel & Van Engen, Charles E., *Communicating God's Word in a Complex World: God's Truth or Hocus Pocus?* (Lanham, MD: Rowman and Littlefield, 2003).

Shenk, Wilbert R., *Changing Frontiers of Mission* (Maryknoll: Orbis, 1999).

Shenk, Wilbert R., "Believing without Belonging? Reflections on the Consultation," *International Review of Mission* 92, 365 (2003), p. 231-239.

Sire, James W., *The Universe Next Door: A Basic Worldview Catalogue* (3rd ed.; Downers Grove/Leicester: IVP, 1997).

Solomiac, Paul, *De Jérusalem à Kuala Lumpur: L'Église mondiale en mission* (Dossiers de Christ seul; Montbéliard: Éditions mennonites, 2011).

Sogaard, Viggo, *Media in Church and Mission: Communicating the Gospel* (Pasadena: William Carey Library, 1993).

Spindler, Marc, *La mission: Combat pour le salut du monde* (Paris: Delachaux et Niestlé, 1967).

Spindler, Marc, *Pour une théologie de l'espace* (Neuchâtel: Delachaux et Niestlé, 1968).

Spindler, Marc & Lenoble-Bart, Annie, eds., *Chrétiens d'outre-mer en Europe: Un autre visage de l'immigration* (Paris: Karthala, 2000).

Stark, Rodney, *The Rise of Christianity: A Sociologist Reconsiders History* (Princeton, NJ: Princeton University Press, 1996).

Stassen, G.H., Yeager, D.M., Yoder, John H., eds., *Authentic Transformation: A New Vision of Christ and Culture* (Nashville: Abingdon, 1996).

Steuernagel, Valdir R., "Social Concern and Evangelization: The Journey of the Lausanne Movement," *Occasional Bulletin from the Missionary Research Library* 15, 2 (1975).

Sticht, Pamela, *Culture européenne ou Europe des cultures? Les enjeux actuels de la politique culturelle en Europe* (Paris: L'Harmattan, 2000).

Stone, Bryan, *Evangelism after Christendom: The Theology and Practice of Christian Witness* (Grand Rapids/New York: Brazos/Harvard University Press, 2007).

Stott, John R.W., *Christian Mission in the Modern World* (London: Falcon, 1975).

Strähler, Reinhold, *Coming to Faith in Christ: Understanding Conversion* (Nairobi: Life Challenge, 2010).

Strauss, Stephen J., "Spiritual Dynamics and Mission," in *Encountering Theology of Mission: Biblical Foundations, Historical Developments, and Contemporary Issues*, ed. Craig Ott et al. (Grand Rapids: Baker, 2010), p. 238-262.

Strauss, W. & Howe, N., *Generations: The History of America's Future, 1584 to 2069* (New York: Quill, 1992).

Susbielle, Jean-François, *Le déclin de l'empire européen: qui domine l'Europe ?* (Paris: First, 2009).

Tan, Kang San, Ingleby, Jonathan, Cozens, Simon, eds., *Understanding Asian Mission Movements* (Proceedings of the Asian Mission Consultations 2008-2010; Gloucester: Wide Margin, 2011).

Tennent, Timothy C., "The Challenge of Churchless Christianity: An Evangelical Assessment," *International Bulletin of Missionary Research* 29, 4 (2005), p. 171-177.

Tennent, Timothy C., *Invitation to World Missions: A Trinitarian Missiology for the Twenty-first Century* (Grand Rapids: Kregel, 2010), p. 191-226.

Thiry, Jean-François, *Donner une âme à l'Europe: Mission et responsabilité des Églises* (Rencontre européenne de culture chrétienne, Vienna, Mai 3-5, 2006; Vienna: Pro Oriente, 2007).

Toncheva, Svetoslava, *Out of the New Spirituality of the Twentieth Century: The Dawn of Anthroposophy, the White Brotherhood and the Unified Teaching* (Berlin: Frank & Timme, 2015).

Ugeux, Bernard, "Questions Which New Spiritualities Pose to Evangelization in Europe," *International Review of Mission* vol. 95, n° 378-379 (July-October 2006), p. 324-328.

Van de Poll, Evert, ed., *Face aux forces du mal: Réflexions sur la pastorale de délivrance* (Hors-série n° 14; Cahier de l'École pastorale; 4ᵉ trimestre 2012).

Van de Poll, Evert, *Europe and the Gospel: Past Influences, Current Developments, Mission Challenges* (London: de Gruyter/Versita, 2013).

Van de Poll, Evert, ed., *L'Église locale en mission interculturelle: Communiquer l'Évangile au près et au loin* (Charols: Exclesis, 2015).

Van de Poll, Evert & Appleton, Joanne, eds., *Church Planting in Europe* (Eugene, OR: Wipf & Stock, 2015).

Van de Poll, Evert, ed., *Mission intégrale: Vivre, annoncer et manifester l'Évangile, pour que le monde croie* (Charols: Excelsis, 2017).

Van der Walt, Bennie J., *The Liberating Message: A Christian Worldview for Africa* (Potchefstroom: Potchefstroom University, 1994).

Van der Walt, Bennie J., "Time Moving 'Past' Man Versus Man Moving 'Through' Time," in *Afrocentric or Eurocentric?* (Potchefstroom: Potchefstroom University, 1997), p. 64-66.

Van der Walt, Bennie J., *Transformed by the Renewing of Your Mind: Shaping a Biblical Worldview and a Christian Perspective on Scholarship* (Potchefstroom: Potchefstroom University, 2001).

Van der Walt, Bennie J., *The Eye Is the Lamp of the Body: Worldviews and Their Impact* (Potchefstroom: Institute for Contemporary Christianity in Africa, 2008).

Vanhoozer, Kevin J., *The Drama of Doctrine: A Canonical-Linguistic Approach to Christian Theology* (Louisville: John Knox, 2005).

Von Balthasar, Hans Urs, *The Glory of the Lord: a Theological Aesthetics* (ed. Joseph Fessio and John Riches; Edinburgh: T. & T. Clark, 1982-1991).

Von Balthasar, Hans Urs, *Theo-drama* (transl. Graham Harrison; San Francisco: Ignatius Press, 1988-2000)

Von Balthasar, Hans Urs, *Theo-logic* (transl. Adrian J. Walker; San Francisco: Ignatius Press, 2000-2005).

Von Rad, Gerhard, "Israel's Ideas about Time and History, and the Prophetic Eschatology," in *Old Testament Theology, vol. 2: The Theology of Israel's Prophetic Traditions* (transl. D.M.G. Stalker; London: Oliver & Boyd, 1965), p. 99-127.

Wagner, C. Peter, *Church Growth and the Whole Gospel: A Biblical Mandate* (New York/San Francisco: Harper & Row, 1981).

Wagner, C. Peter, ed., *Engaging the Enemy: How to Fight and Defeat Territorial Spirits* (Ventura, CA: Regal, 1991).

Währisch-Oblau, Claudia, "Getting Ready to Receive? German Churches and the 'New Mission' from the South," in *Lausanne World Pulse* (July 2008).

Walldorf, Friedemann, *Die Neuevangelisierung Europas: Missionstheologien im europäischen Kontext* (Giessen: TGV Brunnen Verlag, 2002).

Walldorf, Friedemann, "Kontextuelle Missionstheologien für das postmoderne Europa," in *Mission im postmodernen Europa*, ed. Klaus W. Müller (Nürnberg/Bonn: VTR/VKW, 2008), p. 46-66.

Walls, Andrew F., *The Missionary Movement in Christian History: Studies on the Transmission of Faith* (Maryknoll: Orbis, 1996).

Walls, Andrew F., *The Cross-Cultural Process in Christian History* (Maryknoll: Orbis, 2002).

Walls, Andrew F., "Christian Mission in a Five-hundred-year Context," in *Mission in the 21st Century: Exploring the Five Marks of Global Mission*, eds. Andrew F. Walls & Cathy Ross (London: Darton, Longman and Todd, 2008), p. 193-204.

Walsh, Brian J. & Middleton, J. Richard, *The Transforming Vision: Shapening a Christian Worldview* (Downers Grove: IVP, 1984).

Ward, Pete, *Liquid Church* (Exeter: Paternoster, 2002).

Warnier, Jean-Pierre, *La mondialisation de la culture* (Paris: La Découverte, 2003).

Watto, Albert, Ngabana, Jean (interview Jean-François Zorn), "Les évangéliques africains vont-ils rechristianiser l'Europe?" *Perspectives missionnaires* n° 65, 1 (2013), p. 22-29.

Watzlawick, Paul, Beavin, Janet H., Jackson, Don D., *Pragmatics of Human Communication: A Study of Interactional Patterns, Pathologies and Paradoxes* (New York: Norton, 1967).

Wessels, Anton, *Europe: Was It Ever Really Christian? The Interaction between Gospel and Culture* (London: SCM, 1994).

Wiher, Hannes, *Shame and Guilt: A Key to Cross-Cultural Ministry* (Bonn: Culture and Science Publications, 2003).

Wiher, Hannes, "Worldview and Identity across Conversion," *Evangelical Review of Theology* 38, 4 (2014), p. 307-323.

Wiher, Hannes, "Worldview and Oral Preference Learners and Leaders," in *Beyond Literate Western Practices: Continuing Conversations in Orality and Theological Education*, ed. Samuel E. Chiang and Grant Lovejoy (Hong Kong: Capstone Enterprises, 2014), p. 109-125.

Willaime, Jean-Paul, *Europe et religions: Les enjeux du 21e siècle* (coll. Les dieux dans la cité; Paris: Fayard, 2009).

Winter, Ralph, "The Highest Priority: Cross-Cultural Evangelism," in *Let the Earth Hear His Voice*, ed. J.D. Douglas (Minneapolis: Worldwide Publications, 1975), p. 213-225.

Winter, Ralph, "Is It Possible? Global Cross-Cultural Mission Collaboration, 1910 to 2010," *Mission Frontiers* 31, 1 (2009).

Wright, Christopher J.H., *The Mission of God: Unlocking the Bible's Grand Narrative* (Downers Grove: IVP, 2006).

Wright, Christopher J.H., "'According to the Scriptures': The Whole Gospel in Biblical Revelation," *Evangelical Review of Theology* 33, 1 (2009), p. 4-18.

Wright, N.T., *Surprised By Hope: Rethinking Heaven, the Resurrection, and the Mission of the Church* (New York: HarperCollins, 2008).

Yates, Timothy, "David Bosch: South African Context, Universal Missiology – Ecclesiology in the Emerging Missionary Paradigm," *International Bulletin of Missionary Research* vol. 33, n° 2 (April 2009), p. 72-78.

Yèche, Hélène, ed., *Construction européenne: Histoires et images des origines* (Actes des journées d'études du MIMMOC, Université de Poitiers; Paris: Publibook, 2008).

Yoder, John H., "How H. Richard Niebuhr Reasoned: A Critique of *Christ and Culture* », in *Authentic Transformation: A New Vision of Christ and Culture*, eds. G.H. Stassen, D.M. Yeager, John H. Yoder (Nashville: Abingdon, 1996), p. 54-61.

Yung Hwa, "A Systematic Theology That Recognizes the Demonic," in *Deliver Us from Evil: An Uneasy Frontier in Christian Mission*, ed. A. Scott Moreau et al. (Monrovia, CA: MARC, 2002), p. 3-27.

Zorn, Jean-François, "For a Missiology of Western Culture," *International Review of Mission* vol. 95, n° 378-379 (July-October 2006), p. 320-323.

Index of Names

Abraham, William J. 164, 166f, 169, 178, 181, 300, 315
Absalom, Alex 198, 209, 213, 310
Adogame, Afe 146, 157, 217f, 231, 233, 307
Agier, Michel 307
Ahonen, Risto A. 295, 307
Ahrweiler, Hélène 307
Albisser, Judith 139, 216, 307, 310
Allen, Roland 286, 307
Altermatt, Urs 58, 307
Amorth, Gabriele 257, 307
Anzenberger, Raphaël 11, 301, 308
Appadurai, Arjun 308
Appleton, Joanne 261, 302, 327
Asamoah-Gyadu, J. Kwabena 216, 233, 308
Assohoto, Barnabé 163, 308
Athanasius 246, 308
Augustine 17, 111, 264
Avtzi, Kyriaki 295f, 302, 323
Aymard, Maurice 307

Barrett, David B. 285, 308
Barrett, Lois 209, 297, 315
Bartholomew, Craig G. 192, 308
Bastenier, Albert 308
Bastian, Jean-Pierre 130, 292, 308
Bauman, Zygmunt 211, 308
Bavinck, Johan H. 200f, 295, 302, 308
Beavin, Janet H. 196, 329
Bebbington, David 212, 308
Berger, Peter L. 94, 105f, 308
Besse, Jean-Pierre 308
Bevans, Stephen B. 288, 309
Beyerhaus, Peter 11, 240, 253f, 260, 292, 309
Billings, Alan 76f, 87, 309
Blocher, Henri 95, 248f, 309

Blough, Neal 10f, 15, 25, 32, 43, 175, 272f, 288f, 309
Blumhardt, Johann Christoph 250, 309
Bolger, Ryan K. 198, 315
Bonny, Yves 129f, 309
Bosch, David 2, 4, 147, 157, 162-164, 169, 171-173, 175, 177f, 181, 309f, 330
Bousquet, François 31, 46, 310
Breen, Mike 198, 209, 213, 310
Bria, Ion 199, 310
Brown, David 11, 51, 93, 97, 263, 273, 276, 279, 300, 304, 310
Bühler, Pierre 6, 310
Bulangalire, Majagira 278, 310
Bultmann, Rudolf 95f
Bünker, Arnd 139, 216, 307, 310

Cai Zong-Qi 132, 310
Campbell, Thomas 258, 324
Carson, Donald A. 198, 215, 311
Césaire, Aimé 311
Chai, Henri 311
Champion, Françoise 11, 40, 130, 134, 274, 291f, 308, 311, 316
Chiang, Samuel E. 132f, 200, 205, 214, 311, 329
Chilcote, Paul W. 169, 176, 181, 213, 300, 310f, 317, 320
Cholvy, Gérard 36, 311
Clémenceau, Laurent 242, 311
Clouser, Roy 111, 311
Coffinet, Julien 6, 273
Coleman, Robert E. 176, 299, 311
Cook, Matthew 311
Corwin, Gary 6, 109, 325
Coyault, Bernard 278
Cozens, Simon 191, 327
Cray, Graham 198, 209, 213, 312

Cross, John R. 213, 312
Cullmann, Oscar 126, 312

Daniel, Robin 113, 268, 312, 317, 326
Daniel, Yvan 289, 315
Davie, Grace 10f, 30, 37, 41f, 46, 48, 66, 75f, 78f, 85, 87, 114, 135, 210, 275, 290f, 312
Davies, Norman 58, 312
De Beauvoir, Simone 264
De Clermont, Jean-Arnold 311
De Coninck, Frédéric 144f, 311f, 316
Delgado, Mariano 58, 307
Delumeau, Jean 1, 17, 43, 273, 312
Demorgon, Jacques 312
DeYmaz, Mark 145f, 157, 312
Dickason, C. Fred 243, 260, 312
Diprose, Ronaldo 72
Donegani, Jean-Marie 8
Donovan, Kath 131, 313
Dooyeweerd, Herman 106f, 313
Douglas, Mary 123, 313
Dunaetz, David R. 152, 227, 313

Engel, James F. 202f, 213, 299, 313, 315
Engelsviken, Tormod 4f, 295, 313
Escobar, Samuel 191, 313

Faivre, Antoine 313
Faix, Wilhelm 293, 313
Fancello, Sandra 313
Fath, Sébastien 10f, 288, 313f
Ferry, Luc 50, 60, 114, 127, 129f, 314
Flemming, Dean 111, 314
Fox, James 132, 314
Frykenberg, Robert E. 299f, 314

Gantenbein, Jean-Georges 8, 11, 30, 35-41, 43, 46, 197, 278, 292, 314
Garrison, David 209, 302, 314
Gatera, Simon Pierre 298, 314

Gauchet, Marcel 50
Geertz, Clifford 107, 201f, 314
Gibbs, Eddie 198, 315
Gilliland, Dean S. 7, 315
Glover, Terrot R. 263, 315
Godin, Henri 289, 315
Goheen, Michael 192, 297, 308, 315
Gorman, Michael J. 300, 315
Gray, Frank 60, 203, 213, 299, 315
Green, Michael 182f, 206f, 213, 286, 315
Grellier, Isabelle 315
Gretzky, Wayne 261
Griffioen, Sander 106, 321
Guder, Darrell L. 209, 297, 300, 315
Guéroult, Marianne 315
Guillebaud, Jean-Claude 60, 316
Gumbel, Nicky 204, 316

Halik, Thomáš 196, 274, 316
Hall, Edward T. 125, 316
Hall, Mildred R. 125, 316
Hanciles, Jehu J. 217, 228, 233, 316
Hardmeier, Roland 298, 316
Haskell, Rob 311
Hempelmann, Heinzpeter 130, 207, 316
Hervieu-Léger, Danièle 10f, 23, 25, 41, 78, 84, 129, 134, 274, 291f, 311f, 316
Hesselgrave, David J. 189, 299, 316f
Hiebert, Paul G. 6, 107-110, 113f, 188f, 204, 259, 317
Hilaire, Yves-Marie 36, 311
Hillion, Daniel 317
House, Rutba 299, 317
Howe, N. 131, 327
Hunsberger, George R. 169-171, 174, 178, 297, 317
Hybels, Bill 303, 317
Hybels, Lynne 303, 317

Imbert, Yannick 11, 301, 317
Ingleby, Jonathan 191, 327

Index of Names

Jackson, Darrell 317
Jackson, Don D. 196, 329
Jacques, Francis 59, 318
Jenkins, Philip 38f, 43f, 46, 58, 66, 70, 86, 128, 135, 235, 272f, 280, 283-285, 292, 318
Johnson, Samuel D. 217, 318
Johnson, Todd M. 285, 308
Johnstone, Patrick 146, 157, 191, 318
Joncheray, Jean 6, 318
Julian, Ruth 311

Kaempf, Bernard 315
Kaiser, Walter C. 166, 318
Kasdorf, Hans 201, 318
Käser, Lothar 107f, 133, 135, 248, 252, 318
Kearney, Michael 110, 318
Keller, Timothy 7, 11f, 184, 208f, 213, 276, 303, 318, 320
Kim, Kirsteen 318
Kirk, J. Andrew 129, 318
Krabill, James R. 25, 132, 197, 199f, 205, 213, 289, 309, 311, 318
Kraft, Charles H. 7, 107f, 187-189, 258, 299, 315, 319
Kreider, Alan 16, 25, 206-208, 245, 319
Kurian, George T. 285, 308
Kwiyani, Harvey 217f, 223f, 230, 233, 319

Lambert, Yves 35
Latourette, Kenneth S. 287, 319
Lehmann, Léo 276
Lenoble-Bart, Annie 326
Lewis, C.S. 50, 259, 320
Liechti, Daniel 209, 320
Liefeld, Walter L. 176, 320
Lingenfelter, Sherwood G. 120, 125, 135, 320
Lovejoy, Grant 133, 200, 213f, 321, 329
Luca, Nathalie 93

Luckmann, Thomas L. 94, 105f, 308
Lukasse, Johan 302, 321
Luneau, René 294, 321
Lyotard, Jean-François 61, 129, 321

Mandryk, Jason 280f, 321
Mangalwadi, Vishal 62, 66, 87, 321
Margery, Gordon 90
Marshall, Paul A. 106, 321
Mary, André 313
Matthey, Jacques 321
Mayers, Marvin K. 120, 125, 135, 320
Mbiti, John S. 118, 125, 321
McGavran, Donald A. 208f, 302, 321
McIlwain, Trevor 117, 205, 321
McIntosh, Gary L. 131, 209, 211, 302f, 321
Meeks, Wayne A. 206, 321
Mermet, Gérard 321
Meroff, Deborah 9, 12, 300, 322
Meyer, David 246, 308
Micklethwait, John 83f, 86f, 322
Middleton, J. Richard 107, 329
Monet, Gabriel 11f, 130, 198, 209, 212, 299, 303f, 322
Moreau, A. Scott 118, 176, 178, 254, 260, 322, 330
Morris, Richard 248f, 254f, 322
Moser, Felix 42, 322
Mouw, Richard J. 106, 321
Moynagh, Michael 211, 322
Moyo, Anderson 215, 230, 232, 322
Mullen, Bradford A. 258, 324
Müller, Johannes 137f, 215f, 275, 322
Müller, Klaus W. 11, 54, 217, 229, 293f, 296, 301, 318, 322, 328
Müller, Markus 12, 293, 300, 322f
Murray, Stuart 56f, 66, 322
Myors, Ruth 131, 313

Naugle, David 106f, 110-112, 136, 187, 323

Nelson, Édouard 90
Newbigin, Lesslie 11f, 53f, 86f, 95-97, 100, 175, 192f, 197, 208f, 277, 289, 296, 323
Nida, Eugene 189, 323
Nisus, Alain 249, 323
Noort, Gerrit 295f, 302, 323
Nyirongo, Leonard 125, 323

Olofinjana, Israel 142, 216f, 229f, 233, 323
Ong, Walter J. 132, 323
Orr, Graham 268, 323
Osborne, Grant R. 188f, 323
Ott, Bernhard 324
Ott, Craig 208, 213, 254, 260, 303, 324, 327

Paas, Stefan 11f, 51, 210, 295-297, 302, 323f
Packer, James I. 166, 168, 172, 174f, 178, 181-183, 324
Pascal, Blaise 269
Paya, Christophe 11f, 161, 169, 175, 298, 324
Pfister, Jürg 131, 324
Pocock, Michael 147, 152, 157, 227, 233, 313, 324
Pope Jean-Paul II 324
Poulat, Émile 35, 324
Powlison, David 254, 259f, 324
Pownall, André 148, 210, 324
Priest, Robert J. 258, 324
Pytches, David 44

Ramachandra, Vinoth 251f, 325
Reimer, Johannes 11, 153, 304, 325
Riecker, Siegbert 166, 325
Robert, Marie-Hélène 11f, 54f, 87, 110, 276, 295, 325
Rommen, Edward 6, 109, 189, 258, 260, 317, 319, 325
Ross, Cathy 191, 216f, 316, 325, 329
Röthlisberger, Simon 216, 325

Rousselet, Kathy 130, 292, 308
Routhier, Gilles 6, 8, 318
Russell, James C. 11, 25, 43, 188, 272, 287, 325

Sa'a, Yehia 117, 205, 213, 325
Santedi Kinkupu, Léonard 278, 325
Sartre, Jean-Paul 264
Schnabel, Eckhard J. 286, 325
Schroeder, Roger P. 288, 309
Shaw, R. Daniel 113, 254, 260, 299f, 317, 322, 326
Shenk, Wilbert 191, 210, 326
Sire, James W. 53, 326
Sogaard, Viggo 299, 326
Solomiac, Paul 326
Spindler, Marc 198, 240, 253f, 326
Stark, Rodney 206f, 213, 287, 326
Stassen, G.H. 251, 326, 330
Steuernagel, Valdir R. 3, 326
Sticht, Pamela 48, 326
Stone, Bryan 55-58, 66, 87, 101, 326
Stott, John 3, 162, 185, 326
Strauss, Stephen J. 254, 258-260, 327
Strauss, W. 131, 327
Susbielle, Jean-François 82, 327

Tan, Kang San 191, 327
Tanchanpongs, Natee 311
Taylor, William D. 131, 313
Tennent, Timothy C. 210, 240, 327
Thiry, Jean-François 45, 327
Tiénou, Tite 113, 317
Toncheva, Svetoslava 133, 327
Twelftree, G.H. 238

Vallet, Odon 91
Van de Poll, Evert 11, 26f, 29-32, 35, 39, 41f, 46f, 66f, 87, 136, 273, 289, 327f
Van der Walt, Bennie J. 125, 328
Van Engen, Charles E. 25, 326
Vanhoozer, Kevin J. 11f, 129, 192, 297, 318, 328
Vergauwen, Guide 58, 307

Index of Names

Viau, Marcel 6, 8, 318
Von Balthasar, Hans Urs 328
Von Rad, Gerhard 328

Wäfler, Lukas 247
Wagner, C. Peter 209, 258, 302, 328
Wallace, Daniel B. 171
Walldorf, Friedemann 11f, 296, 328
Walls, Andrew F. 191, 217, 288, 316, 329
Walsh, Brian J. 107, 329
Wan, Enoch 147, 152, 157, 227, 233, 313, 324
Ward, Pete 211, 214, 329
Warner, Lacey C. 169, 176, 181, 213, 300, 310f, 317, 320
Warnier, Jean-Pierre 329
Watto, Djamba-Albert 43, 329
Watzlawick, Paul 196, 329

Wessels, Anton 30, 46, 272, 329
White, Mark 258, 319
Willaime, Jean-Paul 129, 314, 329
Wilson, Gene 208, 213, 303, 324
Winkler, Siegfried 231
Winter, Ralph 2, 185, 329
Wooldridge, Adrian 83f, 86f, 322
Wright, Christopher J.H. 5, 166, 183, 192, 239, 260, 329f
Wright, N.T. 11f, 297, 330
Wüthrich, Matthias 216, 325

Yates, Timothy 147, 157, 330
Yeager, D.M. 251, 326, 330
Yèche, Hélène 330
Yoder, John H. 251, 326, 330
Yung Hwa 322, 330

Zorn, Jean-François 329f

Index of Subjects

Abortion 38
Accommodation 188
Acts of the Apostles 184
Adaptation 117, 205, 278
Adoration 134
Affiliation 32, 37, 39-41, 45, 49, 280
Agnostic 9, 49, 116
Allah 116
Alliance 55, 161, 200, 221, 287, 305
Ancient Near East 122, 241
Animism 113-115, 133, 240f, 248, 252, 258f, 318f, 324
Animist 280
Animistic 10, 49, 113f, 122f, 134, 190, 193, 204, 241, 250-258
Animist culture 123
Announce 15, 24, 116, 164, 167-169, 174, 178, 184, 236
Announcement 162, 172, 174
Anthropology 9, 52, 91, 105, 118, 124f, 127, 133, 212
Antioch 146, 215, 230, 232, 246, 322
Apostles 63, 87, 99, 122, 170, 173-176, 178, 184-186, 196, 243, 255, 272, 276
Atheism 8, 40, 51, 58, 254, 293
Atheist 34, 36, 40, 45, 49, 60, 91f, 116, 134, 266
Auto-definition 39f, 45

Baptism 17, 36, 68, 73f, 83, 91, 102, 134, 172-174, 180, 255, 257f, 270, 275
Barrier 4, 47, 49, 51, 53, 55-57, 59, 61, 63, 65, 95, 142, 172, 174, 210, 226, 230, 270
Basic mentality 130

Behaving without belonging 74, 76f
Believing without belonging 10, 36f, 41, 75-77, 210, 275, 291, 312, 326
Belonging without believing 41, 78, 275
Border 44
Bridges 47, 51f, 55, 59, 62, 228f, 263f, 269, 300f
Buddhism 40, 80f, 81, 113-116, 134

Café church 198
Category 76, 109, 172, 209, 258, 297
China 29, 48, 120
Christendom 1, 17f, 22-25, 43, 55-58, 62, 66, 87, 129, 165, 190, 206, 208, 210, 217, 228, 233, 245, 272-274, 287, 295, 316, 326
Christianisation 10f, 18, 40, 43, 57, 193, 247, 274, 287
Chaotic 106, 154, 273
Church cyber 198
Church emerging 11, 86, 99, 129, 188, 197f, 206, 209, 211, 262, 277, 299, 302f, 311, 315
Church ethnic 145, 157, 275, 312
Church fluid 211
Church liquid 198, 211
Church migrant 43, 84, 278
Church messy 198
Church planting 10-12, 145, 152, 182, 198f, 208-210, 213, 216, 227, 261, 272, 277, 286, 295, 297, 302-305, 312-314, 324, 327
Church planting movement 145, 209, 302
Condition human 166, 263-265
Colonial 230
Colonialism 23, 32, 308, 311

Index of Subjects

Commission 5, 96, 170, 176, 268, 280, 295, 304f
Commission Great 170, 280
Communication 7, 10-12, 18, 47, 55, 63, 89f, 95, 109, 122f, 130, 132, 142, 162, 174, 180, 182-190, 192f, 195-200, 202f, 205, 247, 250, 272, 276-278, 286, 290, 298-301, 313f, 319, 326, 329
Communism 61
Community 3f, 25, 39, 56, 61, 71, 76, 81f, 91, 99f, 102, 110, 142, 145, 167, 172-174, 176f, 179f, 188, 193, 198, 208, 211, 220, 222f, 232, 245, 247, 270, 275, 277, 303, 315, 317
Confucianism 114f
Conscience 31f, 38, 60, 72, 105f, 113, 118-125, 127-129, 131-134, 182, 190, 194-198, 200f, 207, 210-213
Conscience orientation 113, 118, 120f, 123-125, 127-129, 131-134, 182, 190, 194-197, 200f, 207, 211-213
Consumer 290
Consumerism 293f
Consumer religion 37, 275
Contextual 212, 295
Contextualisation 7, 23, 35, 118, 177, 189, 206, 229, 276
Contextualisation critical 189, 206
Conversion 16f, 30, 39, 50f, 69, 73, 80, 84, 89f, 114, 117, 121, 163, 172-175, 182, 188, 190, 193-195, 200-208, 212, 214, 219, 245, 265, 275, 277, 287, 299, 317f, 327, 329
Council of Trent 18, 256
Critical contextualisation 189, 206
Cross-cultural communication 162, 189, 192, 205, 278, 300, 314
Cross-cultural evangelism 185, 193, 212, 329
Crusade 32, 38
Cultural diversity 88, 92, 138, 149, 154
Cyber church 198

De-Christianisation 10, 40, 43, 193, 274
Deconstruction 31, 129, 274
Default religion 78f, 275, 291
Destruction 82, 252
Dialogue 3, 6, 9, 11, 18, 53f, 91, 172, 212, 294, 296
Diaspora 139, 143, 146f, 152, 157, 216-218, 227-231, 233, 307f, 313, 320, 322, 324
Dicastery 294
Difficulty 88, 92, 95f, 162, 195, 221, 278
Disciple 5, 17, 65, 97-100, 106, 117, 165, 167-173, 176, 184-186, 189, 191f, 200, 202-205, 213, 236, 254, 265-267, 272, 276f, 279, 298, 310, 321
Discipleship 3, 10f, 54, 57, 60, 87, 97, 102, 117, 147, 172f, 190, 202, 208, 211, 271, 291, 298, 303
Diversity cultural 88, 92, 138, 149, 154
Doxology 254

Ecclesiology 22, 25, 147, 157, 330
Ecumenical Movement 11f
Elohim 235, 237f, 242
Emergence 248
Emerging church 11, 86, 99, 129, 188, 197f, 206, 209, 211, 262, 277, 299, 302f, 311, 315
Encyclical 294
Epistemology 8, 106, 109, 124, 129, 318
Epistles 167, 176
Epistles pastoral 176
Esotericism 40, 113, 133, 135, 240, 248, 294
Esoteric mystical nebula 40, 45, 274, 311
Essence 94, 264
Ethnic church 145, 157, 275, 312
Ethno-doxology 199f
Euangelizô 162, 174, 184-186, 196
Euthanasia 10, 38

Evangelical Movement 10, 21, 106, 167, 288
Evangelisation 1f, 6, 11f, 54, 63, 74, 87, 137, 147, 175, 185, 188, 209, 231, 276, 288, 294f, 301, 309, 313, 315, 320, 325
Evangelisation new 2, 11f, 294f
Evangelise 15, 18f, 22f, 30, 32, 43, 57, 149, 164, 168, 176f, 184-187, 221, 224, 230, 276, 289, 293
Evangelism cross-cultural 185, 193, 212, 329
Evangelist 128, 135, 163, 178f, 182f, 224, 301
Exclusive 3, 22, 38, 50-52, 65, 187
Exhortation 16, 87, 96, 168, 175f, 294, 324

Fluid church 211
France 1, 15, 18, 26, 34-36, 39f, 42, 44, 60, 64, 67f, 73, 84, 88, 91-93, 96, 101, 131, 209, 245, 263, 266, 268, 278, 281, 283f, 288-290, 292, 300f, 304-306, 309-311, 313-315, 320
Fresh expressions 145, 198, 209, 213, 262, 312
Frontier 4, 24, 27, 52, 109, 191, 322, 329f

Globalisation 11, 20, 23, 130, 163, 292f, 308
Good News 3, 16, 64, 95, 99, 116, 162, 166, 174f, 180, 183f, 186f, 268, 276, 296, 302, 323
Great Britain 292
Great Commission 170, 280
Greco-Roman 30
Greek 7, 15, 24, 30, 67, 114, 116, 123f, 126, 133, 162, 171, 174f, 183f, 186, 194f, 200f, 208, 237f, 245f, 251, 273, 296, 323

Hebrew 7, 113-116, 123-126, 132, 184, 194-196, 201, 204, 208, 217, 238, 241f

Hermeneutical spiral 188f, 323
Hermeneutic community 193, 208, 277
Hermeneutic missional 297, 317
Heterodoxy 40, 43
Heterogeneous 76, 146f
Hinduism 40, 79, 84, 113-115, 134
Holy Trinity 44, 283
Homogeneity 145
Homosexuality 36
Human condition 166, 263-265
Human conduct 265
Human history 100, 263, 268
Human identity 264
Human rights 31, 45, 60, 102, 121
Human solidarity 264
Humanity 50, 59, 61, 81, 83, 165f, 183, 192, 208, 235f, 265, 276
Humanity new 147, 263, 265f

Identity 10, 23, 30, 39, 43f, 63, 72, 74, 90, 92, 106, 108, 114, 119, 121, 131f, 138, 142-145, 147, 204, 212, 216, 229, 264f, 270, 273-275, 277, 290, 292, 329
Identity human 264
Immigrant 67f, 127, 131, 139, 152, 190, 199, 217, 223f, 226f, 230-232, 278
Immigration 39, 43, 45, 63, 68, 137, 151, 209, 212, 223, 308, 315, 326
Incarnation 6f, 36, 40, 167, 172, 180, 197, 265, 315
Incorporation 3
Inculturation 296
India 62, 116, 197, 296
Individualism 24, 31, 40, 114, 121, 128, 210, 275, 294
Industrialisation 19, 127f, 191
Insider 80, 138, 230
Institutional 57f, 65, 71, 75f, 94, 210
Intercultural 138, 141-145, 148f, 154, 212, 221, 229-231, 233, 273, 275, 305, 311f, 315

Index of Subjects

Intercultural church 140-142
Islam 9, 12, 38-40, 45f, 58, 66, 70, 79f, 84, 113, 115f, 128, 134, 235, 250, 272f, 275, 283, 292, 294, 318

Jerusalem 174, 195, 215, 236, 326
Jew 16f, 24, 36, 69, 80, 85, 123, 146, 172, 175, 194, 206, 243, 280
Jewish 33, 73, 80, 111, 206, 244, 266, 287
Justification 21, 48, 88, 102, 121f, 124, 201

Keryssô 174, 184, 186

Late modernity 127, 129, 273
Lausanne Movement 2-6, 87, 163, 185, 228, 295, 313, 326
Linguistic 143, 172, 192, 220, 222, 296-298, 328
Liquid church 198, 211
Liturgy 198f, 256, 310
Lystra 90

Majority 5, 20f, 37, 39, 42, 44f, 56, 69, 72, 78, 84f, 97, 117, 123, 134f, 151, 186, 190, 199, 203, 217, 226, 237, 242, 268
Make disciples 170-172, 184, 192, 202
Marginal church membership 71f
Martyreô 174, 184
Megachurches 283, 303
Membership official 74
Mentality 15f, 19, 31, 288
Mentality basic 130
Messy church 198
Migrant 12, 27-29, 36, 43f, 80, 84f, 115, 127f, 131, 134f, 137, 139f, 143f, 146, 150f, 157, 195, 215, 218, 228, 275, 278, 293
Migrant church 43, 84, 278
Migration 64, 143, 145, 149, 216f, 220, 226f, 229, 232f, 305, 308, 316
Minimal church membership 41

Minimal church practice 71f
Minority 20, 23, 36f, 39, 42, 45, 49, 56, 69f, 86, 115, 134, 139, 275
Missiology 1, 6, 8f, 11, 42, 50, 109, 113, 145, 147, 152, 157, 191, 194, 197, 216, 227, 233, 240, 253, 263, 289, 292, 295-297, 299, 302, 304-307, 313, 324f, 327, 330
Missiology Western 129, 318
Missional 1, 9, 211, 213, 215, 230, 297f, 300, 304, 310f, 315-317, 320, 322, 325
Missional church 11, 130, 209, 277, 297f, 303, 315
Missional hermeneutic 297, 317
Modernity late 127, 129, 273
Monocultural 138f, 140, 142, 163, 275
Monocultural church 138f, 140, 142
Mosaic 137-141, 143-145, 147-149, 151, 153-155, 157, 199, 230, 275
Movement ecumenical 11f
Movement evangelical 10, 21, 106, 167, 288
Multicultural 12, 59f, 63, 68f, 78, 100, 138, 145, 148-150, 153f, 206, 208, 212, 221, 223, 276
Multicultural church 142-145, 225, 275, 304
Multi-religious 68f, 81, 206, 208, 212
Music 31, 55, 61-63, 77, 83, 86, 90, 134, 141, 150, 152, 198, 220f, 224, 261, 274
Muslim 12, 17, 27, 33, 36, 38f, 69, 73, 79f, 82, 85, 91, 115, 117, 135, 205f, 224, 226f, 250, 280, 283-285
Mystery 40, 61, 111, 268

Nationalism 252
Nébuleuse mystique ésotérique 40, 274, 311
Neo-platonic philosophy 129
New Age 30, 42, 79f, 83, 133, 247f
New evangelisation 2, 11f, 294f

New German Federal States 35, 38
New humanity 147, 263, 265f
New religious movement 38, 80, 83, 93, 207
Nominal 2, 12, 63, 70-74, 78, 87, 219, 226, 280, 319f
Nominal church member 71, 74, 76, 83
Non-Jew 16, 80, 146, 174, 187, 194, 243
Non-verbal communication 195-199, 203

Obedience 3, 240, 249, 266f
Official membership 74
Official religion 74
Orthodoxy 40, 73, 75, 208
Outsider 80, 230, 268

Palestine 243
Paradox 10, 20, 47, 58-61, 63, 65f, 68f, 109, 130, 196, 239, 241, 273, 277, 291-293, 329
Paray-le-Monial 44
Passerelles 144f, 263, 300f, 310-312, 315
Pastoral Epistles 176
Penal substitution 89, 193f
Persuade 47, 174
Persuasion 3, 95
Philosophy 9, 17, 19f, 106f, 109, 111, 113f, 125, 127, 129f, 212, 240, 258, 272, 274, 278, 288f, 321
Philosophy neo-platonic 129
Pilgrim 10, 60, 80, 84, 291f
Post-Christian 58f, 273f
Postmodern 30, 40, 53-55, 61, 78, 96, 109, 129f, 133, 179, 189, 206f, 262-267, 269, 271, 273, 276-278, 291, 297, 302, 315-317, 321
Postmodernity 10, 31, 44, 127-131, 133-135, 190, 195, 210, 212, 266, 295
Post-religious 274, 276
Post-secular 52, 67, 82, 86

Practitioner 9f, 36f, 292
Praeparatio evangelica 118
Preach 4, 117, 145, 170, 176, 184f, 186, 230, 278
Preaching 8, 126, 163, 166, 168, 175, 185, 187, 197, 220f, 295
Premodern 129f, 207, 259, 272f, 276
Presentation 1, 27, 117, 167f, 185, 193, 199, 230, 251, 256f
Prisoner 121
Proclaim 5, 47, 163, 167, 174, 178, 185-187, 236, 255, 264, 268, 276f, 294
Proclamation 2-5, 55, 162f, 167f, 171, 173-176, 179f, 183, 185f, 272, 277, 294
Promise 40, 86, 170f, 183, 185, 244, 267
Prosperity Gospel 132
Protestantism 18-21, 36, 42, 73, 134, 167, 288, 313-315
Purity 249

Quran 116

Recomposition of the religious 274
Reconciliation 3, 25, 121f, 124, 151, 193f, 201, 304
Reconquista 38
Reductionism 112
Reform 10, 18, 64, 113, 246, 256
Relativism 20, 22, 31, 37, 44
Relevant 1, 10, 50, 93, 104, 109f, 165, 187, 190, 193, 221, 247, 262f, 269, 276f, 289, 304
Religion by default 10, 41
Religion consumer 37, 275
Religion non-Christian 52, 82, 240, 244
Religion official 18, 21, 74
Religion popular 42, 113, 115, 134
Religion mystery 111
Religion vicarious 10, 37, 41f, 78, 275, 291

Index of Subjects

Resource 77, 118, 202, 209, 213, 216, 299
Response 9, 12, 33, 36, 51, 53, 57, 84, 89, 113, 162, 169, 188f, 192, 199, 224f, 245, 253, 294, 300, 317
Revelation 8, 110, 112, 145, 183f, 202, 237, 239f, 265, 330
Reverse 85, 216f, 233, 323
Reverse Mission 217
Revival 10, 22, 84, 86f, 191, 288, 322
Roman 2, 7, 16-22, 27, 55, 123f, 126
Roman Catholic Church 2, 18-20, 35, 43, 54, 72, 83, 92f, 126, 129, 169, 191, 248, 255f, 279, 294
Roman culture 123f
Roman Empire 16, 20, 176, 183, 187, 263, 286f
Romania 17, 34f, 37f, 40, 282, 284

Sciences social 1, 6-9, 84, 105, 109, 118, 201, 311f, 325
Second generation 139, 154, 229, 231f
Second Vatican Council 35, 255f, 294
Secularisation 10, 19, 44, 48-51, 59, 75f, 78, 81-83, 85f, 114, 127, 190, 193, 246, 291
Secularism 19, 49, 91, 135, 259, 273, 294
Sending 42, 103, 132, 163, 169f, 173f, 180, 185, 191, 209, 297f, 315
Septuagint 184, 186, 237
Socialism 35
Social sciences 1, 6-9, 84, 105, 109, 118, 201, 311f, 325
Solidarity 60, 173
Solidarity human 264
Soul Survivor 44
Space 19, 25, 35, 39f, 110, 112f, 166f, 170, 198, 216, 234, 270, 311, 326
Specialist 91, 164, 196, 202, 234, 241
Spiral hermeneutical 188f, 323
Spirituality 1, 30, 40, 42, 45, 52, 55, 60, 76, 79-81, 83, 128, 133-135, 143, 182, 190, 254, 263, 266, 274, 277, 279, 290, 292, 298, 327
Spirituality missionary 182, 190-192, 276
Suburb 120, 278
Syncretism 25, 204, 258

Tabula rasa 21
Taizé 44, 83
Target 6, 8, 10, 32, 45, 109, 145-147, 150, 165, 188-190, 200f, 203, 290
Teaching 16f, 36, 45, 60, 90f, 117, 133, 167f, 171-173, 178, 196, 205, 211, 243, 248, 255, 267, 270, 327
Theo-drama 328
Theology of the Gospel 10, 182, 184, 272, 286
Transculturation 299, 326
Transformation 5, 17, 25, 43, 110-112, 117, 119, 122f, 127, 134, 177f, 187f, 194, 202, 204, 211f, 217, 233, 248, 251, 254, 296, 272, 287, 316, 325f, 330
Trust 57, 90, 98, 152, 154, 167, 187, 230, 237, 253, 266f

United Kingdom 34f, 37, 41f, 131, 229, 282, 284, 296
Unity 26, 44, 133, 137, 141f, 146, 149

Vatican II 2, 295, 325
Verbal communication 184, 196-199
Vicarious religion 10, 37, 41f, 78, 275, 291

Welcome 57, 81, 85, 106, 138, 144, 147, 150, 152, 163, 178, 198, 241, 270
Western Missiology 129, 318
Without religion 36, 40f
World Evangelical Alliance 161, 200

YHWH 126, 236f

Table of Contents

Preface *(Hannes Wiher)* v

Preface to the French Version *(Bernard Huck)* vii

Introduction *(Hannes Wiher)* 1
    Definition of Evangelism, Evangelisation and Mission 2
    Relationship between Theology and Social Sciences........................... 6
    Review of Research 9
    Concluding Considerations... 11

Part One: Understanding Europe 13

Chapter 1: Evangelism in Europe: Historical Background
Neal Blough 15
    Pre-Constantine Epoch 15
    Constantine and the Medieval Epoch 17
    Epoch of Reformation (16th and 17th Century) 18
    Modernity 19
    Five Observations 20
        1. Gospel between Pluralism and Relativism 20
        2. Imported Religion... 20
        3. Logic of Division.. 21
        4. Facing Modernity 22
        5. Strategy towards Contextualisation 23
    Suggestions and Questions 24
    Further Reading 25

Chapter 2: European Context Today and Evangelism
Julien Coffinet.. 26
    Geographical Definition 26
    Demographic Data 27

- Total Population 27
- Population Growth 27
- Fertility Rate 27
- Number of Migrants 27
- Ageing Process 28

Economic Data 29
- Europe, a World Economic Power 29
- Persistant Important Inequalities 29

Urbanisation 29

Heritage of the Great European Ideas 30
- Greco-Roman Roots 30
- Pagan Cults 30
- Enlightenment 31
- Postmodernity 31
- Christian Heritage 31

Religions and Beliefs of Europeans 32
- European and National Statistics 32
  - European Values Survey (EVS) 2008 33
  - Gallup International 2014 34
- Four Particular Situations in Europe 35
  - France 35
  - United Kingdom 37
  - Romania 37
  - New German Federal States 38
- Islam in Europe 38
  - Islam and Anti-Occidentalism 39
- Mystical-Esoteric Nebula and the Recomposition of Religion 40

European Christianity 41
- Typology of European Christians 41
- Religion by Default and Vicarious Religion 41
- Christian Potential for Mission in Europe 42
- Sleepiness and Awakening 43

Conclusion 44
- What Is the State of Europe Today? 44
- What Do the Europeans Believe? 45
- What about the Christian Churches? 45

Further Reading 46

Chapter 3: Paradox of Europe and Christianity: Barriers and Bridges
Evert van de Poll 47

    Why Europe? 48

    The Angle of Secularisation 48
        Major Barrier: Non-Religious Worldview 49
        Secular-3 and the Challenge of Exclusive Humanism 50
        Response: Apologetics 51
        Bridges 51

    The Angle of Post-Modernity 53
        Major Barrier: Unbelief in Absolute Truth 53
        Response: Dialogue and Respect for Others 53
        Bridges 55

    The Angle of Post-Christendom 55
        Major Barrier: the Image of Church 56
        Response: Other Kinds of Churches, New Forms of Evangelism ... 57

    The Paradox of Europe and Christianity 58
        Much Christianity in Secularisation 59
        Postmodern Critique and Christian Experience 61
        Heritage of European Christianity 62

    Ambivalent Attitudes towards Christianity 63
        Attachment and Indifference 63
        Ignorance 64

    Conclusion 66

    Further Reading 66

Chapter 4: How "Christian" Is Europe Today?
Evert van de Poll 67

    Christians in a Secularised and Multi-Religious Society 68
        Special Position of Christianity 69
        A Solid Minority 69
        The Limitations of Quantitative Approaches 70

    Marginal Church Membership 71
        Nominal Church Members 71
        Minimal Church Practice 72
        A Typical European Phenomenon 72

    Different Criteria, Different Variants 73

Believing and/or Behaving without Belonging 74
    Believing without Belonging 75
    Behaving without Belonging – Cultural Christians 76
    Belonging without Believing and/or Behaving 78

Vicarious and Default Religion 78
    Vicarious Religion 78
    Default Religion? 79
    A Typical Example 80

Europe Still Considered a "Christian" Part of the World 81
    In a Cultural Sense 81
    In a Civilisational Sense 82

Moving to Post-Secular Situations? 82
    Return of Religion in the Public Sphere 83
    Secular and Religious Trends 84
    Hope 86

Further Reading 87

Chapter 5: Particular Difficulties Facing our French Fellow Citizens in Understanding and Receiving the Gospel
David Brown 88

Particular Difficulties 89
    Vocabulary 89
    Ignorance 90
    The Worldview Conveyed by French Culture 92
    The Plausibility of the Message of the Gospel 95

How Can Christians Deal with These Mental Representations? 96
    The Life of Each Christian 97
        The Disciple Worships God 97
        The Disciple Trusts God 98
        The Disciple Obeys God and Fights the Good Fight 98
        The Disciple Loves His Neighbour as Himself 99

    The Life of the Local Church 99

    Freedom 100

Conclusion 102

Chapter 6: Interdisciplinary In-Depth Analysis
Hannes Wiher 104

Preliminary Reflections on an In-Depth Analysis 104
   Biblical and Anthropological Approaches to the Deep Structures .. 105
   Operational Approach to the Deep Structures 108
   Role of Models in the Sciences 109
   Worldview as a "Model" 110
   Relationship between Bible and culture 111

Four Operational Models for Worldview 112
   Stratigraphic Model of Creation 113
   Five Basic Soteriological Concepts 115
   Conscience Orientation 118
      Development of the Conscience 119
      Conscience and Personality 120
      Soteriological Model of Conscience 121
      Conscience and Scripture 122
      Conscience and Theology 124
   Time Concept 124

Interdisciplinary In-Depth Analysis 126
   Interdisciplinary Analysis 126
   Cultural In-Depth Analysis 127
      Conscience Orientation 128
      Modernity / Postmodernity 128
      Literate Culture / Orality 132
      Esotericism / Animism 133
      Spirituality / Religions 134

Result of the Interdisciplinary In-Depth Analysis 134

Further Reading 135

Chapter 7: The Mosaic of Cultures:
A Challenge for European and International Churches
Johannes Müller 137

Cultural Diversity in Churches 137
   Monocultural Churches Appreciate Uniqueness 138
   Intercultural Churches Live Unity 141
   Multicultural Churches Experience Diversity 143

Are Mixed Churches Really Necessary? 145

    Homogeneity or Mixing? 145
    On the Move in the Mosaic 147
    We Need One Another 149
    Develop Mixing 150
        Building Contacts and Fellowship 150
        Reducing Uneasiness 151
        Indigenous Churches 151
        International Churches 152
    Contacts with Churches of Other Cultures 153
        Ministry among the Second Generation 154
    Conclusion 154
    Summary Table of the Models 155
    Further Reading 157
    Sources of Photos 157

Part Two: Communicating the Gospel in Europe .. 159

Chapter 8: What Is Evangelism?
Biblical Hints for the European Context
Léo Lehmann 161

    Introduction 161
    What Is Evangelism? 162
    Some Questions to Ask 164
    Biblical Data 165
        God's Missionary Nature 165
        Jesus and the Message of the Gospel 166
            Coming of Jesus Christ 166
            A Message in a Person 167
            A Message that Has to Be Announced 168
        Jesus Sending the Disciples 169
            Order or Promise? 170
            Go and Make Disciples of all Nations 171
            Baptism and Teaching 172
        Example of the Apostles 174

Churches of the New Testament 176
    Exhortations to Evangelise? 176
    Ministry of the Evangelist 178

Conclusion 179

Further Reading 181

Chapter 9: Cross-Cultural In-Depth Evangelism
Hannes Wiher 182

Preliminary Considerations 182
    Theology of the Gospel and of Evangelism 182
    Holy Spirit and Missionary Strategies 187
    Evangelism and Transformation of Deep Structures 187
    Gospel and Culture: Hermeneutic Considerations 188
    Missionary Spirituality 190

Communication of the Gospel in Europe 193
    A New Language 193
    Holistic Communication of the Gospel 196
    Oral and Written Presentation of the Bible 199
    Conversion Process 200
    Learning from the Early Church: A Relational Approach 206
    Church Planting 208

Conclusion 212

Further Reading 213

Chapter 10: Outreach amongst African-led Churches in Switzerland: a Case Study
Johannes Müller 215

The Lord's Hand Was with Them 215

Role of African Christians in the West 216

Survey among African Church Leaders in Switzerland 218

Evangelism through African-led Churches 219
    Approaches to Evangelism 220
        Outreach to the Public Place 220
        Jointly Organised Big Events 221
        Church Programs 222
        Personal and Relational Evangelism 223

    Summary and Complementary Observations 224
    Who Is Being Reached? 225
        Fellow Africans 225
        Swiss People 226
        Other Immigrant Minorities 227
        International Outreach 228

Perspectives for Cross-Cultural Outreach 228
    Readiness to Learn 229
    Contextualisation of Message and Style 229
    Strategic Partnerships 230
    A Key: The Second Generation 231
    What Can Swiss and European Churches Learn? 232

Conclusion 232

Further Reading 233

Chapter 11: Demonology: A Forgotten Dimension
Hannes Wiher 234

God and Gods 234
    Relationship between the Biblical God and the Other Gods 234
    Uniqueness of the Biblical God 235
    Uniqueness of Jesus Christ 236
    Other Divinities 237
    Two Paradoxes 239
    Tripolar Perspective of Religions 239

Demons in the Bible 241
    Demons in the Old Testament 241
    Demons and Jesus 243
    Demons and the Apostle Paul 243

Demons and the European Christian 244
    Demons and the Early Church 244
    Demons and Anthony the Great 245
    Demons and Western Europe 246
    Demons and Western Christians 248
    Modern Idols 251

Antagonistic Dimension of Mission 253

Conclusion 259

Further Reading 260

Chapter 12: What Kind of Church for Postmodern Europeans?
Daivd Brown 261

Introduction 261

Four Bridges 264

1) The Human Condition 264
   Our Human Solidarity 264
   Our Human Identity 264
   Our Human Conduct 265

2) The Church Is the New Humanity 265

3) True Spirituality 266
   Worship 266
   Trust 267
   Obedience: Fighting the Good Fight, Day by Day 267
   Loving People 267

4) The Story Line of Human History 268

Practical Ways towards the Outworking of These Four Bridges 269

Conclusion 271

Conclusion *(Hannes Wiher)* 272

Appendix *(Hannes Wiher)* 280

Appendix 1: European Statistics 280

Religions 280

Christianity 281
   Christian Confessions 281
   Evangelicals 281
   British Megachurches 283

Islam 283

Two Religious Minorities in Europe 1900-2025 285

Appendix 2: Literature Review 286

History of Evangelism in Europe 286

Analysis of the European Context 289

Theology of Evangelism 294

    Communication of the Gospel 298
    Church Planting 302

List of Authors 305
Bibliography 307
Index of Names 331
Index of Subjects 336

Europe: Restoring Hope

Deborah Meroff

The continent known for over 1000 years as the heartland of Christianity has gone into spiritual arrest. Drawing from the experience of many individuals and organisations, this book takes a hard look at four population groups at the centre of Europe's heart trouble: marginalised people, Muslims, youth and nominal and secular Europeans. Here is proof that it is possible to restore hope to this great continent when God's people work together. This practical resource supplies all the motivation and information we need to get started.

"Europe is very likely a battleground for the future of global Christianity... I hope that whoever reads these pages will be encouraged and inspired to prayer and action."

Jiří Unger
Former President of the European Evangelical Alliance

"My wife Drena and I have now been based in Europe for 50 years. Debbie Meroff's book True Grit was one of the most important books in our lives, and her new book on Europe is another cutting edge, must-read!"

George Verwer
Founder and International Co-ordinator Emeritus, OM International

"This book shows that God is still at work in Europe. He is building his church despite many challenges. And he wants to see each one of us playing an active part in restoring hope to Europe!"

Frank Hinkelmann
President of the European Evangelical Alliance

Pb. • pp. 296 • £ 14.95 • US$ 24.95 • € 14.95
ISBN 978-3-941750-06-7

VTR Publications • Gogolstr. 33 • 90475 Nürnberg • Germany
info@vtr-online.com • http://www.vtr-online.com

The Heart of Church and Mission
Bryan Knell

This book brings together a passion for the church and a passion for global mission. It looks at the heart of the UK church, asking whether and how it beats for mission and explores the passion of the mission community, and asks how it involves the local church. You might be forgiven for expecting that the heart of church and the heart of mission would be interwoven and closely linked together, but that has not been the case.

Two significant historical events continue to shape the church and mission in the Western World. Christendom removed mission from the church and the launch of the missionary societies disengaged the local church from mission. Although there is plenty of talk of change, the dominant mind-set is still shaped by these events. Practical suggestions are directed at churches and agencies with the aim of re-establishing, Mission at the heart of the church and the church at the heart of mission.

The world is a different place to when the "modern" Western mission movement developed. Yet many of the same structures exist today, in both churches and mission agencies. The church in the West needs to engage in new and appropriate ways in the world, building on history but not being bound by it. Bryan's prophetic call is to new ways of thinking, new attitudes and clear Biblical principles and deserves a wide audience. The Global Church deserves no less than a fresh approach to obeying His command to join together in God's mission in His world.

Martin Lee, Executive Director, Global Connections, UK

Pb. • pp. 80 • £ 6.00 • US$ 9.99 • € 9.95
ISBN 978-3-95776-037-1

VTR Publications • Gogolstr. 33 • 90475 Nürnberg • Germany
info@vtr-online.com • http://www.vtr-online.com

www.ingramcontent.com/pod-product-compliance
Lightning Source LLC
Chambersburg PA
CBHW050122170426
43197CB00011B/1682